TELELITERACY

TAKING TELEVISION SERIOUSLY

·DAVID BIANCULLI·

A TOUCHSTONE BOOK
Published by Simon & Schuster
New York • London • Toronto • Sydney • Tokyo • Singapore

To Kathy, Kristin, and Mark,
with love

TOUCHSTONE
Rockefeller Center
1230 Avenue of the Americas
New York, New York 10020

First Touchstone Edition 1994
Published by arrangement with the Continuum Publishing Company

TOUCHSTONE and colophon are registered trademarks
of Simon & Schuster Inc.

Manufactured in the United States of America

10   9   8   7   6   5   4   3   2   1

Library of Congress Cataloging-in-Publication Data
Bianculli, David.
    Teleliteracy: taking television seriously/David Bianculli.—1st Touchstone ed.
       p.   cm.
    Originally published: New York: Continuum, 1992.
    "A Touchstone book."
    Includes bibliographical references and index.
       1. Television broadcasting—Social aspects—United States. 2. Visual literacy—
United States. 3. Television in education—United States. 4. Popular culture—United
States. I. Title.
PN1992.6.B49   1994
302.23'45'0973—dc20   93-44352
                                                                        CIP

ISBN: 0-671-88238-4

CONTENTS

PART 3: A MEDIA ROUNDTABLE 161

(Photographs may be found between pages 62 and 63)

ACKNOWLEDGMENTS

This book owes its origin to the early encouragement of Mark Woodruff and Cathy Cook of *Taxi* magazine, who urged the expansion of my proposed TV column idea into the November 1989 "Teleliteracy" quiz and article that resulted. It owes its existence to the enthusiasm and support of Michael Leach, president of Crossroad/Continuum, who identified that article as the seed from which a book-length defense of television should spring. Finally, this book owes its completion to the sharp eyes and mind (and infinite patience) of Evander Lomke, the managing editor of Continuum, and Bruce Cassiday, whose editing saved me from more errors and redundancies than I would ever confess to publicly.

A special thanks goes to those who surrendered their time and trust by agreeing to being interviewed as roundtable participants for this project: David Attenborough, Linda Bloodworth-Thomason, Timothy Brittell, James L. Brooks, James Burke, Ken Burns, James Burrows, Peggy Charren, Bill Cosby, Mark Dawidziak, Shelley Duvall, Linda Ellerbee, Fred W. Friendly, Mark Frost, Robert Geller, Don Hewitt, Peter Jennings, Lindsay Law, William Link, Lorne Michaels, Bill Moyers, Alexander Nehamas, Carolyn Olivier, Fred Rogers, Donald Rosenberg, Robert J. Thompson, Kurt Vonnegut, and David Zurawik.

And though I don't want to overstate it, this seems the proper place to acknowledge the ways in which two of the people listed above had a true impact on my life, personality, or opinions—an impact predating my professional career. When I was a teenager, Bill Cosby's comedy albums helped shape my sense of humor, while his costarring role opposite Robert Culp on *I Spy* reinforced my belief in racial equality (at a time when such reinforcements, on network television, were otherwise very hard to come by). Also in my formative teen years, it was from reading such delightful Kurt Vonnegut novels as *Slaughterhouse-Five, Cat's Cradle,* and *The Sirens of Titan* that I was led to the work of other American literary satirists and humorists. Indirectly, I have Vonnegut to thank for my passion for James Thurber, Robert Benchley, and especially for Mark Twain. More directly, I have Vonnegut to thank for influencing the way I think, write, question, and joke. And that's no joke.

Yet every TV producer, writer, director, newsperson, or host I interviewed for *Teleliteracy* has impressed and influenced me in some way, which is why they were sought out in the first place. Without their input, this book would not be the same. Neither would television.

On a cryptic personal note, I'd like to thank the one other person who read the manuscript from start to finish, as well as the colleague who served as my pace car and confidante throughout. Both of you requested anonymity, but you know who you are.

And finally, because not even dedicating the book to them seems acknowledgment enough, I'd like to thank my wife, Kathy, and our children, Kristin and Mark, for enduring what became a very long and time-consuming writing process.

INTRODUCTION

One of the challenges in writing this book, which sets out to give television credit where it's due, was attempting to paint TV's portrait at a time when it refused to stand still. In 1991, the year the bulk of *Teleliteracy* was written, television presented widespread coverage of an air war, a ground war, a failed Soviet coup, the Clarence Thomas confirmation hearings, the William Kennedy Smith rape trial, and the dissolution of the Soviet Union. (As this book was going to press in 1992, the aftermath of the verdict in the Rodney King case was an even more recent major news event.) When those stories were given wall-to-wall coverage on TV, it was my duty as a TV critic to put the book aside and dive into a comparative analysis of network news coverage—praising the Cable News Network for its initial Gulf War coverage, for example, while later ridiculing it for surrendering so much air time to the Smith trial. The period was such a busy one for TV, "real" and otherwise, that proving the point about TV's impact became easier than finding the time to mount the argument. *Time* magazine called 1991 "one of the most eventful years of this century," and acknowledged television's importance by honoring CNN founder Ted Turner. "For influencing the dynamic of events and turning viewers into instant witnesses of history," the magazine explained, "Robert Edward Turner III is *Time*'s Man of the Year for 1991." Had *Time* been in the business of handing out awards for Medium of the Year, television would have won hands down.

And yet, that same year, a gaggle of predominantly conservative pressure groups launched a "Turn Off Your TV Day" boycott (which, by the way, had no statistical impact), and individual communities—from Andover, Connecticut to Wayzata, Minnesota—supplemented that national protest with their own anti-television campaigns. Television continued to be seen in many circles as the enemy, blamed for everything from the decline of quality in Hollywood movies ("The audiences have become trained to accept less and less because of television," claimed industry power broker David Geffen) to a reversal in the evolution of the human mind ("We're unwittingly rearing a generation of 'different brains,'" insisted author Jane Healy in *Endangered Minds: Why Our Children Don't Think*). Even on occasions when TV seemed to be getting some respect, as when New York's Museum of Television & Radio opened its lavish new facilities, the medium's contributions seldom were taken at face value or discussed with a straight face. The *New York Times* asked at the time, "Are television and radio, though undeniably shapers of society, worthy of a museum's ennoblement, or should they be condemned as corrupters of literacy?"

The general attitude regarding television has not changed that much since 1986, when author and mass-culture professor Mark Crispin Miller said of television that "Everybody watches it, but no one really likes it." Miller called that "the open secret of TV today," and added, "Its only champions are its own executives, the advertisers who exploit it, and a compromised network of academic boosters. Otherwise, TV has no spontaneous defenders, because there is almost nothing in it to defend."

Statements like that would make me angry if they didn't display such laughable ignorance. That's the comment of someone who writes about TV a lot more than he watches it—or, at least, of someone who watches all the wrong things.

I'm more than willing to be a "spontaneous defender" of television, even though it amazes me that such a position has been seen as controversial. I'm not saying all TV is good; the majority of it isn't. I'm arguing that the best of TV is very good indeed, and that the idea of indiscriminately ridiculing or avoiding the medium of television displays no more intelligence than denouncing all movies as fluff, or holding a "Don't Open a Book Day." I'm arguing that television should be taken seriously enough to be judged in context, without preconceptions, on its own merits—as in the pages that follow.

Teleliteracy is divided into three sections. Part 1 puts TV in context, starting with the personal (what TV means to me, and, thanks to an enclosed "pretest," what it means to you) and concluding with the historical— showing that television, like many popular media before it, has been penalized for its very popularity. Part 2 is a Media Manifesto, making the case for television as an art form and defending it against some of its more vocal and critical attackers. Part 3 is an examination of television from several different angles, looking at everything from TV in the classroom to TV on the battlefield.

My own comments on these and other subjects will be complemented, and sometimes contradicted, by a variety of respected producers, performers, professors, and pundits interviewed exclusively for the book, from Bill Cosby and Peter Jennings to Fred Rogers and Lorne Michaels. The men and women included in the following pages are by no means the only ones who create or appreciate quality television. Indeed, some other people whose work I admire tremendously, such as executive producer Bruce Paltrow (*St. Elsewhere*), former network executive Grant Tinker, and *Nightline* anchor Ted Koppel, could have been included as well, just as other critics and professors with similar sensibilities could have been consulted. However, the people contacted for this book amply represent their likeminded peers, and have one crucial thing in common: they use television well and take it seriously.

Isn't it time everyone else did the same?

PART I

A MEDIA PERSPECTIVE

There's no sense talking about what TV is unless we also look at what TV *was*, where it came from—and where, in another sense, *we're* coming from.

I'll start by laying my own cards on the table, and relating what the medium has meant to me as a Baby Boomer-turned-TV critic. Then I'll ask you to show *your* hand by taking the Teleliteracy quiz, and seeing for yourself whether you're fluent in television's shared vocabulary.

Next comes a look at mass media through the ages, which not only shows how distressingly similar our reactions have been to the reigning popular arts, but establishes important connections and chronologies that play a part in later chapters. An appreciation of the history of film and radio, for example, is critical to an understanding of the censorial and ethical battlefield issues that were raised most recently during the Gulf War.

It may be too strong to suggest that if we do not learn from our TV history, we are condemned to repeats. However, I suggest that knowing more about television's past, and watching more of its better offerings from the present, are the best ways to come to terms with it in the future.

1

TELEVISION DAYS

Woody Allen has his *Radio Days*, but he's older than I am. At thirty-eight, my mass-media memories are vastly different. I have *Television Days*, and my earliest video recollections are a montage of brief, flickering, black-and-white images: test patterns and farm reports while waiting for the Saturday-morning cartoons to start. Heckle and Jeckle and Tom Terrific. Month-long countdowns for *Peter Pan* and *The Wizard of Oz*. Looney Tunes, the Road Runner, Gerald McBoing Boing, Captain Kangaroo's Grandfather Clock.

But TV was growing up as quickly as I was, and, for whatever reasons, my parents allowed and even encouraged me to sample at will. Both of them were fervent supporters of John F. Kennedy, so I was allowed to stay up late to watch the Democratic convention and Nixon–Kennedy debates of 1960. Three years later, I watched, along with the rest of America, as the nation mourned JFK's assassination and, astoundingly, witnessed Jack Ruby's shooting of Lee Harvey Oswald on live TV. I was only ten, but that's not the kind of thing you forget. I matured a lot that weekend; so did television.

I had never seen real death on TV before, but, by then, the TV set was a regular and reliable source of horror, thanks to *Alfred Hitchcock Presents, The Twilight Zone,* and a show called *Thriller,* hosted by Boris Karloff, that scared me to death. That, to me, was TV's dark side. On the light side, as I headed into the 1960s, my favorite programs were *Rocky and His Friends* and its closely related successor, *The Bullwinkle Show,* from which I developed my love of bad puns.

In the midsixties, my teen years, I nurtured tastes and ideas that, in retrospect, leave me less than proud. I loved *The Wild Wild West,* for example, and clearly recall telling a school friend that, based on the way Robert Conrad vanquished bad guys seven at a blow, I'd rather fight four or five guys at a time than just one. My friend fixed me with a glance that said, in essence, I watched too much TV. Looking back, I'm certain he was right.

Perhaps, though, my uncritical nature is what led me to become a TV critic by profession. I didn't just watch *Batman* and *Star Trek* and *Get Smart;* I also watched *Have Gun, Will Travel* and *The Defenders* and *Slattery's People.* I caught the Beatles on *The Ed Sullivan Show* and had my consciousness raised by *The Smothers Brothers Comedy Hour.* I watched, with fascination, such unscripted TV events as the moon landing, the evening news reports from Vietnam, and the 1968 riots in Chicago. And surely, I'm not the only American male my age who, as a youth, was overcome by several significant and unforgettable emotions while watching Diana Rigg as Emma Peel on *The Avengers.*

It was television, almost as much as rock 'n' roll, that encouraged me to be different, and think differently, in the late sixties. Tom and Dick Smothers paved the way for me, along with Patrick McGoohan's surrealistic, paranoid, and nonconformist *The Prisoner* series. When the new decade started, my tastes had evolved to encompass the unfettered, short-lived freedom of the PBS anthology series *The Great American Dream Machine* (former home of Andy Rooney, Chevy Chase, Marshall Efron, and others) and the increasingly surrealistic TV addresses by President Richard M. Nixon.

In the first half of the seventies, reality far outstripped entertainment. Aside from a few oddball shows, such as *Kolchak: The Night Stalker,* there wasn't much to compare with the freakishness of the Saturday Night Massacre or the Watergate hearings. Then, in the fall of 1975, came *Saturday Night Live,* which gave my generation a TV voice of its own for the first time. It also, by coincidence, helped me find my voice as well: *Saturday Night Live* was the first TV series I reviewed as a professional TV critic, inaugurating my TV-review column in Florida's *Gainesville Sun.*

I've changed employers many times since, but not my approach. I still watch too much TV. I still find that everything I care about shows up on TV sooner or later, giving me a chance to think and write about music, politics, comedy, drama, science, even the business and technology of television. And, after all these years, I still get enthusiastic when I see good stuff—and upset when the networks mess it up or take it off. It's difficult to describe the joy I got when previewing, and raving about, and steering readers toward, Dennis Potter's *The Singing Detective*—or my amazement when, while interviewing Kurt Vonnegut for this book, he turned out to be just as rabid a fan of that very same miniseries. I also enjoy the sense of continuity that comes when I introduce my own children to something as subversively entertaining as *The Simpsons,* which is to the nineties what *The Bullwinkle Show* was to the sixties.

Am I taking TV too seriously? Maybe—but I'd argue that many people don't take TV seriously enough. The common and easy thing to do is to dismiss TV entirely, or to attack it for its obvious excesses and weaknesses. However, rejecting the entire medium of television on the basis of *Charlie's Angels* is no more logical or defensible—or sporting—than rejecting the entire motion-picture industry on the basis of *Porky's.* Not too long ago, film was as maligned and mistrusted as TV is today, but the movies have since matured into an accepted and admired art form. Television, too, is a modern art, and it's on display—every night—in the largest gallery in the country. Yet perhaps because of that pervasiveness and familiarity, it's either taken for granted or targeted for abuse. Anyone who still thinks of TV as a vast wasteland, though, hasn't checked out the scenery in quite a while.

And even television's past has a significant and continued impact on our present culture. That's where the concept of *teleliteracy* comes in: it's an acknowledgment and understanding of the elements of TV's past and present that are likely to survive well into the future. In essence, anyone who can discuss TV's coverage of the Gulf War or the William Kennedy Smith trial, or laugh knowingly at any of TV's parodies of Roseanne Arnold singing the national anthem, or who can mimic the theme song of *The Twilight Zone,* is demonstrating teleliteracy.

This differs a bit from *Cultural Literacy,* the concept put forth by Professor E. D. Hirsch, Jr., in his best-seller of the same name. The subtitle of that book, it should be remembered, is *What Every American Needs to Know.* By comparison, teleliteracy is, for the most part, What Every American Already Knows.

In the follow-up book *The Dictionary of Cultural Literacy,* written by Hirsch, Joseph F. Kett and James Trefil, the authors stated in their introduction that "cultural literacy, unlike expert knowledge, is meant to be shared by everyone." Sharing is one thing; remembering is another. Most of us "shared" *Beowulf* in junior high school, but that doesn't mean we could spout a cogent synopsis many years later.

I suggest that cultural literacy, while a fine idea, is applying its energies in the wrong direction. If you want to talk about knowledge that is shared by everyone, the area on which to focus is television. Television is our most common language, our most popular pastime, our basic point of reference; it's also where most of our children are first exposed to allusion, satire, and other "literary" concepts.

Look at *Sesame Street,* which is littered with characters and skits poking fun at literature (fairy tales), poetry (nursery rhymes), music, and even TV itself. Or *Square One TV,* a television show that teaches mathematics to preteens. Its most popular segment is "Mathnet," which borrows Jack Webb's monosyllabic *Dragnet* style to teach fractions and decimals. And is there really that much difference between a child's insistence on hearing the same bedtime story night after night and wanting to rewind and review an entertaining installment of *Shelley Duvall's Faerie Tale Theatre?*

As viewers age, and as television ages, the commonly shared experiences pile up. TV has now matured to the point where it's repeatedly self-referential, as when *The Wonder Years* lapses into a dream sequence based on *Star Trek,* or when *Newhart* ends its entire run with an episode suggesting the whole series was a dream—and putting Bob Newhart back into the character, bedroom and bed of his previous hit TV series, *The Bob Newhart Show.* Yes, these are inside jokes—but the point is that, with television, almost everyone's an insider.

Does this mean that literacy, at least in the cultural sense, is doomed to extinction? That the literati who in this century fondly cite the works of Franz Kafka will be usurped in the next century by *tele*literati who prefer to quote from the words of Ralph Kramden? No. But it's time to realize TV must be doing something right to reach and affect so many people, and that teleliteracy is something to be quantified and upgraded and utilized, not ignored. By the time you've digested the history and arguments on the following pages, you may look at television a little differently . . . or, at the very least, with a little less guilt.

2

TELELITERACY PRETEST

Let's get right to the point: what is *Teleliteracy,* and how can we combat it? Basically, teleliteracy is the demonstration of fluency in the language and content of TV—and there's no reason to fight or fear it. In fact, teleliteracy is something to be embraced, not denounced, and this book sets out to explain why. From *Sesame Street* to *60 Minutes,* from the PBS documentary *The Civil War* to the TV coverage of the Gulf War, television is too important and pervasive a mass medium to be dismissed as a crass medium.

That's the pretext. Now for a pretest.

Are *you* teleliterate? *You Bet Your Life*—and if you just thought of Groucho Marx's quiz show of the same name, you've proven my point. To demonstrate that teleliteracy exists, and that a *Bonanza* of TV knowledge has been absorbed even by those who snobbishly maintain they watch little or no television and are much more comfortable discussing the classics, I've prepared a simple quiz—well, half simple, anyway. On one side is the "classics" portion, asking questions about famous works of art and literature; on the other side is the "teleliteracy" portion, asking parallel questions about famous works of . . . television. On one side, Milton; on the other, Milton Berle.

TV or not TV? That is the question. Well, that's *one* question. Here are 150 others.

CLASSICS LITERACY QUIZ

Section I. Lyric Poetry.

Provide the next line from the following poems. (One point for each correct answer.)

1) "In Xanadu did Kubla Khan / A stately pleasure-dome decree . . ."

_____

2) "Theirs not to reason why / theirs but to do or die . . ."

_____

3) "Laugh, and the world laughs with you / weep, and you weep alone . . ."

_____

4) "Under the spreading chestnut tree / the village smithee stands . . ."

_____

5) "Death, be not proud . . ."

_____

6) "I think that I shall never see / a poem lovely as a tree . . ."

_____

7) "Gather ye rosebuds while ye may . . ."

_____

8) "By the shores of Gitche Gumee / By the shining Big-Sea-Water . . ."

_____

9) "Beware the Jabberwock, my son! / The jaws that bite, the claws that catch! . . ."

_____

10) "It takes a heap o' livin' / in a house t' make it home . . ."

_____

Section II. Body of Work.

Put the following works by each artist in their related chronological order—'1' being the earliest, '3' being the latest. (One point for each correctly arranged trio.)

	1	2	3
11) Aristophanes			
a) *The Birds*	—	—	—
b) *The Frogs*	—	—	—
c) *Lysistrata*	—	—	—

TELELITERACY QUIZ

Section I. Lyric Poetry.

Provide the next line from the following TV themes. (One point for each correct answer.)

1) "Come listen to a story / 'bout a man named Jed . . ."

2) "Green Acres is the place to be . . ."

3) "It's a beautiful day in this neighborhood / a beautiful day for a neighbor . . ."

4) "Hey, hey, we're the Monkees / And people say we monkey around . . ."

5) "Here's the story / of a lovely lady / who was bringing up three very lovely girls . . ."

6) "The house is a museum / when people come to see 'em . . ."

7) "Rollin', rollin', rollin' / though the streams are swollen / Keep them doggies rollin' . . ."

8) "M-I-C / See you real soon / K-E-Y / Why? Because we *like* you! . . ."

9) "I'm so glad we had this time together . . ."

10) "The weather started getting rough / The tiny ship was tossed . . ."

Section II. Body of Work.

Put the following works by each artist in their related chronological order—'1' being the earliest, '3' being the latest. (One point for each correctly arranged trio.)

	1	2	3
11) Arthur, Beatrice			
a) *All in the Family*	—	—	—
b) *The Golden Girls*	—	—	—
c) *Maude*	—	—	—

12) Beethoven, Ludwig van
- a) *Pathetique Sonata*
- b) Sonata in F Minor *(Appassionata)*
- c) Symphony No. 6 *(Pastorale)*

— — —
— — —
— — —

13) Da Vinci, Leonardo
- a) *The Adoration of the Magi*
- b) *The Last Supper*
- c) *Mona Lisa*

— — —
— — —
— — —

14) Dickens, Charles
- a) *A Christmas Carol*
- b) *Great Expectations*
- c) *Life and Adventures of Nicholas Nickleby*

— — —
— — —
— — —

15) Dostoyevsky, Fyodor
- a) *The Brothers Karamazov*
- b) *Crime and Punishment*
- c) *Notes from the Underground*

— — —
— — —
— — —

16) Eliot, T. S.
- a) *Murder in the Cathedral*
- b) *Old Possum's Book of Practical Cats*
- c) *The Waste Land*

— — —
— — —
— — —

17) Hemingway, Ernest
- a) *For Whom the Bell Tolls*
- b) *The Old Man and the Sea*
- c) *The Sun Also Rises*

— — —
— — —
— — —

18) Mozart, Wolfgang Amadeus
- a) *The Marriage of Figaro*
- b) Requiem
- c) Symphony No. 41 *(Jupiter)*

— — —
— — —
— — —

19) O'Neill, Eugene
- a) *Ah! Wilderness*
- b) *The Emperor Jones*
- c) *The Iceman Cometh*

— — —
— — —
— — —

20) Stravinsky, Igor
- a) *The Firebird*
- b) *Five Easy Pieces*
- c) *The Rite of Spring*

— — —
— — —
— — —

12) Ball, Lucille
   a) *Here's Lucy*   — — —
   b) *I Love Lucy*   — — —
   c) *Life with Lucy*   — — —

13) Cosby, Bill
   a) *Cos*   — — —
   b) *The Cosby Show*   — — —
   c) *I Spy*   — — —

14) Dey, Susan
   a) *Emerald Point N.A.S.*   — — —
   b) *L. A. Law*   — — —
   c) *The Partridge Family*   — — —

15) Field, Sally
   a) *The Flying Nun*   — — —
   b) *Gidget*   — — —
   c) *Sybil* (miniseries)   — — —

16) Griffith, Andy
   a) *The Andy Griffith Show*   — — —
   b) *Matlock*   — — —
   c) *The New Andy Griffith Show*   — — —

17) Landon, Michael
   a) *Bonanza*   — — —
   b) *Highway to Heaven*   — — —
   c) *Little House on the Prairie*   — — —

18) Morgan, Harry
   a) *AfterMASH*   — — —
   b) *Dragnet*   — — —
   c) *M*A*S*H*   — — —

19) Serling, Rod (writer/producer)
   a) *Night Gallery*   — — —
   b) *Requiem for a Heavyweight* (drama)   — — —
   c) *The Twilight Zone*   — — —

20) Wagner, Robert
   a) *Hart to Hart*   — — —
   b) *It Takes a Thief*   — — —
   c) *Switch*   — — —

Section III. Classic Quotes.

Match each quotation to its proper source. (One point for each correct match.)

21) "Better late than never."   — a. René Descartes
22) "Look homeward, Angel, now, and melt   — b. Euripides
    with ruth."   — c. Ben Franklin
23) "Rome was not built in one day."   — d. John Heywood
24) "A mighty fortress is our God."   — e. Omar
25) "I think; therefore I am."   Khayyám
26) "The gods visit the sins of the fathers   — f. Titus Livius
    upon the children."   — g. Martin Luther
27) "O Brave New World that has such   — h. John Milton
    people in't."   — i. William
28) "A rolling stone gathers no moss."   Shakespeare
29) "A Jug of Wine, a Loaf of Bread—and   — j. Publilius Syrus
    Thou."
30) "There are no Gains, without Pains."

Section IV. Character Studies.

In the following sets of matching questions, match the characters to the work in which they appear. (One point for each correct match.)

31) Aase   — a. *The Faerie Queen,* Edmund
32) Alceste   Spenser
33) Cleonice   — b. *Lysistrata,* Aristophanes
34) Gloriana   — c. *The Misanthrope,* Molière

35) Sir Toby Belch and Sir   — d. *Peer Gynt,* Henrik Ibsen
    Andrew Aguecheek
36) Benedick and Claudio   — a. *Much Ado about Nothing,*
37) Quince and Bottom   Shakespeare
                          — b. *A Midsummer Night's Dream,*
                                Shakespeare
                          — c. *Twelfth Night,* Shakespeare

Section III. Classic Quotes.

Match each quotation to its proper source. (One point for each correct match.)

21) "Baby, you're the greatest."
22) "Live long and prosper."
23) "Na-noo, na-noo."
24) "Don't have a cow, man."
25) "Solid."
26) "Sorry about that, Chief."
27) "Stifle it, dingbat."
28) "Warning! Warning! Danger! Danger!"
29) "Who loves ya, baby?"
30) "You look mah-velous!"

__ a. Archie Bunker *(All in the Family)*
__ b. Bart *(The Simpsons)*
__ c. Fernando *(Saturday Night Live)*
__ d. Linc Hayes *(Mod Squad)*
__ e. Ralph Kramden *(The Honeymooners)*
__ f. Kojak *(Kojak)*
__ g. Mork *(Mork & Mindy)*
__ h. Robot *(Lost in Space)*
__ i. Maxwell Smart *(Get Smart!)*
__ j. Mr. Spock *(Star Trek)*

Section IV. Character Studies.

In the following sets of matching questions, match the characters to the work in which they appear. (One point for each correct match.)

31) Abby
32) Alexis
33) Maddie
34) Sue Ellen

__ a. *Dallas*
__ b. *Dynasty*
__ c. *Knots Landing*
__ d. *Moonlighting*

35) Gomer and Goober
36) Larry, Darryl, & Darryl
37) Lenny and Squiggy

__ a. *The Andy Griffith Show*
__ b. *Laverne & Shirley*
__ c. *Newhart*

Section V. Love and Death.

Mark an X next to the loving couples who were still alive, and together, at the end of their story. (One point for each correct answer, whether a mark or a blank.)

38) ___ Jude Fawley and Sue Bridehead, Thomas Hardy's *Jude the Obscure.*
39) ___ Lenina Crowne and John, Aldous Huxley's *Brave New World.*
40) ___ Pierre and Natasha, Leo Tolstoy's *War and Peace.*
41) ___ Porgy and Bess, Gershwin's *Porgy and Bess.*
42) ___ Wilfred and Rowena, Sir Walter Scott's *Ivanhoe.*

Section VI. Loving Couples.

Match the men in the left column to the women on the right. (One point for each correct match.)

43) Almaviva ___ a) Ada
44) Clyde ___ b) Carmen
45) Jeeter ___ c) Penelope
46) José ___ d) Rosina
47) Odysseus ___ e) Sondra

Section VII. Mythological Deaths.

(One point for each correct answer.)
Who killed . . .

48) Achilles? _____
49) Narcissus? _____
50) Remus? _____

Section VIII. Visual Aids, Nineteenth Century.

Match the work of nineteenth-century art to the decade in which it was produced. (One point for each correct match.)

51) *The Dead Toreador,* Édouard Manet ___ a) forties
52) *Mother of the Artist,* James McNeill Whistler ___ b) fifties
53) *The Peaceable Kingdom,* Edward Hicks ___ c) sixties
54) *Starry Night,* Vincent van Gogh ___ d) seventies
55) *Washington Crossing the Delaware,* Emanuel Leutze ___ e) eighties

Section V. Love and Death.

Mark an X next to the loving couples who were still alive, and together, at the end of their story. (One point for each correct answer, whether a mark or a blank.)

38) ___ Archie and Edith, *Archie Bunker's Place.*
39) ___ Sam and Diane, *Cheers.*
40) ___ Sonny and Caitlin, *Miami Vice.*
41) ___ Jim and Margaret, *Father Knows Best.*
42) ___ Mr. and Mrs. Richard Kimble, *The Fugitive.*

Section VI. Loving Couples.

Match the men in the left column to the women on the right. (One point for each correct match.)

43) Dan ___ a) Hot Lips
44) Frank ___ b) Laura
45) Luke ___ c) Lucy
46) Norton ___ d) Roseanne
47) Ricky ___ e) Trixie

Section VII. Televisual Deaths and Near-Deaths.

(One point for each correct answer.)
Who killed . . .

48) Mrs. Kimble on *The Fugitive?* _____
49) Laura Palmer on *Twin Peaks?* _____

Who shot . . .
50) J. R. Ewing on *Dallas* (that famous first time)? _____

Section VIII. Visual Aids, Twentieth Century.

Match the work of twentieth-century TV to the decade in which it was introduced. (One point for each correct match.)

51) *Charlie's Angels,* ABC. ___ a) forties
52) *Hill Street Blues,* NBC. ___ b) fifties
53) *I Love Lucy,* CBS. ___ c) sixties
54) *The Smothers Brothers Comedy Hour,* CBS. ___ d) seventies
55) *Texaco Star Theater* (Milton Berle), NBC. ___ e) eighties

Section IX. Numbers.

With one point for each correct name, identify the following:

Alexandre Dumas's Three Musketeers
56) _____
57) _____
58) _____

Chekhov's Three Sisters
59) _____
60) _____
61) _____

Book of Revelation's Four Horsemen of the Apocalypse
62) _____
63) _____
64) _____
65) _____

Dostoyevsky's Brothers Karamazov
66) _____
67) _____
68) _____
69) _____

Section X. Miscellaneous.

For each correct answer to the following questions, you earn one point.

What was the name of the dog . . .
70) In Washington Irving's "Rip Van Winkle"?
_____

71) That guards the gates of Hades (and had three heads)?
_____

Identify the son of . . .
72) Sir Lancelot in Sir Thomas Malory's *Le Morte d'Arthur.*
_____

Identify the daughter of . . .
73) Satan in John Milton's *Paradise Lost.*
_____

Identify the captain and first mate of the *Pequod* in Herman Melville's *Moby-Dick.*
74) Captain:_____.
75) First mate:_____.

Section IX. Numbers.

With one point for each correct name, identify the following:

Steve Douglas's *My Three Sons* (any three of four)
56) _____
57) _____
58) _____

The four *Golden Girls*
59) _____
60) _____
61) _____
62) _____

The two men from *U.N.C.L.E.*
63) _____
64) _____

The two astronauts on *I Dream of Jeannie*
65) _____
66) _____

Bonanza's brothers Cartwright
67) _____
68) _____
69) _____

Section X. Miscellaneous.

For each correct answer to the following questions, you earn one point.

What was the name of the dog . . .
70) That Jeff, then Timmy, played with for years?
_____

What was the name of the dolphin . . .
71) That headlined its own TV series?
_____

Identify the son of . . .
72) Cliff and Clair Huxtable on *The Cosby Show.*
_____

73) Lucy and Ricky Ricardo on *I Love Lucy.*
_____

Identify the captain and first mate of the *Minnow* in *Gilligan's Island.*
74) Captain:_____
75) First mate:_____

ANSWERS:

Section I. Lyric Poetry.

1) "Where Alph, the sacred river, ran / Through caverns measureless to man / down to a sunless sea." ("Kubla Khan," Samuel Taylor Coleridge)
2) "Into the valley of death / Rode the six hundred." ("Charge of the Light Brigade," Alfred, Lord Tennyson)
3) "For the sad old earth must borrow its mirth / But has trouble enough of its own." ("Solitude," Ella Wheeler Wilcox)
4) "The smith, a mighty man is he / with large and sinewy hands." ("The Village Blacksmith," Henry Wadsworth Longfellow)
5) ". . . though some have called thee mighty and dreadful / For thou art not so." ("Death," John Donne)
6) "A tree whose hungry mouth is prest / Against the earth's sweet flowing breast." ("Trees," Joyce Kilmer)
7) "Old time is still a-flying." ("To the Virgins, to Make Much of Time," Robert Herrick)
8) "Stood the wigwam of Nokomis / Daughter of the moon, Nokomis." ("Hiawatha's Childhood," Henry Wadsworth Longfellow)
9) "Beware the Jubjub bird, and shun / The frumious Bandersnatch." ("Jabberwocky," Lewis Carroll)
10) "A heap o' sun an' shadder, / an' ye sometimes have t' roam." ("Home," Edgar A. Guest)

Section II. Body of Work.

11) Aristophanes: a-1 (414 B.C.), b-3 (405 B.C.), c-2 (411 B.C.).
12) Beethoven: a-1 (1799), b-2 (1804–7), c-3 (1809).
13) Da Vinci: a-1 (1481–82), b-2 (1495–97), c-3 (1504).
14) Dickens: a-2 (1843), b-3 (1860–61), c-1 (1838–39).
15) Dostoyevsky: a-3 (1879–80), b-2 (1866), c-1 (1864).
16) Eliot: a-2 (1935), b-3 (1939), c-1 (1922).
17) Hemingway: a-2 (1940), b-3 (1952), c-1 (1926).
18) Mozart: a-1 (1786), b-3 (1791), c-2 (1788).
19) O'Neill: a-2 (1933), b-1 (1922), c-3 (1946).
20) Stravinsky: a-1 (1909–10), b-3 (1916–17), c-2 (1911–13).

Section III. Classic Quotes.

21) f.
22) h.
23) d.
24) g.
25) a.
26) b.
27) i.
28) j.
29) e.
30) c.

ANSWERS:

Section I. Lyric Poetry.

1) "A poor mountaineer, / barely kept his family fed." *(The Beverly Hillbillies)*
2) "Faaaarm livin' is the life for me." *(Green Acres)*
3) "Would you be mine? / Could you be mine?" *(Mister Rogers' Neighborhood)*
4) "But we're too busy singin' / to put anybody down." *(The Monkees)*
5) "All of them had hair of gold / like their mother / the youngest one in curls." *(The Brady Bunch)*
6) "They really are a scre-am / The Addams family." *(The Addams Family)*
7) "Rawhide." *(Rawhide)*
8) "M-O-U-S-E." *(The Mickey Mouse Club)*
9) "Just to have a laugh and sing a song." *(The Carol Burnett Show)*
10) "If not for the courage of the fearless crew / The *Minnow* would be lost." *(Gilligan's Island)*

Section II. Body of Work.

11) Arthur: a-1 (1971–72), b-3 (1985–92), c-2 (1972–78).
12) Ball: a-2 (1968–74), b-1 (1951–57), c-3 (1986–87).
13) Cosby: a-2 (1976), b-3 (1984–92), c-1 (1965–68).
14) Dey: a-2 (1983–84), b-3 (1986–92), c-1 (1970–74).
15) Field: a-2 (1967–70), b-1 (1965–66), c-3 (1976).
16) Griffith: a-1 (1960–68), b-3 (1986–91), c-2 (1971).
17) Landon: a-1 (1959–73), b-3 (1984–1990), c-2 (1974–82).
18) Morgan: a-3 (1983–84), b-1 (1967–70), c-2 (1975–83).
19) Serling: a-3 (1970–73), b-1 (1956), c-2 (1959–64).
20) Wagner: a-3 (1979–84), b-1 (1968–70), c-2 (1975–78).

Section III. Classic Quotes.

21) e.
22) j.
23) g.
24) b.
25) d.

26) i.
27) a.
28) h.
29) f.
30) c.

Section IV. Character Studies.

31) d.	**33)** b.	**35)** c.
32) c.	**34)** a.	**36)** a.
		37) b.

Section V. Love and Death.

40) and **42)** get the *X*. Every other couple, in one way or another, got the shaft.

Section VI. Loving Couples.

43) d. Almaviva and Rosina, Rossini's *The Barber of Seville.*

44) e. Clyde Griffiths and Sondra Finchley, Theodore Dreiser's *An American Tragedy.*

45) a. Jeeter and Ada Lester, Erskine Caldwell's *Tobacco Road.*

46) b. José and Carmen, Bizet's *Carmen.*

47) c. Odysseus and Penelope, Homer's *The Odyssey.*

Section VII. Mythological Deaths.

48) Achilles was killed by Paris (shot in the heel).

49) Narcissus was killed by himself—by his own vanity (he starved to death gazing at his reflection).

50) Remus was killed by Romulus.

Section VIII. Visual Aids, Nineteenth Century.

51) c. *The Dead Toreador,* Édouard Manet, 1864.

52) d. *Mother of the Artist,* James McNeill Whistler, 1872.

53) a. *The Peaceable Kingdom,* Edward Hicks, 1845.

54) e. *Starry Night,* Vincent van Gogh, 1889.

55) b. *Washington Crossing the Delaware,* Emanuel Leutze, 1851.

Section IX. Numbers.

56–58) Athos, Porthos, and Aramis.

59–61) Masha (Kuligin), and Olga and Irina Prozorov.

62–65) Conquest, Slaughter, Famine, Death. (Because of varying interpretations, credit is also given for such synonymous descriptions as War, Plague, and Hunger.)

66–69) Dmitri, Ivan, Alyosha, and Smerdyakov the bastard.

Section X. Miscellaneous.

70) Wolf.

71) Cerberus.

72) Sir Galahad.

73) Sin (who, with an incestuous union with her father, gave birth to Death).

74) Ahab.

75) Starbuck.

Section IV. Character Studies.

31) c. **33)** d. **35)** a.
32) b. **34)** a. **36)** c.
                        37) b.

Section V. Love and Death.

Only 41) gets the *X*. Sam and Diane split up, and the other wives died.

Section VI. Loving Couples.

43) d. Dan and Roseanne, *Roseanne*.
44) a. Frank Burns and "Hot Lips" Houlihan, *M*A*S*H*.
45) b. Luke and Laura, *General Hospital*.
46) e. Ed Norton and Trixie, *The Honeymooners*.
47) c. Ricky and Lucy Ricardo, *I Love Lucy*.

Section VII. Televisual Deaths and Near-Deaths.

48) The one-armed man.
49) Leland Palmer (under the influence of Killer Bob).
50) Kristin Shepard.

Section VIII. Visual Aids, Twentieth Century.

51) d. *Charlie's Angels*, ABC, premiered 1976.
52) e. *Hill Street Blues*, NBC, premiered 1981.
53) b. *I Love Lucy*, CBS, premiered 1951.
54) c. *The Smothers Brothers Comedy Hour*, CBS, premiered 1967.
55) a. *Texaco Star Theater* (Milton Berle), NBC, premiered 1948.

Section IX. Numbers.
56–58) Mike, Robbie, Chip, and eventually the adopted Ernie.
59–62) Dorothy, Rose, Blanche, and Sophia.
63–64) Napoleon Solo and Illya Kuryakin.
65–66) Tony Nelson and Roger Healey.
67–69) Adam, Hoss, and Little Joe.

Section X. Miscellaneous.

70) Lassie, on *Lassie*.   **73)** Little Ricky.
71) Flipper, on *Flipper*.   **74)** Skipper.
72) Theo.   **75)** Gilligan.

EUGENE O'NEILLSEN RATINGS

CLASSICS LITERACY	Score	TELELITERACY
Rhodes scholar. (Good as it gets.)	62–75	*Rhoda* scholar. Totally teleliterate.
Peabody award. (Amazing.)	48–61	Sherman and Peabody award. (Your knowledge goes Wayback.)
Honorary doctorate. (Born to be Wilde.)	34–47	Honorary *Daktari*. (Born to be wild.)
Captain Courageous. (Classic scholar.)	20–33	Captain Video. (Classy viewer.)
Classically literate. (You made the cut.)	6–19	Tele-illiterate. (You missed the cut.)
Turn on your mind.	0–5	Turn on your set.

3

MASS MEDIA AND
MASS CONTEMPT

If I were a lawyer, rather than a TV critic, my defense of television would begin with a motion requesting a change of venue—to a place where TV could be judged fairly by an impartial jury and guaranteed a fair trial. Eventually, the case would be settled out of court, or thrown out, because no such place exists.

Ridiculing television, and warning about its inherent evils, is nothing new. It has been that way since the medium was invented, and TV hasn't exactly been lavished with respect as the decades have passed. Just check out the titles of some prominent books about TV's content and impact: Marie Winn's *The Plug-in Drug*, Neil Postman's *Amusing Ourselves to Death*, Wilson Bryan Key's *Subliminal Seduction*, Tony Schwartz's *Media: The Second God*, Harlan Ellison's *The Glass Teat*, and, most blatantly, Jerry Mander's *Four Arguments for the Elimination of Television*. Less prominently, but no less negatively, there are book-length attacks with such threatening titles as *Children and Television: The One-Eyed Monster?* and *Telegarbage*, which may well be the polar opposite of *Teleliteracy*. To paraphrase Bob Dylan, you don't need a Willard Scott to know which way the wind blows.

I suspect, though, that a lot of the fear and loathing directed at television is done so out of a time-honored, reflexive overreaction to the dominant medium of the moment. For the past four decades, television has been blamed for corrupting our youth and exciting our adults, distorting reality, and basically being a big, perhaps dangerous, waste of time. Before TV, radio and film were accused of the same things. And long before that—in fact, some 2,500 years earlier—philosophers were arguing that poetry and drama should be excluded from any ideal city on much the same grounds.

The link between ancient philosophy and modern television was introduced to me by a philosophy professor who sought me out at a dinner party and asked, in enthusiastic tones, what I knew about Plato. "It's been a while," I confessed, "but I remember that it dries up if you don't keep the lid on." After patiently explaining he meant Plato, not Play-Doh, the professor recounted Plato's arguments against poetry and music and theater, and likened them to today's elitist attacks on the mass medium of TV. Taking that idea and running with it, I found a pattern that went through the ages with revealing, and depressing, regularity. While the common people—the consumers—generally were eager to entertain and be entertained by new art forms, the ruling and intellectual elite responded with stubborn conservatism. Invariably, they cherished the old and ridiculed the new—even though the cherished art of old had been treated just as shabbily when *it* was new. So, Sherman, set the Wayback machine for the fourth century B.C., where we'll begin with Plato and Homer, then quickly work our way back to the future.

In book 10 of *The Republic,* Plato—writing in an extended-dialogue style in which his arguments emanate from the mouth of Socrates—attacks epic poet Homer, and other tragedians, on several grounds, all of which have a still-familiar ring. "Their productions are appearances and not realities," he gripes. "Drawing, and in fact all imitation, produces its own work, quite removed from truth," he complains, and quickly lumps poetry, or "imitation by sound," into the same category. Plato may have been the first critic in history to totally denounce the docudrama form on philosophical grounds, but he wouldn't be the last. "The only good docudrama," *New York Times* TV critic Walter Goodman proclaimed in print in 1989, "is an unproduced docudrama."

The audience, as well as the art form, troubled Plato, whose remarks are colored by an implied disdain for the popularity of public performances, "especially in crowded audiences when men of every character flock to the theater." These "common people," as Plato-as-Socrates so charitably calls them, are drawn to "the peevish and diverse character"—including Odysseus and other emotional heroes in Homer's *The Iliad* and *The Odyssey* who engage in such questionable (to Plato, anyway) displays of emotion as "spinning out a long melancholy lamentation" or "disfiguring themselves in grief." To Plato, baring such intimate sorrows is more "a woman's" reaction than a man's, and is not to be condoned. Clearly, Plato would have given thumbs down to the central characters of *Hamlet* and *Macbeth,* and there's no doubt Alan Alda would have had no place in Plato's Republic.

And even back then, community standards was the applicable guideline: "If you receive the pleasure-seasoned Muse of song and epic," Plato warns, "pleasure and pain will be kings in your city, instead of law and the principle which, at all times, has been decided by the community to be best." Finally, Plato sums up his antiarts argument with the cold, sweeping pronouncement that "this poetry is not to be taken seriously."

Alexander Nehamas, an Edmund Carpenter professor of the humanities at Princeton University (and the dinner-party companion who laughed at my Play-Doh joke), calls these ideas "an absolute horror to everybody who loves Plato." Nehamas has studied and written extensively about both Plato and television, and suggests that Plato, rather than being antiart, merely was an elitist. According to Nehamas, Plato wanted to ban poetry readings and live theater because, being free and accessible and raucous and extremely popular, they were the mass entertainment of that era.

"If, instead of 'tragedy' and 'poetry,' or 'Homer' and 'Aeschylus,' you read 'mass entertainment' or 'popular media,' you'll recognize Plato's arguments as the ancestor of all the reasons we have today for being suspicious of television," Nehamas says.

To wit: poetry, by which Plato means drama, confuses us between appearance and reality. The action it presents is too extreme and violent. Most important, it's a corrupting influence, perverting its audience by bombarding it with inferior characters and vulgar subjects—and constituting, in Plato's own words, "a harm to the mind of its audience." Substitute "television" for "poetry" in *The Republic,* and you've got the makings of an FCC commissioner or TV critic, circa fourth century B.C.

If Plato's Republic had become reality, it would have been a republic with a lot of empty libraries, theaters, and museums—if, indeed, those repositories of the arts would have survived at all. Plato's personal utopia never came to pass—but throughout the centuries, wherever and whenever a new medium of artistic expression attracted a lot of people, someone was ready, waiting, and eager to attack its content and fear its impact.

Less than three centuries after the founding of Christianity, Origen, head of the Christian school of Alexandria, ordered that "Christians must not lift up their eyes to stage plays, the pleasurable delights of polluted eyes, lest their lusts be inflamed by them." The more famous St. Augustine, born a century after Origen's death, was in total agreement, and even stronger voice: "Stage plays," he said, "are the most petulant, the most impure, impudent, wicked, unclean, the most shameful and detestable atonements of filthy Devil-gods." (Other than that, St. Augustine, how'd you like the play?)

The point, though, is that one generation's Devil-gods are another generation's demigods, just as one generation's object of low disdain often emerges as a later generation's high art. Today, Aristophanes is lauded as one of the theater's best and boldest early comic playwrights. Back then, Plutarch, a contemporary, dismissed him with a particularly hateful diatribe.

"The language of Aristophanes," Plutarch complained, "reeks of his miserable quackery: it is made up of the lowest and most miserable puns; he doesn't even please the people, and to men of judgment and honor he is intolerable; his arrogance is insufferable, and all honest men detest his malice."

Yet Aristophanes' comedies played to packed houses in their day; the "common people" who attended them were obviously less troubled than Plutarch by Aristophanes' irreverent spoofs of his political leaders and theatrical peers—and much more understanding of the fact that, when it comes to puns, the lower and more miserable the better. (My personal goal, when sticking puns into my newspaper columns, is occasionally to concoct one so painfully "miserable" that the reader will throw down his or her paper in disgust. Now *that's* entertainment.)

Some of Aristophanes' comic plays, including *The Frogs*, survive, and college professors teach them today as revered works of the era. What's more, *The Frogs* was a small fish in a big pond: in classical Athens, government-sponsored marathon stage and poetry festivals were staged often and essentially free of charge, with several plays a day presented for several days. Citizens came to applaud, boo, throw vegetables, interact, relax, share ideas, and enjoy themselves—kind of like a succession of ancient Woodstocks.

William Shakespeare, too, was a popular playwright of his time, and by no means an elitist figure. It's common to hear TV producers today say if Shakespeare were alive, he'd be writing for television. And, like television, Shakespeare attracted his share of detractors through the years, from those who questioned his authorship of the plays to those who ridiculed their content.

The first published series of critical articles examining Shakespeare's work appeared in the periodical *The Adventurer* in 1754, written by an appreciative yet sometimes critical critic named Joseph Warton. "This drama is chargeable with considerable imperfections," he says of Shakespeare's *King Lear*, including the allegedly excessive violence of "the cruel and horrid extinction of Glo'ster's eyes, which ought not to be exhibited on the stage."

"Shakespeare's name, you may depend on it, stands absurdly too high and will go down," Lord Byron wrote in 1814. "He had no invention as to stories, none whatever. He took all his plots from old novels, and threw their stories into a dramatic shape, at as little expense of thought as you or I could turn his plays back again into prose tales."

Byron guessed wrong, but the real tragedy is that Shakespeare's reputation has been so universally and formally inflated that many of today's young readers now fear and reject him purely on the basis of his "classic" stature. As Mark Twain remarked, a classic is "a book which people praise but don't read." Twain, too, is an author whose literary stock has risen and fallen over the years. (He also, in a witty but unconvincing volume called *Is Shakespeare Dead?*, argued that Shakespeare could not possibly have been the author of his plays, but that's beside the point.) Twain's *Adventures of Huckleberry Finn*, now widely and wisely treasured as one of the finest works in American literature, was initially dismissed for the most part as a children's adventure story—and not always praised as *that*. An earlier manifestation of *Life* magazine ran a review in 1885, dripping with ridicule, recounting how Huck faked his own death in the book by having "killed a pig, smeared its blood on an axe and mixed in a little of his own hair, and then ran off," and suggesting sarcastically that "this little joke can be repeated by any smart boy for the amusement of his fond parents." More seriously, the Public Library committee of Concord, Massachusetts, immediately banned *Huckleberry Finn* from its shelves with the explanation that it included "a series of experiences not elevating," was "more suited to the slums than to intelligent, respectable people," and was regarded as "the veriest trash." Even today, more than one-hundred years after its publication, Twain's masterpiece is attacked often as being too incendiary, too racist, or too much of a bad influence on impressionable youth.

These two truths seem to be self-evident. Whenever a medium or work of art catches on with the masses, it's blamed for a variety of societal ills—and not fully appreciated as "art" for at least a generation. In other words, where there's progress, there's protest. Plato lost his argument with poetry and drama and art, but the battle has been waged ever since, with critics always on hand to denounce new works until they've aged enough to be appreciated as "classics." The most literal example of this is "classical" music, whose very description reflects the warm benediction of the passage of time. Yet its history, too, is studded with the grumblings of skeptics wary of new forms.

As part of the movement in which the Renaissance succumbed to the Baroque period, Italian composer Claudio Monteverdi broke away from the polyphonic practices of his musical predecessors to create what he called the "second practice" of music. Monteverdi's experimentation led to his 1607 music drama *Orfeo* (credited by some as the first true opera), yet Monteverdi and his peers were attacked at the time by music theorist Giovanni Artusi, who wrote in outraged tones that this modern music was ignoring the rules established by centuries of fine tradition. It was a theme that, with minor variations, would recur throughout musical history, and many now-standard works were greeted with critical scorn. Giuseppe Verdi's 1851 opera *Rigoletto*, now a beloved standard, was dismissed by the *Times* of London as "the most uninspired, the barest, and the most destitute of ingenious contrivance," adding that "to enter into an analysis would be a loss of time and space"; *La Gazette Musicale de Paris* proclaimed it Verdi's "weakest work," and predicted that *Rigoletto* "has hardly any chance of being kept in the repertoire."

Two years later, in 1853, a critic for Boston's *Daily Atlas* reflected on a symphonic work that, to his dismay, had recently celebrated its silver anniversary with no reduction in its number of popular performances. The piece was Beethoven's Symphony No. 9, and the critic disliked almost all of it, especially the "Ode to Joy" choral movement that provides its powerful, evocative finale. "If the best critics and orchestras have failed to find the meaning of Beethoven's Ninth Symphony," he wrote, "we may well be pardoned if we confess our inability to find any. The *adagio* (the third movement) certainly possessed much beauty, but the other movements, particularly the last, appeared to be an incomprehensible union of strange harmonies. Beethoven was deaf when he wrote it." Just as lethal a critical barb was aimed at Tchaikovsky, whose public unveiling of a new musical work prompted this review in an 1875 issue of the St. Petersburg publication *Novoye Vremya:* "Tchaikovsky's First Piano Concerto, like the first pancake, is a flop."

Even composers, contemporaries, and crowds got into the heady act of music-bashing. *The Barber of Seville* composer Gioacchino Rossini ridiculed Richard Wagner's "music dramas" (Wagner's term for his often lengthy stage productions) by noting that "Wagner has good moments, but bad quarter-hours," while Mark Twain got off an even better barb by insisting that Wagner's music was "better than it sounds." The catcalls, boos, and fistfights prompted by the 1913 premiere of *The Rite of Spring*—a reaction spurred by both Igor Stravinsky's volatile music and Vaslav Nijinsky's erotic choreography—remain legendary. And, as always, some critics were ready and willing to suggest that exposure to this "new" mode of expression could be, to recall the words of Plato, "a harm to the mind of its audience." The music critic for the *New York Tribune,* for example, reviewing the 1918 premiere of Sergei Prokofiev's Piano Concerto No. 1 in D-flat Major, Opus 10, wrote, "Mr. Prokofiev's pieces have been contributions not to the art of music, but to national pathology and pharmacopoeia. . . . They are simply perverse." The same *New York Tribune,* six years later, sent music critic Lawrence Gilman to attend the premiere of an ambitious and beautiful jazz piece, George Gershwin's *Rhapsody in Blue,* but Gilman found in it neither ambition nor beauty. "How trite and feeble and conventional the tunes are; how sentimental and vapid the harmonic treatment, under its disguise of fussy and futile counterpoint!" he wrote in the *Tribune.* "Weep over the lifelessness of the melody and harmony, so derivative, so stale, so inexpressive!"

The *Tribune* is dead; long live Prokofiev and Gershwin.

It's almost as though something can be accepted by the critical elite as "art" only after it's rejected by the mass audience in favor of something else. Literacy itself, it should be remembered, was once an elite activity—with Greek and Latin texts valued more than the common vernacular, and with "common" translations of those "great works" anything but common. In early colonial America, books were relatively rare, usually found in urban seacoast towns, and either religious or scholastic in nature. Cotton Mather, who had what was considered the largest private library in late-seventeenth-century New England, valued what he termed "Devout and useful Books," and scorned most English literature and other books of "delight and amusement."

Historian Daniel Boorstin, who describes Mather's library in *The Americans: The Colonial Experience,* also notes how the printing press—specifically, the rise of almanacs and newspapers—spread literacy as well as news. The newspaper became a truly democratic mass medium, yet even some of its most famous practitioners were concerned about its possible negative side effects. "The Reading Time of most People," Boorstin quotes Benjamin Franklin as writing in 1786, "is of late so taken up with News Papers and little periodical Pamphlets, that few now-a-days venture to attempt reading a Quarto Volume."

And isn't that basically the same complaint lodged about the Viewing Time of most People who are of late so taken up with Tele Vision? Not that all Quarto Volumes were created equal. In *Walden,* Henry David Thoreau grumbles about the local popularity of a series of romance stories, collected in a multi-volume set of books called *Little Reading* ("which I thought referred to a town of that name which I had not been to," Thoreau writes, in what for him is a veritable knee-slapper). Besides dismissing the writing as "on a very low level, worthy only of pygmies and manikins," Thoreau warns that overexposure to such inferior literary works is dangerous to your health.

"The result," Thoreau writes, "is dullness of sight, stagnation of the vital circulations, and a general deliquium and sloughing off of all the intellectual faculties." (He may have a point, too, because I had to look up *deliquium;* it means a softening with age.) Elsewhere in the nineteenth century, and into the twentieth, such "pulp literature" as the so-called penny dreadfuls attracted critics who warned of the cheap and sensational stories' deleterious effects upon "the young and the less well-educated."

The twentieth century began by instituting Rural Free Delivery, which in turn led to wider and faster dissemination of newspapers, magazines, and mail-order catalogs. Those catalogs sparked national interest, even in rural areas, for new consumer goods and services—and were as widely (and vainly) decried then for their ads, claims, and negative impact as TV ads are today. And every invention that came along, it seems, simultaneously was embraced by the public and feared by the guardians of the status quo.

For example: Thoreau, again in *Walden,* writes, "We are in a great haste to construct a magnetic telegraph from Maine to Texas; but Maine to Texas, it may be, have nothing important to communicate." So much for the concept of *united* states.

Not even the invention of the phonograph, which enabled people to listen to recorded musical performances privately and repeatedly, was free from criticism. The famous marching-band composer and conductor John Philip Sousa, no doubt fearful that attendance at his national tours would decrease once the music was available on disc, wrote a magazine article in 1906 called "The Menace of Mechanical Music." In it, he predicted that, as sheet-music sales fell and record sales increased, the result would be "a marked deterioration in American music and musical taste." Actually, Sousa was closer to the mark in predicting another unwelcome side effect: noise pollution of outdoor environments by portable mechanical music-makers. Sousa had envisioned hand-cranked phonographs instead of battery-powered boom boxes, but give the guy some credit.

Music and musical tastes thrived and expanded after the phonograph was introduced, and recordings of musical "classics," as well as popular songs, became part of the phonograph owner's home library. In 1917, little more than a decade after Sousa's anti-"mechanical music" salvo, the Victor label released its first jazz record, by the all-white "Original Dixieland Jazz

Band." Other labels and bands (black performers as well as white) quickly followed suit, and the freewheeling new sound, thanks largely to its accessibility through phonograph records and the infant medium of radio, soon captivated the era to the point where it's now known as the Jazz Age. "It wasn't only an innovation," a young Jimmy Durante enthused, "it was a revolution!"

Once again, though, the nay-sayers were armed and firing, with some of them marching to Sousa's drumbeat. Four years after the first jazz record was released, an article in the *Ladies' Home Journal* asked disapprovingly, "Does Jazz Put the Sin in Syncopation?"—and that was nothing compared to the reception rock 'n' roll would receive when it surfaced in the 1950s.

Film, like the record album so feared by Sousa, was an invention that froze and captured performances for later examination, like so many artistic fossils. Unlike records, though, the movies didn't start out as a "collectible" medium. Films didn't come to you; you went to them, first for crude but entertaining little silent "flickers," then for increasingly involved and imaginative narratives, and eventually for full-length epics with sound and spectacle, presented in movie "palaces" and preceded by fanciful cartoons and astoundingly timely (at least for that time) newsreels. Because of its rapid and radical development, the motion picture had to prove itself all over again with each advance. Novelist and screenwriter Graham Greene, who served as a film critic for London's *Spectator* in the thirties, later laughed at himself regarding his own narrow intolerance of films that broke new ground. "I was horrified by the arrival of talkies (it just seemed the end of the film as an art form)," Greene wrote in retrospect, "just as later I regarded color with justifiable suspicion." He was not alone in being wary of this new technological marvel.

In May 1896, only two months after the first public exhibition of film in Britain (a program that included such nonfiction shorts as *A Visit to the Zoo, Rough Seas at Dover,* and *The German Emperor Reviewing His Troops*), an essay entitled "The Cinematograph" appeared in the *New Review.* In it, essayist O. Winter mocked the enthusiasm with which people were greeting these little flickers—and predicted movies would have no artistic future because, as one source summarized Winter's argument, "their apparent realism was a delusion."

Almost simultaneously, the first American film to feature professional actors was released: *May Irwin Kiss,* an 1896 short whose title was a description, not a request. In the movie (also known as *The Kiss*), May Irwin and John Rice acted out, for the camera, a scene from the current Broadway comedy *The Widow Jones.* Even though the action on film was the same as that witnessed from the stage each night by New York theater patrons, the intensity and relative closeness of the moving-picture image made for a particularly vivid impression. It was the cinema's first kiss—and, almost predictably, prompted the earliest known film review. A brief article in the June 15, 1896, issue of *Chap Book* branded *May Irwin Kiss,* and its noteworthy cinematic breakthrough, "absolutely disgusting." The brand-new Vitascope Hall of New Orleans, America's first cinema and the host theater for *May Irwin Kiss,* was no doubt helped, more than hurt, by this outraged rejection, and business boomed. Patrons were charged ten cents for admission, an additional ten cents to see the Edison Vitascope projector, and, for yet another dime, could purchase a frame of discarded film. Another visceral early hit was the 1903 *The Great Train Robbery,* one of the first Westerns and narrative stories on screen: reportedly, its scene of a gun pointing at the screen and firing caused some patrons to flee or faint.

The sex and violence in those early films triggered responses that are echoed today in complaints about the content of certain TV shows. In Chicago, social reformer Jane Addams lobbied for police and citizen groups to "supervise" what could properly be shown in these new neighborhood nickelodeons, yet suggested that they could develop into a positive social influence. The powerful *Chicago Tribune,* on the other hand, printed an editorial insisting that, since such films "minister . . . to the lowest passions of childhood," it was "proper to suppress them at once." The editorial called for the enactment of a law that would "absolutely forbid" nickelodeon admittance to anyone under eighteen, thus protecting children from their "wholly vicious" influence. The *Tribune* ended its call to action by claiming, "There is no voice raised to defend the majority of five-cent theaters, because they cannot be defended. They are hopelessly bad." In 1907, the nation's first motion-picture censorship law was passed—by the Chicago City Council, which prohibited "immoral or obscene" pictures. (One of the first offenders: a 1908 Vitagraph production of Shakespeare's *Macbeth,* on the grounds that the stabbing scene was too predominant.) A year later, New York City Mayor George B. McClellan, concerned about the growing popularity and content of the films shown in the more than six hundred movie houses in his city, closed them all on Christmas Eve. The exhibitors were back in business, thanks to a court injunction overruling McClellan, the day after Christmas—although the city quickly enacted an ordinance barring children under sixteen from admittance to any film without being accompanied by an adult.

But then as now, kids comprised a sizable segment of the movie audience, and concerns about the effects of film fantasy on impressionable youth only increased as the movies matured, and as the cinema began to create popular, influential stars. At first, the actors in early films were unidentified by the studios—an intentional omission aimed at keeping the actors' profiles, and consequently their film-budget salaries, to a minimum. (In view of the multimillion-dollar salaries for movie stars in the 1990s, those early film producers may have been right.) However, there was no need for the poor, neglected performers to band together in a sort of Actors Anonymous. Some actors didn't want credit in this new medium. But as audiences grew exponentially, so did the demand to know who was starring in the most popular films. Taking the hint from theatrical road companies, which often prominently advertised recognizable cast members to help sell more tickets, the cinema finally followed suit in 1910. The most famous and successful early example came when Florence Lawrence, the actress known as "The Biograph Girl"—and, up to that point, known *only* as the unidentified yet familiar face from many Biograph films—was hired by rival producer Carl Laemmle of IMP, and given name billing as "Miss Lawrence, The Imp Girl." A year later, a different actress was given the perhaps dubious honor of being the first movie performer identified by name in a review. The publication was *Variety*, the year was 1911, the film was *The Italian Barber*—and the actress was Mary Pickford, hailed by the reviewer for her "cute ways and girlish manner." Before long, she would be nationally revered as "America's sweetheart."

Meanwhile, as the first identified screen performers were starting to make names for themselves, a few established "name" performers from the legitimate stage began to relent and agree to dabble in this new upstart medium. In 1912, New York's Lyceum Theater held a premiere screening of *Queen Elizabeth,* an imported, ambitious fifty-minute costume drama starring French sensation Sarah Bernhardt. The film was such a success that its American distributor, Adolph Zukor, made a fortune—and spent it to establish Famous Players, a film production company whose slogan was "Famous Players in Famous Plays." Stage actor John Barrymore and infamous stage beauty Lillie Langtry, the English actress known as "The Jersey Lily," were two of Zukor's early Famous Players; a third was Mary Pickford, who by then was nearly as famous for her film appearances as her new colleagues were for their stage work.

When the opulent Strand Theater opened on Broadway in 1914, the opening-night crowd was treated to operatic interludes, a stage act, dancing fountains, a newsreel-type showcase that showed plays from a baseball game held that very day—and *then* the movie, a nearly two-hour Western called *The Spoilers.* The account in the next morning's *New York Times* attested to both the cynicism that had attended the early growth of film, and the speed with which it was now growing:

> I must confess that when I saw the wonderful audience last night in all
> its costly togs, the one thought that came to my mind was that if anyone
> had told me two years ago that the time would come when the finest-
> looking people in town would be going to the biggest and newest theatre
> on Broadway for the purpose of seeing motion pictures I would have
> sent them down to visit my friend, Dr. Minas Gregory at Bellevue Hospi-
> tal. The doctor runs the city's bughouse, you know.

That review was written by Victor Watson, the paper's drama critic—because, at that point, no regular film critic had yet been appointed. Not that an absence of official critics meant an absence of criticism. Even in *Motion Picture World,* a young publication that you would expect to be largely supportive of film, there were attacks on specific movies and general cinematic trends—such as, in this essay from 1911, the amount of sex and violence (what else?) in Westerns. "The accumulation of abhorrent incidents given in Indian and cowboy plays under the pretense of picturing actual life," wrote Louis Reeves Harrison, is so repulsive in its low savagery, so beastly and unsavory, that it might be just as well to cut out such plays indiscriminately. . . . They are repellant to the cultivated, and even cease in the course of time to stimulate the jaded appetites of the unwashed. . . . I have seen decent people before a theater entrance turn away at the sight of a poster announcing one of these dramas of blood and nastiness, and many refuse to go inside of a picture show because of them.

Actually, by then, it seemed that millions more people were seeing and enjoying movies than avoiding and attacking them. To measure how quickly and completely movies were sweeping the country, all you have to do is shift the focus over to the *Chicago Tribune*, which had attacked nickelodeons so passionately in 1907. Seven years later, in 1914, that same *Tribune* became the first general newspaper in America to employ a regular film critic, John Lawson. His replacement, Audrie Alspaugh, quickly became a powerful film critic in the Midwest, and many in show business grew to fear the pen name under which she wrote: Kitty Kelly. (That's spelled a little differently than the current, "no-relation" Kitty Kelley, whose unauthorized biographies of celebrities have generated their own share of fear and loathing—but it's an amusing coincidence nonetheless. The more things change. . . .)

With critics, of course, came criticism—and the early critics, like critics of any era, didn't always recognize a classic, or a class act, when they saw one. "In general," charged Henry MacMahon, writing in the *New York Times* in 1915 (reacting to several negative reviews of D. W. Griffith's *The Birth of a Nation* and other contemporary film criticism), "the most learned critics of the pictures seem to be as far behind the art form they are criticizing as the Edinburgh Reviewers were hopelessly to the rear of Wordsworth, Shelley, Keats, Coleridge, and Byron, whom they vainly attempted to extinguish while upholding the time-worn art of Dryden and Pope."

This helps explain why, when critics got their first look at Buster Keaton's 1927 Civil War comedy-drama *The General*, many of them saw not a masterpiece, but, in the words of New York's *Herald-Tribune*, "the least funny thing Buster Keaton has ever done." Robert E. Sherwood of *Life* criticized Keaton for "gruesomely bad taste," just because he had dared to include scenes of killing in a film billed as a comedy. The entire history of cinema, as with any true art form, is riddled with critical missteps, from the aforementioned Graham Greene's underinflated opinion of Greta Garbo (whom he likened to "a beautiful Arab mayor") to the respected James Agee's overinflated opinion of Charlie Chaplin's *Monsieur Verdoux*. "It is permanent," he wrote in the *Nation* in 1947, "if any work done during the past twenty years is permanent."

The qualifying "if" in Agee's remark is especially telling, because, even as late as the forties, there was little sense that the Hollywood filmmakers were making movies that would last. D. W. Griffith spoke for the industry at its infancy, and for a generation, when he said, "Movies are written in sand. Applauded today, forgotten tomorrow. Last week the names on the signs were different. Next week they will be changed again." That attitude would change, ironically, with the arrival of television, which usurped movies as *the* visual mass entertainment medium, while ironically providing movie studios with an insatiable outlet for their inventories of old films—the ones, that is, they'd bothered to save.

Until then, the general feeling in Hollywood was that, if any images from movies were to linger, they would do so largely in the minds and memories of the audience. "That's the great thing about the movies," Jimmy Stewart said once, in his endearingly halting manner. "You're giving people little—little, tiny pieces of *time*—that they never forget."

There were, however, those fervent visionaries who felt that movies were of lasting importance, or at least worthy of serious consideration, almost from the start. Author F. Scott Fitzgerald said, "As long past as 1930, I had a hunch that talkies would make even the best-selling novelist as archaic as silent pictures." MGM producer Irving Thalberg once said of movies that "the medium will eventually take its place as art because there is no other medium of interest to so many people." Thalberg didn't live to see his prophecy disproven. He died in 1936 B.T.—Before Television.

It's encouraging, when looking back at the early years of film history, to see that not all film critics were narrowly critical. A few, in fact, articulated both the excitement and possibilities of the motion picture. While it's true that *Life* magazine objected to "the constant shifting of scenes" in Griffith's landmark 1915 film *The Birth of a Nation*, it's also true that the *New York Times*'s MacMahon countered with the opinion that "the 'constant shifting of scenes,' instead of being a blemish, is the very virtue of this new dramatic-musical-photographic form." The same year *Birth of a Nation* was released, James Shelley Hamilton, in an article for *Everybody's*, recognized and applauded Griffith's cinematic achievements in impressively detailed fashion:

> Griffith . . . saw that the story must be told wholly by action, that the introduction of long, explanatory subtitles was just as awkward a method of construction as it would be in a spoken play if each character were to advance to the footlights and explain to the audience who he was and how he came to be there. He saw that past action had to be presented visually, and that often it had to be recalled to the audience to give point to the present action; so he invented the "flash-back," which is a view of a past or distant scene, inserted almost as an illustration is inserted in a story. To give emphasis to a particular character, a face, or an important bit of stage property, he invented the "close-up". . . . He introduced, too, the device of simultaneous action, the method by which the last part of *The Birth of a Nation* is made so exciting.

Even E. E. Slosson of the *New York Independent*, who was bitterly (and correctly) critical of the racist, pro-Ku Klux Klan elements in *The Birth of a Nation*, was nonetheless intelligent, prescient, and objective enough to look past the trees and see the forest. In 1915 he wrote:

The film play, compared with its rival, the stage play, has certain serious defects, notably the absence of sound and color. But on the other hand it has certain compensating qualities of its own, and producers are very wisely laying more stress on these instead of imitating what the stage can always do better. For instance, the film playwright can use all outdoors for his background instead of a painted and rumpled backdrop. He can change the scene oftener than the Elizabethan dramatist. He can dip into the future or the past as though he were in Wells's Time Machine. He can use literally an army of supernumeraries in place of a dozen attendants with spears. He can reveal the mind of his characters in two ways, neither of them possible on the stage, first by bringing the actor so close that the spectator can read his facial expression, and second, by visualizing his memories or imaginings. He can, if he so desires, wreck a train, burn a house, sink a ship, or blow up a fort, since he does not have to repeat the expense every night.

The "serious defects" noted by Slosson—the absence of sound and color—were quickly overcome, but not necessarily the skeptics. Many critics, like Greene, were suspicious of each new cinematic advance, and even the movie industry itself was riddled with skepticism. *Variety* trumpeted the start of production on *The Jazz Singer* with a 1927 front-page banner headline reading FIRST ALL-TALKING PIC STARTS—but the subhead, in slightly smaller type, was "Only a Fad," Say Experts.

Even so, early champions existed, and persisted. Welford Beaton, reacting to that first full-length "talkie" in his 1928 *Film Spectator* review of *The Jazz Singer*, began his review with a brazen, accurate declaration. "*The Jazz Singer*," he wrote, "definitely establishes the fact that talking pictures are imminent. Everyone in Hollywood can rise up and declare that they are not, and it will not alter the fact. If I were an actor with a squeaky voice I would worry." Later in the same review, Beaton added:

> If I were a producer I would give sound devices my major attention and I would develop artists who can talk and directors who know color, for if there be anything certain about the future of pictures it is that in two years or less we will be making talking pictures in color and that no others will be shown in the big houses. . . . *The Jazz Singer* will have a definite place in screen history, and Warner Brothers are to be congratulated upon blazing a trail along which all other producers soon will be traveling.

Another critic at the time impressed by the possibilities of talking pictures was Alexander Bakshy, who wrote a 1929 essay called "The Talkies" for the *Nation* (where, decades later, James Agee would toil as a film critic before becoming a successful screenwriter). Discussing the motion picture medium's advantages over the stage, Bakshy noted:

> On the stage the actor moves in real space and time. He cannot even cross the room without performing a definite number of movements. On the screen an action may be shown only in its terminal points with

all its intervening moments left out. Similarly, in watching a performance on the stage the spectator is governed by the actual conditions of space and time. Not so in the case of the movie spectator. Thanks to the moving camera he is able to view the scene from all kinds of angles, leaping from a long-distance view to a close-range inspection of every detail. It is obvious that with this extraordinary power of handling space and time—by elimination and emphasis, according to its dramatic needs— the motion picture can never be content with modeling itself after the stage. The fact that it has now acquired the power of speech will certainly not make it any more willing to sacrifice its freedom and individuality.

Bakshy's keenest observation, however, was one that is as true today about television as it was then about the movies. "It is a sad reflection on the limitation of intellectuals and artists all over the world," he complained, "to see history repeat itself in the contemptuous resentment with which they are greeting the arrival of the talking picture. Just as twenty years ago when the silent movies began to stir the world, so today the patrons of art and the theater refuse to see in the talking picture anything but another vulgar product of our machine civilization."

At the time Bakshy wrote that essay, the movies were at the absolute height of their popularity, with 95 million Americans attending the cinema each week in 1929. The production of motion pictures in the United States had risen from a dozen films in 1913 to 841 five years later; by the end of the twenties, the new-movie count had leveled out at about 500 per year, or nearly ten movies per week. Stars rose fast and burned brightly, and their accessibility—at least on the silver screen—gave them a stature unparalleled in show-business history. "Over the years," film critic Arthur Knight has noted, "the movies have furnished America with its nearest equivalent to Europe's royalty." The late mythologist Joseph Campbell put it even more precisely when he said, "There is something magical about films. The person you are looking at is also somewhere else at the same time. That is a condition of the god. . . . He is on another plane. He is a multiple presence."

As movies and movie stars became more popular, they also became a more popular target. Former Postmaster General Will H. Hays began to put his stamp on the movie industry when, in 1922, he accepted the presidency of the self-regulating Motion Picture Producers and Distributors of America. One of his first moves was to issue an edict banning Fatty Arbuckle from pictures, less than a week after he was acquitted of the manslaughter of "good-time girl" Virginia Rappe. In 1927, the Hays office produced a list of what George Carlin might call "The Eleven Things You Shouldn't Do in Movies," a laundry list of "don't" guidelines that included "pointed profanity," "any licentious or suggestive nudity," and "scenes of actual childbirth." Red-flagged for "special care" in an additional list, and similarly discouraged, were scenes of "excessive or lustful kissing," "deliberate seduction of girls," and "man and woman in bed together." A stringent, more official Production Code soon followed, calling for reforms and decrying such early-thirties films, now considered classics, as gangster movies

Little Caesar and *The Public Enemy* (too violent) and Mae West vehicles such as *I'm No Angel* (too suggestive). In 1933, on the heels of all those films just mentioned, Mary G. Hawks, president of the National Council of Catholic Women, addressed a meeting of that organization and leveled an attack on the movies that, in the 1990s, sounds uncannily similar to modern denouncements of television.

Movies, she said, were "a menace to the physical, mental and moral welfare of the nation. . . . These injurious effects are greatly enhanced by the shameless sex appeal of the advertising. Constant exposure to screen stories of successful gangsters and 'slick' racketeers, of flaming passions and high-power emotionalism, may easily nullify every standard of life and conduct set up at home and will almost inevitably effect a moral decline at the very outset of life's adventures."

But if you want parallels—spooky ones—between today's damning generalities about TV and its effects on children, and the kinds of warnings and accusations being tossed around when the cinema was the dominant medium, the single best source is *Our Movie Made Children*, Henry James Forman's collection of the first social studies supposedly measuring the effects of films on the young. Published in 1933, *Our Movie Made Children* is bursting with blame, pointing the finger at the movies for inciting everything from sex and violence to larceny and lethargy. The crimes TV is accused of today, the movies were being tried for in 1933. Try these on for size:

Although the motion picture is primarily an agency for amusement, it is no less important as an influence in shaping attitudes and social values. The fact that it is enjoyed as entertainment may even enhance its importance in this respect.

Daily broadcasting of the passions and caprices and adventures of men and women in plays and on the screen, interpreted by ill-equipped authors and directors, cannot but be destructive of ideals that have proved to be wholesome and worthy of preservation.

Only the Bible and the Koran have an indisputably larger circulation than that of the latest film from Los Angeles.

The vast haphazard, promiscuous, so frequently ill-chosen, output of pictures to which we expose our children's minds for influence and imprint . . . is extremely likely to create a haphazard, promiscuous and undesirable national consciousness.

This type of daydreaming (after watching movies and fantasizing) becomes in reality a sort of drug.

The motion picture is for the great masses a more significant educational influence than most of the school work done in the country.

There is probably something socially wrong, something subversive of the best interests of society in the way a substantial number of present-day movies are made, written, conceived. . . . The road to delinquency, in a few words, is heavily dotted with movie addicts . . . .

One social scientist, who says of gangster films that "Fagin's school was child's play to this curriculum of crime," insists that "crime technique may be learned from the motion pictures," and says of his sample study of teen criminals that "in numerous instances the direct suggestions and influence of motion pictures propelled the spectators towards acts of delinquency and crime."

Another researcher warns that the sexual content of movies "may stimulate impulses and whet appetites." That "conclusion" is supported, throughout the book, by testimony from actual movie-watching teenagers, who confide their innermost thoughts to the note-taking social scientists. A high-school girl says, "I have learned from the movies how to be a flirt." Another girl, sixteen, remarks, "No wonder girls of older days, before the movies, were so modest and bashful. They never saw Clara Bow and William Haines. . . . I think the movies have a great deal to do with present-day so-called wildness. If we did not see such examples in the movies, where would we get the idea of being 'hot'? We wouldn't." And what social study, loaded with a quote such as the one from this teenaged girl, wouldn't prompt concerned parents to circle the wagons and aim at the cinema?

"When I see a fellow and girl in a passionate love scene," this youngster is quoted in a study called "Sex-Delinquency and Crime," "such as The Pagan, I just have a *hot* feeling going through me and I want to do everything bad."

Because of their visual immediacy and wide reach, movies are the closest parallel to television—but other twentieth-century media suffered just as many slings and arrows of outrageous accusers, especially when it came to the potential corruption of America's youth. Gilbert Seldes, in a 1924 essay praising the virtues of the newspaper comics pages ("*Krazy Kat,* the daily comic strip of George Herriman, is, to me, the most amusing and fantastic and satisfactory work of art produced in America today," he wrote in The Seven Lively Arts), actually was exultant that conservative pressure groups had yet to discover the violence and anarchy of the daily comics: "Mutt and Jiggs and Abie the Agent, and Barney Google, and Eddie's Friends have so little respect for law, order, the rights of property, the sanctity of money, the romance of marriage, and all the other foundations of American life," he wrote, "that if they were put into (popular) fiction the Society for the Suppression of Everything would hale them incontinently to court and our morals would be saved again." Sure enough, in the 1950s, a psychiatrist named Dr. Frederic Wertham published a study called *Seduction of the Innocent,* in which he insisted that the reading of comics and comic books was causing "the ruination of children."

And after disc jockey Alan Freed brought a three-day "Rock 'n' Roll Show" to Hartford, Connecticut, in 1956, local psychiatrist Francis J. Braceland testified at a public hearing that rock music was "a communicable disease, with music appealing to adolescent insecurity and driving teenagers to do outlandish things"—such as dancing together in public, an activity that Cleveland, Ohio, city fathers had already deemed illegal unless accompanied by an adult (an absurd ruling, based on a dusty 1931 city ordinance, that quickly proved unenforceable). Hartford's Braceland also called rock 'n' roll "cannibalistic and tribalistic," revealing the arguably racist "roots" of his remarks. In December 1957, the week after Elvis Presley's "Jailhouse Rock" had topped the Billboard singles chart, Sammy Davis, Jr., moderated a syndicated radio roundtable discussion devoted to rock 'n' roll. One of the panelists was recording star and Columbia Records executive Mitch Miller, who, siding with Davis, dismissed rock 'n' roll as "the comic books of music."

From the fear of Elvis's pelvis in the fifties to the recent court declaration that the music of 2 Live Crew is officially obscene, the history of rock music is a constant refrain of critics, clergy, and concerned parents railing against the musical expression of youth. Rock has gotten a bad rap; so has rap. Tipper Gore, spearheading a group of congressional wives who are upset about the content of rock 'n' roll lyrics and music videos, is living, complaining proof that the current generation of authority figures can be just as frightened of a popular art form as those in generations past. Meet the new boss, same as the old boss.

Rock 'n' roll, like jazz and blues before it, expanded its reach exponentially thanks to radio—but not even radio was greeted with universal acclaim. It, too, was an object not necessarily to be trusted. In 1922, when WHAS radio began broadcasting in Louisville, an angry farmer visited the fledgling broadcasters and informed them, "Yesterday afternoon I took a walk across my farm. A flock of blackbirds passed over. Suddenly one of them dropped dead. Your radio wave must have struck it. . . . Suppose that wave had struck me?"

One early periodical article from that same period, probing the possible relationships between radio and illegal activities, was titled "Ether Waves vs. Crime Waves." Another asked, "Is Radio Hurting the Church?" In the 1920s, radio began by following the lead of the earliest silent films, and kept its announcers intentionally anonymous—then, like film, did an about-face and pushed its popular performers into the spotlight. Another parallel between the two media is that with radio, as with film, there were some bullish and prescient early supporters. The first issue of *Radio Broadcast*, in 1922, suggested that "some day in the future the popularity of a political party in office may hinge entirely upon the quality of broadcasting service," and that "the people's University of the Air will have a greater student body than all of our universities put together." And radio, like other forms of popular entertainment, had its share of detractors, and sparked more than a few interesting controversies.

In 1938, five years after *Our Movie Made Children* was published, Orson Welles's *Mercury Theatre on the Air* accidentally terrorized many Americans, young and old, with its updated Halloween-night version of H. G. Wells's *War of the Worlds*—proving the power of radio in a remarkable way, as many people, believing the radio reports about a Martian invasion, fled their homes in panic. That was when radio was king, Orson Welles was young, prewar jitters were high, and the convincing ballroom music and "emergency" broadcasts sounded so authentic—partly because no one expected to be fooled, and partly because Welles's company so skillfully mimicked the sounds of the popular music shows, news bulletins, and announcers of the time. At the time, that artistry was attacked, not applauded, and Welles found he had to apologize for a show he couldn't believe that *anyone* believed. A dozen brief years later, the problem with radio wouldn't be that it was taken too seriously—but that it wasn't taken seriously enough. Comedian Fred Allen, who did exceedingly well on radio, nevertheless remarked quite objectively about the public's general attitude toward it.

"Radio was the first free entertainment ever given to the public," Allen wrote in his 1954 memoirs *Treadmill to Oblivion*.

> Since it was piped into homes, it was a service similar to running water. When the novelty of the shows wore off, many people had more respect for running water than they did for radio. A houseowner who would never think of speaking disrespectfully of the water in his house would rant around his radio set, sounding off about the dubious merits of some program he had just heard.

Radio, like the movies, built its own superstars, borrowed others, and ruled the roost—but, like the movies, began to lose its audience by the millions around the year 1950, when television came into the home, and into its own.

For more than four decades now, television has been the primary popular-arts villain of our society. It has been attacked from within as well as from without, and accused of spreading the same social ills and dastardly side effects as, in a very different and distant era, *The Iliad* and *The Odyssey*. From that Homer, the Greek, to Homer Simpson the geek, the blame's the same—and it's time to put the blame to rest.

4

INSTANT REPLAY: A BROAD LOOK AT BROADCAST HISTORY

Some people, perhaps most, believe that television history began with the advent of the so-called Golden Age, circa 1950, but TV actually began to take shape a generation before that. The word television, in fact, was used in *Scientific American* as far back as 1907. However, the early development of television was a case of *tubus interruptus*—stalled initially by the Wall Street crash of 1929 just as deep-pocketed investors were sorely needed to finance experiments, then stalled again by World War II just as the technology became feasible. TV was slowed further by the fact that radio, still a relatively young medium in its own right, was such a money machine and star-making vehicle that diving into untested TV waters wasn't exactly a high priority for either the owners or performers of network radio. For all intents and purposes, TV's programming achievements don't begin in earnest until the late 1940s, but television's technology and potential were visible much, much earlier. And yes, that means another blast to the past.

Understanding the development of TV, and how it drew from and eventually proved more popular than vaudeville, the dramatic theater, movies, and especially radio, is the key to understanding its impact, its uniqueness—and many of the hostile and condescending verbal grenades thrown at it over the years. Once we get to those specific grenades, I'll lob them back, one by one, in the directions from which they came—but first, a look back to what might be called TV's "Stone Age."

First off, it's gratifying to learn that, with television as with film, there were a few brave, often lonely people who could look at an infant technology and see the future—*any* future. What may well be the first television "review" in history was printed in the June 21, 1923, issue of *Variety*. "Moving Pictures By Radio Successfully Demonstrated," the headline announced, and the story told of Washington, D.C. inventor C. F. Jenkins's "radio eye" transmission system, where a camera in one location sent moving images to a nearby receiver. "The fingers of Mr. Jenkins were wiggled before this device and their movement faithfully reproduced," the reporter noted enthusiastically, though he finished the sentence with the qualifying comment, "although somewhat indistinct." (Everybody's a critic.)

Apparently, moving fingers were a handy element of TV's earliest experiments. In a 1924 article for London's *Kinematograph Weekly*, reporter F. H. Robinson provided a short but enthusiastic account of a visit to the Hastings laboratory of John Logie Baird, where Robinson witnessed what he called "radio vision." It was a very early test of "the transmission of moving images by wireless," and Robinson, like the invention he described, was beaming. "I myself saw a cross, the letter 'H,' and the fingers of my own hand reproduced by this apparatus across the width of the laboratory," Robinson wrote. "Undoubtedly wonderful possibilities are opened up by this invention."

To put it in perspective, this was only a few years after the first commercial *radio* station in America, Pittsburgh's KDKA, had gone on the air in 1920. Amazingly, both Jenkins's "radio eye" and Baird's "radio vision" demonstrations actually had predated the incorporations of future radio giants NBC (1926), and CBS and England's BBC (both 1927). A public demonstration of Baird's invention, somewhat refined, took place in 1926, and public unveilings of the latest advances in this new visual medium quickly became accepted practice. That same year, General Electric's Dr. E. F. W. Alexanderson proposed a TV system based on revolving mirrors, and predicted at a press conference that such a system, adopted globally, would allow people at home to "view the Rajah of India on parade, a future world championship boxing match, or heads of nations may hold a conference by television." *(Nightline,* anyone?) There was action as well as talk: in 1927, the same year the motion-picture industry was stunned by the technological marvel of *The Jazz Singer,* Bell Telephone Laboratory's Dr. Herbert E. Ives placed a tap dancer on the roof of the Bell skyscraper in New York, and, using telephone wires and a gas-filled picture tube, displayed her dancing image to astounded laboratory visitors on a floor below. This was a case of literally tapping the line, but no one seemed to mind. On the contrary: *New York World* reporter Bill Laas, after witnessing Ives's televised tap dancer, wrote a Sunday feature story headlined "When Television Comes to Every Home," predicting a TV in every home—the mass-media equivalent of a chicken in every pot—within ten years. If not for the Great Depression and the war, he may have been right.

General Electric had begun broadcasting the first regular TV programs in May 1928, three times a week, via its WGY station in Schenectady, but to an audience so small—and so dominated by engineers equipped with the special Alexanderson TV receivers—that it seemed less a technological innovation than an existential question ("If a TV signal is broadcast, but no one sees it, was it ever broadcast at all?"). In September 1928, using its radio sister station to boost the audio portion, Schenectady's WGY ambitiously mounted the first live television drama—a forty-minute presentation of *The Queen's Messenger,* J. Hartley Manners's one-act play. Maurice

Randall and Izetta Jewell starred, but were outshone by the novelty of the event. The *New York Times* covered it in a story that was more news report than drama review: The headline was a no-nonsense "Play Is Broadcast by Voice and Acting in Radio-Television," and the story noted that the play was "chosen for the experiment because its cast contains only two actors, who would alternate before the television cameras." Actually, the TV production was a bit more populated than that; because the bulky TV cameras were virtually immobile, two other actors were employed to play the characters' hands, so that certain actions could be photographed in close-up using a separate camera and lens. (Notice, once again, the prominence of fingers in TV's early days.)

Technically, *The Queen's Messenger* was a hit: "For the first time in history," noted the *Times* in its next-day coverage, "a dramatic performance was broadcast simultaneously by radio and television. Voice and action came together in perfect synchronization." The *Times* failed, however, to notice another "first" attached to that particular telecast. It was presented in the afternoon and performed again that evening—making it television's first official prime-time rerun.

And while that one article in the *New York Times* seemed to approve, most of these early TV signals attracted more venom than viewers. The *New York Telegram* warned in 1928 that if this new medium of television was used "to distribute miniature billboards into the home, its growth will be stifled at the outset." (With predictions like that, no wonder the *Telegram* went out of business.) The same year, stage actor Lionel Barrymore warned that the rise of television would "scrap theaters throughout the country." He needn't have worried—it was the imminent stock market crash that would start scrapping theaters by the dozens, all but kill vaudeville, and put the development of TV largely on hold. With the onset of the depression, the prognosis for the future of television became . . . well, depressing. Instead, radio and the movies picked up most of the slack. And the momentum, and the majority of the talent looking for work when the theatrical circuit began to short-circuit.

The media that thrived during the depression were the ones with the most beneficial methods of distribution. At the start of the twentieth century, vaudeville had risen to prominence hand-in-hand, and often in the same theaters and on the same bills, as the early silent films; vaudeville and the movies enjoyed such success together that they eventually split apart, seeking—and getting—separate audiences and all-day showcases. When the Palace Theatre opened on Times Square in 1913, it gave vaudeville performers and writers everywhere a dream, and a goal, that held firm until the crash of 1929. The phrase "to play the Palace" meant to appear at the apex of the national vaudeville circuit, and there was no shortage of talent. Vaudeville veterans who graced the Palace, and other vaudeville stages, included Fred Astaire, Jack Benny, Milton Berle, Fanny Brice, George Burns, and Gracie Allen—and those are just some of the *A*'s and *B*'s. Other headliners at the Palace included W. C. Fields, Ethel

Merman, Kate Smith, and a comedy act known as the Marx Brothers. In a 1924 *Life* review of the Marx Brothers' participation in the Broadway revue *I'll Say She Is*, humorist-critic Robert Benchley raved about their antics at length, then added a comment containing a highly revealing parenthetical: "There must be thousands of you who have seen them in vaudeville (where almost everything that is funny on our legitimate stage seems to originate) and who know that we are right."

Benchley's offhanded defense of vaudeville was pretty brave, because the "mass medium" of vaudeville, despite its abundance of talent, was largely dismissed by most critics at the time. Even the distinction separating vaudeville variety shows from Broadway revues on the "legitimate" stage employed the word *legitimate* as yet another semantic slap at a popular mass medium. But semantic slaps were the least of vaudeville's worries, for it was about to be hit head-on by the force of the depression. Vaudeville shows and staged plays had to be remounted day after day, at relatively great cost; motion pictures, conversely, were literally in the can, and, unlike stagebound acts, could appear anywhere and everywhere at the same time. Once the film itself was produced, all that remained were the costs for duplication, distribution, and promotion. Attending a movie was at least five times cheaper than going to a live show, and radio—once you built or bought a receiver (average cost: ten dollars)—was free. No wonder movies and radio rose, and vaudeville and the theater fell or stalled, after the crash.

"Hard times have added millions of persons to the radio audience, while taking millions from the (theater) audience," noted L. B. Wilson, a radio station and movie-chain owner, early in 1933. "You can get Eddie Cantor on the air for nothing. It costs you fifty cents or more to get him at the theater. You may need the fifty cents for food or clothing. So the theater loses a patron and the radio gets a listener. In previous depressions, there was no radio, and people had to have something to get their minds off their worries."

During Broadway's 1929–30 season, seven out of ten musicals, and nearly nine out of ten dramatic productions, were financial failures. Robert Benchley, then serving as drama critic for The *New Yorker*, couched the gravity of the situation in his trademark wit, but made his point just as effectively. "This business of opening a play and then closing it just as this department gets the review in type has ceased to be funny," Benchley wrote on December 21, 1929. "If the managers are trying to wear me down by this policy of closing shows after they have run only a week, they are succeeding. . . . We can't go on just registering deaths." In that same column, Benchley reviewed a new play, *Family Affairs*, which he predicted would last "for at least six weeks" on the basis of its star, Billie Burke (who, ten years later, would play the Good Witch in *The Wizard of Oz)*. In the next week's *New Yorker* column, though, Benchley vented his frustration after noting *Family Affairs* had become the latest Broadway casualty, closing the night after he wrote his review.

"O well, the hell with it!" Benchley wrote, depressed by the depression.

> Go ahead and close your old shows and see if *I* care! I'll do my duty. I'll
> get all dressed up and go to the openings. I'll make little notes on my
> program which I can't read when I get seated at my typewriter, and I'll
> write out the notices and send them to the printer, just as if there were
> a real play under consideration. And *then* I shall stop worrying my pretty
> little head about it. If it closes, all right. If it runs, all right. I don't want
> to hear about it again, please.

If the "legitimate" Broadway houses were having a hard time luring audiences and keeping their shows afloat, vaudeville was doing even worse—partly because, as radio reached out for talent in the early thirties, the singers and comedians of vaudeville proved more easily and instantly presentable out of context than full-length plays. Before long, vaudeville had little to offer that wasn't already available on radio—except, of course, sight as well as sound. But, by the thirties, the movies had that, too. Ironically, one scheme concocted by the owner of a chain of vaudeville theaters to draw customers, a proposal described in a 1930 *Variety* headline as a "Boon to Vaudeville," was the public exhibition of television. The idea actually came to pass in 1930, as Proctor's Theater in Schenectady offered the "world premiere" of a talking TV picture as a theatrical attraction. The pictures were shown on an experimental seven-foot screen—mammoth for a home, but hardly exciting in an oversized movie palace. In such a setting, the television pictures, like vaudeville's future, looked small and fuzzy.

Within four years of the start of the depression, the number of vaudeville theaters nationwide had dropped from about two thousand to fewer than six hundred. Attendance dropped sharply also, which, right there, is the major difference between movies and vaudeville after the depression. Movies, which had just discovered sound, gave audiences a whole new reason to attend, and weekly attendance at the American movie houses jumped from 65 million in 1928 to 95 million the following year, and held at 90 million in 1930. More than eight-thousand cinemas closed between 1929 and 1935, but those that remained open did very well; average weekly attendance at the movies remained between 80 and 90 million from 1936 through 1949. As for radio, which had only begun commercially in 1920, it was still riding an impressive, stratospheric growth curve.

It was an astoundingly rapid rise for a new technology, especially one that was the stuff of science fiction less than a decade before. David Sarnoff, an employee of the American Marconi Company, had written an internal memo in 1916 proposing a plan in which a "radio music box" could become "a household utility," capable of tuning to several different wavelengths and offering such diverse programming as music, lectures, "events of national importance," and "baseball scores." He was proven exactly right with alarming speed, and both he and his company profited as a result. Marconi became RCA in 1919, and RCA soon dominated the field as the leading distributor of radio sets.

Women had just been given the vote in 1920, and, thanks to another constitutional amendment, liquor had just been taken away. The Westinghouse Electric and Manufacturing Company, setting up a new enterprise in its home town of Pittsburgh, Pa., established the country's first radio station, KDKA. Horne's department store, seeing an opportunity to get in on the ground floor of the "wireless receiver" business, ran in the *Pittsburgh Sun* an ad, looking deceptively like a news story, about the station's pre-launch broadcast tests. "Victrola music, played into the air over a wireless telephone, was 'picked up' by listeners on the wireless receiving station which was recently installed here," the Horne's ad gushed. This ersatz "news report" included a positive critique ("Two orchestra numbers, a soprano solo—which rang particularly high and clear through the air—and a juvenile 'talking piece' constituted the program") and a blatant concluding sales pitch ("Amateur Wireless Sets, made by the maker of the Set which is in operation at our store, are on sale here, ten dollars up"). Five weeks later, KDKA was launched officially, timed so that its inaugural broadcast would be coverage of the returns of the 1920 presidential election—instantly fulfilling Sarnoff's prediction that "events of national importance" could be relayed by radio.

Sarnoff had also predicted radio would deliver baseball scores; within five years of his prediction, it was delivering entire games. KDKA was first here, too, when an employee took his "wireless telegraphy" equipment to an August 1921 game between the Pittsburgh Pirates and Philadelphia Phillies, set up his equipment behind the home-plate screen at Forbes Field, and described the afternoon game live for the station's local listeners. WJZ in Newark, one of the country's first radio stations, made baseball and broadcasting history that fall when it set up a relay system to provide "live" reports—reports that were actually phoned in to, then repeated by, a studio announcer—of the 1921 World Series between the New York Yankees and the New York Giants. "Re-creating" games remained a common practice for decades, and its skillful practitioners, who relied on their own baseball knowledge and acting skills to inject excitement and information between "pitches," included such still-familiar figures as Red Barber, the respected and beloved announcer whose sportscasting career spanned four decades (1934–66), and . . . Ronald Reagan, who, before moving out west to become a movie star, used to re-create Chicago games for WHO radio in Des Moines.

WJZ made a different type of radio history in 1922, by presenting the first stage show presented on radio. It featured vaudeville star Ed Wynn in *The Perfect Fool*—and Wynn, true to the occasion, did a perfectly foolish thing. Wynn was so thrown by having to do his comedy routines for only a radio microphone, without any immediate feedback or laughter, that the announcer of the live broadcast hurriedly corralled everyone on the premises—electricians, telephone operators, janitors, even other actors— to gather around and act as Wynn's studio audience. Their vocal and supportive enjoyment of his jokes helped Wynn get through the program.

Unfortunately, that also gave radio, and then television, the precedent for what's now known as the laugh track.

When Wynn played *The Perfect Fool* that year, there were more than two-hundred stations across the country, broadcasting to ever-growing, ever-enthusiastic audiences. By the following year, 1923, more than 2.5 million sets already were in use. In those early years of radio, the programming was spotty, the performers unpaid, the announcers unidentified—but, as with the advent of silent movies, that practice of toiling in anonymity soon changed. Graham McNamee, whose career in radio began in 1923, broadcast under his own name while announcing the 1925 World Series for New York's WEAF, and received an amazing fifty-thousand letters as a result. This was at a time when WEAF's signal was limited to a hundred-mile radius, and when owning a radio was still the exception, not the norm. If any station owner, or performer, wanted proof of the reach, power, and future of broadcasting, there it was.

McNamee became so popular and prominent so quickly that police would usher his car into and out of the ballpark ahead of any other reporter; that sudden popularity, naturally, sparked jealousy in some of McNamee's print peers. "I don't know which game to write about," grumbled Ring Lardner in one of his baseball pieces. "The one I saw today, or the one I heard Graham McNamee announce as I sat next to him at the Polo Grounds." But McNamee also had his defenders. Red Barber, who eventually would succeed McNamee as radio broadcaster for the World Series, wrote admiringly that "the greatest sports announcer we ever had was Graham McNamee." And McNamee's stature as a radio star is most evident from his assignment behind the mike for one of the biggest news stories, and live radio triumphs, of the decade: Charles A. Lindbergh's triumphant return to Washington, DC, after completing his transatlantic flight to Paris in 1927.

Almost from the start, radio operators recognized and exploited the value the medium's immediacy could give to news and sports: no more waiting for the next day's paper, or the latest newsreel, to see or hear what was happening. Chicago's WGN, in a daringly different display of radio programming, broadcast in 1925 the final days of the Scopes "Monkey Trial," in which attorneys Clarence Darrow and William Jennings Bryan locked horns on the issue of evolution. Predictably, there arose an immediate cry from a minority of Congressmen to ban from radio all discussions of evolution—but radio itself was evolving too rapidly to be stopped.

Responding to such an array of programming, consumers kept buying and listening to radios. The 2.5 million radio sets in use in 1923 had doubled to 5 million by 1926. That's when RCA's Sarnoff was given the approval and budget to establish a subsidiary—co-owned with minority partners, and gung-ho radio manufacturers, General Electric and Westinghouse. The new venture was called NBC, and was designed to produce blocks of programming that would be distributed to affiliated stations via a pair of different networks. The flagship station for the NBC "Red Network," introduced in 1926, was New York's WEAF, the station that had generated such notice with its broadcast of the previous year's World Series. The NBC "Blue Network," which began in 1927, was led and fed by WJZ, the pioneering Newark station that had broadcast the first radio-delivered World Series, and had since moved to New York. NBC charged its affiliated stations a small fee for producing and providing the programs, but the parent company RCA was more motivated by the fact that better shows, and bigger market saturation, meant the manufacture and sale of more radios. (Forty years later, when NBC would push color programs to sell RCA color televisions, the same plan would be used all over again, just as successfully.) NBC made an early mark for itself by providing the first coast-to-coast coverage of the Rose Bowl in 1927, but for radio to really take off, as had the moving pictures, it would take stars—and NBC saw them on the horizon, plain as black and white.

It's noteworthy, given the influx of stage talent that would run to radio during the depression, that radio's first significant superstars were a pair of white comics who had developed their act in vaudeville, working in blackface. Vaudeville, after all, was the unofficial blueprint for early radio, from the division of its entertainment offerings into specific increments at set intervals, adhering to a printed schedule, to the dependence upon vaudeville's writers, actors, and performers. On the radio, in a 1926 series for Chicago's WGN called *Sam 'n' Henry*, Freeman Gosden and Charles Correll dispensed with the blackface and concentrated on the characters and voices. In 1928, the series changed stations (to Chicago rival WMAQ), and titles, and became known as *Amos 'n' Andy*. The change of ownership gave Gosden and Correll a visibility—or at least an audibility—far outside of the Windy City, for WMAQ approved the duo's plan to record and distribute recorded discs of the shows to other stations nationwide, so long as the program was performed live on WMAQ. This crude method of distribution, involving thirty stations and utilizing primitive ten-inch, five-minute wax discs, not only paved the way for the concept of program syndication, but also made *Amos 'n' Andy* a household word throughout America.

NBC, which had begun life the same year as *Sam 'n' Henry*, paid a mammoth one-hundred-thousand dollars per year in 1929 to acquire exclusive radio rights to *Amos 'n' Andy*—and struck gold, depression or no depression. The show became such a popular network hit that listeners scheduled their activities around it, and many movie theaters, adopting an if-you-can't-beat-'em attitude, slotted time on *Amos 'n' Andy* nights to pipe in broadcasts to their patrons as part of the evening program, rather than lose the audience altogether.

Also in 1929, a young man named William S. Paley purchased CBS, and countered both the NBC competition and the oncoming depression by offering to give certain portions of his network programming away free to affiliated stations, a total of up to twelve hours per day, rather than charging them for the privilege. Paley reasoned he could more than make up the money by charging advertisers higher rates if the size of the audience increased, and it was a brilliant gamble. (Selling the audience base to advertisers, as newspapers and magazines did, would become not only the norm in broadcasting, but the overwhelming driving force.) The number of radio stations signing on as CBS affiliates nearly doubled overnight, as did Paley's profits. With NBC having an early and significant jump in the field of entertainment, Paley seemed at a huge disadvantage, but the onset of the depression and the collapse of vaudeville made a great deal of talent available very quickly. Paley also had a gift for building new talent on his own: he gave nearly daily exposure to young singers Kate Smith and Bing Crosby. Equally important was his early commitment to build broadcast news into something respectable and important (hiring Ed Klauber of the *New York Times* to establish CBS News was a crucial first step). The growth of CBS News, along with the growing roster of entertainment stars, helped Paley's CBS to battle Sarnoff's NBC head-on. The winner, of course, was the radio audience.

By the early thirties, NBC, in either its "Red" or "Blue" Networks, boasted a very strong lineup. In addition to *Amos 'n' Andy*, NBC boasted shows starring Eddie Cantor, Bob Hope, Al Jolson, and Rudy Vallee, whose radio variety series quickly usurped the Palace Theatre as *the* place to be for vaudeville talent. CBS offered Jack Benny, Fred Allen, George Burns and Gracie Allen, and even Ed Wynn. Radio became the nation's most popular source of entertainment—and, in certain conservative circles, a popular source of irritation.

Pressure groups, such as the National Congress of Parents and Teachers, began arguing as early as 1933 that radio was "venal" and "tiresome," and should be a government operation. The group argued for the institution of "public ownership and operation of broadcasting" rather than "a commercial monopoly which is already going over the heads of parents in an effort to influence children in their homes." (In time, commercial and public broadcasting would exist side by side, in both radio and television.) Angry about the over-the-air use of recorded music, the Music Publishers Protective Association began printing warning labels on its artists' records—warnings aimed not at consumers, but at engineers. "Not licensed for radio broadcast," they were stamped. But all music-publishing representatives capitulated, and negotiated, as radio and its audience continued to grow exponentially.

As it entertained people by the millions, radio also began to inform and even soothe them. When President Franklin Delano Roosevelt delivered his inaugural address in March 1933, he used the same style of speech that had been heard, in person or on the radio, whenever a politician had spoken before a crowd: booming, forceful, usually formal. That same week, a series of bank collapses prompted the new president to take to the air waves again—but this time in an intimate, unprecedented type of political broadcast. Instead of a "standard" broadcast in which radio listeners heard a politician boldly and loudly addressing a large gathering, listeners tuning in to that special radio address heard their president speaking, in essence, softly and directly to them. It was a new type of public speaking for radio—and, at the same time, a new type of radio. Roosevelt's seemingly casual addresses came to be known as "fireside chats," and were broadcast regularly, though sparingly, throughout his presidency: that first year, Roosevelt delivered only four such "chats," spaced at least two months apart. He was well aware, though, of the intent and impact of his low-key performances. Partway through his presidency, Roosevelt told Orson Welles there were two great actors in America at that moment; Welles, he said, was the other one.

Radio had definitely arrived by then, but TV already was waiting in the wings. NBC, heady with its head start in network radio, had launched its own experimental flagship TV station, New York's W2XBS, in 1930. Close on NBC's heels, television manufacturer Allen B. DuMont broadcast a half-hour TV test special via two New Jersey stations the same year, and CBS launched its experimental New York TV operation over W2XAB in 1931. The inaugural CBS broadcast was TV's first true "special," giving the audience at home the chance to see, as well as hear, some exciting, noteworthy talent. Kate Smith, fast becoming a star thanks to constant exposure on CBS radio, sang "When the Moon Comes over the Mountain," and George Gershwin played his "Liza"—a song from the musical *Show Girl*, which had closed after 111 performances in 1929. Even so, the future of television appeared as blurry as the image on those flickering, shadowy, round TV tubes.

In a special article on television published in the 1931 edition of the *Encyclopaedia Britannica*, TV was saluted for its potential ability to relay "speakers or athletic events to audiences at a distant point," but denigrated because "the practical and economic barriers to transmitting really satisfactory images are so great as to oppose very serious obstacles to the general use of television." This could be tossed away as just another pessimistic, ill-informed reaction against a new medium, except that the author of that special *Britannica* article was, if anything, very healthily informed: he was the same Herbert Ives who had wowed people with his tap-dancing TV demonstration four years earlier.

For a while, Ives was proven more right than wrong. New York's CBS station, the aforementioned W2XAB, ran a one-hour test special in October 1932 called *Broadway on Parade*, headlined by Helen Morgan. It prompted, from *Variety*, the grim observation (or nonobservation) that "Few of the entertainers on the bill were approachably recognizable." A pioneer West Coast station, Los Angeles's W6XAO, exploited its hometown Hollywood connections by running live interviews in the early thirties, with such stars as Tom Mix and Jean Harlow, and even showing such recent films as *The Texan* (a Gary Cooper Western from 1930). However, the sixty-line resolution was so poor, Cooper may as well have been starring in an Eastern. And though TV and TV technology advanced during the thirties, it was a very slow advance. "The talk of television among the experts is, on the whole, pessimistic. 'It will be a long time' is the gist of the statements," reported J. C. Furnas, in his 1936 book *The Next Hundred Years.*

> There are always a few optimists who say, "Next year. Television in every third home. Satisfactory." Still the years roll on. Each one brings something new, but no one has yet solved all the difficulties. The movie people struggled for thirty years to get a little sound in their performances and the sound people (radio) have been working just as hard and almost as long to get a little vision in their act.

Furnas was not, however, totally without hope, or vision. "It is my hope," he writes in that same book, "and I see no reason why it should not be realized, to be able to go to an ordinary movie theatre when some great national event is taking place across the country and see on the screen the sharp image of the action reproduced—at the same instant it occurs. This waiting for the newsreels to come out is a bit tiresome for the twentieth century." Later in the same century, people wouldn't even have to leave their homes to see such sights, and Furnas predicted that as well, though with one final dash of skepticism:

> Some time later I hope to be able to take my inaugurals, prize fights, and football games at home. I expect to do it satisfactorily and cheaply. Only under those conditions can a television set get into my house. . . . I am waiting for my television but I cannot live forever.

He didn't have to. The very next year, 1937, video advances included the development and demonstration of a much clearer TV picture by RCA-NBC (with Felix the Cat, not a wiggling finger, as the test image), and the hookup of a ninety-mile coaxial cable connecting Philadelphia and New York. NBC's W2XBS station even broadcast a production of Arthur Conan Doyle's Sherlock Holmes story *The Three Garridebs* that year. One of the visitors checking out a laboratory demonstration of the latest TV advance was author and essayist E. B. White, who took his lasting impressions from that visit and drew on them for an essay he wrote for *Harper's* in 1938. This was at a time—postdepression, prewar—when radio, not TV, was on everyone's mind and in everyone's parlor (well, 91 percent of the parlors, anyway, as of 1938). To put it in perspective: live, coast-to-coast radio coverage of the Hindenburg disaster had occurred only the year before, and Orson Welles's infamous *War of the Worlds*, broadcast in 1938 the night before Halloween, was still a few months away. Exposure at the New York World's Fair would bring TV a much higher profile the following year—but in 1938, White had this to say about television:

> I believe television is going to be the test of the modern world, and that in this new opportunity to see beyond the range of our vision we shall discover either a new and unbearable disturbance of the general peace

or a saving radiance in the sky. We shall stand or fall by television—of that I am quite sure . . . .

Television will enormously enlarge the eye's range, and, like radio, will advertise the Elsewhere. Together with the tabs, the mags, and the movies, it will insist that we forget the primary and the near in favor of the secondary and the remote. More hours in every twenty-four will be spent digesting ideas, sounds, images—distant and concocted.

This is before TV networks even existed, much less before they began broadcasting regionally, nationally, internationally, or over twenty-four-hour periods. White's remarks also predate, by thirteen years, the premiere of the 1951 Edward R. Murrow-Fred Friendly collaboration *See It Now* on CBS, which opened with the very enlarged "Elsewhere" vision of simultaneous live views of the Brooklyn Bridge in the East and the Golden Gate Bridge in the West. It was one of the first, and most literal, uses of the coast-to-coast TV hookup, which in 1951 finally connected California and New York by coaxial cable. "We are impressed," Murrow told viewers then, "by a medium in which a man sitting in his living room has been able for the first time to look at two oceans at once."

Murrow, of course, made his initial reputation as a CBS reporter working overseas prior to and during World War II, with his unforgettable live broadcasts that began "This . . . is London." Radio in general, and CBS and CBS News in particular, thrived throughout the forties; even so, it was America's entry in the war, more than anything else, that delayed TV's usurpation of radio as the reigning mass medium.

This doesn't mean TV was either inactive or invisible during the pre-war and war years. In May 1938, in a front-page story, Bob Landry, a critic on *Variety*, gave the trade press's first full-blown analysis of a TV show. It was a 25-minute dramatization of a horror story, writer-director Thomas Hutchinson's *The Mysterious Mummy Case*, that was performed before a live audience and broadcast by NBC's W2XBS in New York. Dorothy McGuire was one of the stars, and the story told of an evil-exuding mummy case "whose macabre influence killed a series of men and finally sent to the bottom of the ocean the *S.S. Titanic.*" The review was, in *Variety* terms, boffo.

The Mysterious Mummy Case qualifies as cathode ray television's first important milestone from a purely story-telling, entertainment-technique standpoint. . . . RCA–NBC experimenters used a combination of five sets, employing live talent, and the auxiliary interpolation of moving picture footage, slides, and special effects . . . .

For the first time television got beyond the close-up of a ticking watch, the blurred reproduction of newsreels, the contrasting of a 441-line smudge with a 343-line smudge, and the photographing of company executives.

Naturally, any praise was accompanied by reservations. Later in the review, Landry noted, "Images do not permit easy recognition of the characters," and added that "television is still crude. Very crude. It is still a long way off. . . . But compared to the rain-streaked flickers of the nickelodeon days the entertainment offered by *The Mysterious Mummy Case* is relatively advanced." The review itself, significantly, was accompanied by a sidebar caveat from the *Variety* editors. Headlined "Television Warning," it doubtless headed off a lot of nay-saying letters to the editor by remarking "there is nothing immediately hot or revolutionary about the present status of television," and that "there is still a great distance to travel before it can be placed on the market."

Flying in the face of such caution, local TV in general, and NBC's W2XBS in particular, kept conducting experiments. A week after televising *The Mysterious Mummy Case,* the New York NBC station presented the first local TV broadcast of a full-length motion picture: *The Return of the Scarlet Pimpernel,* released the previous year in Great Britain. (It's no surprise the movie came from abroad; Hollywood, even at this early point, and despite its previous cooperation with a local Los Angeles station, had nothing but contempt for the concept of television.) Another RCA–NBC experiment, this one in the summer of 1939, was a special called *Pinky Lee and Co.,* starring the vaudeville comic and two assistants. It, too, earned a review in *Variety,* one more or less prefiguring the success of TV's first superstar, Milton Berle. The reviewer (Landry again) observed, "It appears that television, like the early cinema, has an affinity for slapstick. . . . Some things may not be promising for the sky-pictures, but custard pie seems to lose nothing in the transfer."

That same summer, on that same station, Noël Coward's *Hay Fever* was adapted—costarring, in a lost yet tantalizing appearance, Montgomery Clift as Simon Bliss. Television continued to rack up performing "firsts," which, according to several sources, included Fred Waring as the first "name" band to appear on TV, and Ann Miller as the first tap dancer.

As noted, RCA introduced its TV system to visitors at the New York World's Fair in 1939, and television received a lot of press attention. Naturally, not all of it was positive. "The problem with television," declared the *New York Times* in March 1939, "is that people must sit and keep their eyes glued on the screen; the average American family hasn't time for it. Therefore, the showmen are convinced that for this reason, if for no other, television will never be a serious competitor of (radio) broadcasting." The *Times* neglected to mention that the same "problem" applied to, say, reading a book—or, for that matter, the *Times.*

CBS unveiled its prototype for a color TV system in 1940, a system that, though impressive, was incompatible with current black-and-white broadcasting standards. After soaking up millions of dollars and years of effort, it was abandoned. Meanwhile, on July 1, 1941, something else new came to the fledgling medium of television: commercial sponsors.

That was the day advertising sponsorship of television programs was declared legal in America. The CBS station W2XAB became known as WCBW then, but was too busy fiddling with a whole new concept of color

TV technology to get too worked up about TV sponsorship. Conversely, NBC's New York station, now called WNBT, had lined up sponsors in anticipation of the ruling. It rolled out several sponsored programs that very day; one was Lowell Thomas's regular fifteen-minute radio newscast, simulcast on television for the first time. NBC's camera showed Thomas reading the news in his studio—a TV image punctuated by occasional close-ups of cans of Sunoco Oil, the TV show's sponsor. *Variety,* while noting that news reports were as valuable to television as to radio, groused, "There is nothing very glamorous about . . . men reading either news digests or commercials from scripts." That, too, would change quickly.

Yet before newscasters could dominate things, the news did—and the war abroad had such serious repercussions on the home front that most broadcasters across the country quickly pulled the plug on their TV operations. In New York, the CBS and NBC stations all but ceased operations in the fall of 1942, and didn't resume again until after the war—but that left open the door for some area rivals. Schenectady's General Electric operation, which had presented *The Queen's Messenger* back in 1928, started its WRGB TV station and, in 1942, presented a one-hour dramatization of *Uncle Tom's Cabin.* DuMont's first TV station, W2XWV in New York, had only begun experimenting in 1941, and didn't begin regular operation until the summer of 1942—so it was reluctant to go dark during wartime. DuMont's founder had been right in the thick of things during TV's experimental broadcasts of the early thirties, and envisioned a DuMont "network" that would eventually compete with stations offering CBS and NBC programs. Throughout the war, DuMont's New York station televised between five and ten hours of TV programming per week—which, according to *Television Daily,* made it "the only television station in the U.S. to maintain a regular program schedule." The DuMont station, which in 1944 changed its call letters to WABD, hogged virtually all of the TV review space in *Variety,* but logged few triumphs. One of its few noteworthy wartime efforts was a May 1943 variety special called *Cafe Television,* headlined by future *Broadway Open House* host Jerry Lester. Checking out the casual talk-and-variety format, *Variety* said, "This is a feature that has promise, despite a number of rough edges."

For the most part, though, there were few TV shows to see, and few sets to see them on. Production on TV sets was halted during the war years, and, when production resumed in 1945, only about one hundred sets were manufactured—and those went to people who had signed up on prewar waiting lists.

After the war, things were different. Television was ready to do battle with radio, and the participants in that battle were a mixture of the familiar and the new. CBS was there, of course, as was NBC—or, technically, half of NBC, since the government had forced NBC to divest itself of its "Blue Network" in 1943. Under new ownership, the "Blue Network" became ABC, which eventually got its own New York flagship TV station in 1948. And there was, for a while, a fourth network: DuMont, which had laced together enough interested affiliates to claim true network status. DuMont had some early, noteworthy successes: Jackie Gleason, for example, developed most of his memorable characters, including Ralph Kramden, for DuMont's *The Cavalcade of Stars* in 1950, two years before defecting to CBS. However, DuMont could match neither the salaries nor the station lineups of its competitors, and DuMont's fall corresponded with ABC's slow rise; DuMont eventually collapsed in 1955.

Yet DuMont's eventual failure was overwhelmingly overshadowed by the success of just about everything else related to television—and each fresh success, it seemed, had some strong relationship to previous successes in previous mass media. NBC, which had scored such memorable coups with sports broadcasting in the formative days of radio, presented the first network TV broadcast of a World Series in 1947, which could be seen on NBC stations in New York, Schenectady, Philadelphia, and Washington, DC. In those four cities, the televised baseball games—in which the Yankees beat the Brooklyn Dodgers in a thrilling seven-game series—were viewed by an estimated 3.9 million people. That's a fairly remarkable statistic, because a full 3.5 million of those people were watching on barroom TV sets.

Television sets were not yet a common piece of furniture in the home, but that first televised World Series sold an awful lot of sets, as did other exciting offerings from TV that year. People who bought, say, a General Electric ten-inch "Daylight Television" for $325 in 1947 could be the first, and maybe the only, people on their block to see the first telecast of *Howdy Doody*, and NBC's *Kraft Television Theatre*, and *Meet the Press*, as well as regular shows featuring wrestling, roller derby, and singing cowboy Gene Autry. If they lived in or around Chicago, they could also see a local children's show named *Kukla, Fran and Ollie*, which went network a few years later. There was even a weekly prime-time soap opera in 1947: DuMont's *Faraway Hill*, a weekly series that had actually begun the year before. None of it, though, impressed the influential writer and critic H. L. Mencken, whose October 30, 1947, diary entry says of television: "I can imagine only very stupid people looking at it, at least in its present form. It is not even as well developed as the movie was in the days of *The Great Train Robbery*."

The very next year, ABC and CBS joined NBC and DuMont in providing network fare, and interest in TV exploded. By 1950, there were 3.8 million TV households equipped with television—a large number, but still less than ten percent of total homes. By 1955, the number had shot to 30.7 million, with a TV set in nearly two out of three households.

Once you get to 1948, the history of television becomes so familiar it hardly needs recounting; reputations, if not memories, resonate to this very day. Vaudeville may have been dead by then, but its spirit and jokes lived on in the spirit of Milton Berle, whose antics on NBC's *Texaco Star Theater* made him the medium's first superstar—he was to TV what *Amos 'n' Andy* was to radio, and caught on just as quickly.

Berle was signed to guest host only the first four installments of *Texaco*

Star Theater, but his summertime debut was such a smash that, by fall, he was permanent host. Days after his June debut, *Variety* raved that Berle was "one of those naturals," and coined a new term: *Vaudeo.* " 'Vaudeo'— the adaptation of old-time vaudeville into the new video medium—came of age last Tuesday night . . . in a performance that may well be remembered as a milestone in television." The term *Vaudeo* soon was Deadeo, but *Variety* was more correct when noting that the TV success of Berle and his wide variety of guests, ranging from Pearl Bailey to Señor Wences, "tipped off the practicability of integrating the vast reservoir of . . . variety talent into the industry's newest offspring." The reviewer, George Rosen, even noted that "it was all whipped together into the old Palace format," suggesting television had not killed vaudeville after all, but merely absorbed it.

By the end of 1948, Berle's show was seen each week by an estimated eighty percent of all TV owners. Both *Time* and *Newsweek* put Berle on their covers the same week in 1949, and, later that year, Philip Hamburger of the *New Yorker* wrote with accuracy, but without much enthusiasm, "When the history of the early days of commercial television is eventually written, several chapters will no doubt be devoted to the strange art of Milton Berle." Vaudeville also resurfaced in the looseness of *Arthur Godfrey's Talent Scouts* and the sheer variety presided over by Ed Sullivan in *Toast of the Town* (later renamed *The Ed Sullivan Show*), both of which, like Berle's *Texaco Star Theater*, began in 1948. Sullivan, however, got less-glowing initial reviews from the press, perhaps because his peers were jealous that one of their own had made the jump from the printed page to network television. *Variety* said dryly that "Sullivan, as an emcee, is a good newspaper columnist."

Also that year, TV borrowed from the more serious Broadway tradition, as well as from radio's successful dramatic anthology series, to launch such ambitious regular showcases as *Philco Television Playhouse* and *Studio One*. It borrowed from the movies, specifically the "B" Westerns, to mount a successful cowboy series starring Bill Boyd as his established Saturday-matinee character of Hopalong Cassidy—and recast a radio hit on TV by hiring Clayton Moore to play a visible version of *The Lone Ranger.* Television became, with astonishing speed, the country's chief celebrant and purveyor of popular culture—delivering, for the first time in history, both the sights and sounds that had drawn people to previous mass media and popular performances.

Television had the visual punch of movies and the stage as well as the immediacy and intimacy of radio. TV drew from all of it—and sometimes lampooned it. In *The Admiral Broadway Revue* (later and better known as *Your Show of Shows*), which began in 1949, Sid Caesar and his brilliant stable of performers and writers lampooned everything from ballet and opera to silent, current, and foreign movies. Meanwhile, Ed Wynn, one of the first vaudeville performers to cross over to radio, made a similar leap of faith by starring in CBS's *The Ed Wynn Show* in 1949, the first TV show to originate from Hollywood. Writers, directors, comedians, actors, singers, announcers, newscasters—some of them warily steered clear of television, but others flocked to it, eager to try something new or, at the very least, able to read the writing on the wall. Weekly movie attendance tumbled from 87.5 to 60 million, a drop of nearly one-third, between 1949 and 1950, and television was the reason. Radio, too, was hemorrhaging, losing audience to this bold new medium. As a result, many radio stars could soon be seen as well as heard.

Jack Benny took his CBS radio show to CBS television in 1950, when *The Jack Benny Show* made its debut. George Burns and Gracie Allen, Kate Smith, Frank Sinatra, and Bob Hope got their own TV shows that year, too, and there were TV incarnations of such familiar radio shows as *Your Hit Parade* (which showcased and often acted out popular songs, like an early MTV) and *The Adventures of Superman*. Movie stars, as well as radio stars, emigrated to television that year: Groucho Marx began a whole new career by hosting *You Bet Your Life* (first for radio, then for TV), and *The Roy Rogers Show* brought yet another likable big-screen cowboy buckaroo to the small screen.

By 1951, television's supremacy was assured, and the range of programming truly invigorating. That was the year of *I Love Lucy;* of Ernie Kovacs's playful brilliance with TV technology; of Gian Carlo Menotti's *Amahl and the Night Visitors,* the first opera written for television; of the heavyweight fight, carried by NBC, in which Rocky Marciano defeated Joe Louis; of the TV debut of *Amos 'n' Andy,* with black actors Alvin Childress and Spencer Williams (and Tim Moore as the Kingfish) inheriting the roles played on radio by the show's white creators; of *The Chevy Show,* ending with Dinah Shore's trademark kiss; of Murrow's *See It Now*; and of the Senate crime hearings, which made stars of such questioners as Estes Kefauver (a Democratic senator from Tennessee) and questionees as Frank Costello, whose stardom arose, paradoxically, from his reluctance to be shown on camera. As a compromise, television covered Costello's halting testimony by photographing only his hands as he spoke. (It might have been the moment TV was rehearsing for all those years when its earliest cameras honed in on all those "moving fingers.") A *Broadcasting* editorial that year suggested that coverage of the Kefauver hearings had "promoted television in one big swoop from everybody's whipping boy—in the sports, amusement, and even retail world—to benefactor, without reservations. Its camera eye had opened the public's."

There were things TV still lacked in comparison to radio, but not many. One was the diversity of available programming, another was the hours of operation, and a third was an active participation on the part of the audience. Such popular radio shows as *Lights Out,* certainly, could feed greater horrors through the power of imagination than visual special effects could ever hope to duplicate. The power of the Orson Welles radio version of *The War of the Worlds* doubtlessly was due, in no small part, to the willingness of many listeners not only to suspend disbelief, but to flesh out the images described to them in intricate and intimidating detail. Radio, at its best, not only permitted you to imagine, but required it.

"How, for example, would you ever 'zoom in' on Fibber McGee's closet?" Brock Brower wrote in the April 1960 issue of *Esquire*, lamenting the passing of "old-time" radio.

> That avalanche of roller-skates, vacuum-cleaner parts, and bottles of Johnson's Glo-Coat, then the epic pause, and finally the falling dinner-bell: it was pure sound, and it's a relief to find NBC's innocuous revival of *Fibber McGee and Molly* keeping at least that closet sacred—and off-camera. Or Jack Benny's Maxwell. It was an internal combustion that Mel Blanc brought out of his own gut and had nothing to do with the visible automotive world. Or that door Raymond opened on *Inner Sanctum*. It wasn't a door. It was a ghastly rasp that climbed up your spine.

Yet what the familiar medium of radio offered could hardly compete with the new frontier of television. The shifting media landscape was like an earthquake, in a rapid and constant state of upheaval—as was obvious from the daily audience figures for usage of each medium. In 1947, the average family listened to radio 4.32 hours per day; by 1951, the first year for which comparative figures with television were available, daily listening had decreased to 3.39 hours, while TV viewership was measured at 1.43 hours daily. In 1954, TV would take the lead from radio and get credit for just under three hours of daily use, while radio had slipped to 2.5 hours. Television never looked back; radio had no choice but to look elsewhere—and counterprogram. In 1948, the most popular forms of network radio programming were dramatic shows—which occupied nearly one-third of the broadcast week—and music performed live. A decade later, the dominant form on network radio was the recorded-music show, followed by news.

Fred Allen, who had gone from vaudeville and the stage to radio and loved it, then from radio to TV and loathed it, vented his frustrations about the new dominant medium by making two points in his 1954 memoirs. One point was exactly right: "Comedy has changed with the coming of television," he noted.

> The radio listener saw nothing; he had to use his imagination. It was possible for each individual to enjoy the same program according to his intellectual level and his mental capacity. In radio, a writer could create any scene that the listener could picture mentally. In television, a writer is restricted by the limitations imposed on him by the scenic designers and the carpenter. With the high cost of living and the many problems facing him in the modern world, all the poor man had left was his imagination. Television has taken that away from him.

Of course, not even the curmudgeonly Allen would level the same charge at the motion picture, and suggest that the comedy of the Marx

Brothers was impaired by the tacky stage sets. But in terms of TV taking over and imposing a new type of audience involvement, Allen was correct. Where he really messed up was with this assessment:

> There was a certain type of imaginative comedy that could be written for, and performed on, only the radio. Television comedy is mostly visual and the most successful of comedians today are disciples of the slapstick. Jack Benny, with his comedy show, has been a star in radio for more than twenty years. I am afraid that twenty years from today none of the current crop of TV comedians will be found cutting their elementary didoes before the camera.

The first thing to understand about Allen's remark is that *didoes,* a seldom-used word today, means a showy, insubstantial act. The second thing is that he made that statement in 1955, when "the current crop of TV comedians" he was dismissing as quick flashes in TV's pan included Jackie Gleason and Art Carney in *The Honeymooners,* Lucille Ball in *I Love Lucy,* the inventive genius of Ernie Kovacs, and the TV work of such old vaudeville and radio colleagues as Groucho Marx, George Burns, and even Jack Benny. That supposedly transitory class of 1955 also included Bob Hope, who, at this writing, is *still* cranking out top-rated TV specials for NBC. In the 1990s, more than thirty-five years later, the "elementary didoes" of every one of those celebrated comics are displayed daily on cable TV and in national syndication. All those comics who stayed with and thrived on TV are, with the exception of Groucho, more known and revered today for their TV routines than for their work in other media. Fred Allen, ironically, is most strongly associated with television too—but only as a man who tossed withering insults in its direction.

"The reason why television is called a medium," Allen said, in his most-repeated, often-jumbled quote, "is because nothing on it is ever well done." Allen defined television as "a device that permits people who haven't anything to do to watch people who can't do anything." (Which may be the inspiration for Frank Zappa's quoteworthy dismissal of rock-music criticism as something written by people who can't write, about people who can't play, for people who can't read.) Allen's verbal attacks on TV have become part of its history and mythology, much like former FCC commissioner Newton Minow's "vast wasteland" phrase and Marshall McLuhan's joint declarations that "the medium is the message" and, later, "the medium is the massage." McLuhan, though, was making specific points, and not at all hostile ones, in his own catchy fashion. Minow and Allen were attacking television—an activity that, since the medium was invented, has been one of America's most popular spectator sports. Especially among nonspectators.

As early as the late forties, at the very beginning of network broadcasting, TV was being called an electronic babysitter . . . or words to that effect. Jack Gould of the *New York Times,* one of the first and best TV critics to serve on an influential newspaper, noted the phenomenon in 1948: "Children's hours on television," he wrote, "admittedly are an insidious narcotic for the parent. With the tots fanned out on the floor in front of the receiver, a strange if wonderful quiet seems at hand." That same year, an NBC script executive, concerned about the mesmerizing properties of television, wrote an internal memo suggesting daytime TV soap operas be written for the ear as well as the eye, to free up women viewers to do chores while "listening" to the TV set. Otherwise, he warned, "The audience must watch a television play to receive full enjoyment. And if the housewife does that for too many hours each day and for too many days each week, the divorce rate may skyrocket."

In the fifties, the attacks came from many, and sometimes unexpected, quarters. Kefauver, who had felt firsthand the power of television as a "star" of his televised 1951 Crime Commission hearings, turned right around in 1952 and conducted a Senate inquiry into the relationship between radio and television violence and juvenile delinquency. The House of Representatives, not to be outdone, conducted an investigation into "immoral or offensive" radio and TV programming the same year. Both panels urged voluntary restraint, and Kefauver's committee eventually released a report urging that the Federal Communications Commission establish minimum guidelines for children's programming, but the advice fell short of creating congressional mandates for the content of entertainment programming. The Kefauver committee had been unable to prove a link between TV and juvenile crime—like the link so "firmly" established with film and juvenile crime in *Our Movie Made Children*—but at least walked away with the satisfying knowledge that it had been unable to *disprove* a link. The official summary noted that the committee had been unable to find "irrefutable evidence that young people may *not* be negatively influenced [italics mine] in their present day behavior" by televised crime and violence. So much for the innocent-before-proven-guilty concept. . . .

The committee would have had more to complain about very shortly, when Warner Brothers reversed an earlier stand against cooperating with the TV networks (Jack L. Warner had explained his studio's refusal to provide films to television with the simple argument, "If people can get something for free, I see no reason why they should want to pay for it"). Warner Brothers became the first major Hollywood studio to film a weekly series for television. Among its first productions were *Colt .45* and *Cheyenne*, which premiered in 1955 and started a flood of backlot, bullet-filled TV Western series. By 1956, a *Reader's Digest* article suggested a call to action—against TV action—that began with its clear and active title: "Let's Get Rid of Tele-Violence."

Every decade since then has brought with it an intensified interest in, and debate on, the content and impact of television. The sixties could claim a reasoned, credible 1961 study *(Television in the Lives of Our Children*, by Wilbur Schramm, Jack Lyle, and Edwin B. Parker) that concluded, "It is not scientifically justifiable to say that television is good or bad for children. The relationship is always between a *kind* of television and a *kind* of child in a *kind* of situation." Also part of the sixties, though, were Minow's "vast wasteland" remark, and the introduction of such statistically damning studies of TV violence as those of George Gerbner and his team at the University of Pennsylvania. (Both of those will be addressed more fully in the next part of the book, when I throw down the gauntlet and attack TV's attackers.)

The sixties also gave us Mason Williams, who wrote for (and performed on) *The Smothers Brothers Comedy Hour,* a wonderful highlight of that decade's TV history. Even so, to Williams it was a more confining than liberating experience. Network constraints prompted Williams to leave the show and, like Fred Allen, subsequently rail against television from a former insider's viewpoint, with a gifted comic writer's deadly aim and staccato one-liners. "I am qualified to criticize television," Williams wrote in *The Mason Williams F.C.C. Rapport,* "because I have two eyes and a mind, which is one more eye and a mind more than television has." He also wrote, "Television doesn't have a job, it just goofs off all day." And "Television is doing to your mind exactly what industry is doing to the land. Some people already think like New York City looks."

Not all television criticism is that much fun to read. Some of it is hysterical, all right, but in a different way. In the seventies, there were such anti-TV books as Gregg Lewis's *Telegarbage,* which included a foreword that said of television, "Every year millions of people become its willing captives, unaware that their minds are being programmed by a dazzling, bloody array of violence and sex unprecedented in electronic communication history." The same book also echoed a *Movie Made Children* refrain by quoting a crook who said he'd learned criminal behavior from TV—"Once, after watching a *Hawaii Five-0* episode, I robbed a gas station," he said, adding, "The show showed me how to do it." And, puzzlingly, the book quoted a German study in which volunteers who were denied the use of TV suffered adverse side effects. "Tension and quarrelling increased, even wife-beating reached a new intensity, and the volunteers' love life took a nose dive," it reported. What lesson is supposed to be learned from this? That too *little* TV can cause violence?

Oddly enough, by 1977, one anti-TV critic was going on record as pining for the "delightful, refreshing, and full of fun" good old days—of the sixties. "Today, by contrast," Mary Lewis Coakley wrote in her 1977 book *Rated X: The Moral Case against TV,* "nearly all TV offerings are soiled by an obsession with sex and a sneering attitude toward the traditional underpinnings of American society.... It is not so much that any one particular program is, for instance, violent, or reeking with sick sex, or oozing anti-Americanism; rather it is that almost every program is tinged or tainted to some degree." She likened each offense to a snowflake, and all of TV to a veritable blizzard: "It is the cumulative effect, the constant, ever-falling stuff that does the trick—that implants ideas and corrodes the national soul."

In another TV book from the seventies, *The View from Sunset Boulevard,* author Ben Stein reports with authority, but without citation, that "scientists have found that the TV news, with its constant diet of sneers and negativism, makes regular viewers hostile and apathetic." He does not address, however, the constant diet of sneers and negativism aimed at TV itself—but it's quite a menu. I haven't even gotten to the surgeon general's 1972 report on TV violence (which basically reached the wimpy conclusion that there was evidence of a "causal relationship" between violence on TV and the behavior of *some* children under *certain* circumstances). Or the "Family Viewing Time" fiasco of the midseventies, which literally tried to impose taste by committee. Or such essayists of the eighties as Neil Postman (who, in *Amusing Ourselves to Death,* declared that "the best things on television *are* its junk" and called *Sesame Street* a "threat to our public health") and Allan Bloom (who, in *The Closing of the American Mind,* remarked of MTV's music videos that "Hitler's image recurs frequently enough in exciting contexts to give one pause," and called MTV a purveyor of life as "a nonstop, commercially prepackaged masturbational fantasy"). Is it mere coincidence that one of Bloom's other books is a translation of Plato's *Republic?*

Nor have I mentioned Terry Rakolta's recent nationwide campaign against Fox's *Married . . . with Children,* or some of the headlines that have made the newspapers so far in the nineties. "Is TV Spawning a Generation of Non-Thinkers?" and "TV Adds to Math Problems" are some of the typical TV-hating headlines. "TV and Jobs Cut Into Reading Time," claims the headline of one *USA Today* article. I'm sure it's a fascinating story. Unfortunately, I've been too busy watching TV, and being a TV critic, to read it.

And now, *as* a TV critic, I'm about to step up and take my turn at bat. From Plato to Postman, it's been open season on the most popular mass media—and it's about time somebody fired back. Ready? Aim. . . .

An early TV Heavyweight: One of the Golden Age examples of TV productions inspiring subsequent movie treatments is this 1956 Rod Serling drama, written for the CBS anthology series *Playhouse 90*. Jack Palance starred as the tragic fighter in the live television presentation, flanked here by Ed Wynn (who, by that time, already had contributed greatly to the histories of vaudeville, radio, and early experimental TV) and Keenan Wynn, Ed's son. In the 1962 film version, Anthony Quinn inherited Palance's role.

"And now, here's something we hope you'll *really* like!": Rocky and Bullwinkle, two of the Jay Ward cartoon characters whose offbeat sense of humor entertained, and influenced, more than one generation of delighted viewers. (Jay Ward Productions)

Peter, Peter, TV teacher: Early exposure to literary references, reinforcing the joy of reading and storytelling in even the youngest viewers, is provided by such shows as The Disney Channel series *Jim Henson's Mother Goose Stories*. In this episode, young actor Sam Preston plays the Knave of Hearts, and plays opposite Muppet Workshop puppets of the King and Queen, in a retelling of "Queen of Hearts." (© Disney; ©Henson Associates, Inc.)

LEFT: **One giant leap for TV kind:** The giant (Carel Struycken) hovers over Dale Cooper (Kyle MacLachlan), who has recently been shot, in an ABC *Twin Peaks* cliffhanger alluding to the famous "Who shot J.R.?" episode of *Dallas*. As popular phenomenon, TV literature, and teleliteracy grab bag, *Twin Peaks* had it all—at least for a while. (© 1990 Copyright Capital Cities/ABC, Inc.)

RIGHT: **Good golly, where's Wally?:** Jerry Mathers and Barbara Billingsley, still famous after all these years for their portrayals of June and Theodore (the Beaver) Cleaver on *Leave It to Beaver*, make a joint appearance on the Fox Network series *Parker Lewis Can't Lose!* Here, they flank Melanie Chartoff, who plays the school principal. (© 1991 Fox Broadcasting Company. Photo credit: Brian D. McLaughlin)

Love, love them do: The Beatles, in their first appearance on *The Ed Sullivan Show*, did more than provide CBS with a top-rated program. They sent out a simultaneous musical and cultural wake-up call to an entire nation of young viewers. (CBS)

Necessary zoom: The popular NBC *Saturday Night Live* characters of Wayne (Mike Meyers) and Garth (Dana Carvey), stars of the TV-show-within-a-TV-show "Wayne's World," went from poking fun at media coverage of the Gulf War to starring in their own hit Hollywood movie, *Wayne's World.* (NBC and Paramount Studios)

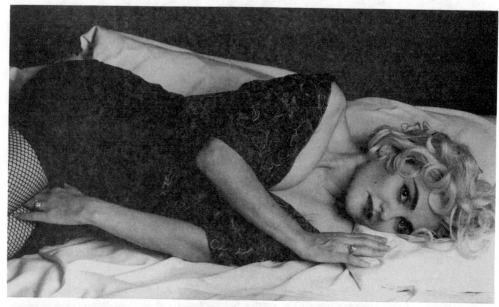

Like, a version: Julie Brown spoofs Madonna's *Truth or Dare* movie and early videos by mounting a full-length musical Showtime cable spoof called *Medusa: Dare to Be Truthful.* (© Showtime Networks Inc. 1991)

Baby, they're still the greatest: In a detailed and very reverent extended sequence, the cast members of ABC's *Perfect Strangers* recall and imitate the characters from *The Honeymooners.* From left, Rebeca Arthur (Mary Anne) plays Trixie, Bronson Pinchot (Balki) is Ed Norton, Mark Linn-Baker (Larry) is Ralph Kramden, and Melanie Wilson (Jennifer) is Alice. (© 1991 Lorimar Television)

LEFT: **Can you say "satire," boys and girls?:** On NBC's *Saturday Night Live,* Eddie Murphy lampoons a TV star, and becomes one, while appearing in a "Mr. Robinson's Neighborhood" sketch very loosely based on the children's TV series starring Fred Rogers. (©1990 National Broadcasting Co., Inc. Photo by: R. Lewis)

RIGHT: **It's a wonderful day in the petting zoo:** Meanwhile, the *real* Fred Rogers, seen here visiting the San Diego Wild Animal Park with Joan Embery, takes a field trip as part of a creature-filled theme week on the durable and delightful PBS children's series *Mister Rogers' Neighborhood.* (PBS. Photo: Kira Corser)

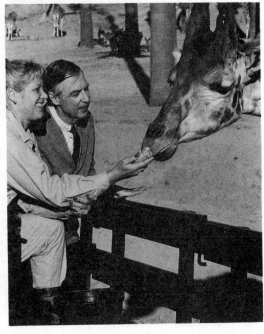

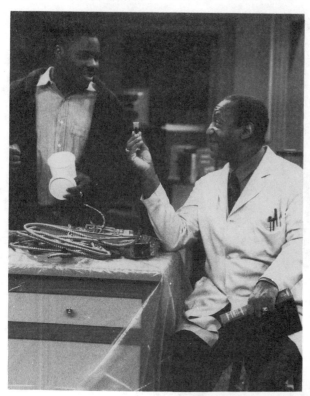

Prime time Theo-logy: Bill
Cosby as Cliff Huxtable, and
Malcolm-Jamal Warner as his son
Theo, discuss Theo's new job re-
sponsibilities as a counselor in an
episode of NBC's *The Cosby Show.*
Throughout the entire run of
this series, Cosby fought for the
goals and ideals he wanted the
show to embrace and embody.
(©1991 National Broadcasting
Co., Inc.)

It's Bart, but is it Art?: Yes, if
sales prices for animation cels
from Fox's *The Simpsons* are
any indication. Matt Groening's wickedly sarcastic cartoon
series, depicting the life and
times of the delightful but
dysfunctional Simpson family,
is today's TV answer to *The
Bullwinkle Show*—but is Bart
Simpson a rebel without a
cause, or merely an undiag-
nosed dyslexic? (TM & ©Twen-
tieth Century-Fox Film Corp.
1990)

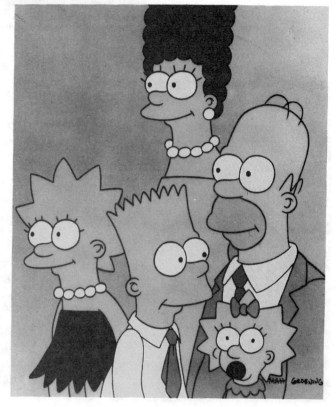

Yesterday's mythology via today's technology: When Bill Moyers (left) conversed with the late mythologist Joseph Campbell (right) for a six-part PBS series called *Moyers: Joseph Campbell and the Power of Myth,* TV demonstrated its power as a very effective and accessible teacher. (PBS)

Taking the mystery out of history: Historian Shelby Foote, left, and *The Civil War* documentarian Ken Burns, became unlikely media stars as a result of the enthusiastic national response to their excellent 1990 PBS series. (PBS. General Motors Mark of Excellence Presentations)

General literacy: During TV coverage of the Gulf War, the briefings by Central Command Chief General H. Norman Schwarzkopf were as precise, powerful, and impressive as the "smart bomb" footage and battle tactics he unveiled and narrated on live television. (AP/Wide World Photos)

A peace of the action: After the Gulf War, and his retirement from active duty, Schwarzkopf lent his strong presence, and considerable military expertise, to a 1991 CBS fiftieth-anniversary program about Pearl Harbor. Schwarzkopf, out of uniform, and Charles Kuralt served as hosts. (© CBS Inc.)

Go Western, young man: He may not be young, but Robert Duvall had no reservations about moving from the movies to television to star as Augustus McCrae in the 1979 CBS miniseries *Lonesome Dove*—a Western every bit as good as, and maybe better than, the classic large-screen cowboy epics. (CBS)

Way above the Norm: The characters and story lines on *Cheers* have been delighting audiences for a decade, and, though largely taken for granted, are fine and funny examples of TV as art. Two wonderful parts of the *Cheers* comedy equation: John Ratzenberger as pompous, factoid-spouting Cliff Clavin, left, and George Wendt as genial, beer-guzzling Norm Peterson. (© 1990 National Broadcasting Co., Inc.)

A true TV masterpiece: Michael Gambon starred as a tortured writer, and his more assured fictional alter ego, in Dennis Potter's deliriously multilayered BBC-TV miniseries *The Singing Detective*, shown on PBS in 1988. Am I right? Or am I right? (BBC/PBS)

PART II

A MEDIA MANIFESTO

Because television is so widely and convincingly attacked, it isn't easy to come to its defense without being put on the defensive. It's as though, by taking TV seriously, you automatically prevent *yourself* from being taken seriously. That may be why some TV critics continue to reflect more disdain than enthusiasm in their approach to the beat, because to reflect enjoyment or appreciation might make them seem less erudite. That's nonsense. I'm as tough a TV critic as the next guy (or gal): my standards for TV excellence are high, and my tolerance level for bad TV is low. I'm the first to admit that 90 percent of television is, in a word, crap. But I'm also aware of, and in agreement with, science-fiction writer Theodore Sturgeon's well-known "Sturgeon's Law," which says "90 percent of *everything* is crap." Don't put Danielle Steel at the top of your best-seller lists, or *Home Alone* at the top of your annual box-office lists, and tell me the most popular TV shows—such as *Cheers* and *60 Minutes*—don't measure up.

There's another reason my arguments in support of television should be bolstered, rather than eroded, by the fact I've been a TV critic for more than fifteen years. Simply put, TV critics watch more television, in terms of both quality and quantity, than anyone else. The general public certainly watches a lot of TV, but people don't watch shows they don't like—at least not for very long. Professors and social critics who attack TV—and even those few who defend it—often base their opinions and analyses on a relatively small body of programming. Even if they're well-intentioned, the demands of their full-time positions often preclude regular immersion in the ever-churning waters of daily television. Ironically, even the people who *make* television, as a general rule, are too busy producing it to be fluent in what their peers are doing elsewhere on the small screen.

TV critics, on the other hand, watch it all. We are—or should be—equally fluent in the good and the bad, the important and the trivial, the brilliant and the banal. We *have* to watch shows we don't like; it's part of the job description. But we're also the first to see—and get excited about—such works of art as the miniseries *The Singing Detective* and the documentary series *The Civil War*.

So if I say—and I do—TV is better now than it was in the "Golden Age" of TV, and the best of television compares favorably with the best Hollywood films, and TV deserves more respect than it's getting, I'm delivering the carefully considered opinion of a *professional* TV viewer—someone who's been reporting from the trenches, day in and day out, *Today* and *Tonight* and tomorrow. And because I've seen more TV than most people who enthusiastically attack and dismiss television, it's fairly easy, in turn, to attack and dismiss *their* arguments.

That's what I'm about to do in the following ten chapters, while stating my own argumentative positions in support of the medium of television. Consider this a quickie course in "TV Appreciation," and my own Media Manifesto—or, if you prefer, the Ten Commandments of Good Television:

1. TV Is Too Important to Turn Off.
2. TV Is *Not* a Vast Wasteland.
3. Links Between TV and Violence Should Be Taken with a Grain Assault.
4. TV Can Be Literacy's Friend as Well as Its Foe.
5. Marshall McLuhan Was Right: There *Is* a Global Village.
6. Marshall McLuhan Was Wrong: The Medium Is *Not* the Message.
7. Television Deserves More Respect.
8. Some Television Is Literature—and Vice Versa.
9. Television Deserves Serious Study.
10. Teleliteracy Is Here . . . So Telefriend.

5

TV IS TOO IMPORTANT
TO TURN OFF

"I never watch TV, and neither should you."

This position—distilled in Jerry Mander's *Four Arguments for the Elimination of Television*—is the most sweeping and absurd attack of all. It's the video equivalent of an illiterate proudly proclaiming, "I never read books or newspapers, and neither should you." Dismissing television in its entirety makes no more sense than dismissing the printing press. Yet some respected academics and scholastic institutions have no qualms about doing just that—and about challenging those who feel otherwise.

Robert Thompson, an associate professor at Syracuse University's Newhouse School, is a specialist in media studies—a thirtysomething professor who's also a *thirtysomething* professor. He's a verbal and visible advocate of television as a serious subject, and even has appeared *on* TV in support of it. In 1989, he was one of several professors profiled in a *60 Minutes* piece about TV as a university subject. On that occasion, he told correspondent Morley Safer, with more pride than shame, "I have a BA from the University of Chicago in Political Philosophy. Did my thesis on *The Divine Comedy*. I have an MA and a PhD from Northwestern. I read the great books of the Western world. I *love* television."

Not everyone shares his enthusiasm. I met Thompson in 1991; since then, we've exchanged letters, compared ideas, and been mutually intrigued by the parallels and prejudices concerning our respective jobs. Thompson says he's lost track of how many of his professorial peers have informed him that TV has no place in an institute of higher learning—and, in fact, should not be viewed at all. "I don't watch it, it's garbage," they tell him, which Thompson likens to "indicting an entire body of material based on instinct." Thompson has published articles about television in education journals, and those articles elicit often vehement responses. One letter, from an associate professor in Virginia with a PhD, typifies the anti-TV argument:

"Television is a rare thing, a technology wholly without redeeming features," this professor wrote Thompson.

> The influence of TV on our society has been uniformly malign, and there is not a single social problem we face which has not been caused by or exacerbated by television. . . . I believe there is only one cure for the social illness television has caused: abolition. The collection and destruction of all TV sets, broadcasting facilities and tape libraries would be a long step on the road back to sanity for the world.

Another concrete example of anti-TV bias surfaced as I was doing an interview for this book with ABC News anchor Peter Jennings. Jennings's prime-time specials, like his colleague Ted Koppel's, are impressive and usually important, and his demeanor and sensibility on ABC's *World News Tonight*—and especially in moments of breaking news coverage—are both comfortable and comforting. I still remember the day of the Challenger explosion in 1986, when ABC first played the tape showing Christa McAuliffe's parents reacting—in a grief-stricken close-up—as the space shuttle blew up with their daughter aboard. After watching it along with the rest of ABC's audience, Jennings said coldly he didn't think we'd be seeing *that* again—a clear and firm message to his viewers as well as his control room. The fact that Jennings could be offended by one of his network's own news images—and veto it immediately—was an impressive display of good taste. Jennings clearly is a man who takes his television seriously.

It is not, however, a universal trait. During our interview, Jennings mentioned, almost as an aside, that the school his son attends has a blanket don't-let-your-kids-watch-television philosophy. When I told Jennings I assumed it was a private school, his formerly affable expression hardened into a somewhat challenging stare. "Why do you assume that it's a *private* school?" he asked, presumably resenting what he thought was an unfair inference based on his financial and social status. "Because," I replied, "a *public* school wouldn't care." Jennings laughed and said, "Smart answer," and went on to explain his feelings about the value of television. While noting emphatically that people who get their news only from television are "underinformed," Jennings expressed the opinion that people who consciously *avoid* television are robbing themselves of a different type of education.

"If you don't watch television," Jennings says, "you will never have the chance to see an American attack on Baghdad. You will not have seen Challenger, you will not have seen Neil Armstrong, you will not have seen John Kennedy's funeral, you will not have seen Martin Luther King make his speech [at the Lincoln Memorial]." And throughout the interview, Jennings would keep adding to his list of memorable TV moments, from the entertainment of *Cheers* and *L.A. Law* to the deadly seriousness of "the young man in front of the tanks in Tiananmen Square."

Think about some of those news images, and the impact and value of television become crystal clear. Newspaper photographs of the Challenger disaster can freeze that tragic twin plume of smoke, but only television can track the flight from start to fiery finish, following the tragic trail as the flaming wreckage makes its free fall back to earth. Still photographs from the moon can show Neil Armstrong on the ladder of the lunar module, about to take that giant leap for mankind, but only television can show the reduced-gravity, pseudo-slow-motion descent leading to man's first steps on the moon—and show it while, literally, a whole world is watching. And while the still photo of that lone Chinese student, bravely stepping in front of a column of Chinese tanks to impede their progress, is an incredible image in its own right, it's even more powerful as a moving picture, when you can watch the tanks rumble to a stop, turrets slowly rotating, as the man waves his arms and implores his countrymen to turn back.

Don Hewitt, executive producer of CBS's *60 Minutes*, is a man whose career stretches as far back as the beginnings of network TV itself. As a news director and/or producer, he was involved in some of TV's most memorable news events—the 1960 Nixon-Kennedy debates, CBS's 1963 coverage of the John F. Kennedy assassination and funeral—and created the newsmagazine format with a series that, nearly a quarter-century after its premiere, finishes in television's Top 10. Dan Rather and Diane Sawyer honed their craft on *60 Minutes*; Mike Wallace, Morley Safer, and Harry Reasoner thrived on it; and a countless procession of newsmakers, artists, and con men appeared on it. The varied content in the average hour of *60 Minutes*—ranging from a hard-hitting interview with some foreign leader to a softball commentary by Andy Rooney—exemplifies what Hewitt feels is one of TV's strongest attributes. Television, Hewitt says, serves many functions. It's sometimes a stage, sometimes a sports arena, sometimes a cinema, sometimes a newspaper or newsmagazine, and sometimes—in an analogy Hewitt has used many times before—a chapel.

Television, Hewitt says, is where "Americans go ... and ask Dan Rather, Peter Jennings, and Tom Brokaw to heal their wounds after our spacecraft burns up in the atmosphere, or if a president gets assassinated, or any one of many national catastrophes. They don't go to Oral Roberts. They don't go to Jerry Falwell. They don't go to Pat Robertson." They go, instead, to what Hewitt calls "Walter's ministry," in honor of Walter Cronkite's reassuring effect after the 1963 assassination of President Kennedy. "I was there when it started, when Cronkite did that after Kennedy was assassinated. They came and they said, in effect, 'Walter, tell us everything is all right, that we're going to get through this.' "

A brief review of TV's coverage of that event, printed shortly thereafter in *TV Guide*, prefigured—and supported—Hewitt's analogy of TV as a video chapel:

Television's remarkable performance in communicating news of President John F. Kennedy's assassination and the events that followed was a source of sober satisfaction to all Americans. It acted swiftly. It acted surely. It acted intelligently and in impeccable taste. On that unforgettable weekend in November 1963, television provided a personal experience which all could share, a vast religious service which all could attend, a unifying bond which all could feel. I take this opportunity to add my voice to those who already have recognized television's historic contribution.

The review was signed: Lyndon B. Johnson, president of the United States.

"During those four days in 1963," Kathleen Hall Jamieson writes in her book *Eloquence in an Electronic Age*, "television delivered the contemporary equivalent of the Gettysburg Address. But where Lincoln's words were long remembered, the pictures from the Kennedy eulogy survive. Where Lincoln's eulogy was heard only by those crowding a Pennsylvania field, Kennedy's was seen by over 90 percent of the homes in the United States and by the citizens of twenty-two other nations. Where the Gettysburg Address was inaccessible to those not fluent in English, the visual images of the Kennedy eulogy spoke a universal language." Continuing the Lincoln-Kennedy comparison, and underscoring the speed and value of electronic media, Tony Schwartz says in his book *Media: The Second God*, "When President Lincoln was assassinated, it took eight months before 85 percent of the people in the United States knew about it. The entire country knew about the assassination of John F. Kennedy in a matter of minutes." Those figures are questionable, but the difference a century makes is not.

Joseph Campbell said that TV's coverage of the Kennedy assassination and funeral was a "deeply significant rite" of passage, with the mass medium of TV facilitating "an enormous nation, made those four days into a unanimous community, all of us participating in the same way, simultaneously, in a single symbolic event."

It's not that anyone defending TV as a medium has to reach back nearly thirty years for a persuasive example. On the contrary, TV's coverage of the Kennedy assassination was such a momentous, galvanizing national event, it's virtually incomprehensible to imagine anyone *since* then rejecting television as without value. Television can inform in ways, and at speeds, that no other medium can touch—and its speed increases all the time. How in the world—and I mean that literally—can a history teacher deny his students the use of TV when the collapse of the Berlin Wall in Germany, the release of Nelson Mandela in South Africa, the demonstrations by student protesters in China, the start of the air war against Iraq, and an attempted Soviet coup are all covered live by television?

How can professors condemn a medium that, at its best, embraces and popularizes some of *their* best? Joseph Campbell is better known in death than he was in life, thanks to Bill Moyers's six-part interview series *Joseph Campbell and The Power of Myth*. Campbell's books surged to the best-seller lists after his conversations with Moyers were broadcast—and it's a trick television, and Moyers, have pulled many times. In July 1991, for example, two entries on the *New York Times Book Review* best-seller lists—*Iron John* by Robert Bly (#1) and *Fire in the Belly* by Sam Keen (#6)—owed much of their popularity to TV in general, and Moyers in particular, since both writers had been interviewed previously by Moyers in well-received, reputation-enhancing specials. "Television can stir emotion," Moyers told a reporter, while books "invite reflection." Used together properly, they're a very potent team.

Moyers's long and distinguished reporting and commentary for CBS, his thought-provoking documentaries for CBS, CBS Cable, and PBS, and his intellectually challenging and enriching PBS series and specials make him a one-man argument against those crying for the abolition of television. At political conventions, Moyers often was the sole voice posing questions more philosophical than political. In his network documentaries, Moyers often runs counter to the prevailing social moods—delving deep into the controversies of race and education, religion and broadcasting, politicians and Iran-Contra cover-ups. Through his conversational TV shows, Moyers exposed many viewers, for the first time, to Campbell, Bly, Keen, and, over the years, dozens of others. Some may ridicule us for not getting there first—but at least we got there. And TV, in the person of Bill Moyers, led the way. Yet Moyers, in persuading intellectuals to take part in his *World of Ideas* PBS series and other video ventures, sometimes confronts the same anti-TV bias already described by Thompson and Jennings.

"I suspect that intellectuals regard television as oversimplified," Moyers says, "and therefore, understanding the complex nature of reality, they are suspicious of it." Once they get involved, though, some become converts. Moyers tells a story of one professor—a physician and philosopher—who "didn't want to do television, wouldn't *look* at the television," but consented, finally, to an interview on *World of Ideas*. The conversation turned into a two-part installment that was successful both with viewers and with the subject himself, who returned three years later with a tip on an academic conference Moyers should televise. Perhaps the way to get more intellectuals to support television, rather than dismiss it, is to get more of them *on* television.

In the meantime, a blanket condemnation of television by any anti-TV elitist automatically rejects works of art, music, theater, and literature that same person no doubt would embrace in any other form. Forget, for a moment, about arguing the worth of popular sitcoms and dramas (although I'll get to that a little later). Instead, stab these no-TV snobs in their high-culture Achilles' heel. If "all TV is worthless," that means Leonard Bernstein's televised concerts and music workshops are worthless; viewing Dustin Hoffman in a CBS production of Arthur Miller's *Death of a Salesman* is a wasted three hours; nothing is to be gained by watching Bill Moyers talk with Joseph Campbell; and sitting in front of the TV set to watch a seventeen-hour production of Wagner's complete *Ring* cycle is no more worthwhile an endeavor than sitting in front of the washing machine to watch a complete rinse cycle.

And if *those* are deigned worthy of viewing, then TV is no longer a total waste of time. It becomes a matter of opinion and degree—and when you begin discussing individual worth instead of total worthlessness, you're talking criticism rather than condemnation. You're talking value judgments about things that can, and often do, have value. Whether you like it or not, you're talking art. And if you refuse to watch it, you no longer have any idea what you're talking about.

Harlan Ellison, who has written both for and about television, complained in the introduction to *The Other Glass Teat,* his second volume of articles from his days as a TV critic, "There's still that hateful snobbishness about TV. Dips my age put it down without fail, without redeeming remark, without a suggestion that the medium has a saving grace. Yet every night, if one selects one's viewing with anything greater than the brain power of a maggot, one can find at least an hour or two of worthwhile programming." That was written in 1975, when television offered much less variety than it does now. Yet though TV has improved, attitudes haven't always kept pace. Ellison himself, by 1977, had soured to the point where, after learning I had chosen a career as a TV critic, he advised me to "go out and get some honorable job—like putting animals to sleep or something."

Walking away from television isn't the answer, though. Its potential is too great, its reach too vast. A top-rated TV program such as NBC's *The Cosby Show* reaches tens of millions of viewers each week—and Bill Cosby himself, while critical of many aspects of TV, nevertheless champions its value as a social force.

Cosby, in fact, is particularly well positioned to address the medium of television from several different angles. Not only did he star in—and help guide—the most successful TV series of the eighties, but he has also shown a long-time commitment to prosocial children's television by appearing in such series as *Sesame Street, The Electric Company,* and *Picture Pages.* His work in the animated series *Fat Albert and the Cosby Kids,* with some of the same concerns for shattering stereotypes that later infused *The Cosby Show,* helped him earn a doctorate in education from the University of Massachusetts. Like Peter Jennings, Cosby uses television responsibly. He seeks out, rather than hides from, experts in psychology and education who can evaluate the possible interpretations of—and hidden messages within—a given dialogue line or plot twist. He's also very funny, and it's the humor that allows him to get across his messages to such receptive and massive audiences.

Cosby says his belief in the power of television as a positive force was developed long before he became a TV star or attended graduate school. It happened when he was a student at Temple University, listening to a teacher give a gloom-and-doom lecture about what would happen when George Orwell's *1984* predictions of a TV-ruled society were outdone by the Big Brother media conditions of the *real* 1984.

"The professor was standing there, just glowing about *1984* and how TV was going to own us someday," Cosby recalls, "and it was so blatant that no one was looking at the other side. Yes, it's true, all that negative that we talk about. But if something is that powerfully negative, there's got to be something that powerfully *positive* about it. It's clearly our own fault. . . . I think it's possible to take all of this on, and compete successfully in a commercial market, if you put together all of the things you care about. . . . "The fact is," Cosby adds, "I do believe that this tube can turn things around for us."

I agree—but first, the people who ignore it have to turn around and start watching it.

6

TV IS *NOT* A VAST WASTELAND

First, let's put that famous 1961 remark by Newton Minow in its full context. It was made at a National Association of Broadcasters convention where Minow, who recently had been appointed head of the FCC by President Kennedy, was addressing TV station managers for the first time. In part of his speech, Minow praised certain television efforts, singling out such broadcasts as the 1960 Nixon-Kennedy debates, Murrow's *See It Now,* the anthology dramas *Kraft Television Theatre* and *Playhouse 90,* and even *The Twilight Zone* and the Mary Martin TV production of *Peter Pan.* The part of the speech that's remembered, though, is where Minow turned into a shark.

"When television is bad, nothing is worse," he told the suddenly solemn broadcasters.

> I invite you to sit down in front of your television set when your station goes on the air and stay there without a book, magazine, newspaper, profit-and-loss sheet or rating book to distract you—and keep your eyes glued to that set until the station signs off. I can assure you that you will observe a vast wasteland. You will see a procession of game shows, violence, audience participation shows, formula comedies about totally unbelievable families, blood and thunder, mayhem, violence, sadism, murder, Western badmen, Western good men, private eyes, gangsters, more violence, and cartoons. And, endlessly, commercials.

Minow was giving an example with a built-in handicap—limiting the view of the TV landscape to a single station, sign-on to sign-off. True, the ability to take the blinders off and avert one's glance to a competing station, thus widening the view of what Minow perceived as a desert landscape, wouldn't have made *that* much of a difference in 1961. But if you were offended by, say, the violence of CBS's *Wanted: Dead or Alive* with Steve McQueen, you could always flip to ABC's *The Adventures of Ozzie & Harriet.* And on whichever network you looked at that time, there was more than one prominent oasis in Minow's "vast wasteland." Minow himself singled out a few. What he didn't, or couldn't, recognize is that the 1961 vintage of TV series included such "formula comedies" as *The Andy Griffith Show,* such "Western badmen" and "Western good men" as, respectively, Richard Boone as Paladin in the classic *Have Gun, Will Travel* and the Cartwright cowboys of *Bonanza,* and such unfairly dismissed "cartoons" as *Rocky and His Friends.*

But that was then; this is now. The sheer number of alternatives available suggest that even if the "vast wasteland" existed in 1961, it has long since been irrigated and harvested. When Minow gave his speech, there were no UHF stations, PBS was nearly a decade in the future, and cable networks offering original programming was a concept more suited to science fiction than FCC consideration. Quantitatively as well as qualitatively, TV has grown exponentially over the decades—and even Minow might agree with that, at least in part.

On May 9, 1991, Minow gave a thirtieth-anniversary speech to mark the occasion of his "vast wasteland" speech. He admitted the development of cable television, with its varied program services, has turned "a vast emptiness" to "a vast fullness," but voiced concern that cable is neither available nor affordable to all. His greatest worry, though, is this: "I think the most troubling change over the past 30 years is the rise in the quantity and quality of violence on television. In 1961 I worried that my children would not benefit much from television, but in 1991 I worry that my grandchildren will actually be harmed by it."

Which leads to . . .

7

LINKS BETWEEN TV AND VIOLENCE SHOULD BE TAKEN WITH A GRAIN ASSAULT

. . . **B**y which I mean it's not too hard to throw sand in the works of anyone too worked up about concrete links between the violence people watch on TV and the violence they commit in real life. That's not to say one has nothing to do with the other—only that a definite link is all but impossible to prove. You can't witness the positive side effects of television, such as the marked increase in library-card registrations that occurred nationwide after Henry Winkler's Fonzie applied for one on *Happy Days*, without wondering about the negative side effects of less laudable behavior. To measure and document those effects is something else entirely. Comparative scientific studies work on a simple principle: to study the effects of a particular variable in any given equation, all you have to do is establish two sets of identical conditions, remove the variable from one, and compare. In the case of television, what this requires, for a fully convincing study to be mounted, is for a researcher to identify two separate communities whose attributes and citizens are similar in every single respect—except that one community has been totally untouched by television. Good luck finding one.

As for quantifying violence on television, that's no problem. The problem, instead, is in the definition of what *constitutes* a violent act—and in the press's often unquestioning acceptance of every TV-violence statistic that wends its way into a press release. The National Coalition on Television Violence, for example, is an Illinois-based organization whose chairman and research director is Thomas Radecki, a psychiatrist who has distributed his statistics-filled, TV-attacking *NCTV News* for more than a decade. Many people take it very seriously; Minow, in fact, appears to have relied directly on NCTV statistics in his 1991 speech when noting the "troubling" increase in televised violence. Indeed, the closer and longer you read *NCTV News*, the more interesting it gets—though not necessarily for the reasons its editor intended.

In May 1991, Radecki's NCTV distributed a press release announcing that "at the recent annual meeting of the American Psychiatric Association, researchers from across the country linked television to 50 percent of the crime in our country and suggested that it may play an important role in teen suicide as well." The use of the plural *researchers* was technically accurate, because one researcher had presented a paper about the supposed TV-and-crime link, while another had presented a paper showing that teen suicide rates have increased since the introduction of television. But it's hardly the national consensus implied by the headline on the press release. The figures, though, are what stand out—as both fantastic and familiar.

A decade before, in the summer of 1981, Radecki had appeared before members of the Television Critics Association (TCA), to whom he announced that "50 percent of the violence in real life is directly or indirectly related to TV." When some critics began pressing for the facts behind his matter-of-fact figures, Radecki was either unwilling or unable to define his interpretation of "indirectly related," and, when pressed to cite a single study proving a causal link between TV violence and aggressive behavior, failed to do so. That may explain why, when Radecki appeared later that year at the 1981 TV violence hearings held by the House Subcommittee on Telecommunications, his assessment had been modified slightly to read, "Television and film violence is probably responsible for from 25 to 50 percent of all real-life violence in our society." Presto: within six months, Radecki's official estimate relating half of all "real" violence to television *alone* had been amended so that it was a *probable* link of perhaps as little as half that amount, and with *film* thrown in as a coconspirator. Yet Radecki's statistical claims in front of that committee elicited at least one rave review: "The strongest testimony came from Dr. Thomas Radecki," said the newsletter released and edited by Dr. Thomas Radecki.

Even when the data are more specific, they're not necessarily more persuasive. According to the NCTV monitoring results for spring 1991, one of the season's ten most violent network shows in prime time was the CBS cartoon series *Toon Nite*— which consisted of Bugs Bunny and *Peanuts* cartoons, reruns of *The Bullwinkle Show,* and other "High Violence" programming. *Toon Nite* was monitored as having twenty-six acts of violence per hour—more than four times as many as the documentary series *Cops*, which escaped with a milder "Some Violence" rating. The idea of not differentiating between the police's real gunfights and Snoopy's aerial dogfights is ridiculous on its face—yet many "TV violence" researchers rely on, and swear by, just such an all-encompassing approach. George Gerbner, former dean of the Annenberg School of Communications at the University of Pennsylvania, was among the first researchers to study and measure television violence. His definition of violence has remained constant over the decades: "The overt explicit expression of force intended to hurt or kill, or the action of actually hurting or killing." In the beginning, Gerbner's reports were blow-by-blow, show-by-show, much as Radecki's still are today. But perhaps because Gerbner's broad definition resulted in some similarly hard-to-explain specific results—for example, *I Dream of Jeannie* being identified as the most violent series of 1968—his methodology soon shifted from isolating individual programs to assessing the networks as a whole.

I have no quarrel whatsoever with Gerbner's statistical methods, but I don't buy his definition of violence. "So long as the act is credible," Gerbner told me in the late seventies, "it is considered violent. Cartoons and slapstick can be terribly violent; the fact that it is couched in a humorous context is irrelevant. It's still violence. Humor is like the sugar coating on a pill. And so far as a work of fiction is concerned, there is no such thing as an act of nature. The earthquake, which takes lives, is there only because the scriptwriter wishes it to be there. He created the earthquake, not God, so it is counted as an act of violence."

A shotgun blast from *The Terminator*, a whack on the head in *The Three Stooges*, the spinning tornado in *The Wizard of Oz*—in the eyes of Gerbner and his research staff, all would register equally on the violence scale. And that's a pill I can't swallow, no matter how statistically it's sugar-coated.

The main question, though, is what all this counting adds up to. In 1980, a group called the National Federation for Decency, monitoring profanity instead of violence, released its results for the previous fall season, listing the ten most "profanity-oriented" programs. *Archie Bunker's Place* (formerly *All in the Family*) topped the list, which was no surprise. But the miniseries *Holocaust* was third, *M*A*S*H* fifth, *The Love Boat* ninth—and those results *are* surprising. Any system that equates a "hell" muttered by Archie Bunker with a "hell" used to describe prison conditions in Auschwitz—and ranks the somber, important *Holocaust* as more profane than the silly, disposable *Love Boat*—is one hell of a system. It's so busy quantifying the individual elements of a show that it never steps back to take into account the context of those moments, or the program's overall quality. Most of the TV violence studies fall into the same trap. In Radecki's spring 1991 study, *Cheers* was given a much higher violence rating than *Babes*—but that doesn't make *Babes* a better show. *Hill Street Blues*, at times, was an awfully violent show, but it also was awfully good. These violence counters attempt no such distinctions.

If all you do is count acts of violence, then where does William Shakespeare's *Titus Andronicus* rate—or any of his other corpse-strewn dramas, up to and including *Hamlet*? Do you damn the miniseries *Jesus of Nazareth* because of its flagellation and crucifixion scenes? And what of the Bible itself? If you're looking for a source of violent scenes and a high incidence of the words *hell* and *damn*, what better place to begin?

Television didn't invent violence—it's just the latest mass medium to be blamed for it. As for that study pointing out that teen suicides have risen since the introduction of television—well, the ozone layer has depleted since then, too. Why don't we just blame *that* on TV while we're at it? British writer Christopher Dunkley has noted, correctly though somewhat flippantly, "It was not an addiction to *Starsky and Hutch* which sent Genghis Khan on his wicked way . . . . The whole of recorded history shows that the absence of sadistic television does not by one iota reduce the incidence of sadistic crime." And Don Hewitt, in the final chapter of his *Minute by Minute . . .* book on *60 Minutes,* takes a similar tack when responding to a criticism that TV violence led to the attempted assassination of then-President Ronald Reagan: "How much television do you think John Wilkes Booth watched before he shot Lincoln, or Cain watched before he slew his brother Abel?"

In much more recent history—the mid-1970s—Ellis Rubin, a Florida attorney, tried to defend a teen accused of murdering his elderly neighbor by claiming that the boy had been a victim of "involuntary subliminal intoxication" of television violence. (The way that plea was worded, Rubin was lucky he wasn't charged with reckless redundancy. How can something subliminal be voluntary?) The trial, ironically, was televised; Rubin lost the case, but it made for some interesting TV.

Television can be, and often is, blamed for just about anything. One of my favorite instances occurred in 1979, when the Florida Orthodontic Society went so far as to blame television for crooked teeth. "When a child watches TV," the organization claimed, "he often leans on one hand, pushing in on his teeth. Changing that habit early on can save a bill for braces later on." One solution is to have the child watch less television. Another, equally effective solution is to allow the child to watch just as much TV as before, but to switch hands half the time.

Even in those cases where blame seems to be placed correctly—in whichever media—issues of cause and effect are seldom, if ever, clear-cut. Was J. D. Salinger, by writing *A Catcher in the Rye,* responsible for the murder of John Lennon, just because a dog-eared copy of the book was found in the back pocket of Mark David Chapman? Were the Beatles, by writing and recording "Helter Skelter," responsible for Charles Manson's murder spree? Was Jodie Foster at fault for starring in *Taxi Driver,* or Paul Schrader for writing it or Martin Scorsese for directing it, when John Hinckley claimed he shot then-President Ronald Reagan to impress her after seeing that movie? Tom O'Brien, film critic for *Commonweal,* tackled that touchy question head-on in his book *The Screening of America.*

"Was *Taxi Driver* the only violent film Hinckley had ever seen?" O'Brien asks.

> Had he idolized gun-toting heroes long before? What other life events— or other movies—might have contributed to his dementia? If you want to blame *Taxi Driver* for John Hinckley, you have to indict other assassination movies such as *The Manchurian Candidate, Suddenly,* or even, for all its comedy, *Bananas. . . .* The list gets long, the blame diffuse—and unfair. John Wilkes Booth was partly "inspired" in his assassination of Lincoln by Shakespeare's *Julius Caesar;* he even used a theatrical setting for the shooting. But Booth was guilty, not theater and not Shakespeare.

St. Augustine, of course, would have had no problem blaming Lincoln's murder on those petulant, impure, impudent, wicked, unclean, shameful, detestable, filthy Devil-god stage plays. He warned us, you know.

8

TV CAN BE LITERACY'S FRIEND AS WELL AS ITS FOE

Cleveland State University professor Jane Healy, author of *Endangered Minds: Why Our Children Don't Think*, attacks the long-running PBS children's series *Sesame Street* by saying, "It's truly amazing that everyone seems to have bought the notion that the program will teach kids to read, despite the fact that the habits of mind necessary to be a good reader are exactly what *Sesame Street* doesn't teach." Jerome L. and Dorothy G. Singer, a husband-and-wife team of psychologists at Yale, agree. They accuse *Sesame Street* of creating "a psychological disorientation in children that leads to a shortened attention span, a lack of reflectiveness and an expectation of rapid change in the broader environment." Neil Postman, author of *Amusing Ourselves to Death* (and another Big Bird basher) warns, "*Sesame Street* makes kids like school only if school is like *Sesame Street*." The inference is clear: if one of the TV shows most generally accepted as beneficial to children is actually *bad* for kids, then why should parents let kids watch TV at all?

The inference, like the argument, is dead wrong. Empirically, early studies showed that, after six weeks of watching *Sesame Street*, those students were significantly more proficient than nonviewers at the tasks of recognizing letters, associating sound with letters, and identifying different geometric forms. Artistically, *Sesame Street* has developed into a wonderful show; as both a TV critic and a parent, I applaud it, and encouraged my children to watch it. Pragmatically, it's neither the responsibility nor the function of *Sesame Street* to—as Postman puts it—*make* kids like school. That's the teacher's job, and the parent's. *Sesame Street* is there to encourage children while entertaining them—to introduce them to concepts so they'll be more prepared for the scholastic experience when their education truly begins. Anyone who sees *Sesame Street* as an enemy of education, rather than an ally, is misunderstanding the impact and potential of television. Educators who fear TV and run from it are heading in the wrong direction; they ought to use it and run with it.

Peggy Charren, who founded Action for Children's Television almost twenty-five years ago, has been lobbying networks and producers to create more responsible children's TV ever since. She knows, and speaks out, when children's TV is irresponsible and bad. But, unlike the directors of other so-called pressure groups, she is just as quick to recognize the reverse. When it comes to such shows as *Sesame Street* and *Mister Rogers' Neighborhood,* she's ready and willing to attack their attackers.

"I think most of the people who attack any public-TV shows for children," Charren says, "are trying to get on the *Today* show. You can't make noise if you perpetuate the conventional wisdom. . . .

"*Sesame Street*—there's a program that really has a goal of doing things right. It has the goal of educating children. People who attack *Sesame Street* never look at the rest of the stuff children watch, because they *know* it's junk. It's beneath them." Charren, who has kept tabs on *Sesame Street* since its inception, says the show reacted to early criticism by becoming "even better than it was." It slowed its pace, added more women and Hispanics, presented children with disabilities, and, like Fred Rogers on *Mister Rogers' Neighborhood,* began to acknowledge and explore some of the major, serious issues of growing up: divorce, death, prejudice. "It's a very meaningful messenger," Charren says, "starting at the right age." She also dismisses the argument that *Sesame Street* wrecks children's attention spans by saying, "Any terrific teacher doesn't say that. It's the lazy teacher who can't figure out how to teach."

A similar opinion of television comes from a somewhat unexpected source: *Cultural Literacy* author Hirsch, whose book included a surprisingly TV-tolerant passage:

> It will not do to blame television for the state of our literacy. Television watching does reduce reading, and often encroaches on homework. Much of it is the intellectual equivalent of junk food. But in some respects, such as its use of standard written English, television watching is acculturative. Moreover . . . the schools themselves must be held partly responsible for excessive television watching, because they have not firmly insisted that students complete significant amounts of homework, an obvious way to increase time spent on reading and writing.

Hewitt of *60 Minutes* is more specific, and generous, with his praise: "I think *Sesame Street* is maybe the best contribution that television has made to America. . . . [It's] the best example of using this medium for what it can do, which is to bring people out of environments that they feel trapped in, and introduce them to the world they may have never met if they didn't have a television set in their living room." Cosby, too, cites *Sesame Street, The Electric Company,* and *Mister Rogers' Neighborhood* as being among those children's shows that "were and are very, very important."

Even the Singers, who criticize *Sesame Street* so strongly, have kind words for the efforts of Fred Rogers. In their 1990 book *The House of Make-Believe,* they state, "One TV program that is especially sensitive in helping the pre-school child make sense out of a confusing world is *Mister Rogers' Neighborhood.* The host, Fred Rogers, acts as a surrogate parent, explaining through verbal repetition, music, puppets, special guests, and trips to various locations some of the confusing elements in a child's environment. . . . He can help a child deal with a first day at school, a visit to the doctor, or a stay in the hospital." This is high praise indeed, especially from Jerome Singer, who suggested on another occasion that children might be better off if denied television completely until their reading and learning habits are well formed.

That extreme position, though, draws fire from another direction. Carolyn Olivier is director of admissions at Landmark College, an institution in Putney, Vermont, specializing in teaching students with learning disabilities, such as dyslexia. She has heard such advice before, and soundly rejects it. "If people have to wait to watch TV until they can read and write," she says, "there'll be a whole part of the population who as adults will never get to watch TV."

Another commonly voiced complaint about TV is that it robs the viewer of time to do other things—that when children are watching television, for example, they aren't reading, doing homework, or playing outdoors. "They're not playing in the street, either," ACT's Charren says, her flippancy revealing her impatience with that particular attack on TV. Again, this argument against the use of television dispenses with any evaluation of individual worth, and pits medium against medium rather than content against content. It may sound like a sin for a child to watch four hours of television on a Saturday afternoon—but if that child is watching the miniseries version of *Anne of Green Gables,* or a handful of episodes from David Attenborough's nature series *The Trials of Life* (two recent examples from my own home and neighborhood), I argue that's a fine use of their time *and* their television sets. "Watching *some* TV," says Charren, "especially some terrific television, is as good as going to a terrific movie and reading a terrific book."

The same thing holds for adults, and for entire families. Before reacting with alarm to the latest statistic showing that the average TV household watches seven or eight hours of TV a day, or that the average child will have seen five-thousand hours of TV before entering first grade, ask *how* those viewers are watching—whether it is intently, with the TV set being the focus of their attentions, or as radio with pictures, a background complement to whatever else they happen to be doing. More important, ask *what* they're watching.

Let's take the "eight hours a day" family viewing estimate. For me, an average Monday viewing day might begin with a fifteen-minute look at the Weather Channel, to see how our kids should be outfitted for school. Then, not counting any viewing I'd do as part of my job, the rest of my viewing day probably would include an evening newscast, an hour or two of prime time (on Mondays, *Evening Shade* and *Northern Exposure*), and, if the subject is interesting, *Nightline.* That's close to three hours of "pleasure" viewing just for me, and that's hardly atypical. Give my wife the same viewing allotment, though not necessarily with the same programs, and you're up to six hours a day already. If my two children each watch an hour of TV a day—which, on weekdays, is basically their limit—that's eight hours of family viewing right there. Are we slaves of the "boob tube"? No. Are we sitting there, zombielike, forfeiting all opportunities to interact, exercise or read? No. We're using the television when we want, to watch what we want. People who complain about TV's constant availability, like those who complain about its profane and violent content, seem to forget that every set comes equipped with both a channel changer and an on-off switch.

In his early editions of *Baby and Child Care*, Dr. Benjamin Spock had a notably tolerant view regarding the use of mass media by school-age children. "In general," the famed child authority wrote in his 1963 edition, "if a child is taking care of his homework, staying outside with his friends in the afternoon, coming to supper, going to bed when it's time, and not being frightened, I would be inclined to let him spend as much of his evening with television or radio as he chooses." As noted in Marie Winn's *The Plug-in Drug*, Dr. Spock had backpedaled a bit by the mid-seventies, advising that "the hours for watching television should be limited," and that children and parents "come to a reasonable but definite understanding about which hours are for outdoors, for homework, for meals, and for programs."

The change in tone is indicative of a growing fear and dislike of television as a resource, though it doesn't always deserve the abuse. Sylvia Anne Washburn, a third-grade teacher at Marshall Elementary School in Toledo, Ohio, was given the first Teacher of the Year Award by the Disney Channel in 1991—and immediately was asked, at a press conference held for the nation's TV critics that summer, whether she saw the irony in her getting a teacher's award from the very medium that had stolen so much homework time from students. "There may be an irony in that," Washburn replied, "but if children were guided by their family in watching the TV shows that they *should* watch, then there wouldn't be the problem." A caring parent, she said, "will sit there during a television show and use it as a lot more than just a baby-sitter, and will use it as an educational tool."

Bill Moyers has done more to prove television's worth as an educational force than almost anyone else you could name—yet even he is defensive when it comes to TV's ubiquitousness. Nor does he see it as stealing time only from children. "I guess, overall, television is probably a negative force in our society," Moyers says, "because . . . when you are watching television, you are not doing anything else. You are not talking to your wife, playing with your kids, attending a town meeting, writing a letter to your congressman."

Robert Thompson has heard that argument many times before—so many times that his response to it is immediate and passionate. "The assumption there," he says, "is that by doing one thing, you're not doing the other. By watching television, you're *not* learning to read. You never hear a music professor say, 'You attend so many ballets; you should be attending operas.' No one says that when someone is listening to good music, or taking a trip to the science museum, those activities are all taking away from time they could be spending reading."

In Thompson's own academic circles, he says, his support of television as a subject worthy of scholarly scrutiny often is misconstrued as an assault on reading and literacy. "Because you're arguing in defense of television," he says, "they think you're therefore arguing for abolition of study of the classics. To them, it's like matter and antimatter. I don't think intellectuals can understand that a person could in the morning read Shakespeare, and in the afternoon laugh at *Laverne & Shirley.*"

And since the same time-wasting arguments were leveled at radio before TV, and at movies before radio, and at theater before the movies, and at certain kinds of books and newspapers before that, it's a position that grows less convincing with each repetition. Blame television for a drop in the literacy rate, and in national Scholastic Aptitude Test scores, if you want to. But even if you could prove a direct link, which is doubtful, that would merely identify the problem, not solve it. Television isn't going away—not until another, more popular mass medium usurps it. And even if television *is* part of the problem, it's also part of the solution.

PBS, more than any other network, has recognized that—not only with the alphabetical wordplay on *Sesame Street,* but with such fine series as *Reading Rainbow,* which is designed specifically to create an enthusiasm for reading, books, and libraries. In 1992, PBS and the Children's Television Workshop—the creators of *Sesame Street*—plan to unveil a new series called *Ghostwriter,* aimed at the seven-to-ten age group. Its goal: to use state-of-the-art TV technologies, outreach programs, supplementary materials, and other tricks to improve reading, writing, and comprehension skills, and provide young viewers "with compelling opportunities to read and to write."

Even older viewers can become more literate—and experience more literature—by watching the right kinds of television. In *Fields of Vision,* British writer D. J. Enright—no great fan of television—admits that "television adaptations of Dickens, Trollope, Jane Austen, among others, have the effect of sending some viewers back to the novels, to renew acquaintance, to spot what has been left out, to clear up obscurities caused by truncation. The effect on other viewers may be to send them to the novels for the first time; pious hope would have it so." That hope may be pious, but it's not mistaken. TV producer William Perry generated many TV adaptations of stories and novels by Mark Twain, including the excellent PBS dramatization of *Life on the Mississippi,* starring David Knell as young Sam Clemens. "When we released *Life on the Mississippi,*" Perry said in 1989, "we ran a survey of libraries around the country. And for the month that followed that show, the circulation of Twain's book had gone up 50 percent—and that was true of other Twain books as well." To those who say TV fosters illiteracy, Perry says to tell them "to ride the subway after *Shogun* has been on."

Robert Geller, another longtime advocate of TV as a "literate" me-

dium, created *American Short Story*, that fine American-literature precursor
to the current *American Playhouse*. The twin joys of *American Short Story*,
launched in 1977, were its tasteful adaptations of wonderful stories and
its reliance upon gifted young talent. Shelley Duvall in F. Scott Fitzgerald's
Bernice Bobs Her Hair. LeVar Burton in Richard Wright's *Almos' a Man*.
Outside of the *American Short Story* umbrella, Geller has continued to work
with literary adaptations—from 1979's *Too Far to Go*, an NBC telemovie
amalgam of John Updike stories that was later released theatrically, to *Seize
the Day*, a 1989 *Great Performances* dramatization of the Saul Bellow story,
starring Robin Williams. During his *American Short Story* years, Geller recalls, "I would get fascinating letters from kids I least expected to hear
from. I don't want to turn this into Spencer Tracy and *Boys Town*, but I'd
hear from boys who had never read Fitzgerald, girls who had never read
Bernice, and what resonated through them." As for the idea that TV can
inspire reading, Geller says, "Go to bookstores after *Lonesome Dove* is shown.
That's proof. It's not sophisticated proof—but that's proof."

Some would call it heresy to discover that Geller's adaptations of Fitzgerald and Updike share library space with the printed originals—but it's
been that way since 1988, when the John T. and Catherine R. MacArthur
Foundation arranged for the duplication and dissemination of selected
PBS programs at special rates to public libraries. Episodes of *American
Short Story* and *American Playhouse* are included, along with Perry's version
of *Life on the Mississippi* and a half-dozen dramatizations from *The Shakespeare Plays* series. The same package included such landmark nonfiction
works as *Alistair Cooke's America*, Jacob Bronowski's *The Ascent of Man*, Kenneth Clark's *Civilisation*, *A Walk through the 20th Century with Bill Moyers*,
Fred Friendly's *The Constitution: That Delicate Balance*, and two superb nature series from David Attenborough, *Life on Earth* and *The Living Planet*.
It should be pointed out that these quality packages were by no means the
first videotapes to cross the threshhold of public libraries. In fact, more
than four-thousand libraries nationwide had already established video-
lending facilities when the PBS package was organized.

The thought of books and videos as intellectual neighbors, if not
equals, is relished by David Attenborough himself. In his nature documentaries, he uses television astoundingly well, both as a personal communicator and an effective educator. His most recent series, the ambitious and
lengthy *The Trials of Life*, is, quite simply, a television masterpiece; its companion book, written by Attenborough, is more complementary than du-
plicative. Taking advantage of the TV medium to create interest in a book
with the same title, then taking advantage of the strengths of the printed
page to add and reorganize other information in that book, is a trick used
by Moyers (in *The Power of Myth*, among others), Attenborough, and others
equally comfortable in print and on TV. It's accurate to say TV does some
things better than others, and that TV should never supplant reading. But
it's absurd to say that, when it comes to education and literacy, TV has no
strengths, and no place, at all.

"One has to analyze what it is that television does best," Attenborough says, entertaining the concept of teleliteracy quite seriously. "What television does best is to light flames of enthusiasm, and to give smells and whiffs and sparks of excitement. And what it doesn't do, not nearly as well, is carry on abstract lines of thought, which is what books are good at. . . .

"TV can be used in a multitude of ways, just as printing can. There are some differences, of course. You can't go back as easily as you can in a book. But it's like generalizing about printing: It's what it *means*, it's what people put *into* it. Television is good at igniting. It is not so good at carrying ideas, even simple ideas. . . . You won't be able to go into enormous detail. In the ideal circumstance, you produce a double package."

Another example of TV and books as happy bedfellows fell into my lap—or, to be precise, sat in the next seat—as I was taking an airplane flight to Chicago in July 1991. I was well into the writing of this book by that time, and was flying to Northwestern University to be a guest lecturer at one of Robert Thompson's summer classes for visiting high-school media students. By coincidence, the man seated next to me was a public high school teacher, a man with ten years of teaching experience and with very strong opinions about the use of television in and out of the classroom. What began as a conversation quickly turned into an interview, for just as I considered myself a grunt soldier in the TV battlefield, so could Timothy Brittell—this stranger on a plane—be considered a representative soldier on the front lines of American education. (Besides, the chance meeting was too serendipitous to overlook.)

Brittell is a social studies teacher at Leota Junior High School in Woodinville, Washington. Not an average teacher, I suspect, for an average teacher wouldn't go to the trouble of dressing up as Thomas Jefferson or Adolf Hitler just to keep his students interested—or take the time to write his own supplementary materials whenever using TV as a resource. And just as Brittell uses print materials to complement television, so he uses television to complement some of his classroom texts. "Our books are woefully inadequate," he says, citing both age and content. The school system's primary history textbook, Brittell says, talks about "President Carter" in the present tense. What's even more galling to him is the conservative political process behind the selection of textbooks, which can stifle rather than foster scholarly debate and a questioning attitude.

"I worked for the state textbook committee for Oregon," recalls Brittell, unearthing a previous job experience as a pertinent parallel. Each textbook submitted for possible adoption by the state school system had to be judged using a standard questionnaire, and, in Brittell's opinion (and mine), judged rather narrowly. "The first question on the form," Brittell says, "was something like, 'Does this textbook criticize our founding fathers or the Constitution in any way?' If it does, you close the book. That's as far as it goes."

That's why, when Brittell supplements some of his classroom textbooks with pertinent TV programming, his students sometimes ask, "Why is it we're never told these things?" After Brittell's students watched the first segment of the documentary series *The Civil War*, Brittell noticed that the school library's copy of Frederick Douglass's autobiography was checked out constantly, by student after student, for the rest of the year. In some cases, it's clear, TV can inspire people *to* read—but even if it merely informs or inspires them, isn't getting the information via television better than not getting it at all?

There's a well-known quote by Ed Murrow describing the then-fledgling medium of television in enthusiastic yet reserved tones. "This instrument can teach, it can illuminate; yes, and it can even inspire," Murrow said. "But it can do so only to the extent that humans are determined to use it to those ends. Otherwise, it is merely wires and lights in a box." That's the famous portion of Murrow's quote, and it has lasted more than a generation as the TV equivalent of the "garbage-in, garbage-out" (or GINGO) warning label leveled at the computer industry. However, Murrow's remarks didn't quite end with that memorable "wires and lights in a box" phrase. Next came a plea to include television in the arsenal of national education and enlightenment: "There is a great, perhaps decisive battle to be fought, against ignorance, intolerance and indifference. This weapon of television can be useful."

In 1955, some twenty years before the introduction of the home videocassette recorder, Murrow and producer Fred W. Friendly collaborated on a book version of *See It Now*—one of TV's earliest hardbound spinoffs. The book reprinted some of the best transcripts from the show's first four seasons, including interviews with physicist J. Robert Oppenheimer and poet Carl Sandburg, and Murrow's controversial report, defending an Air Force officer accused of Communist ties, called "The Case of Lieutenant Milo Radulovich." Back in those pre-VCR days, publishing the transcripts in book form was the best means of saving the content of those shows for posterity, and for serious study and prolonged enjoyment. In the foreword to the hardcover version of *See It Now*, Murrow and Friendly collaborated on a passage that explained their comfort with TV words on a printed page. They weren't just making a case for TV and literacy; they were arguing for the concept of TV as literature.

"We expect," Murrow and Friendly wrote, "that all good literature has not been written on a typewriter or with a pen or dictating machine. We believe that Sandburg talks as well as he writes, that Sir Winston Churchill converses as well as he orates, that President Eisenhower ad-libbed the best copy he ever wrote." Listing some of the other individuals interviewed for the *See It Now* reports, Murrow and Friendly remarked that some of them "may never write a book, but under the pressure of the moment and armed with the conviction born of conflict, they composed compelling literature."

Make that *tele*literature. I'll get to that a little later. Right now, it's time to move on to another TV concept treasured by Murrow—using the medium of television to bridge time, and especially space.

9

MARSHALL McLUHAN
WAS RIGHT:
THERE *IS* A GLOBAL VILLAGE

It was Marshall McLuhan, the media theorist, who pegged that phrase in *The Gutenberg Galaxy: The Making of Typographic Man,* when he wrote, "The new electronic interdependence recreates the world in the image of a global village." That was in 1962—one year before the John F. Kennedy assassination demonstrated television's reach, power, and importance beyond a shadow of a doubt, and years before battlefield images from the war in Vietnam, halfway around the globe, would warrant Michael Arlen's unshakable description of it as "the living-room war." A generation later, the information flow had become a two-way street. When other media were denied access during the 1991 war with Iraq, American viewers could get reports from Baghdad courtesy of CNN and Peter Arnett—and know that other countries and leaders around the world, including Iraqi officials, were receiving and watching the same information at the same time. In August 1991, the impact of global telecommunications was demonstrated by a no less striking example: the attempted overthrow of Soviet president Mikhail Gorbachev.

The coup story broke on Sunday, developed on Monday, exploded on Tuesday, and reversed course on Wednesday. As with the Gulf War, covering it as a TV critic meant watching four to six TV sets at once, VCRs running, in marathon sessions—taking notes, analyzing coverage, tracking network exclusives, analyzing commentary, filing daily stories, and generally trying to ride the beast while it's running wild. Most other TV critics were busy doing the same thing, commenting on the story—and the storytellers—as TV delivered its first rough draft of history. Here, as merely a personal example, are excerpts from my *New York Post* TV column for Thursday, August 22, 1991—the day after the coup attempt collapsed.

The staggering, fast-moving events of the last few days can be interpreted in many ways, but one thing, at least, is crystal clear: 1991 is the polar opposite of *1984*. Big Brother isn't watching us. Thanks to TV technology, we are watching Big Brother.

No less than politics, passion, and perseverence, it was technology that played a crucial role in the unraveling of the attempted coup in the Soviet Union. In turning back the military forces that had arrested President Mikhail Gorbachev and surrounded Russian federated republic president Boris Yeltsin, the key weapons weren't guns and tanks—but phones, fax machines, ham radios, amateur camcorders, and access to foreign news broadcasts and broadcasters.

Locally and globally, Yeltsin was able to amass supporters and inform reporters without leaving the relative, though tenuous, safety of the Russian Parliament building. Once the word got out, so did tens of thousands of Soviet citizens—and television, by keeping its cameras and attention trained on Moscow and the issue, may have affected the very outcome of the story. . . .

If ever a current event typified the worth and power of a so-called global village, this was it. In isolation, the leaders of the coup may have pulled it off; with the world watching, they quickly became outnumbered and outmaneuvered.

That's one overall round of applause that television, as a mass medium, has earned this week. Another is the speed with which it was able to chase and advance the convoluted and often conflicting developments. It's true that TV sometimes added to the confusion—but it added to the knowledge base even more. And yesterday morning, especially, the very speed with which rumors flew and attitudes changed was a strong indication that something major was happening.

Never before has so much been available to so many so quickly. In some ways, that's a frightening thought; in other ways, though, it's thrilling. From wide-eyed child to well-informed adult, television can open windows of observation—and opportunity—that otherwise would be unavailable or incomprehensible.

Before the start of this century, parents could pretty much control the amount and content of their children's knowledge of the "big wide world"—the area outside their immediate physical and emotional experience. Authority figures were seldom if ever challenged, and concepts clashing with the parents' personal beliefs could be withheld from the child merely by keeping all printed matter—and adult discussion—out of their reach. In this context, "Out of sight, out of mind" meant controlling what they knew and when they knew it. Literate children could read only what they could obtain—and those who couldn't read at all were excluded even more hopelessly and completely from a wider range of intellectual experience.

The movies were the first medium to change that imbalance in a substantial way; in fanciful films and realistic newsreels, youngsters could marvel at places they'd never visited, decipher accents they had never heard and witness people, places, and things they'd never even imagined. Radio carried just as much impact, only in actual or perceived "real time," and without any exclusionary barriers. A child listening to a radio announcer, even one whose voice was carried on a faint signal from a faraway city, felt as if that announcer were speaking directly and exclusively to him or her— and, in a way, the announcer was doing precisely that. Even if jazz or rock 'n' roll records weren't allowed in the house, a properly tuned radio could smuggle the same sounds into the home—breaking the protective barriers erected by the parents.

Similarly, all the studies in *Our Movie Made Children* support the idea that children of the thirties flocked to the movies to learn about things they couldn't experience anywhere else. Those social scientists saw movies as a threat to the status quo, rather than an opportunity for education and sophistication. The danger for the older generation was the thrill for the younger one: what they had been denied in print, they could now—via movies and radio—see and hear for themselves. Television, of course, eroded the barriers almost entirely. "Just as the printing press five centuries before had begun to democratize learning," Daniel Boorstin wrote in *The Americans: The Democratic Experience,* "now the television set would democratize experience, incidentally changing the very nature of what was newly shared."

"When I was young," writes Ernest L. Boyer, former US Commissioner of Education,

> there was no television in our home. I was twelve years old before we purchased our first radio. We did receive a daily newspaper and the *National Geographic,* which I eagerly devoured as soon as it arrived. Our Model A took us on short excursions from our Ohio home, rarely more than 100 miles or so. School was *the* central learning place and the teacher was the key source of knowledge. For students coming to our schools today, that world I knew is ancient history, and the glimpses of the outside world I found in the *National Geographic* have broadened into expansive vistas available at the flick of a switch.

Tony Schwartz, in *Media: The Second God,* calls this "the postliterate age," and says, by watching television, "our children have received a vast store of information about the world we live in without requiring the ability to read or write, a lack that would have condemned them to utter ignorance in a previous age." Looking back to a pre-TV age, Schwartz writes,

> Formerly, a city child of two or three who could not yet read had no idea of how a field of wheat sways in the breeze. Today this urban child recognizes the field of wheat from his experience of television. The same preschool child has some understanding of space travel, natural disasters such as tornadoes and floods, and even the terror of war. The Midwestern child knows something of how the child in China lives. The child in Istanbul can recognize the skyline of Manhattan. Little children can identify the voices of national leaders and many other public figures,

and they can identify other sounds that television and radio alone have made familiar to them.

Many media theorists, critics, and educators have bemoaned this technological advance as a sociological retreat, especially where children are concerned. Most definitely, television has brought more sex, violence, and harsh language into the home—but it's also brought more music, art, laughter, news, and positive role models. The challenge—and the responsibility—is to use television wisely, as a resource, rather than indiscriminately.

One of the more rational (and readable) authors addressing this issue is Joshua Meyrowitz, professor of communications at the University of New Hampshire and author of the provocative *No Sense of Place: The Impact of Electronic Media on Social Behavior.* In his chapter on "The Blurring of Childhood and Adulthood," Meyrowitz notes that television has served to educate children about many formerly unknown topics, including the private behavior of their own parents. As a pre-TV example, Meyrowitz quotes resourcefully from *The Diary of Anne Frank.* Hiding from Nazis and locked in the same tiny room as her parents, Anne witnessed them behaving in ways they had previously been able to keep private from her. "Why do grownups quarrel so easily, so much, and over the most idiotic things?" she wrote. "Up till now I thought that only children squabbled and that that wore off as you grew up."

Meyrowitz then suggests that the first generation of TV kids learned the same lesson under far less grim circumstances, merely by watching such sitcoms as *Leave It to Beaver* and *Father Knows Best.* On those programs, parents radiated an all-is-well attitude to their children, yet agonized and sometimes argued privately about what to do with the kids and each other. By watching those shows at home on TV, Meyrowitz says, children witnessed both the "onstage" and "backstage" behavior of the TV parents, and perhaps took from it the lesson that their own parents were similarly insecure and less than perfect. Meyrowitz is also the author who, in addressing the accessibility of young viewers to TV's global village, coined the eminently quotable phrase that television "escorts children across the globe even before they have permission to cross the street."

But is that such a bad thing? When the Gulf War erupted, and became an unavoidable concern for young children as well as adults, television responded to the situation by using TV to speak directly and frankly to children. Peter Jennings hosted a Saturday-morning Gulf War special for ABC. Linda Ellerbee addressed Nickelodeon's young viewers on the same topic. And Fred Rogers—the friendly face, soothing voice and guiding light of PBS's *Mister Rogers' Neighborhood*—was asked to create and appear in a series of public-service announcements aimed at children, talking to them about their war-related questions and fears. "That was such an opportunity," Rogers recalls. "I didn't want to get involved, and get in the fray of the whole thing—but when I heard that kids were really scared, then I felt, 'Put those feelings aside, Rogers, and do what you can.' That's when television can be at its best."

Rogers knows a lot about TV at its best, especially when it comes to children. An ordained minister of the United Presbyterian Church, he has been ministering to young people, through television, for nearly forty years—a remarkable demonstration of dedication and TV longevity. Rogers's career as a children's TV personality began in 1954 as a puppeteer on *Children's Corner,* a local TV show on WQED in Pittsburgh, Pennsylvania; Josie Carey was the host, and an unseen or costumed Rogers worked the puppets, including a still-familiar Daniel S. Tiger. Rogers began production of *Mister Rogers' Neighborhood* for the Canadian Broadcasting Corporation in 1964, sold it to the Pittsburgh ABC affiliate in 1965, and expanded his audience via public television in 1966.

I've interviewed Rogers several times over the years, and if one thing remains constant, it's his unwavering loyalty to his audience, rather than the medium through which he addresses it. Once, while visiting Philadelphia, Rogers politely turned down an invitation to appear on that evening's *Nightline,* even though the topic was "death and children." The reason for Rogers's refusal? He had come to town to speak to a kindergarten class the following morning, and felt they deserved his full and rested attention. Rogers is no less focused or forthcoming regarding his reservations about the medium of television: "I'm not a fan of television," he says simply. His own work, however, demonstrates the value of honest discussion of previously "hidden" issues facing children (death, disability, divorce)—and Rogers sees value in TV's ability to be a window on the world.

"Fine art, civilized speech, thoughtful ways of interacting with people—children's introduction to such things can come early, on television," Rogers says. "Some children wouldn't have the opportunity of some of those cultural riches—even to know what an opera or a symphony or a cello was—if not for television."

That's just as true for adults, of course, and TV provides an opportunity to cut across cultural, ethnic, economic, and educational lines. In 1955, one of Murrow's guests on CBS's *Person to Person* was Francis Henry Taylor, director of New York's Metropolitan Museum of Art. Here's what Taylor told Murrow more than thirty-five years ago: "I would think that television is the most important vehicle for the dissemination of art that has ever come to hand. I think it is just as important as the invention of printing in the 15th century. After all, before words we had picturegrams—we had images to express ideas. And today we are able, though television, to transmit ideas in visual form to mass audiences who have never had that type of visual experience in their lives."

What is true for art is true for all arts. *A Chorus Line,* during its record-setting fifteen-year Broadway run, played 6,137 individual performances that were seen by a total of 6.5 million people. Compare the immense success of that stage show to the ratings "failure" of another piece of musical entertainment—television's *Cop Rock,* which wound up as the lowest-rated ABC series of the 1990–91 season. Even so, each *individual* episode of Steven Bochco's *Cop Rock* was seen by more than 9 million viewers. On the other end of the scale, an episode of NBC's top-rated *Cheers* can draw more than 40 million viewers. On public television, shows of wonderful artistic merit routinely reach an audience in the millions. When people think of the "global village," they normally think of breaking news from foreign lands—but what about the worldwide telecasts of Live Aid and the Oscars, or the cultural exchanges of TV programming worldwide? When England's BBC-1 shows *Cagney & Lacey* in prime time, or America imports *Rumpole of the Bailey*, isn't that basically a double bill at the Global Village Duplex?

To hone in on a single, superb example, look at the output of the PBS anthology series *American Playhouse*. In its first decade of operation, *American Playhouse* has presented an astounding array of dramas and comedies, musicals and tragedies, cultures and perspectives. *Longtime Companion*, released theatrically prior to its PBS premiere, was a *Playhouse* production. So were *The Thin Blue Line, Testament,* and *Stand and Deliver,* to name but a few. The long list of *Playhouse* productions includes a brilliant adaptation of Philip Roth's *The Ghost Writer*, a delightful version of Kurt Vonnegut's *Who Am I This Time?*, and TV-adapted stage productions of everything from Sam Shepard's *True West* to the Stephen Sondheim-James Lapine musicals *Sunday in the Park with George* and *Into the Woods*.

American Playhouse, all by itself, embodies the best attributes of what people remember, with their selective memories, of TV's so-called Golden Age. Lindsay Law, executive producer of *American Playhouse* since its inception, has been a reliable source of thoughtful, ambitious, artistic television—and of insightful comments about the medium's possibilities and impact. Law tells a "global village" story about *Sunday in the Park with George*—a Broadway musical revolving around the creation of a Neo-Impressionist painting by French painter Georges Seurat. Producing a version of it for *Playhouse* in 1986, Law says, "was one of those completely selfish decisions, because I just thought it was one of the most remarkable musicals I had ever seen on stage. . . . I knew no one would watch it." But partly because he loved the show so much, and partly because he felt Sondheim was largely unknown outside of New York and Los Angeles ("His shows don't go on tour—except *A Funny Thing Happened on the Way to the Forum*, which is the only one that had your normal bus-and-truck tour"), Law pushed a TV version of *Sunday* through the *Playhouse* production process.

On the day *American Playhouse* broadcast *Sunday in the Park with George* over PBS, Law was on a movie set in Billings, Montana, and rushed back to his hotel room in time to see it on the local PBS member station.

"I was in the tallest building in all of Montana," Law says, "which means I was on the ninth floor. I turned on my television set and this announcer comes on and says, 'Next, Stephen Sondheim's Pulitzer Prize-winning musical.' I just found it unbelievably moving, in a certain way, that . . . this should get out there, and in Billings, Montana, which is not cabled, and they've only got about seven of the thirteen channels that even have a picture on them. I suddenly said, 'Anyone sitting in Billings, Montana—or anywhere else in Montana that night—and turning through their dials can see Bernadette Peters and Mandy Patinkin doing this show.' I found it astonishing. And then the great story, on top of it all, was that it actually had a huge audience—and I had never expected anyone to watch it."

Thanks to television, cultural offerings from specific parts of the country emanate to interested audiences nationwide: opera and classical concerts *Live from the Met*, Paul Simon live from Central Park, folk music from Wolf Trap, country music from the Grand Ole Opry. These shows bring distant voices closer and allow viewers at home to experience sensations and ideas from afar. The same is true of documentaries, and certainly of talk shows. "I love to watch the *Donahue* show," playwright Arthur Miller said in 1984. "You *see* this country."

One of the most significant changes instituted by television—and one with a direct correlation to the "global village" concept—is that lines between local, national, and international news have blurred to the point of invisibility as television has developed. In the late forties, CBS's *Douglas Edwards and the News* and NBC's *Camel News Caravan* (with John Cameron Swayze) became the first network news programs. Like the few existing local TV news programs at the time, these shows were fifteen minutes long and closer to radio than television: news reports were read from wire reports, unencumbered, for the most part, by related video footage. In 1962, Telstar and Relay communications satellites were launched, allowing, for the first time, instant transmission of TV pictures across the Atlantic. Not at all coincidentally, that also was the year McLuhan coined his "global village" phrase. One year later, network newscasts—specifically, *The CBS Evening News with Walter Cronkite* and NBC's *The Huntley–Brinkley Report*—doubled to thirty minutes in length, and a portion of that time was devoted to relaying news and pictures from afar. The system worked both ways, of course: no greater use of satellite technology occurred in 1963, or at any time since, than when the American networks relayed to the rest of the world their nonstop coverage of the John F. Kennedy assassination.

Throughout the sixties, television played a pivotal role in domestic and international affairs by its news coverage of events in America and abroad—coverage that, in addition to the facts, conveyed such visceral elements as fear, outrage, cruelty, and determination. It's no coincidence the American civil rights movement didn't really take hold until the advent of television. It was only when all of America could see, on their nightly newscasts, the civil disobedience and police brutality occurring in places like Selma and Montgomery in Alabama, or Watts in Los Angeles, that the issue of civil rights became a national concern rather than a series of "isolated" local events. Television, by relaying reports from troubled cities to an entire nation of TV watchers, let viewers know the scope of the discontent. What was more important, it informed the disenfranchised, wherever they lived, that they were not alone.

The same thing happened with the antiwar movement and the Woodstock generation. TV's coverage of the riots at the 1968 Democratic Na-

tional Convention, the massive gathering at Woodstock in 1969, and the
Kent State shootings of 1970 let members of the younger generation know
what was happening to their peers, and stirred emotions that led many to
action. It wasn't just the news footage from Vietnam that fanned the flames
of the antiwar movement; it was also the footage from cities around the
country, showing the volume and intensity of local protests.

Just as television could show America itself in times of dissent, it could
also define, relay, and even create moments of national solidarity. In 1954,
Murrow's brave, challenging *See It Now* analysis of McCarthyism ("This is
no time for men who oppose Senator Joseph R. McCarthy's methods to
keep silent") gave a national voice to the quiet whispers of dissent. Shortly
thereafter, the McCarthy era came to a close—actually, slammed shut—as
the nationally televised Army–McCarthy hearings showed Army counsel
Joseph Welch challenging the senator, who was attempting to tarnish the
reputation of a young lawyer. "Let us not assassinate this lad further, Senator," pleaded Welch, whose quiet testimony of the young man's innocence
stood in stark contrast to McCarthy's boisterous bullying. "You've done
enough. Have you no sense of decency, sir, at long last? Have you left no
sense of decency?" In *Eloquence in an Electronic Age,* Kathleen Hall Jamieson
wrote that the contrast in styles and substance, as relayed through television, made the difference. "At close range, Welch proved credible—Mc-
Carthy did not."

"When viewers could watch history being made right before their
eyes," a television historian, Irving Settel, wrote, "the Image involved the
American people in public affairs more directly than ever before, including
millions who scarcely ever read a newspaper." McLuhan, in his 1964 book
Understanding Media: The Extensions of Man, noted, "It was no accident that
Senator McCarthy lasted such a short time when he switched to TV. . . .
Had TV occurred on a large scale during Hitler's reign he would have
vanished quickly. Had TV come first there would have been no Hitler at
all."

That's debatable, because there has been no shortage of dictators since
the emergence of television. Also, the concept that some leaders are
"made" by television, and others destroyed, gives too little credit to the
American viewer. The same Richard Nixon who was ill-served by TV in
the 1960 Nixon–Kennedy debates was well-served by it eight years earlier,
when his live "Checkers" speech saved his vice-presidential spot on the
Republican ticket.

What is true, in each case, is that TV relayed the information and
images instantly, allowing each viewer to form his or her own opinion.
Nationally and globally, TV has trained its cameras at newsmakers and
news events and thrust certain stories and issues into the national consciousness. When Morley Safer's 1965 CBS report from Cam Ne showed
a US marine using a lighter to set fire to an elderly Vietnamese couple's
home—in retaliation for gunfire emanating from somewhere in that village—his "Zippo lighter" report helped the conduct of American soldiers

in the Vietnam War become a burning issue in the United States. Literally, it was a case of a village going global.

"Television has become the national nervous system," Tom Wicker wrote—and it's a terrifically appropriate analogy. When things are running smoothly, it's taken for granted; at times of crisis, its functions become crucial, and every variation is zealously monitored and analyzed. At all times, you can read the national temperature simply by tuning in.

There are human-interest stories that, by being reported and repeated through TV's vast network of stations, turn local events into national fascinations: whales stuck beneath the ice in Alaska, for example, or little Jessica McClure stuck deep in an abandoned well in rural Texas. Yet television's fascination with such stories is by no means a recent or unexpected development. In 1949, when a child named Kathy Fiscus was stuck in a well in San Marino, California, Los Angeles's KTLA-TV broadcast rescue efforts nonstop for more than twenty-seven hours, and competing station KTTV was not far behind. The live coverage proved so riveting that people without TV sets crowded in front of appliance stores, staring for hours at the TV sets in the display windows. "The telecasts of the tragedy gave a glimpse into the future coverage of big news events by video once the coaxial cable is laid across the country," an unsigned *Variety* report suggested, noting that "nearly every tele receiver within signal range of the two TV stations was turned on" as people watched the ongoing rescue efforts. "Interest was so great in the heroic rescue work of the child that it would have attracted millions on interconnected networks."

Sometimes those millions are already tuned in, expecting one event but witnessing another—the 1972 massacre at the Olympic games in Munich, the 1989 Bay Area earthquake just prior to Game Three of the World Series at San Francisco's Candlestick Park. (Both times, ironically, ABC sports announcers slipped impressively into the role of newscasters, with Jim McKay covering events at Munich and Al Michaels serving as on-location anchor after the quake.) Other times, it's the event itself that draws viewers—with enormous speed and in astounding numbers—to their television sets.

Finally, there's one other aspect of the "global village" worth celebrating. Thanks to the widespread development and popularity of videocassette recorders and camcorders, news now travels from the bottom up as well as the top down. In 1968 at Chicago and 1965 in Watts, television transmitted astounding and volatile pictures, but the only things shown were those that had been captured by the networks' bulky, obtrusive cameras. Imagine the abuses that could have been captured and corroborated on video had VCRs and camcorders been common in the sixties. Or look—without having to imagine—at the national furor sparked by the amateur videotape showing some Los Angeles police officers beating Rodney King in 1991. Those grainy, blurry, but indisputable images showed three patrolmen beating a helpless man as a dozen other officers stood by and watched. Relayed nationally and repeatedly by TV newscasts and debated heatedly on everything from *Donahue* to *Nightline,* that video—taken by local resident George Holliday, who filmed from inside his home across the street—gave an instant visual representation, and shared redefinition, of the term *police brutality.*

"This is going to be the defining incident in police brutality; it's going to be the historical event for police in our time," Jerome Skolnick, law and sociology professor at the University of California at Berkeley, told the *New York Times* two weeks after the beating occurred. Stephan Talty, writing in *Film Comment* magazine, said, "When the video was broadcast on national television, it was as if a long-standing rumor had been confirmed by a new technology, as if a new microscope now widely available to the public had given us pictures of a ravaging, diseased cell." Talty, by "reviewing" the video, also put a finger on the source of its power. "The sheer duration of the beating, lash after lash after lash with the nightsticks, is at the core of the incident's terror. Video showed it to us in real time, coolly bringing out the savageness involved. Had photographs been taken, the officers could have claimed that King resisted between the shots. But the video froze the event into a solid image that must be answered to."

The same sort of ground-level video accountability is happening worldwide, and gaining a worldwide audience. Two decades ago, black poet and composer Gil Scott-Heron wrote a song warning that "the Revolution will not be televised." Since the invention of camcorders, though, it has been—many times. In Hungary, South Africa, Poland, and Romania, dissidents have used camcorders to gather visual evidence of abuses and triumphs, an international underground network of VCR owners to duplicate and disseminate that evidence, and satellite technology to beam uncensored images and information across otherwise closed borders. Ted Koppel, in a brilliant 1989 ABC special called *The Koppel Report: Television—Revolution in a Box,* collected many examples of newsworthy scenes taped by amateur camcorder operators: a driver unknowingly plunging his car off a collapsed section of the Bay Bridge, a gun-turret explosion aboard the *USS Iowa,* three different camcorder angles of an air-show tragedy in West Germany. Koppel contrasts this to the JFK assassination in 1963, when only one man, Abraham Zapruder, had the equipment, inclination, and "lucky" timing to be filming as bullets began to fly. Zapruder got the murder (though not the murderer) on 8-mm. film, and sold the film, after a bidding "auction" attended by select print and TV representatives, to *Life* magazine—which printed only selected frames, and for years zealously kept the entire film from being shown to the American public.

Don Hewitt, who at the time was executive producer of *The CBS Evening News with Walter Cronkite,* learned about the Zapruder film from Dan Rather, whose CBS radio report on Kennedy's death had scooped the competition. Rather, on the phone from Dallas, told Hewitt on the phone that he was poised to deliver another exclusive: he was the only TV reporter invited to attend a screening of, and bid for rights to, Zapruder's incalculably important film. Hewitt told me his instructions to Rather were to grab the film from Zapruder ("Hit him if you have to," Hewitt recalls saying), run back to the station, make a taped copy, then run back and return the movie. "All they can get you for is assault," Hewitt says he advised Rather, "because you've returned the film. . . . Let the CBS lawyers get into the act, and let them argue about price and everything else, but at least we've got it. But give it back to him right away." Hewitt laughs, and continues the story: "He said, 'I'll do it, I'll do it! It's terrific. I'll do it right away!' And I thought, 'Holy [expletive deleted], what have I said?' So I called him back and said, 'Dan, for Christ's sake, don't do that.' And he said, 'Well, I was prepared to do it, until you called back.' . . . I caught him before he went out the door." Rather, in *The Camera Never Blinks*, remembers it a bit differently. He claims the notion to "knock him down and grab the film, run back to the station, show it one time, and then let him sue us" as his own, and adds, "Later someone at the network suggested half jokingly, but only by half, that I should have done just that." If Rather, in his book, was protecting an unnamed Hewitt, both versions could be considered correct. In any case, Rather responded with physical restraint but journalistic aggressiveness, bolting out of the room right after seeing the film to run back to CBS and describe, on live TV, what he had just witnessed.

The chance of any publicly attended event generating a similarly invaluable and exclusive piece of footage in the future is almost nonexistent. "If something like that were to happen today," Koppel said in his TV special as a hazy snippet from the Zapruder film was projected over Koppel's left shoulder, "fifty home-video cameras would capture the event from twenty different angles." If anything, that's a lowball estimate. In the nineties, it's not unusual to see fifty camcorders at a grade-school music recital. And while the amateur equipment can be used to preserve something that personal and banal, it can also record tracer bullets fired by Romanian secret police, abuses in hospitals and day-care centers, and images of Iraqi corpses that never made the network evening newscasts. One public television series, fittingly titled *The 90's*, contains nothing but pieces recorded and reported by independent and amateur video enthusiasts. Another public-TV series, *South Africa Now*, used videotape shot by citizens and amateurs to break the censorship ban against press coverage imposed by the South African government.

Jack Nachbar, a professor of popular culture at Bowling Green University, told *Newsweek* he sees the home video camera as a "new truth-telling device that can cut through lies." That presumes, though, that seeing is believing—which isn't always the case. The motivation of the camcorder photographer must always be taken into account, and video, like still photography, can be staged and even faked. When and if propagandists make room in their budgets for such state-of-the-art computer-generated effects as digital compositing (which brought the T-1000 to life in *Terminator 2: Judgment Day*), believing what your eyes see won't be as easy as it looks.

However, even if seeing isn't automatically believing, at least seeing is seeing—and in some repressive regimes, that's the fastest road to freedom.

"George Orwell was wrong," Koppel said in *Television—Revolution in a Box*. "The media, which he predicted would become the instrument of totalitarian control, has become, instead, its nemesis." It's an assessment that's incisive and poetic—and, since it comes from television itself, deliciously ironic. Television, at least, is paying attention to the impact of new video technologies, and to its worldwide reach and audience. Others should, too.

10

MARSHALL McLUHAN WAS WRONG: THE MEDIUM IS *NOT* THE MESSAGE

When MTV: Music Television launched its music-video network on August 1, 1981, the first video played was "Video Killed the Radio Star," by an obscure group called the Buggles. The song and video were two years old, but the title was too perfect to let a lack of timeliness stand in the way: it was a declaration of war, based on the assumption that, once rock music could be "seen" as well as heard, radio—and artists more interested in music than image—would be a thing of the past. As it turned out, MTV thrived, but so did radio and radio stars. Each created stars that made music, and money, for the other. Instead of extinction, there was cohabitation.

I was watching MTV that night, and reviewed the launch for the next edition of the *Akron Beacon Journal* in Ohio. As a critic, I had sort of made it my business—because it was—to live in areas wired by cable TV, and to subscribe to everything I could get. At first, it happened purely by accident. I was living in Gainesville, Florida, working as a TV critic and earning my master's degree, when Ted Turner began beaming the signal of his Atlanta station WTCG via satellite in 1976. Only a handful of cable stations picked up and relayed the signal at first, but my local system was one of them. The most memorable offering—and the one I singled out for review—was a late-night news show starring Bill Tush. Unlike Turner's later venture in the cable news business, Tush's show was played strictly for laughs. (Eventually, the call letters for WTCG were changed to WTBS, then changed again to the current TBS.)

In Fort Lauderdale, as critic for the *Fort Lauderdale News* in the late seventies, I subscribed to HBO—which, back then, used to go dark between movie presentations, and broadcast only a part of each day. I also subscribed to Showtime when it went national in 1978, and, in 1980, covered the cable network launches of Cinemax, CNN, and The USA Network. By the time I moved to Akron, in 1981, living in a cabled neighborhood was a must; when I left for the *Philadelphia Inquirer* in 1983, I chose the suburbs over the city, at least partly because the city wasn't yet wired for cable. Which, now that I've gotten around to it, is precisely my point.

By living in smaller communities, I was able to subscribe to and evaluate cable networks on an ongoing basis—while, in most major cities, cable had yet to arrive, which meant critics and journalists at larger papers had little direct experience. Consequently, a lot of the stories trickling down from the major urban publications betrayed a lack of understanding of either cable TV's appeal or its weaknesses. Stories were either too negative (who needs more than four or five channels, anyway?) or too positive (Warner–Alex's interactive QUBE system got rave reviews from visitors, but yawns and catcalls from local critics more familiar with its shortcomings). Those critics and viewers who had lived with cable for years, though, had seen enough to treat it as neither television's salvation nor its assassin. It was just another delivery system—one more medium in the modern mix.

CBS, NBC, and ABC scoffed at cable at first, then trumpeted dire warnings about how "free TV" was in jeopardy—and finally, when the profit-margin potential of cable networks became clear, tripped over one another to buy into existing cable ventures and launch new ones. CBS tried, and failed, early with CBS Cable. Currently, ABC has cable ties to ESPN and Lifetime; NBC has bought into SportsChannel America, Bravo, CNBC, and the Financial News Network; and NBC and ABC are joint partners, along with the Hearst Corporation, in the Arts and Entertainment Network (A&E). Strange bedfellows? Not where money is concerned and survival is an issue. The three-network share of audience decreased substantially in the 1980s, but TV viewership didn't. Cable networks, independent stations, public television, videocassettes, and videodiscs all competed for attention—and, in varying degrees, earned it.

Lengthy conjecture about whether the networks will survive, like yawn-inducing debate about whether the networks or the independent producers should reap the most profits from financial syndication, is wasted energy. Whether the networks live or die, and regardless of who profits most from producing it, TV programming will come from somewhere. Until, that is, TV is replaced by another, more appealing mass medium—at which time the best and most popular aspects of television will be absorbed into the new medium. Here's where McLuhan missed the point: it's the message, not the medium, that's the message. Television didn't kill vaudeville; it absorbed it. MTV didn't kill the radio star; it helped make new ones.

Before the invention of the phonograph, people who wanted to listen to music either had to be musically inclined—in which case they could buy the sheet music and play it at home—or had to sit still for private or public live performances. With the phonograph record, music enthusiasts could hear what they wanted when they wanted, and by whom they wanted. With sheet music, it was the music they were after; once records came in, it was both the music and the performer. A few generations later, with the coming of MTV, the sight of a video often figured in the equation as well—but always, at the core, was the music. Every new format introduced—from 78 RPM records to compact discs—has been blamed in advance for either its inferior musical reproduction or its sinister potential misapplications. What invariably happens, though, is that the new delivery system—even if makes an old delivery system obsolete—serves to make more of the music available than before. Similar shifts happen in all media, all the time.

Adults in the nineties, who lived through the sixties, should have gotten the message by now—the message that the message *is* the message. How many hardware changes have we lived through in the past thirty years? With TV, we went from black and white to color, then to projection and oversized screens. With video, we went from Betamax to VHS; with camcorders, we shifted from clunky, two-part Beta and VHS decks to sleek, eminently portable 8-mm. video. With music, we packed a century's worth of format changes into a single generation. Mono to stereo LPs. Reel-to-reel recorders to eight-track tapes, then (if, like myself, you were *really* gullible) quadrophonic eight-track, then cassettes—and, finally, compact discs. Except finally is much too strong a word, now that Digital Audio Tape (DAT) is here and recordable CDs aren't far behind. Technology is moving so swiftly, the DAT format may well be outmoded by the time this book is published.

When Sony unveiled its first consumer compact disc player in the early eighties, I attended a demonstration in Akron at the nearest (and only) area dealer licensed to sell the state-of-the-art unit. Because of its $1,000-plus price tag, it was targeted to high-income, highbrow audio enthusiasts—and because few release agreements had been negotiated for rock artists regarding CD rights, classical-music recordings dominated the music catalog at the outset. (In fact, the relationship of classical music to the development and early popularity of the compact disc cannot be overstated; the reason Japanese designers set storage capacity of more than an hour on the five-inch CD was to ensure Beethoven's Symphony No. 9 would fit on a single disc.) Consequently, I attended the demonstration with Donald Rosenberg, now the classical music and dance critic of the *Pittsburgh Press*, who was evaluating the technology and the sound reproduction of CDs for the *Akron Beacon Journal* and other Knight–Ridder newspapers.

At the time, I was most impressed by the salesperson's dramatic demonstration of a compact disc's durability. He dropped it on the carpeted showroom floor, stepped on it, and ground it into the carpet, then put it back in the CD player and let us hear the results: no pops, no skips, no flaws of any kind. (The flaws, I realized eventually, were in my own gullible brain. The information on a CD is encoded on its underside, so the salesperson—with full knowledge, no doubt—was protecting the vulnerable side of the disc while "punishing" the blank side.) In retrospect, though, what impressed me most about that day was Rosenberg's studied but enthusiastic acceptance of a new technology many of his peers ridiculed at the time—and still do.

"People still say it about CDs—that they have terrible sound, that it's unrealistic, that they're not going to last," Rosenberg says. "And of course they are—unless they get superseded by something else. I mean, the LP is going to be dead soon. But I don't think it's unusual for people to resist the new. People don't want the change." Yet Rosenberg, despite having collected thousands of vinyl classical LPs over the years, welcomes it. "I'm so immersed in CDs now, I rarely put anything else on," he says.

Yet as CDs elbow vinyl LPs out of the record stores, they make room for more music than those stores offered before. Record labels have reissued long-out-of-print albums for the CD market, and the popular success of such definitive CD boxed sets as *Robert Johnson: The Complete Recordings* have reintroduced vintage artists to a new generation in an easily accessible way. Recordings once consigned to the vaults, when rereleased, now fill other vaults with profits. A similar gold mine was tapped in 1958, when Columbia Records released Johnny Mathis's *Greatest Hits* on LP. The album defied the recording industry's conventional wisdom that consumers wouldn't buy a collection of songs available on other records—and, upon its release, almost instantly topped the charts. The Mathis package remained on the *Billboard* charts for 490 consecutive weeks—more than nine years—and "greatest hits" LPs became common practice, just as major-compilation "boxed-set CDs" are today. The LP may die, but the music and its greatest performers won't die with it. And actually, because vinyl records are more easily damaged than CDs, the value of mint LPs are sure to be worth more to future collectors than "mint" CDs.

With television, the lines separating the various delivery systems have all but vanished. Programs originating from first-run syndication *(Star Trek: The Next Generation)* and Fox *(The Simpsons)* can be equal or superior to the efforts of major networks CBS, NBC, and ABC. Telemovies made originally for cable *(Mandela)* show up later on broadcast TV in syndication. Telemovies made by both broadcast and cable networks show up on videocassette, repackaged to look like regular film releases. Video stores have shelves full of old TV shows available for sale and rental. Pay-per-view cable systems allow viewers to select from a menu of specials and movies each night, paying only for what they want to see when they want to see it. Viewers can rent movies—and almost anything else—for their VCRs, and discriminating film buffs can enjoy videodiscs that bring their favorite movies to life in letterboxed format and CD stereo—plus, on some versions, alternate audio tracks that provide a sort of mini-film course as running commentary. Voyager's Criterion Collection release of *The Last Picture Show,* for example, includes a fully restored version of the 1971 film, including nine minutes of footage cut from the theatrical release, in a wide-screen, letterbox format. On a separate audio track, which viewers can access at the push of a button, director Peter Bogdanovich talks about each scene as it's being shown. And after the movie is over, the videodisc keeps going, with such "extras" as *Last Picture Show* star interviews, original screen tests and movie promos, and frame-by-frame, page-by-page reproductions of the original screenplays for *The Last Picture Show* and its sequel, *Texasville.* As videodisc technology catches on, expect to see more films—and even TV series—given such grand treatment.

There are so many nightly options now on the television schedules—and so many others outside those "normal channels"—viewers no longer have to settle for what Paul Klein, former NBC Entertainment President, once dubbed the "Least Objectionable Program." The average home in 1990 had a choice of thirty-two program channels—compared to an average of ten channels a decade earlier. Remote control devices have turned many viewers into "grazers"—and if they don't find something interesting on broadcast or cable TV, they can switch to VCRs, videodiscs, or computers to satisfy their video urges. It's all part of the new freedom—what Stewart Brand, creator of *The Whole Earth Catalog* and author of *Media Lab: Inventing the Future at MIT,* calls "Personal Renaissance."

Brand writes in *Media Lab,* "We've seen people use VCRs to stop being jerked around by the vagaries of network scheduling, build libraries of well-loved films, and make their own videos." The "personal library" of videos is a routine concept today, and a popular one: in 1990, for the first time, Hollywood generated more money from sales of videocassettes than rentals. The home-video library, though, is a very recent development. When I was in college (in the pre-Betamax midseventies), a film professor who owned personal copies of selected movies was considered by his students to be part god and part outlaw. However, the search for a wider range of entertainment options—and the means to enjoy them at a time of one's own choosing—is nothing new.

The fancy picture-in-picture TV sets of the nineties, with multiple images available simultaneously, sound like the latest in modern technology—but listen to this 1961 newspaper ad for a De Forest TV console, which featured two or three sets in the same cabinet. "The great networks are sharpening their weapons—competitive performances at the same hour—you simply can't jump all round the dial and take a small bite—there's too much to miss. But De Forest double or triple screen TV lets you see all—all the time." It was an obvious early cry for some form of viewer control of the situation, even though this particular triple-image solution didn't catch on. Perhaps people couldn't see De Forest for the threes.

An even earlier clarion call against network tyranny—and a virtual commercial for the then-unknown concept of time shifting—can be found in a very unlikely place: Arthur Miller's *Death of a Salesman,* written in 1948. It's the scene in which Willy Loman goes in to appeal to his boss—but, instead of getting sympathy and understanding, gets an enthusiastic lecture about the virtues of modern technology's newest miracle, the wire recorder. Wire predated reel-to-reel tape, and Willy Loman's boss was excited about its time-shifting possibilities . . . for radio.

"You can't do without it," he tells Willy. "Supposing you wanna hear Jack Benny, see? But you can't be home at that hour. So you tell the maid to turn the radio on when Jack Benny comes on, and this automatically goes on with the radio! . . . You can come home twelve o'clock, one o'clock, any time you like, and you get yourself a Coke and sit yourself down, throw the switch and there's Jack Benny's program in the middle of the night!" When unveiling the Betamax in 1976, Sony ran print ads that—like Willy Loman's boss—stressed that audiences at home need no longer be dictated to by network programmers. The ads proclaimed, "Now you don't have to miss *Kojak* because you're watching *Columbo*."

Entertainment's so-called Personal Renaissance has grown exponentially ever since. Network TV research has shown that, especially on weekend nights, the usage of VCRs—now in more than 65 million households—eats significantly into the available audience. ABC's Saturday-night programming of *China Beach* and *Twin Peaks,* according to the network, was a calculated gamble to win back some of those VCR defectors. It was a gamble that failed, though, and both *China Beach* and *Twin Peaks* were canceled at the end of the 1990–91 season. ("I think *China Beach* turned out to be a bit more serious, perhaps a little bit too brooding, for the Saturday night audience," Robert A. Iger, president of ABC Entertainment, told TV critics that summer. As for *Twin Peaks,* Iger said it suffered from both "mistakes made on the creative side" and from being a serialized drama. "If we were going to attract viewership to a show such as *Twin Peaks* on Saturday night, we had to do it with a show that didn't require the viewer to be there every week.")

On the movie front, Hollywood studios now generate more revenue from video sales of their films than from box-office receipts in movie theaters—much more, in fact. The home-video market generated $10.3 billion for Hollywood in 1990, whereas domestic receipts from movie theaters accounted for $5.1 billion—less than half as much. Movie studios in the nineties can plan and market their film rosters accordingly, and in some cases choose to finance a property because video sales and rentals can be relied upon to turn a theatrical loss into an overall profit. One videocassette wholesaler has said that, where certain movie releases are concerned, studios "are counting on video to be the cake, not the icing." In addition to providing a profitable afterlife for certain films, the increasingly formidable home-video market has also provided a new life for old movies and TV shows. On videocassette as well as videodisc, movies and TV series are being repackaged—and often restored—as collectors eagerly build their own individual video libraries.

Television networks are struggling, and failing, to maintain a delivery system that no longer makes sense. What good is a much-ballyhooed "fall season," when many of those shows are canceled by December? Why offer weaker programming during the summer months, traditionally the most lucrative season for home-video rentals? And what good are reruns, when each show's most devoted viewers are likely to have taped the program the first time around? Nicholas Negroponte, founder of the Media Laboratory at the Massachusetts Institute of Technology, predicts that the networks' future will be built almost totally around live programming—a return, ironically, to its technological infancy. "Sports and elections probably will remain synchronous and shown live," Negroponte says in *The Media Lab.* "The rest won't. The rule might be: if you can bet on it, you won't see it out of real time. . . . The traditional 'mass media' will essentially disappear." In his vision, the next years, and certainly the next century, will see a melding of the computer, publishing, broadcast, and motion-picture industries.

James Burke, author and TV commentator, has melded most of those industries together already. He relies on volumes of often arcane books and articles when researching his science specials, then converts that knowledge into TV shows by using the latest computer technology to assist the graphics, and his own affable show-biz presence to serve as host. In his native England and throughout TV's global village, Burke's specials are loaded with original insight and challenging opinion. His ten-part documentary series *Connections,* imported by PBS in 1978, was an utterly fascinating overview of inventions and inventors, and how certain inventions changed the shape and direction of certain societies. In terms of an audience draw for PBS, it was to the seventies what *The Civil War* was to the nineties—the most popular documentary series shown on PBS up to that time. Burke explored a similar concept in a later series, *The Day the Universe Changed,* that was just as delightful and provocative. And in 1990, Burke wrote and hosted *After the Warming,* a TV special that looked at the effects of global warming not only by looking back through history, but by looking ahead to the year 2050, which Burke visualized with help from the latest in image-generating computer technology. A key part of the special is a typical network "newscast" from 2050, although, privately, Burke questions whether the networks will even survive that long.

"I think that all sorts of mass media are doomed," Burke says. "They are, after all—as you know—a nineteenth-century phenomenon, and they will go. . . . Just as large, centralized plants bringing thousands of human beings to do exactly the same activity three million times a day from nine to five, they will go, too. With electronic telecommuting, you won't even be doing it physically any more. So I think the day of a mass *anything,* its days are numbered. There will be an electronic net on which we will all live, and we will dip in or stay out as you choose—a sort of balanced anarchy."

A less extreme scenario is envisioned by Warren Littlefield, whose interest is definitely vested: he's president of NBC Entertainment. "By the year 2000," he said in a January 1991 speech to advertisers, "we'll probably have about 100 million TV homes. Cable could be reaching 70 to 75 percent of those homes, with an even higher penetration of VCRs. High-definition and interactive television will have arrived. The choices and fractionalization of the audience will continue, but I have no doubt that the commercial networks will still be around, and be a force to contend with."

Personally, I suspect "real time" television will not vanish entirely. The instant availability of all types of music—on record albums, singles, cassettes, and CDs—hasn't killed radio. People continue to gravitate towards "star" personalities, and there's a lot to be said for the shared communal experience of a simultaneous national broadcast. Radio used to provide it; now television does. Even if tomorrow's version comes via satellite, or fiber-optic transmission, or a massive home-entertainment database, there will always be room for "real time" transmission and enjoyment of entertainment—not just news, sports, and weather. The likelihood is that viewers at home eventually will be able to call up any program they like—at any time—from a massive national network of databases, and store it on disc or tape (at a set fee, naturally) for retrieval and reviewing at their own leisure.

If anything's at risk under this new delivery system, it's the video rental chains—except that it's equally easy to imagine a "Blockbuster Video Database" establishing a major foothold there, too. Most probably, any asynchronous delivery system—in which viewers decide what and when they will be watching—will complement, rather than replace, what we now know as simultaneous "network" delivery of program offerings. Television without a set of "live" options would be like a restaurant without a menu. You don't *have* to visit that restaurant—but when you choose to go there, it's nice to have a basic selection. Otherwise, a choice that's truly unlimited can be somewhat overwhelming.

Admittedly, I could be wrong about this—but so could everybody else. Hollywood is no more scientific or reliable in predicting the future than in predicting hits, and the only thing trickier than guessing which road will be traveled is guessing the speed limit on that particular path. When I chose to become a TV critic in the midseventies, it was partly to be in place to document the coming video revolution. I guessed correctly, back then, that home videocassettes and personal computers and cable television and pay-per-view would all be part of the growing media landscape. Where I guessed wrong was in underestimating that growth.

In 1980, VCR penetration was so low—in about 1.5 million homes at mid-year—that almost no programs were produced originally for the home-video market. "It's pretty hard to justify original products when the potential sales volume is so low," one home-video executive said then, explaining why the first original entries in the home-video field included an ABC Video Enterprises news-clip compilation called *The Pope in America: A Journey For Understanding*, a live-on-tape music show called *Teddy Pendergrass in Concert*, and the medium's first full-length "rock-video album," Blondie's *Eat to the Beat*. "In theory," I wrote then, "the advent of videocassettes was going to bring us Broadway, Brahms, and Baryshnikov. In practice, it has given us Deborah Harry, Teddy Pendergrass, and Pope John Paul II."

In the early eighties, reviewing such text-adventure computer games as *Zork* was part of my job description, as was going to the local video arcade and analyzing the appeal of such games as *Asteroids* and *Pac-Man.* The joke was on me, though. In all those cases, the technology and appeal mushroomed so quickly that entire jobs were created to cover them: newspapers began syndicating columnists who wrote exclusively about computer hardware and software, computer games, and the home-video market. In the nineties, there's bound to be a similar growth in writers specializing in videodiscs: the industry predicted sales of 12 million discs in 1991, a figure double the sales for 1990.

Every once in a while, I'll dip into those technological waters to take their temperatures for an article—but for the most part, those media babies have outgrown the general parameters of the TV critic's job, and become the responsibility of other specialists. It's all we TV critics can do to hold on to cable. And as thrilled as I am about the prospects for high-definition television, and the multimedia video work stations combining state-of-the-art audio, video, CD, and database facilities, I'm afraid when they get here, they'll arrive at such a speed that it'll be tough for TV critics to jump on board. In the 1967 movie *The Graduate,* the secret word was *plastics.* A quarter-century later, the secret word is *fiber-optics.*

No matter how uncertain I am of the future, though, I feel sure the idea of a "mass media" will survive in some fashion—simply because, as a culture, we enjoy and seek out certain common frames of reference. There is a value in the feeling of being up-to-date and in the know—discussing last weekend's Madonna skit on *Saturday Night Live,* or the Baghdad dispatches of CNN's Peter Arnett—and it's an opportunity provided only when masses of people are reached at the same time.

Pauline Kael, in an essay comparing film to television, focused on the real-time transmission as a crucial part of its appeal. "Just as it sometimes seems that even a teenager locked in a closet would pick up the new dance steps at the same moment as other teenagers," she writes in *Kiss Kiss Bang Bang,* "these television watchers react to the same things at the same time. If they can find more intensity in this box than in their own living, then this box can provide *constantly* what we got at the movies only a few times a week."

Kael's point about the shared experience is well taken, even if her tone is notably overwrought. She acknowledges its power, but not its glory. By dismissing it as "this box," she identifies it by its package, not its content—looking at what TV *is* rather than what TV *does.* It's the "medium is the message" idea again. But if more people focused on what television presented at its best, they might be less inclined to disregard it as "this box." Or that boob tube.

11

TELEVISION DESERVES
MORE RESPECT

In 1953, NBC's *Philco Television Playhouse* presented an original Paddy Chayefsky teleplay called *Marty,* starring a then-unknown Rod Steiger as a homely and lonely Bronx butcher. It won no awards. Yet it didn't exactly go unnoticed. "People from all over the country and all different walks of life, from different races and religions and creeds, sent me letters," Steiger wrote in his memoirs. "The immense power of that medium!"

Overnight, Chayefsky became much in demand, while talent formerly reluctant to become involved in TV began flocking to anthology dramas. Meanwhile, Delbert Mann, who had directed *Marty* for TV, went in the opposite direction: Hollywood hired him to direct a movie version starring Ernest Borgnine. Released in 1955, *Marty*—this former live TV show—won four Oscars, including best screenplay, best actor, and best picture. Other TV directors, such as Sidney Lumet, John Frankenheimer, George Roy Hill, and Arthur Penn, quickly followed. Directors, writers, actors—reputations were being made overnight, and cashed into opportunities in other media, during TV's Golden Age.

"In those few years between, say, 1953 and 1957," Arthur Penn recalled in *Premiere,* "the studios realized that the new troupe of actors and directors and writers was probably going to come from television. And it was true. Charlton Heston, Paul Newman, Eva Marie Saint—almost everyone who became a new star, from the late fifties on, probably had their start in live TV." Newman starred in a 1956 *U.S. Steel Hour* drama, *Bang the Drum Slowly,* that predated the Robert De Niro movie by seventeen years. Also for *U.S. Steel,* Cliff Robertson starred in *The Two Worlds of Charlie Gordon,* based on the short story "Flowers for Algernon"; remade in 1968 as the movie *Charly,* it earned Robertson a Best Actor Oscar. Another Robertson TV role, opposite Piper Laurie in the 1958 *Playhouse 90* production of JP Miller's *Days of Wine and Roses,* went to Jack Lemmon, who starred with Lee Remick in the 1962 film version; both the TV and movie versions received raves for their realistic depiction of an alcoholic couple. Reginald Rose's teleplay of *The Twelve Angry Men* won an Emmy after its *Studio One* broadcast in 1954; Robert Cummings won an Emmy, too, but he was replaced by Henry Fonda for the 1957 film version it "inspired." On occasion, TV's live anthology series presented programs that later inspired stage *and* film versions—as in the cases of *The Miracle Worker* on *Playhouse 90* (starring Patty McCormack in the role that later won Patty Duke an Oscar) and Andy Griffith in *No Time for Sergeants* on *U.S. Steel.*

In January 1955, when *Kraft Television Theatre* presented a dramatization of Rod Serling's *Patterns,* his services became in immediate demand. Serling was by no means an overnight success—he had written seventy-one previous teleplays—but, thanks to the impact of *Patterns,* he was a success overnight. "One minute after the show went off the air my phone started to ring," Serling said later. "It's been ringing ever since." In the *New York Times,* TV critic Jack Gould predicted *Patterns* would "stand as one of the high points in the TV medium's evolution." A year later, Serling topped himself, and overshadowed *Patterns* in the TV history books, by writing *Requiem for a Heavyweight* for *Playhouse 90.* At the Emmys, *Heavyweight* walked away virtually undefeated: Jack Palance won for best actor, Serling for best teleplay, Ralph Nelson for best direction, and *Requiem for a Heavyweight* for best single show of 1956. Nelson got to direct the 1962 film version, but Palance was replaced by Anthony Quinn. Live television was the place to make reputations—but not, sadly, to stay put.

In the British model of show business, people moved effortlessly among film, TV, and the theater—an artistically acceptable flexibility encouraged by the fact that all three industries were based primarily in London. In America, you had Broadway and live television in New York, and the film industry in Hollywood. Broadway retained clout because of its exclusivity—its small, upscale audience. The more popular television became, the less respect it got in show-business circles. Television became a means, not a goal.

"The Golden Age was golden largely in the sense of opportunity," said Gore Vidal, who wrote dramas for *Studio One* and a book musical for *The Milton Berle Show* back then. "There was an awful lot of drama. Television was still new and exciting. Everybody watched. You would walk down the street the next day and you would hear people talking about it." Robert Geller, who carried on the anthology-TV tradition with his *American Short Story* series, recalls why he was so taken by the Golden Age dramas—specifically citing Chayefsky's *Marty* and "anything Reginald Rose was writing" as fond memories.

"The characters usually resonated what I might be vicariously experiencing, because I was a contemporary," Geller says. "The emphasis was on language and character. And for somebody who loved literature, it offered the possibility of being entertained by the ambiguous. . . . It's thirty-plus years ago, so I was not as much of a 'sophisticate' then, but it just seemed to be magic to me."

Besides Gore Vidal, another now-best-selling author who wrote for TV during its Golden Age is Kurt Vonnegut, who adapted a handful of his magazine short stories into TV scripts and sold them to various anthology series in the fifties. One early effort, based on his short story "D. P.," appeared on *General Electric Theater* in 1955 under the title *Auf Wiedersehen*, starring Sammy Davis, Jr. The same story was adapted for *American Playhouse* in 1985, with Stan Shaw in the lead; that version, called *Displaced Person*, won an Emmy.

Vonnegut also has been represented on television by *Between Time and Timbuktu* (a 1972 *NET Playhouse* amalgam of several Vonnegut stories and characters, starring William Hickey); *Who Am I This Time?* (a clever 1982 *American Playhouse* adaptation of his story, starring Susan Sarandon and Christopher Walken, and directed by Jonathan Demme); and, most recently, a 1990 trilogy of short-story adaptations for Showtime cable's *Kurt Vonnegut's Monkey House*. Except for *Between Time and Timbuktu*, television has served him well every time. However, that doesn't mean Vonnegut is uncritical of television—which is where the author of *Slaughterhouse-Five*, *Cat's Cradle*, and *Breakfast of Champions* figures into this look at TV's Golden Age history.

"I was a magazine writer, and that's how I made my living, when television came along. In the short story business, you could operate out of a mailbox," Vonnegut remembers. "You just put a story in the mail and waited to see whether they wanted it. It paid extremely well. When television started out, it was largely centered here in New York, and so it operated on the same basis early on. You mailed them a script, and they'd call you up and tell you how to fix it on the phone, or whatever, but you could do business at a distance." The Golden Age of Television, in Vonnegut's opinion, "wasn't all that good," and he says much the same thing about Broadway's "Golden Age" of the twenties and thirties.

"I think about the Golden Age of the theater, when people got all dressed up and saw the latest George S. Kaufman comedy . . . and everybody's sentimental for that."

Vonnegut laughs. "It's nothing but a sitcom. The couch, the stairway off to one side. The difference is, there were maids in those shows. Nobody has maids any more," Vonnegut says, laughing again. "But it wasn't so damned great, and they might have been pilots. These things would run for six months on Broadway, and they might have been pilots for mediocre sitcoms—you know, the madcap daughter who's fallen in love with the bad guy. There was Eugene O'Neill, and there were some other greats, but most of it was on the level of very mediocre TV."

Discourteous as that sounds, it's merely Vonnegut's refusal to sentimentalize the past merely because it has been supplanted or overshadowed by art forms of the present. "Each new technology creates an environment that is itself regarded as corrupt and degrading," Marshall McLuhan wrote in 1964. "Yet the new one turns its predecessor into an art form." This is another example of McLuhan's being right. It's another way of saying each current mass medium is rejected critically as it's accepted popularly, while the previously dominant mass medium becomes more celebrated as "art" in hindsight. During TV's Golden Age, the finest dramas produced were praised by critics, popular with audiences—yet were seen as less important than the subsequent movie versions they inspired. Generally, TV got little respect then, and gets even less today.

When radio was the dominant medium, it was dismissed and disparaged almost as cavalierly. In 1938, an article in *Fortune* magazine surveyed the radio landscape, and declared it the aural equivalent of a vast wasteland—but instead of blaming broadcasters, as Newton Minow did in his famous speech about 1961 television, *Fortune* put the blame on consumers. "You cannot criticize the output of radio as a whole without criticizing the taste of the American public. . . . It may be distressing to be told that the chief entertainment of 129 million people is a ventriloquist's dummy, swing bands, Broadway wise guys, and . . . assorted fluff, gush, and drivel. . . . But there you are." In time, the antics of such "Broadway wise guys" as Jack Benny and George Burns would be remembered as treasures, not fluff, and the musical contributions of Benny Goodman, Duke Ellington, and the like would be called genius, not drivel.

The pattern of mass-medium artistic assimilation—initial disparagement, followed by revisionist acceptance and eventual adoration—is almost comically predictable. When something is right under our noses, whether it's jazz music, movies, TV, or any other popular culture, Americans almost always react by sticking those noses up in the air. "Notoriously, Europeans—and particularly the French—have recognized, researched, praised (and sometimes overpraised) the American arts—our movies, our jazz, our comics—before we have," note Bill Blackbeard and Martin Williams in their introduction to a Smithsonian Institution collection of newspaper comics.

> And it would perhaps not be too chauvinistic to point out that we have produced these things, after all, and loved them, and that scholarship, art criticism, and cultural history are secondary pursuits. At the same time, many of our own historians of the arts, having borrowed their principles, procedures, and attitudes largely from European cultural historians, have proceeded to apply those principles only to such traditional categories as we have borrowed directly from abroad—to literary history, to the theater, to concert music and the like, sometimes pausing to scorn or reject those artistic genres that are particularly American, like the movies, jazz, and the comics.

Filmmaker William Wyler summed up this transatlantic relationship when he joked, "In Europe they're just as snobbish as they are in New York. They like foreign pictures." Unfortunately, we can't expect the French to rescue us when it comes to our attitudes about television: American TV isn't as widely exported and embraced there as are our musical and movie products. Fortunately, the slow but steady acceptance of the American motion picture, even without foreign intervention, suggests a path that American television could—and should—follow.

In a previous chapter, I singled out some important early examples of positive film reviews—ones that saw potential in the medium, and art in some of the movies themselves. Even in the forties and fifties, however, such reviews were uncommon, and limited largely to championing epic works. "The movies have produced one of their rare great works of art," James Agee wrote in 1946, praising Laurence Olivier's film version of Shakespeare's *Henry V*—a movie imported from Britain. But Agee stood out, like Pauline Kael after him, because he also wrote glowingly and passionately of silent comics, screwball comedies, and even Bugs Bunny cartoons ("It killed me," he said of *Rhapsody Rabbit)*, and came to bat for the medium as a whole. In 1945, he wrote in the *Nation*, "If you compare the moving pictures released during a given period with the books published during the same period—or with the plays produced or the pictures painted or the music composed—you may or may not be surprised to find that they stand up rather well."

That may not sound like a bold statement from today's perspective, but consider the tone of W. H. Auden's 1944 letter to the editor in the *Nation*, praising Agee's film criticism. Agee gained instant respectability after being lauded publicly by such a revered literary figure. Yet at the same time Auden was applauding Agee's movie reviews, he was dismissing the movies themselves. "I do not care for movies very much and I rarely see them; further, I am suspicious of criticism as the literary genre which, more than any other, recruits epigones, pedants without insights, intellectuals without love," Auden admitted.

> I am all the more surprised, therefore, to find myself not only reading Mr. Agee before I read anyone else in *The Nation* but also consciously looking forward all week to reading him again. . . . What he says is of such profound interest, expressed with such extraordinary wit and felicity, and so transcends its ostensible—to me, rather unimportant—subject, that his articles belong to that very select class . . . of newspaper work which has permanent literary value.

Not that I'm against critics getting praise when it's due, but the idea that a critic could gain respectability—while the art he's analyzing is denied it—is absurd. Is the "literary value" of Agee's words in his *Nation* reviews any less significant than the value of Agee's words in his subsequent screenplay adaptation (with director John Huston) of *The African Queen?* Or, because *The African Queen* is a movie, does that make Agee's "extraordinary wit and felicity" automatically seem "rather unimportant"?

Once again, the French came to the rescue. French film critics not only looked closely at the content of individual movies, but looked for connecting threads in both the subject matter and the styles of creators and contributors. In 1946, the same year Agee was praising *Henry V*, critic

Jean Pierre Chartier, in *La Revue du Cinema*, was applying the newly minted phrase film noir—literally, "black film"—to such movies as *Double Indemnity, Murder My Sweet,* and *The Postman Always Rings Twice.* The essay's translated title: "Americans Also Make 'Noir' Films." In the fifties, *Les Cahiers du Cinema,* under the direction of André Bazin, made a brilliant, bold, and durable case arguing for the importance of cinema. And just before the end of the decade, a French compendium titled *Vingt Ans de Cinema Americain* gave lavish, appreciative A-to-Z listings of American directors and their works.

America finally followed suit—and woke up—at the start of the sixties. In *Film Culture* magazine, critic Andrew Sarris published his now-famous two-part American version of the French critics' auteur theory—crediting certain directors with consistent agendas and artistry, and giving fresh credence to such previously overlooked filmmakers as John Ford and Alfred Hitchcock. The impact of that essay was such that it had a formative impact on some of today's most celebrated directors, including Martin Scorsese. "I started reading Sarris's work in *Film Culture* magazine in '60, '61," Scorsese told *Premiere* magazine thirty years later.

> It was a funny thing. Back then, the only serious films were foreign films—French and Italian new wave, Bertolucci, Godard, that kind of thing. Sarris made me realize I didn't have to hide the fact that I liked *The Searchers.* At the time, you know, that was thought of as just another John Wayne film. Same with films like *Rio Bravo,* and Sam Fuller movies. They were all just Westerns. Sarris made me realize that we had great art in our own backyard.

Richard Levinson and William Link, the talented writer–producer team that created *Columbo* and such landmark telemovies as *The Execution of Private Slovik* and *That Certain Summer,* prefaced their 1981 book *Stay Tuned* with a defense of television. In that opening chapter, defiantly titled "Notes from the Wasteland," they cited a professor of humanities who felt TV was poised to be "the coming prestige medium," using the slow but steady respectability of film as an applicable model.

"He reasons that the cultural establishment dismissed most of the motion pictures of the thirties and forties as mindless mass entertainment," Levinson and Link reported. "Fiction and the theater were the preeminent forms, and the *films noirs* of the period were either ridiculed or overlooked. But fashions change and now the trend-setters, and particularly the young, are praising the very same films that were largely ignored when they were released. Movies are screened in museums, dissected by cineasts, beloved by the French." Levinson and Link added, "Tomorrow's children may well hold up the Archie Bunkers, the Kojaks, and the Fonzies as icons, much as we have a collective soft spot for the heroes of our youth—the Bogarts, Cagneys, Garfields, and Edward G. Robinsons."

In the same essay, the authors staked a claim for TV that echoed, in spirit and almost in language, James Agee's bold defense of movies a generation before: "It's our view," wrote Levinson and Link, "that . . . in any given year the best television movies are better than all but a few theatrical motion pictures and plays for the legitimate stage."

But movies, by having a head start, also have the edge on claiming respectability. Sarris's *Film Culture* essays were followed in the sixties by such seminal cinematic studies as Pauline Kael's *The Citizen Kane Book* and François Truffaut's *Hitchcock/Truffaut*—each of which, by the size and scope of their scholarship, made a persuasive case for taking film *and* film criticism seriously. Truffaut, who went from being a movie critic for *Cahiers du Cinema* to a movie director of such acclaimed films as *Jules and Jim* and *The 400 Blows,* tied the presixties underappreciation of film directly to their popularity. Alfred Hitchcock's suspense films were greeted warmly by audiences, and his hosting chores and droll introductions on his *Alfred Hitchcock Presents* series made him a recognizable celebrity. Yet that very visibility, Truffaut charged in *Hitchcock/Truffaut,* cost Hitchcock respectability. "American and European critics made him pay for his commercial success," Truffaut wrote, "by reviewing his work with condescension, and by belittling each new film." Truffaut's book changed all that for Hitchcock, and articles and books by other passionate, revisionist critics changed things for other Hollywood filmmakers and stars. Throughout the sixties, current as well as vintage films were analyzed and assessed, and the movies—after some fifty years of widespread popularity—became accepted, without much argument, as art.

By that same yardstick, television is about due for some overdue respect. It became popular in the forties, which means the nineties should be the half-century point marking TV's critical reassessment. The only problem is, part of the reason film rose to "art" in the sixties is because television started absorbing most of the critical flak. The condescension Truffaut saw heaped upon Hitchcock by critics is nothing compared to the daily critical condescension heaped upon television, and in the decades since TV became dominant, no other medium has surfaced to deflect the heat.

Television continues to draw fire from all sides. Intellectuals make uninformed and erroneous generalizations about it. Many people who *make* television—make, in fact, some of the very best shows on television—have little respect for the medium in which they work. Almost all film critics, and even many TV critics, consider television unworthy of serious consideration. And there's a long-standing pecking order in show business that, in essence, places film beneath the theater, and television beneath contempt. Even from those individuals who have done a lot to shape and improve the medium, a tone of defensiveness or ridicule often surfaces.

Don Hewitt, the creator of *60 Minutes,* says, "I've always thought what's principally wrong with television is the American public, because they expect too much from it. You buy a television set for five-hundred dollars. You divide that over the next ten years, you pay fifty dollars a year—and I can't believe there isn't fifty dollars worth of enjoyment from that set every year. The problem is, people are looking for fifty dollars a night. Nobody gets those kinds of odds. Those odds are ridiculous."

David Attenborough, too, is concerned about the audience's expectations of television, but on the other end of the spectrum. "If people say, 'Well, there's nothing to watch on television, it's all just a joke,' then the only time you turn it on is when you want a piece of chewing gum," Attenborough says. "But if you turn it on and there's some guy talking about evolutionary theory, you think, 'Oh, to hell with that. That's not what I turned it on for. If I wanted that I'd take a book, thank you very much.' And then you'd look around until you *find* chewing gum. Once you get into that downward curve, that abyss, it's like hell to get out of it."

James Burke, Attenborough's fellow warrior in the battle for quality television, says of the medium, "I think it is a prime educational tool, and I think that it has been seriously misused. What we would accept as a standard definition of television—broadcast television, cable channels, etc., that kind of stuff that has been around since after the Second World War— has been desperately theatrical. It has been pulled down below a common denominator by the need to sell cans of beans and whatever."

Fred Friendly, with a résumé that includes a journalistic partnership with Ed Murrow, ex-president of CBS News, and his just-concluded Columbia University PBS seminars on significant media and moral issues, has all but assumed the role of TV's official curmudgeon. Supporters admire his experience and ethics, while detractors say he's too quick to criticize anything that smacks of the modern TV news era. Indeed, Friendly is blunt and often critical, but backs up that belligerence by producing— and, until very recently, moderating—some of the modern TV era's more challenging televised discussions.

Interviewed for this book, Friendly began by repeating a phrase he had uttered in testimony before Senator John Pastore's Commerce Committee Subcommittee on Communications back when public TV was debated and designed: "In commercial television, the networks make so much money doing their worst, they can't afford to do their best." That was in the sixties. Since then, Friendly says, the costs and profits have risen tremendously—but not the quality. "There's so much money in doing crap. That's the scary part," Friendly says, looking at television today. "They've created a junk TV market, just like they've created a junk food market. Just like there's an appetite for McDonald's, Burger King, and those pizza places, they've created an appetite for junk television—for junk docudramas, for junk news."

That may sound like the crankiness of old age, but in TV, youth can be just as cranky. The most celebrated young documentary filmmaker of our time, Ken Burns, is somewhat leery and scornful of television, even though it was the PBS production of *The Civil War* that shot Burns to prominence. Burns was the nonfiction miniseries' director, coproducer (with brother Ric Burns) and co-writer (with Geoffrey C. Ward and Ric Burns), and the recipient of the series' auteur credit: "A Film by Ken

Burns." Calling *The Civil War* a "film" rather than a TV series is somewhat of a giveaway about how Ken Burns regards television, but it's hardly an attitude requiring close scrutiny to unearth. Ken Burns, as a documentary filmmaker whose fine works include *Brooklyn Bridge* and *Huey Long*, sees TV from the perspective of a wary outsider.

"I've always been aware of it as a manipulative medium.... And I really do feel, in the midst of all of this celebration, this is a slothlike animal that uses so little of its brain," Burns says of television. "It tends to lull us to sleep. With *The Civil War*, it demanded something of them and they responded. And in that response was a quickening of their own pace."

All those concerns and criticisms come from TV's "reality" side, but those on the creative end—producing the medium's plays, dramas, and comedies—voice similar sentiments. *American Playhouse's* Lindsay Law talks about network television in a manner that's as pointed as Attenborough's, as disparaging as Friendly's, and as self-deprecating as Hewitt's.

"The preoccupation with gossip, and everything that is perverse, I find really grotesque. I mean, all of these reality shows," Law says, shaking his head in disbelief. "God, talk about guilty pleasures.... Diane Sawyer being reduced to interviewing Marla Maples—I mean, it's just astonishing," Law says, referring to the ABC *PrimeTime Live* coanchor's highly promoted interview with the alleged mistress of millionaire Donald Trump. "I did nothing but complain about it all week, and I said, 'Oh, they have *done* it, they just *ruined* her as a journalist.' But of course I *watched*," he adds, laughing. "So, like, you can't have it both ways.... The ratings go up, and they realize, 'Aha, we've got to find someone else out there like Marla Maples, because everyone watched.' And it's true. It caters to perhaps the less good side of us, maybe, too often. If there was a balance, it would be one thing ... but there isn't."

Also pointing an accusatory finger at the baser appetites of viewers is *Columbo* cocreator William Link. Despite mounting an eloquent and defiant defense of television in his *Stay Tuned* book with the late Richard Levinson, Link feels modern tastes, and modern technology, play a part in what he sees as a reduction in the demand for serious TV programs.

"Mostly, you know, the networks get crucified—not without cause— and the creative community in Hollywood. Again, not without cause. But no one has laid any of the blame at the doorstep of the audience," Link says. "Obviously, it's not a smart thing to do, because you don't want to alienate your watchers. But I think you have an increasingly ill-educated audience out there, with an increasingly diminishing attention span.... And the remote control, they use it like an Uzi weapon. They do what John Updike calls 'channel surfing.' And you're given a short period of time in which to hook them, and I think the audience really is in the business of looking for sensations. And you get 'sensation' television, all the reality-oriented things, and the sleaze factor comes in ...

"I find it in all the arts. I find it in the tremendous pollution of rock music—which, if you want to compare it to rock music of the sixties, when you had people like the Beatles and Dylan, etc., around, I think there's been a tremendous deterioration in quality. I think you'll find it in the concert hall. Even intelligent people now who like music—you're hard-pressed to name any new important or interesting American composers. You really have to root around to find them. And new American music—or, for that matter, new European music, or new Asian music—gets a world premiere in your concert hall, and that's the last time it's ever played.

"You find it in books and literature. . . . Most of the books are junk. Ballet I don't know. In art, you had the eighties, in which anything worked. You had a postmodern period, and you had artists really rooting around just to find something new that was away from abstract expressionism . . . and doing something to evolve since 'pop' and 'op.' But you find, again, a bankruptcy in the field of painting. I happen to know, because I collect art. I just find there's a general malaise out there. The creative spark is somewhat extinguished. I don't know why. It's a combination of a lot of things, and probably, we in television are responsible for some of it—to a lesser degree than the attacks have tried to show."

If Link sounds like a sentimentalist, unthinkingly preferring the past to the present, that's not the case. Like Vonnegut, his opinion of the past is relatively unclouded by nostalgia. "I grew up, when I was a kid, on radio," Link says, "and radio did not come under the same scrutiny and hostility as television has. Yet if you look back, and listen to the Golden Age of radio dramas, the stuff is pretty lousy." Link has listened to a collection of old radio tapes recently, and says, "It's really the same kind of junk getting on networks and cable TV today. You had the Ed Murrows . . . but mostly it was a mass audience entertainment scene that wasn't very good. Again, poor writing. I'm stunned listening to these old radio dramas. They're pretty awful. *The Shadow, The Lone Ranger*—this is really pabulum."

Finally, after pointing to the audience, the technology, and the particular times in which we live, Link points to the new generation of TV makers. In his opinion, television is getting worse because the executives and producers who make it have little understanding or appreciation of past achievements in TV and film. "People I meet in the business now," Link says, "have very little if any knowledge of great movies or great television." Link tells a story of a young TV executive who, when meeting actor-producer Jack Webb to entertain a proposal for a new series, asked Webb to recite some of his credits ("They don't even remember *Dragnet!*" Link says). It's an outlandish example, though Link swears it isn't apocryphal. Either way, he stands by his assertion that the younger generation brings to TV a different background and value system.

"For one generation, the American motion picture industry began with *Easy Rider*. For the next generation, it began with *Star Wars*. Anything before that is literally the Dark Ages. . . . There's a great swamp of ignorance there. When you talk to them, you can make references to current pictures of the last ten years. If you go back further than that, you begin to get into trouble. . . . And I just don't find the love of the medium that

I saw many, many people had thirty years ago. They get into business for different reasons now: money, glamour, power. Power is a *big* thing." When it is pointed out to Link that the people interviewed for this book have demonstrated both knowledge and passion in impressive degrees, Link counters, "The people you're talking to, obviously, are very bright."

One of those people—one representing a younger generation—is Lorne Michaels, creator of *Saturday Night Live*. In addition to creating, overseeing, and eventually reviving *Saturday Night Live*, Michaels has been executive producer of some of modern TV's finest rock 'n' roll specials: *The Paul Simon Special*, the satirical *The Rutles: All You Need Is Cash*, the Central Park concerts with Simon and Garfunkel and with Simon alone, *Randy Newman at the Odeon*, and others. Michaels's passion for music and film has been a constant throughout his life. Significantly, though, his early enthusiasm for television had pretty much waned by the time he broke into TV as a comedy writer in the sixties.

"I was twenty-three or twenty-four years old when I started on *Rowan & Martin's Laugh-In*," Michaels says, "and the people I was working with were more like fifty-two or fifty-three. They had worked in *radio*. That generation moved naturally into television, whereas my generation broke through first in music, then in the movies. The last bastion was the networks. . . . Remember, *Lucy* was still in flower when *Saturday Night* came out," Michaels says, referring to Lucille Ball's *The Lucy Show.* [Actually, that flower had wilted the year before.] Network television of the midseventies was so "disconnected from the main currents of the time," Michaels says, he intentionally drew the first guest hosts for *Saturday Night Live* from the fields of movies, music, and stand-up comedy, rather than TV. "It was important to stake out the movie and record audience, and let them know that this was a show for them," Michaels says. His "young and judgmental" anti-TV prejudice was nearly universal; he wouldn't even write for *The Mary Tyler Moore Show*, which ran from 1970–77, because he then perceived it as part of the TV establishment. (Michaels now laughs at that story, and himself, calling it a "dumb brag.") "There was very little on TV in 1975 that I had any respect for," Michaels recalls. "I'm from the 'What I really want to do is direct' generation. . . . Movies were an *art*. Television was sort of—well, it had come out of radio somehow."

Oddly enough, one of the young writers who got his start cranking out scripts for some of television's truly terrible series of the mid-seventies—namely, *The Six Million Dollar Man* and *Lucas Tanner*—would return to network television, and to great acclaim, a decade later. In between, Mark Frost wrote for the stage and created documentaries for PBS, but got his best and most important credit after joining the production and writing staff of Steven Bochco's innovative, invigorating NBC series *Hill Street Blues* (cocreated by Michael Kozoll). After that series ended, Frost linked up with film director David Lynch, and the two of them concocted the equally innovative and invigorating *Twin Peaks*. In the last twelve years, only *St. Elsewhere* has stretched conventions or encouraged experimentation as much as those two series; Frost may be so adept at stretching the envelope because he's so *familiar* with the envelope. In direct opposition to Link's stereotype of a young producer, Frost has both experience in TV and an appreciation of film and literature—an obvious appreciation, because he and Lynch injected dozens of literary and movie references in *Twin Peaks*. When asked why they did that, Frost gives a very teleliterate answer.

"I love literature, and I have grown up with books and American movies, and I guess it provides a kind of cultural melting pot," Frost says. "Everything is grist for the mill. And in the absence of any collective mythology, which America sort of seems to be lacking, we have instead the movies. We have images like James Dean on a motorcycle. What I think we are trying to do in those kinds of images is pass on a form of mythology of ourselves. . . . They somehow give us a sense of something being authentic, as opposed to another show that's shot out in the San Fernando Valley with two guys in a cop car."

Frost may or may not feel television has a mythology of its own, but it's certainly generated some mythic generalizations from its critics. The only people who seem to disparage TV more than those who make it are those who *watch* it—although, in a lot of instances, I question just how much they really watch. Even praise, from certain quarters, is suspect, given their probable unfamiliarity with day-to-day television. George Will, *Newsweek* columnist and *This Week with David Brinkley* panelist, writing glowingly of *The Civil War* miniseries, said, "If better use has ever been made of television, I have not seen it." I don't doubt the veracity of that statement one bit, but I *do* question the true scope of Will's praise. Outside of the occasional documentary, talk show, and baseball game, how much TV *does* Will watch? And if you don't sample from commercial and cable as well as public broadcasting, how can you compare or generalize?

The answer is: easily. Generalizations about television come from all over, span the spectrum—and rarely hold up to closer scrutiny.

"Every television program must be a complete package in itself," Neil Postman writes in *Amusing Ourselves to Death*. "No previous knowledge is to be required. There must not be even a hint that learning is hierarchical, that it is an edifice constructed on a foundation. . . . Television undermines the idea that sequence and continuity have anything to do with thought itself." In 1965, that would have been a fair observation in prime time; drama series, like comedies, were constructed of relatively interchangeable parts. How, though, does Postman's statement jibe with the serial format of soap operas, carried over from radio? The characters and situations in that format are nothing if *not* hierarchical and sequential. And by 1985, when Postman's book was published, prime-time network television had given us such weekly dramas as *Hill Street Blues* and *St. Elsewhere*, where complex, continuing story lines were developed over weeks, months, and even years.

Screenwriter, novelist, and essayist William Goldman—author of the book and film versions of *The Princess Bride* and *Marathon Man* and the screenplays for *Butch Cassidy and the Sundance Kid* and *All the President's Men*—is a terrific writer whose sharp eye and sharper wit make him one of the most entertaining and illuminating chroniclers of the movie business. His essays on Hollywood for *New York* magazine are delightful, and his 1983 book *Adventures in the Screen Trade* is loaded with an insider's insight about films and filmmaking. In that same book, though, Goldman makes several digressive forays into the world of TV criticism—and presents several uninformed opinions, in ways barely disguising his disgust for the small screen.

"This paragraph contains all that I know about writing for television," Goldman writes. "They need a hook. And they need it fast. Because they're panicked you'll switch to ABC. So TV stuff tends to begin with some kind of a grabber." Goldman can be released on good behavior because of the use of *tends* as a qualifier. Yes, many sitcoms and dramas depend on "cold openings" to get the viewer's attention, but no one who saw the opening of the miniseries *Centennial,* or of the telemovie *Duel,* could accuse TV of always going for the hook.

Goldman's major critical crime in *Adventures in the Screen Trade,* though, occurs in an otherwise-persuasive discussion of what he calls a "comic-book movie"—something that, basically, has few surprises, little resonance, and no grounding in reality. To define his terms, Goldman talks about television, and says this: "The only prime-time entertainment series that is not a comic-book program is *M*A*S*H.* Not because of its outstanding quality, but because every scene in *M*A*S*H,* no matter how wildly farcical, is grounded in the madness of death." The same two series I used earlier to dispute Postman's thesis, *Hill Street Blues* and *St. Elsewhere,* would seem to disprove Goldman's thesis as well—and both were on the air in 1983, when Goldman wrote that sweeping dismissal of every TV show but *M*A*S*H.* Had he failed to notice the madness of death in which those shows were grounded? Had he failed to notice those shows at all? Or was it, at least partly, that *M*A*S*H* carried the art-by-association that came from its origins as a book and film, whereas both *Hill Street Blues* and *St. Elsewhere* were created originally for television?

I don't mean to pick on Goldman specifically, but if one of the best writers in Hollywood can trash TV so cavalierly and completely in print without a second thought, how ingrained must the anti-TV feelings be? For an answer, let's shift to one of the best writers who *isn't* in Hollywood— Dennis Potter. Potter, author of the brilliant British miniseries *Pennies from Heaven* and *The Singing Detective,* has devoted the majority of his long and bold writing career to television. Since writing his first teleplay in the mid-sixties, Potter has heard all the usual remarks about television—and, in the preface to a printed collection of his selected teleplays, Potter tells about reading a book including yet another slap at the medium of television.

First, Potter quotes from the book itself, a scholarly examination of TV detectives and private eyes: "Because television is so two-dimensionally bland, favoring amiable anonymity," writes the unnamed author, "the only way it can ensure a character's individuality is to burden him with a tic, deface him with a quirk—Kojak's lollipop, Columbo's scruffy raincoat, Rockford's beaten-up trailer." Then, without bothering to attack the specifics of the charge, Potter takes aim at the general tone.

> The tone is as unmistakable as it is predictable. An academic taking the poodle of his prejudices for a little walk. Freshly burdened, now, with a tic, and defaced with a quirk, I acknowledged that there is very little written about television which does not eventually betray smirking condescension or a rather less culpable unease. I have conceded elsewhere—though with one fist dangling low for a counterpunch—that to trundle the adjectival noun *Television* in front of the noble old word *Playwright* is not entirely dissimilar to placing "processed" right next to "cheese."

One academic whose poodle has a very long leash is Allan Bloom, who displays a notably closed-minded approach to TV in *The Closing of the American Mind.* When he writes that "educational TV marks the high tide for family intellectual life," there's no question he intends it as a snide insult, even though I'd argue truly intellectual programming can be found easily and often. (This, of course, would put me at odds with the college faculty member who wrote that aforementioned vitriolic letter to Robert Thompson. "In terms of keeping the human mind active and working above the most primitive level," he told Thompson, "the finest PBS special is no more valuable than the crudest soap-huckstering sitcom.") And when Bloom talks about the "typical" MTV viewer message, his colorful language reveals a lot, though not necessarily about MTV. Bloom describes the MTV viewing experience like this: "A pubescent child whose body throbs with orgasmic rhythms; whose feelings are made articulate in hymns to the joys of onanism or the killing of parents; whose ambition is to win fame and wealth in imitating the drag-queen who makes the music. In short, life is made into a nonstop, commercially prepackaged masturbational fantasy." Clearly, when it comes to television, there is no love in Bloom.

Not only does he attack or dismiss it with every mention, but he fails to mention it when he should. "Students today," Bloom insists,

> have nothing like the Dickens who gave so many of us the unforgettable Pecksniffs, Micawbers, Pips, with which we sharpened our vision, allowing us some subtlety in our distinction of human types. It is a complex set of experiences that enables one to say so simply, "He is a Scrooge." Without literature, no such observations are possible and the fine art of comparison is lost.

That statement could not be more wrong. Students today, if they're literate when it comes to television, *do* have some complex, yet singularly identifiable characters from which to choose. Even *The Dictionary of Cultural Literacy,* in its Fine Arts section, lists "Bunker, Archie" as an entry—and to dismiss a TV anchor as a "Ted Baxter" pretty much says it all. Because this thesis gets to the heart of the argument for teleliteracy, the question was posed to some of the people interviewed for this book: has TV generated any durable archetypical characters who are the television equivalent of Ebenezer Scrooge?

Linda Bloodworth-Thomason, creator and coexecutive producer of *Designing Women* and *Evening Shade*, is an especially qualified TV writer-producer to address that question. Not only does she specialize in comedies where laughs come more from character than situations, but she was an English major and high-school English teacher before embarking on a career in television. Her love of language is apparent in every episode she writes, and she's prolific enough to write a lot of them. Her answer to the question is short, immediate, and to the point. "I guess," she said, "Archie Bunker would be the closest." Then, after a while, she names two more: Hawkeye Pierce of *M*A*S*H* and Mary Richards of *The Mary Tyler Moore Show.*

"I think Hawkeye Pierce is a legendary character," Bloodworth-Thomason says, "and I think he's as interesting as a lot of people you read about in novels—maybe not as fully fleshed out, but pretty interesting. And he sticks *with* you. You know, my whole life, I will feel like I *knew* Hawkeye Pierce from watching that show. . . . And I think most people, particularly most women of my generation, feel like Mary Richards was an old friend. And most of us really haven't had old friends—old fictional friends—since we were children. You remember the fictional friends you had when you were little, and you really don't ever get them again unless you get them through television, because people don't read much."

James L. Brooks, cocreator of *The Mary Tyler Moore Show*, was another person contacted. His track record in television, in terms of artistic as well as popular success, is astounding: Brooks's other credits as cocreator, coexecutive producer, and writer include *Taxi, Lou Grant,* and *The Simpsons.* Even the less popular series he's helped bring to television, such as *The Associates* and *The Tracey Ullman Show,* have been a delight. (All six of those series, in fact, would land on my list of all-time favorites.) What's more, his achievements in television are mirrored by equal success in the motion-picture arena. He directed, produced, and wrote the screenplay adaptation for *Terms of Endearment,* and was writer-producer-director on *Broadcast News.*

Asked if he felt TV generated archetypical characters worthy of Charles Dickens and Scrooge, Brooks says: "I haven't thought about this at all, and I can't approach it academically, but I wonder if *any* form has had blue-collar heroes that entered the consciousness *more.* I mean, Ralph Kramden is *somewhere* in there. . . . And I always thought *All in the Family* was just—it made you understand what popular culture can be. It united us. In some strange way, with the characters in that show, it provided some kind of common ground."

Link, like Bloodworth-Thomason and Brooks, mentions the *All in the Family* character in his unprompted reply. "Archie Bunker. Hasn't that gone into the lexicon of America?" Link asks. "You say Archie Bunker, you're talking about a redneck family man—a guy who supposedly has all-American values, but who is also a very consistent bigot. That's *easily* available to anybody who knows popular culture.

"Has he *watched* television?" Link asks suddenly—referring not to Archie Bunker, but to Allan Bloom. "That comment seems very off-base. . . . When you say *Dallas*, when you say J. R., you know in a flash you're talking about a duplicitous, likable, but corrupt multimillionaire." Link also mentions characters on *M*A*S*H*, several Norman Lear comedies and, when pressed, the Levinson–Link character of Lieutenant Columbo. As played by Peter Falk, *Columbo* is recognized and beloved worldwide: it's the top-rated TV series in Israel, and a hit even in Japan.

Part of the appeal is the mystery series' inverted formula, where the murderer is revealed at the outset, but most comes from the universality and recognizability of the Columbo character. "He's a character who is humble and obviously middle class, or maybe even lower on the socioeconomic scale," Link says, "and it's literally as if the Columbo character is kidnapped by helicopter from Yankee Stadium each week and dropped into the backyard of some Beverly Hills millionaire who's just committed a murder. . . . As a type, he's a tenacious, humorous, extremely bright, highly persistent detective character."

Mark Dawidziak, TV critic for the *Akron Beacon Journal,* is quite familiar with, and enthusiastic about, that Levinson-Link series. Yet instead of starting his list of Scroogelike TV archetypes with Columbo, he prefers to challenge the scope of the original argument.

"When you talk about universal flash points, I would maintain that literature has given up very few of those," Dawidziak says. "Scrooge. Simon Legree. OK—now keep going. You won't find very many others. . . . After a while, you realize we're not a very literature-oriented society. Play the game all the way through, and you'll find TV has actually given us more such characters than literature. I would argue that what pops immediately to mind is Ralph Kramden, which has given us the idea of the blue-collar, not-so-bright guy with a heart of gold. And Chester Riley before him, and even Fred Flintstone after him. No other medium has given us those archetypes as effectively as television."

"King Lear is a wonderful figure, but he doesn't represent too many people in society," Dawidziak insists. "But Ralph Kramden does—he represents a whole segment of people. A generation who grew up with television now uses those archetypes to describe somebody. And TV has given us not just the archetype characters, but also these archetype settings and families and entire contexts. You hear the term *Dickensian* to describe a condition or a plot or a style unto itself. TV, in many ways, can frame things that way too."

In other words, merely the titles of *The Brady Bunch* and *The Waltons* are recognizable synonyms for supersweet families, while *The Twilight Zone*—the title *or* the four-note theme music—is an almost universally evocative shorthand definition of weirdness. And if you acknowledge the TV audience's widespread command of popular TV characters and programs past and present, that single-handedly negates the arguments of both Postman and Bloom. As Ella Taylor writes in *Prime-Time Families*,

> Television is often criticized on aesthetic grounds for its formulaic character. Yet all genre conventions, whether in television, the novel, or the epic poem, are formulaic to the degree that they build on prior forms and can be understood and recognized, or "placed," in relation to other forms by their audiences. Viewers may recognize Archie Bunker not just as a sociological type—the working-class bigot—but also as the direct descendant of Ralph Kramden and Chester Riley.

Having defended television from attacks by almost every other quarter, I now turn to critics themselves. William Link says, "Radio did not come in under the same scrutiny and hostility that television has," and he's right. Almost alone among the major critical disciplines, television criticism fosters—and often encourages—an overt antagonism toward the medium being analyzed. A film critic displaying constant contempt for that medium would soon be replaced; a TV critic with the same attitude would likely be promoted. This attitude developed as television did, as newspapers perceived TV as an ever-increasing threat. Yet while that explains a certain hostility from some members of the first generation of critics, it doesn't explain why those feelings sometimes persist. Read a week's worth of TV columns in your local newspaper or national magazine, and the odds are better than even you'll encounter prose suggesting the writer has an inferiority complex about television. Even the positive reviews can contain negative connotations: watch, for example, for a high-quality telemovie to be described as "terrific by TV standards" or, even more damning, "good enough to be a real movie."

Some of the most celebrated critics are guilty of such TV inferiority complexes. Tom Shales of the *Washington Post*, probably America's best-known TV critic, wrote that "TV-movies are to cinema what the Rolodex is to literature," at a time when *Duel, Too Far to Go,* and *The Execution of Private Slovik* were among his options. Michael Arlen, when he wrote television criticism for the *New Yorker*, didn't exactly elevate the field when he likened TV viewing to something more personal. "Above all it is a private act, an act that we perform by ourselves and with ourselves, even though other people may sometimes share the room and engage in it themselves. What it resembles most, I think," wrote Arlen, "is masturbation."

It would be nice to think that new TV critics, being hired in the nineties, approach their chosen beat with more respect for it—but that's not always the case. Walter Kirn, hired in mid-1991 by *Mirabella* to be its media critic, explained in an interview why he accepted that post rather than take another job as a magazine editor: "I chose to become a critic . . . because generally I don't like it," Kirn said, adding, "For someone who's set himself up as a media critic, I probably watch less TV than my friends." Where else but in the land of TV criticism are prejudice and ignorance considered assets?

The prejudice against TV is so deeply felt, it can inflict even those who *are* deeply interested in the medium. David Zurawik, a journalist who studied specialized reporting and pop culture in graduate school, got a job writing about television, and other aspects of popular culture, for the *Detroit Free Press* in the late seventies. A few years later he switched beats, to the city desk and hard news, because he suddenly felt TV criticism was beneath him. "I had a crisis," Zurawik recalls. "I thought, 'This is not something an adult should be doing.' " But after spending months filing stories as part of a team covering the Haitian and Cuban boat lifts, Zurawik got frustrated when the newspaper stories carried little impact—and even *more* frustrated when, after CBS News sent out a camera crew and interviewed them, their brief appearance on the *CBS Evening News* sparked national outrage at the boat-lift conditions. "TV seems to have *much* more reach," Zurawik recalls thinking. That's when he decided to start writing about TV again. He's now TV critic at the *Baltimore Sun,* and pursuing a doctorate in American studies—with a specialty in popular culture and television—at the University of Maryland.

Don't expect similar epiphanies from most critics, though, for television is more easily ridiculed than reassessed. It's true of many TV critics, and it's even truer of most film critics. A classic demonstration of this occurred at a Television Critics Association panel in 1983, when guests Gene Siskel and Roger Ebert (then of *At the Movies*) went heads-to-heads with Neal Gabler and Jeffrey Lyons (then of *Sneak Previews*). The subject turned to *Hill Street Blues,* which Gabler viewed regularly—and which Siskel and Ebert had seen recently for the first time. Gabler, who took to the show's defense, made sense; Siskel and Ebert, on this particular subject, made noise.

GABLER: In some ways, *Hill Street Blues* is the product of cross-fertilization of film into television.

EBERT: Not cross-fertilization—ripping off. The basic insight behind *Hill Street Blues* is somebody's half-perceived notion of what Robert Altman once did: the intercutting stories, the cute little hangling-dangling plots that are going to be picked up later, the laconic dialogue. If you did this in a movie, it would seem kind of laughable.

GABLER: But I think there's something very interesting here, too. . . . If you only see that in isolation, Roger, and I happen to watch the show just about every week, you miss one of the ingredients that makes it a television series. . . . You do gain a familiarity with the characters. They develop. They evolve in a way, unfortunately, that they can't in a two-hour or three-hour film. . . .

SISKEL: I thought the whole thing with television was revisiting familiar characters as opposed to watching them change.

GABLER: That's not the case with *Hill Street Blues.* I don't want to defend a show that you haven't seen, because we'll be talking at cross-purposes. And I don't think that's very fair to you. But as a regular watcher of

Hill Street Blues, I think it is in some ways one of the best examples of what television can do well—and that is, give us an ongoing saga in which we have an emotional investment in the characters every single week. And we see them go through various evolutions. . . .

EBERT: They go through Identi-Kit emotional fixes.

GABLER: You can't say that on the basis of one viewing, Roger. I think that's unfair.

EBERT: It isn't likely that any other show would have been any better or worse than the one I watched.

GABLER: But you wouldn't judge a film on the basis of five minutes . . .

EBERT: I was accused by a gentleman in the front row of being a film snob. And I will say this: there aren't very many television snobs. The fact is, the best movies are so much better than any television that has ever been done that it frankly isn't even a contest.

Those are fighting words—especially coming from Roger Ebert, the man who wrote *Beneath the Valley of the Ultravixens* for Russ Meyer under the pseudonym "R. Hyde." Well, he can Hyde, but he can't run. In some ways, I guess I *am* a television snob, and more than eager to turn Ebert's "TV vs. Movies" contest into a critical reality.

But actually, what I'd rather do is petition for equality, and encourage the demolition of all these walls we've constructed to isolate television, film, and the theater from one another, and to isolate all of them from printed literature. Take just one author, for example—the one who created the aforementioned Ebenezer Scrooge.

Charles Dickens wrote some of his most beloved books in serial form, writing them in weekly installments for a mass-medium newspaper audience. David Lean's 1946 movie adaptation of *Great Expectations* brought Pip and Mrs. Havisham and the rest to vivid life, enchanting not only those who *had* read the original novel, but those who hadn't and, in some cases, couldn't. Television's miniseries version of *Bleak House* did justice to that novel's richly textured characters and sprawling plot, while the London and Broadway theater borrowed from TV's long-form format to present, in essence, a spectacular "live" Dickens miniseries: *The Life and Adventures of Nicholas Nickleby.* Those who attended those stage shows saw a marvelously realized comedy-drama, but so did those who watched the subsequent TV miniseries version of that same production, featuring the original cast. Later, Dickens's *Little Dorrit* comes out as a six-hour, two-part miniseries— but for the movies, not for television. Within a few months, though, *Little Dorrit* had been broadcast on cable TV and released on home video. Newspaper column, leather-bound book, wide-screen movie, Broadway stage, broadcast TV, home-video cassette—when it's good, it's good, and the medium is *not* the message. When the Dickens will all those "film snobs"— and stage snobs and book snobs—wake up and accept that?

There's irony in the fact that television, the medium for which Siskel and Ebert voice such utter disdain, is the very thing that's given them such visibility and clout in the first place. Ebert previously had been awarded a

Pulitzer Prize for film criticism, but the vast majority of people outside of Chicago had neither heard of nor read anything by those film critics until PBS launched *Sneak Previews* nationally in 1978. And since, at this writing, Ebert is the only film critic in history to win a Pulitzer, that must mean TV critics are four times as good as movie critics—because TV critics Shales, Ron Powers, William Henry III, and Howard Rosenberg have all been awarded Pulitzer prizes for their TV columns. Faulty logic? Simplistic conclusions? Sure. But since those seem to be the weapons of choice, I thought I would play along for a while.

It's totally illogical, for example, that many film critics refuse to keep abreast of television's output and talent, and acknowledge people and subject matter only when they surface on the large screen. Television critics—most of them—make a point to keep up with the latest films, because they're aware talent travels on a two-way street. Film people and film ideas come to television, just as television people and ideas go to film. The "film snobs," though, see it as a one-way street, and it's an exit only. Until it exists on film, it doesn't exist. They don't feel the need to watch or acknowledge television, because it's such an inferior medium—which means they have no idea what they're missing. Or, in some cases, what they're watching.

Let's start with a favorite subject of true film snobs—movies from abroad. *Das Boot,* so wisely and enthusiastically praised by Siskel and Ebert as a foreign film, actually was an even better six-hour television show—a German miniseries cut by almost a third, but not otherwise altered, for theatrical release. (The full-length version was shown in America by the Bravo cable network.) Another German TV miniseries, Rainer Werner Fassbinder's *Berlin Alexanderplatz,* was given a limited run in America's most "art-conscious" movie houses—befitting its fourteen-hour length—before being televised by PBS. Ingmar Bergman's *Scenes from a Marriage,* a superb miniseries shown both in America and abroad, is one of Bergman's finest works of the 1970s; should it have been dismissed by critics because it was made for television? When American movie critics praised *Mona Lisa,* starring Bob Hoskins and Michael Caine, were they aware they were reviewing a British telemovie? And, if they were, should that have made a difference?

Speaking of Hoskins, he's a perfect example of the two-way talent street. I first became aware of Hoskins, and raved about him, when he starred in Dennis Potter's seven-and-a-half-hour BBC miniseries *Pennies from Heaven,* imported by public television in 1978. That's a full six years before many film critics "discovered" him in *The Cotton Club*—and three years before Hollywood cranked out a big-budget, big-bomb movie version starring Steve Martin in the role originated by Hoskins. The miniseries version was so much better in every respect—darker in tone, subtler in character development, richer in plot and subplot, better in every key ingredient from caliber of performances to quality of musical material—that comparisons with the movie version seem almost unfair. Even with a script adapted by Potter himself, the opulence of the Hollywood production numbers and the relatively short running time doomed the movie version to inferior status. Vonnegut, who calls the *Pennies from Heaven* miniseries "one of the greatest things I've ever seen on television," agrees it "was ripped off by Hollywood and not done nearly as well." To use Ebert's phrase, it frankly isn't even a contest.

The same is true of *The Life and Loves of a She-Devil,* a deviously deviant four-hour British miniseries imported by the A&E cable network in 1987. Julie T. Wallace, a hulking, expressive comic actress, gave the finest performance of that TV season as the downtrodden housewife turned vengeful life wrecker. The ghastly yet powerful climax of that miniseries came when the so-called She-Devil, now rich and powerful, endured painful cosmetic (and other) surgeries to turn herself into the spitting image of her ex-husband's glamorous mistress—not to please him, but to tease him. When Hollywood made its version of the Fay Weldon story, called *She-Devil,* it lopped off the crucial climax altogether, and gave the part of the She-Devil to Roseanne Barr (now Arnold), pairing her opposite Meryl Streep's glamour role. Barr was all wrong for the part—not because she came from TV, but because she didn't have the range or the chameleonic talent to do what the part required, much less what Julie T. Wallace had added to it. The TV version of *She-Devil* was inspired; the film version, by comparison, was insipid.

All the TV programs mentioned so far have originated abroad, but American TV, too, has created excellent programs that have either inspired movies or been released *as* movies.

Too Far to Go, executive producer Robert Geller's 1979 NBC telemovie adaptation of several John Updike stories, starred Michael Moriarty, Blythe Danner, and Glenn Close, and was a superb, intimate, literate drama. *Too Far to Go* was rereleased as a theatrical film in 1982, three years after its TV premiere—and the same year film critics "discovered" Glenn Close in *The World According to Garp.*

Duel, Steven Spielberg's ambitious 1971 telemovie, was released theatrically in 1983 with fifteen minutes of extra footage added. The padding wasn't necessary. The streamlined TV version—marrying Spielberg's complex, intensely visual direction to Richard Matheson's simple plot (a motorist and a truck driver engage in an escalating battle of wits in a dangerous cat-and-mouse game on a lonely highway)—was wonderful as is, and contained dozens of camera angles, editing concepts, and even sound effects that would resurface in *Jaws* and *Raiders of the Lost Ark.* Yet, as Levinson and Link point out in another book about television, *Off Camera,* "Steven Spielberg . . . directed a breathtaking Movie of the Week called *Duel,* but . . . had to wait until he 'graduated' into motion pictures before he was discovered."

Testament, a powerful telemovie made for *American Playhouse* in 1983, starred Jane Alexander as a survivor of an unexpected nuclear strike. It was shown in theaters, as a full-fledged film, *before* being shown on PBS. Since then, the roster of acclaimed theatrical films emanating from the

American Playhouse system, and eventually premiering on that anthology series, includes such wide-ranging, ambitious projects as *El Norte, Heartland, Smooth Talk, Stand and Deliver, The Thin Blue Line,* and *Longtime Companion,* an intimate drama about a man dying of AIDS. Executive producer Lindsay Law, pondering those films for which *American Playhouse* has provided varied degrees of funding, guidance, and other support for a decade, says that without the intervention and often the instigation of TV's *Playhouse,* "most things we make would probably never get made." As for *Longtime Companion,* he adds, "That one, one can definitely say without a second guess, would have *never* been made."

On the more commercial side of things, we have the TV series *Star Trek,* which spawned six theatrical films; *The Twilight Zone,* which inspired a movie version; *Police Squad!,* a short-lived 1982 TV series (rerun in 1991), created by Jerry Zucker, Jim Abrahams, and David Zucker, who went on to reprise the concept and characters—and to rehire Leslie Nielsen as the leading man—in two *Naked Gun* motion pictures. And when movies are given credit for breaking so-called new ground, it is often ground that television has plowed already.

Dances with Wolves revived the Western genre in 1990? Sure—after TV's *Lonesome Dove* led the way in 1988. *Rain Man* took the brave step, in 1988, of making an emotional, uncompromising drama about a brother's reluctant and not-altogether-successful attempts to establish a bond with his mentally impaired brother? Sure—after TV's *Promise,* starring James Garner and James Woods as a man suddenly and reluctantly reunited with his schizophrenic brother, did it in 1986. *Bull Durham* broke new ground, in 1988, by combining baseball action and romantic comedy in a fanciful story about a minor-league player and a sexy, wily baseball groupie? Sure—after TV's *Long Gone,* starring William L. Petersen and Virginia Madsen in roles markedly similar to those played in *Bull Durham* by Kevin Costner and Susan Sarandon, laid down the recipe in 1987. These aren't just breezy comparisons of plot synopses, either. You put the performances and scripts and images of *Dances with Wolves* up against *Lonesome Dove,* or *Rain Man* against *Promise,* or *Bull Durham* against *Long Gone,* and it *is* a contest. I would go so far as to argue, in the first two cases, that the TV productions are a shade better. But even conceding a dead heat on content, TV wins points for initiative. In all three cases, it was there first.

And in other cases, neither the timing nor the comparison is even close. The 1982 *American Playhouse* miniseries *Oppenheimer,* for example, explored the same characters and events as the Paul Newman vehicle *Fat Man and Little Boy:* the development of the atomic bomb. TV's *Oppenheimer,* starring Sam Waterston in the title role, predated the *Fat Man* film by seven years—and was infinitely more entertaining, intelligent, and detailed.

Yet Hollywood insiders, and most movie critics, retain a blatant, and sometimes laughable, blind spot when it comes to television. *Chicago Tribune* film critic David Kehr, in a lengthy 1989 essay, recounts and analyzes the successful careers of actor Clint Eastwood and director Steven Spielberg—

and not once, in either case, does he so much as allude to their origins in television. Kehr says of Eastwood that he "entered the film industry in the late 1950s," but "had to go outside the system to become a star—to Italy and the spaghetti Westerns of Sergio Leone." Kehr forgets to mention a little TV Western called *Rawhide*, which premiered in 1959 with Eastwood as the star. Neither the show nor the star exactly went unnoticed; by its second season, *Rawhide* was the sixth most popular series on television. Only in the wake of that success did Eastwood visit Italy between seasons and film *A Fistful of Dollars*—which, when it finally was released in 1964, turned Eastwood into a *movie* star. His experience and exposure on American television, however, was hardly an irrelevant part of the equation—and for Kehr to overlook Spielberg's TV origins is equally sloppy.

Film critics are not really to blame for this attitude. They are merely reflecting what, for decades, has been Hollywood's status quo. As Levinson and Link noted in *Stay Tuned*, "Because of an outmoded but lingering caste system, those who control the nation's films often pride themselves on their ignorance of television. They are oblivious to the fact that many of the actors, directors, and writers they employ have done their best work for the small screen."

"I don't know where we got this disdain for the small screen," says Linda Bloodworth-Thomason. "I don't know where that came from. I don't know if it stems from the movie industry being afraid of television in the twenties—I can't imagine how it got started. But it permeates our culture today . . . and there *is* that pecking order." The running joke in Hollywood, she says, is that feature films look down on prime-time television, prime-time looks down on late-night TV, late-night looks down on daytime TV— "and daytime looks down on View-Master."

The attitude, according to Bloodworth-Thomason, prevails. "I don't think it's changed too much," she says, citing the case of Jim Brooks, who went from writer–producer on *The Mary Tyler Moore Show* and *Taxi* to writer–producer–director of *Terms of Endearment* and *Broadcast News*. "What made me angry," Bloodworth-Thomason says, "was that when he did that, so many people said, 'Well, who would have thought that he could have done these wonderful features?' And I said, 'Who *wouldn't* have thought it?' I mean, a wonderful writer is a wonderful writer. Why would he be any less if he was writing an hour and a half longer?"

Critic Mark Dawidziak says, "It's obviously a very artificial and snooty kind of thinking: theater is the height of art, film is second, and TV a lowly third. . . . That caste system doesn't exist in probably the snootiest of all societies, and that's England. In a country where the class system still hasn't broken down, it *has* no class system when it comes to acting. It makes no difference if you're doing a commercial or a movie or a play or a TV show. They all bounce around."

Lindsay Law says, "I remember when Laurence Olivier did the Polaroid commercial, and everyone said, 'Oh, my God, a famous actor is on television and *selling*.' It is frustrating, to a degree, because in England—

since London is the center of stage and the center of film and the center of television—people just move from one to another without a second thought. And here, you know, a feature film is the only thing you're working toward. On the way there, television is *possible*, and at the start, I suppose you can do some theater—but don't you *ever* do it again. There really isn't that 'Let's go back and forth and work on these different media' idea. . . . They think it's a backward step to go to television, which is too bad. But it's less that than it used to be. . . .

"Unless you are Meryl Streep, there is not enough work in feature films. Not unless you're in that top 5 percentile of actors, directors, or writers, and you get asked to do everything that's wonderful—then you're fine. But who's that? That's ten writers, ten directors, and ten actors. And the worst thing you can do as an artist, in whichever of those fields you're in, is only work occasionally. That's the worst thing that can happen. So if nothing else, television is just a great field to go in and sharpen your skills." Noting that Barry Levinson, director of *Good Morning Vietnam* and *Avalon*, is directing an HBO version of Sally Bedell's book on William S. Paley, Law says of Levinson, "He can get movies made, but he can't turn *that* into a movie—or he doesn't want to, it's too big a story. So HBO says fine, let's do it as a miniseries, and he says, 'Yeah, I'll do that.' "

Robert Geller, like Law, continues to fight to get the best talent available to work in television, and to fight the established anti-TV prejudice. Using different figures than Law, but similar language, Geller says, "I don't know of that many 'Top Five' actresses or actors who cross over to television." Geller, in fact, suggests many veteran movie stars turn to TV only because they're "long in the tooth," and feels one reason television lacks respect from Hollywood and critics is that "there are no brand-name auteurs who can get a film reviewer excited." It's a harsh assessment, and one with which Robert Thompson and David Marc, also a media professor, strongly disagree. They, at least, are excited enough about the auteur status and implications of such TV writer-producers as Levinson and Link, Brooks, and Bochco to have written a book about them published earlier this year: *Prime Time, Prime Movers*. And, ironically, one of TV's most dedicated auteurs—a producer who has hosted and championed anthology series in the eighties and nineties the way Rod Serling and Alfred Hitchcock did in the decades before that—got interested in the anthology TV form after starring in one of Geller's *American Short Story* installments.

That producer is Shelley Duvall, who already had carved out a career as a successful film actress before embarking on a second career in television. Discovered by director Robert Altman, Duvall starred in his *Brewster McCloud* and *Thieves like Us*, appeared in *Nashville*, and got raves (including the Best Actress Award at the Cannes Film Festival) for her central performance in Altman's *3 Women*. After that, while appearing in the title role in an *American Short Story* dramatization of F. Scott Fitzgerald's *Bernice Bobs Her Hair*, Duvall had a hand in the casting process as well—helping to suggest and land Bud Cort, Dennis Christopher, and others in costarring roles. "I loved doing that," Duvall said in 1986. "It was the first production-type thing I ever did." From there, she went on to create and host *Shelley Duvall's Faerie Tale Theatre, Tall Tales and Fables,* and *Nightmare Classics* for Showtime, *Mother Goose Rock 'n' Rhyme* for The Disney Channel, and other ambitious, usually charming projects.

By tapping her own social circle of friends in show business—and enticing others by offering the chance to star in something their children could enjoy, or which they themselves enjoyed as children—Duvall attracted a barrier-busting roster of talent for *Faerie Tale Theatre.* Even so, she agrees with Geller and Law that those barriers still exist.

"It's more or less the agents," Duvall explains, "who say, 'I don't want so-and-so to do television, they have a chance at a really great movie career.' But take a look at the top stars in movies right now. Eddie Murphy, he's from *Saturday Night Live.* Robin Williams came from *Mork & Mindy.* Geena Davis, she was on *Buffalo Bill.* Take a look at any number of stars, and you'll find they all came from television."

OK, let's do it—and let's start with Meryl Streep. Were the film critics who raved about her supporting performance in 1978's *The Deer Hunter* aware of her even more substantive work earlier that year in NBC's *Holocaust,* portraying a Catholic woman who eventually becomes a concentration-camp victim? *Holocaust* was, and remains, one of the top-rated miniseries of all time, so it's not as though Streep's first major acting role went unnoticed—except by film snobs. Critics certainly noted Streep's talent at the time, as did her peers in the TV industry: Streep won an Emmy that year as Outstanding Lead Actress in a Limited Series. (The man playing her husband in *Holocaust* was just as impressive: he was James Woods, in a showcase role that led to his 1979 feature-film break, *The Onion Field.)*

Though Hollywood loves the occasional TV-rags-to-movie-riches story, those modern folk tales invariably leave out a few key parts. To say that Sally Field went straight from the depths of TV's *Gidget* and *The Flying Nun* in the sixties to the heights of the cinema's *Norma Rae* in 1979 neglects Field's superb, Emmy-winning work as a multiple-personality case in the 1976 miniseries *Sybil.* And to any film critics who want to quibble with that, and claim that the true turning point in Field's career as an actress came when she played a loose woman in the film *Stay Hungry* (released the same year as TV's *Sybil),* I'd counter with her similar role in *Mongo's Back in Town,* a telemovie made in 1971.

Similarly, Farrah Fawcett outlasted and outgrew the exploitive embarrassment of *Charlie's Angels* not by turning to movies, which gave her such empty roles as the ones in *Logan's Run* and *Sunburn,* but by returning to television, which challenged her with her first serious dramatic roles—*Murder in Texas,* then *The Burning Bed.* Only after that, when Fawcett starred in the film version of *Extremities,* did most movie critics take her seriously as an actress. Even so, she continues to find and do her best work on TV, as in her chilling portrayal of an amoral killer in the 1989 miniseries *Small Sacrifices.*

The continued perception of a Hollywood caste system almost defies logic—not to mention box-office figures. As long ago as 1987, according to rankings in *Screen World,* the three most popular stars in the entire movie industry had come from television: Eddie Murphy *(Saturday Night Live),* Michael Douglas *(The Streets of San Francisco),* and Michael J. Fox *(Family Ties).* All three of those actors still were in the Top 10 two years later, in 1989, along with some other TV "graduates": Robin Williams *(Mork & Mindy),* Tom Hanks *(Bosom Buddies),* and Kathleen Turner (daytime TV's *The Doctors).* Indeed, in movie stars of the current generation, TV experience and exposure is more the norm than the exception.

Saturday Night Live and *Second City TV* alone gave us Eddie Murphy, Chevy Chase, Bill Murray, Steve Martin, John Candy, Rick Moranis, Gilda Radner, John Belushi, Dan Aykroyd, Albert Brooks, Billy Crystal (who earlier starred in *Soap),* Martin Short, and Catherine O'Hara. Woody Allen worked his way up through TV; so did Mia Farrow, who rose to stardom in the prime-time TV soap opera *Peyton Place.* The list of other current film stars with prior TV series credits—as series *regulars,* mind you, not guest stars—is almost numbingly long. Here's just a sample tally of some of the others not already mentioned:

Michael Keaton *(Working Stiffs,* two different Mary Tyler Moore variety series); Cher *(The Sonny and Cher Show);* Goldie Hawn and Lily Tomlin *(Rowan & Martin's Laugh-In);* Michelle Pfeiffer *(Delta House, B.A.D. Cats);* Kim Basinger *(Dog and Cat,* TV's *From Here to Eternity);* Bruce Willis *(Moonlighting);* Danny DeVito *(Taxi);* Jodie Foster (in TV's series versions of *Bob & Carol & Ted & Alice* and *Paper Moon);* Melanie Griffith *(Carter Country,* the 1976 miniseries *Once an Eagle);* Meg Ryan *(One of the Boys, Wildside);* John Cleese *(Monty Python's Flying Circus, Fawlty Towers);* Alec Baldwin *(Knots Landing);* Nick Nolte *(Rich Man, Poor Man);* Johnny Depp *(21 Jump Street);* River Phoenix (TV's *Seven Brides for Seven Brothers);* Tom Selleck *(Magnum, P.I.);* Beau Bridges *(United States);* Denzel Washington *(St. Elsewhere);* Ted Danson *(Cheers);* Don Johnson *(Miami Vice);* John Travolta *(Welcome Back, Kotter);* and Charles Bronson *(Man with a Camera, The Travels of Jaimie McPheeters).*

The crossovers and connections are almost limitless. Demi Moore and Patrick Swayze, the stars of the incredibly popular *Ghost,* worked previously on TV in, respectively, *General Hospital* and the miniseries *North and South.* In 1985, before Hollywood was handing out leading roles to Kevin Costner, Steven Spielberg showcased him in a one-hour special edition of *Amazing Stories*—an episode costarring another talented young actor, Kiefer Sutherland. Costner's first acting role, for that matter, was a small part in the *American Playhouse* production of *Testament.*

Arnold Schwarzenegger, before pulling down multimillion-dollar film salaries, starred as bodybuilder Mickey Hargitay in the 1980 telemovie *The Jayne Mansfield Story* (Loni Anderson played the title role); in 1990, Schwarzenegger made his *directorial* debut with an episode of HBO's *Tales from the Crypt.* Robert Duvall, who guest-starred many times on such sixties series as *The Defenders, Route 66, The Fugitive,* and *The Naked City,* returned as a headliner to star in the miniseries *Ike* and *Lonesome Dove.* Dustin Hoffman has appeared on TV in a brilliant filmed adaptation of *Death of a Salesman,* and as a guest voice on *The Simpsons.* Jane Fonda crossed to television to make *The Dollmaker,* and George C. Scott has both a TV series *(East Side/West Side)* and many telemovies and miniseries (among them the fabulous *A Christmas Carol*) among his credits. Warren Beatty started out with a recurring role on *The Life and Loves of Dobie Gillis,* and TV can even claim to have gotten there first at two key points in the career of Marlon Brando. After his Broadway triumph in *A Streetcar Named Desire,* but before making his first movie, Brando starred in a 1949 live TV drama, *I'm No Hero,* on the ABC anthology series *Actors Studio.* Thirty years later, the reclusive Brando resurfaced to play George Lincoln Rockwell in ABC's *Roots: The Next Generation.*

That would seem a lengthy and impressive enough list of precedents to give TV its due. What's more, the list gets even longer and better if you add the past and present anthology series, all of PBS's series and specials, and the hundreds of telemovies and miniseries made each year for broadcast and cable TV. I'm not suggesting all, or even most, of these talents were used to their best advantage. But some were. John Malkovich and Gary Sinise left a powerful impression in their 1982 TV debut in the *American Playhouse* production of *True West,* for example, and others displayed obvious talents even in inferior vehicles. By watching the early efforts of actors on television, many TV critics were able to predict stardom for Eddie Murphy, Michael Keaton, Meryl Streep, Nick Nolte, and others. The point isn't that we were right about them, or wrong about others. The point is that we were *watching.*

Behind the scenes, the cross-pollination of film and TV talent is no less prevalent, or significant. America's film critics voted Scorsese's *Raging Bull* the best film of the eighties, and each new film of his is closely and eagerly scrutinized—even his 1989 half-hour contribution to 1989's *New York Stories,* a film anthology also featuring short works by Woody Allen and Francis Ford Coppola. So why should his direction of *Mirror, Mirror,* a 1986 installment of *Amazing Stories* that's as long as his *New York Stories* piece, be of any less value or interest? What about Spielberg's prodigious TV output—not only as creator and occasional writer-director of *Amazing Stories,* but his earlier direction of the telemovies *Duel* and *Something Evil,* and his episodic work for *Columbo* and *Night Gallery?*

Coincidentally, *Night Gallery* is where Leonard Nimoy made his directorial debut, filming a moody and effective vampire episode (starring Lesley Ann Warren) in 1972. More than ten years later, after directing *Star Trek III: The Search for Spock* in 1984 and *Three Men and a Baby* in 1987, Hollywood finally took Nimoy seriously for his directorial skills. Not that he's the only successful TV actor turned movie director, of course. Ron Howard, young veteran of both *The Andy Griffith Show* and *Happy Days,* went on to direct *Splash, Cocoon, Parenthood,* and *Backdraft.* Penny Marshall, star of *Laverne & Shirley,* went on to direct *Big* and *Awakenings.* Rob Reiner, costar of *All in the Family,* went on to direct *This is Spinal Tap!, Stand by Me, When Harry Met Sally . . . , Misery,* and *The Princess Bride.* And Garry Marshall, director of *Pretty Woman,* previously created and acted as executive producer for *Happy Days* and its sister series, *Laverne & Shirley.* Is it possible none of them learned *anything* from working in television?

The list of film directors who have done work in television begins with Delbert Mann of *Marty* fame—and never stops. Alfred Hitchcock, the most visible of TV's directors, not only hosted *Alfred Hitchcock Presents* and its successor, *The Alfred Hitchcock Hour,* for a ten-year stretch (1955–65), but directed eighteen of those shows himself, as well as single episodes of two rival anthologies, *Suspicion* and *Ford Star Time.*

However, even the inexhaustible Truffaut didn't ask Hitchcock about his TV work, though it has clear ties to his feature films of the same period. *Psycho,* perhaps Hitchcock's most famous movie, was filmed largely by the same crew assigned to *Alfred Hitchcock Presents* (including cameraman John L. Russell), and the creepy Bates house in *Psycho* had previously been used, and seen, in a number of episodes in the TV series. Robert Altman, Sydney Pollack, and William Friedkin also directed episodes of the Hitchcock series, and worked for other TV anthologies as well.

In fact, anthology series developed, then drew from, the best directors around. In the old days, John Badham, Blake Edwards, Sam Peckinpah, and Michael Powell directed for TV. In the "new days," anthology series have nurtured the likes of Jonathan Demme (Vonnegut's *Who Am I This Time?* on *American Playhouse)* and Tim Burton (who concocted the animated *Family Dog* episode of *Amazing Stories),* and attracted many, many others. Robert Zemeckis, Joe Dante, Todd Holland, Danny DeVito, Tobe Hooper, Clint Eastwood, Ken Russell, and Walter Hill all have directed for television—before, and in most cases *after,* making their directorial reputations on the big screen. And to those who say feature-film directors and television are mutually exclusive, I have four words to say: David Lynch. *Twin Peaks.*

Finally, look at the writers, producers, and hyphenates (writer-producers, writer-producer-directors, etc.) who have come from television, and who often opt to return there, and you've struck the final blow in the argument against film snobbery: Woody Allen. Mel Brooks. Paddy Chayefsky. Rod Serling. Horton Foote. Carl Reiner. Larry Gelbart. John Sayles. And, of course, James L. Brooks.

"Why do I like working in TV?" Brooks asks. "It's immediate. It's honest. There's almost no room for delusion. . . . When you're in a rewrite night, and you pitch out a line, it doesn't matter who pitches it out. If it gets a laugh in the room, it's a contender, and if it doesn't, you have egg on your face. And there's something grounding and *right* about that for me." Asked whether he agrees there used to be a caste system dividing those in the TV and film industries, Brooks replies without hesitation.

"There used to be more than a caste system. There used to be a barrier," says Brooks, whose first "film" credit was as writer of the 1974 telemovie *Thursday's Game* (it took five more years before he finally landed a movie job, writing the screenplay adaptation of *Starting Over*). "And now there's none whatsoever. I don't know how anything could change more dramatically in as short a period of time. Nobody who worked on TV had a chance to get a job in movies. It was that simple. They used to say that Steve McQueen was the only one who made it. I mean, actors, directors, writers—it was just a stigma. And there's not only none of that now, there's open courtship. It's very difficult to have any success at all writing for television without getting an offer for a movie.

"Television has always been *the* place for people who cared about comedy to go, or to start, and suddenly it's so writer-oriented," Brooks adds. "Almost everybody I worked with on the Paramount lot in the late seventies and early eighties is now prominent in motion pictures. If I really put my mind to it, I could probably list twenty names."

Lorne Michaels agrees the shift has occurred already, and traces it back to the midseventies—after the premiere of his *Saturday Night Live* series. The 1978 movie *National Lampoon's Animal House* turned John Belushi from Not-Ready-for-Prime-Time Player to well-received movie comedian, and other *SNL* regulars and alumni began getting film roles and drawing big audiences. "Suddenly," Michaels says, "Hollywood realized that people wanted to *see* these people." And Michaels, again agreeing with Brooks, thinks the fast track for success has gotten even faster.

"I think we're in a more vulgar age right now," Michaels says. "There's a tremendous fear, with the proliferation of channels. You have so many outlets that . . . the idea of having to wait for an opportunity doesn't exist any more.

"Say you were a writer on *Saturday Night Live* in the first five years. You would fight for your work to get on, and over the course of the five years, if you didn't have a voice already from print—where people could automatically tell your kind of stuff, the way they could, say, with Michael O'Donoghue—you *developed* a voice. And you were one of many, and you got beaten up occasionally, and celebrated occasionally, and you put in those hours, and there was a craft level that was expected, and you learned it just by doing. Someone like, for example, Jim Brooks, who had done series television, it took him probably fifteen to twenty years to get to write a movie that got made—let alone *direct* a movie. . . . And what happens now is, if a writing team is successful and are working on something for more than one season, they can be under contract to one of the studios, to Fox or whatever, to write and develop and produce their own series."

James Burrows, without question, is part of one of TV's most successful partnerships right now. Along with Glen and Les Charles, he's cocreator and coexecutive producer of *Cheers*, which at the end of the 1990–91 season ranked as television's most popular series. Burrows also directs the vast majority of the *Cheers* episodes, a field he broke into on *The Mary Tyler Moore Show*. Burrows was resident director on *Taxi*, where he worked with executive producers Brooks, Stan Daniels, David Davis, and Ed. Weinberger. In those three series alone, Burrows has directed a good share of television's best comic actors. Unlike Brooks, Burrows has continued to focus on directing for TV—though, as he makes clear, not because he feels a caste system exists any longer.

"That's totally wiped out," Burrows says. "I think the crossovers now are tremendous—Jim Brooks, Danny DeVito, Judd [Hirsch]—it's all changed." Not necessarily, he adds, for the better.

"I just think movies have come down to television. That's the problem. I think there are more and more heads of the movie studios who used to be television executives, and that's what's happening. So the kind of stuff that made great movies is just not being made as much any more."

Another semisour note is sounded by William Link, who feels the lowering of the barriers often is accompanied by a lowering of the standards—and the motives.

"Most of my friends who are basically motion-picture producers," Link says frankly, "want to get into TV now. But by waiting this long, they've sort of missed the boat. Network TV is in a rapid state of deterioration. But there's this little family secret in Hollywood—there's more money in TV than there is in theatrical motion pictures. . . . Many motion-picture producers would like to flock into television, aesthetics aside." As for those aesthetics, Link is of the opinion that TV's visual style is reflected more and more on the large screen. "Television direction has influenced movie direction more than vice versa," Link says. His tone, however, is far from complimentary.

Lindsay Law is less convinced than the others that the walls have already tumbled down—but, like Brooks, he enjoys working in different media. "This job, it's a little of everything," he says of his *American Playhouse* post. "So if you go to work on feature films, then you can't go off from it and do little monologues which Jon Robin Baitz wrote (in *Three Hotels*), or you can't go and do *Lemon Sky* as a film with Kevin Bacon. You can't do those. And that's just as interesting to me as going off and doing *Stand and Deliver*. It's just getting more toys in the sandbox," he says, laughing.

So are the walls up or down? In the final analysis, both.

They are still up because, though the potential profits of television have won many converts from the movie industry, the programming has not—or, at least, few people in Hollywood have seen enough television lately to revise opinions formed long ago. Jack Lemmon, Anthony Hopkins, Louis Gossett, Jr., and Brian Dennehy are a few of the immensely talented actors who have no qualms about moving between film and television in search of the best project. Yet other gifted actors, such as Jack Nicholson, Robert De Niro, and Tom Cruise, have so far refused.

But those walls are crumbling, and ready to fall, because the new power in television is beginning to mass around the writer-producer. In the movies, writers are often seen as interchangeable minor parts. In television, such writer–producers as Brooks and Bloodworth-Thomason now carry an enormous amount of weight on their shows, just as star Cosby does on his. We're not at the point yet where the writers get top billing, as they do on British TV, but the writing is becoming the most important part of the package. And in the long run, the caliber of the writing is what will attract even the most stubborn of film-snob holdouts.

For different reasons, two of the people interviewed thought the whole notion of walls and caste systems was ridiculous. Mark Dawidziak calls it ridiculous because he refuses to accept the concept: "You can't say the walls are breaking down between film and TV, because the walls were never really there to begin with," he says. "Nor were they there between movies and plays, or plays and literature. . . . You can't know the history of television without knowing the history of film, of theater—pretty much without knowing the history of mankind. . . . There's no question that all of this is interconnected, and you can't pull television out of the equation."

Conversely, Bloodworth-Thomason thinks the caste system still exists, but calls it ridiculous anyway. And she, too, has a sense of history. "I don't understand all this seriousness. . . . I love Paul Newman because he has his picture on a spaghetti jar," she says. "I don't understand why actors posture as people who would never do commercials. I mean, we are *all* doing commercials, we are *all* selling a product, we are *all* entertainers. And we are really nothing more than those court jesters of centuries ago, who were trying to entertain the king and his subjects.

"People have found various artificial ways to try to elevate themselves, but it doesn't work. It doesn't wash, in my opinion. We're all pretty much doing the same thing, and we're all trying to make money doing it. But there are certain people in features who, I think, try to *act* like they're not trying to make money."

12

SOME TELEVISION IS LITERATURE— AND VICE VERSA

When Dennis Potter's BBC-TV miniseries *The Singing Detective* premiered in America in January 1988, I raved about it in the *New York Post* and predicted it would stand as the best original TV drama of the decade. It did. And when *The Singing Detective* was repeated that summer, Vincent Canby—film critic of the *New York Times*—wrote an effusive article calling *The Singing Detective* "better than anything I've seen this year in the theater." With it, Canby said, Potter has "single-handedly restored the reputation of the screenwriter, at least in television. He's made writing for television respectable and, possibly, an art."

It's nice to have as respected a film critic as Canby backing me up on this one. At the same time, it's a little annoying to witness the ease with which Canby slipped over to TV's side of the fence to deliver his opinion. I agree with him completely: there *was* no movie released in 1988 that came close to the artistry of *The Singing Detective*. But if film critics are going to erect snooty barriers between movies and television, the least they can do is stick to their side. I mean, you don't see me running out to review a terrific movie simply because it's better than anything I've seen that year on television. And what, I wonder, would film snob Roger Ebert have to say about all this?

As for the "art" part of Canby's pronouncement, there's no "possibly" about it. If *The Singing Detective* isn't art, then neither is *Citizen Kane*. In different respects and degrees, I'd also argue that *Cheers* and *Taxi* are art— and *St. Elsewhere* and *Twin Peaks*. If people participating in and analyzing the TV industry can do what Canby did, and look at the content instead of the delivery system, the idea that TV can be art and literature would be accepted as obvious, not absurd.

Anyone reading the published teleplays of Potter's *The Singing Detective* and *Pennies from Heaven* is, inarguably, reading literature. In the same respect, it's easy to read some works of literature—and see television. The connections and comparisons are there, at least to those willing to entertain them.

David Mamet, the playwright who adapted Anton Chekhov's *Uncle Vanya* for television, noted "there is little difference between *Hill Street Blues* and Chekhov." Analyzing the same series, novelist Joyce Carol Oates saw mythic overtones in the stories of *Hill Street:* "The Hill Street police are figures of Sisyphus rolling their rocks up the hill and the next day rolling them up again, and again. . . . It is always the next morning, it is always roll call."

Potter—a man, I should add with both pride and envy, who is a former television critic—defended TV as literature in a 1988 interview. "It probably sounds like political humbug," he told Alex Ward in the *New York Times Magazine,*

> but I've long had this dream of a common culture, and I knew that print would never do it because words of different syllable lengths would be either rejected or received according to what kind of education you had, whereas pictures could impel all the things that great literature does. . . . Dickens, all of them, were willing to adapt and use the serial form because it was the most popular means in their day—people would wait anxiously for the serializations to appear. The writers weren't dragged down by that form, they flew with it. And to me, that implies a confidence in a common culture, an assumption that people are very much brighter than the market men say they are—something in them is capable of responding to things that are very complex. If Dickens were alive today, I'm not sure he wouldn't have written television serials.

Others involved in studying or making television have similar observations. Robert Thompson notes that when Dante wrote *The Divine Comedy* in the fourteenth century, he bucked tradition by defiantly writing his epic story in the more commonly accessible Italian, rather than in Latin or Greek. "He produced a masterpiece in what was thought of as a 'schlock' language, because he said we should talk in the language of the people," Thompson says, then laughs. "If Dante were alive today, he'd be writing for television." And Mark Dawidziak independently makes the same observation as Dennis Potter—that Dickens and TV were made for each other.

"Dickens wouldn't have been able to *resist* it," Dawidziak says. "I think Twain would have been all *over* it. I think they would have been hyphenates—writer–producers. Dickens, particularly. He was a writer–publisher in Victorian England; why wouldn't he be a writer–producer in Hollywood? . . . And you don't think Dickens would have looked at the miniseries and said, 'I can do *that!*'?" Robert Geller, who has spent much of his career adapting literary works for his Learning in Focus TV company, agrees that Charles Dickens's novels are "incredibly visual," and adds, "When you think of memorable quotes from Dickens, there probably aren't as many quotes as images. . . . He is a guy who makes images come to life."

Sergei Eisenstein, the Russian film director whose 1925 *Battleship Potemkin* was a ground-breaking classic, long ago compared Dickens's serialized stories to motion pictures, noting their cinematic qualities and common-man sympathies. Stories from both Dickens and the movies, Eisenstein said, "mill the extraordinary, the unusual, the fantastic, from boring, prosaic, and everyday existence." Eisenstein could just as easily be describing *The Honeymooners*.

"I hope we never lose the primacy of the written word," says Mark Frost, "because I think that speaks to people in a very different and direct *private* way. But you look at something like the adaptation of *Bleak House* that was done a few years ago," he says, referring to the 1985 *Masterpiece Theatre* adaptation of that Dickens novel. "Or even *Little Dorrit*. They gave you the sense of scope and power in those stories." Asked if he thought the day would ever come when TV at its best would be regarded as the Dickens of its day, Frost says, "I think it's real possible." *Hill Street Blues*, after all, is discussed seriously by serious writers, and Frost himself took his *Twin Peaks* duties very seriously from a literary standpoint.

"It's a large canvas we're working on," he said while the series was still in production. "It's almost the equivalent of a filmed novel, where we're shooting every page. And when I think of it—on my best days and the next-best days—that's what I try to imagine. You know, what would Dickens have done if he could shoot every page of *Oliver Twist*?"

"I think if Mark Twain were alive today," Linda Bloodworth-Thomason told TV critics in 1991, "he would be writing in television. I think he would be doing audio-visual literature, which is what television can be. . . . The characters would be memorable, like characters from novels.

"Now I don't want to get up on my soapbox, but I used to teach English, and so I've read a lot of the great American novels, and I just reread *Little Women* not too long ago. And you know, it was pretty boring. I mean, Jo cut her hair. I didn't think a lot happened. Not to disparage a great American novel, but I did *not* think those four women were any more interesting than [her *Designing Women* characters] Mary Jo, Julia, Suzanne, and Charlene."

"All art is practical joking," says Kurt Vonnegut, while contemplating possible original story lines should Showtime order more episodes of *Kurt Vonnegut's Monkey House*, "and I've thought about a whole lot more practical jokes to be played for a half hour on TV." In spirit, Vonnegut may well be the author closest to Mark Twain we have today—which lends further credence to the claim that, if Twain were alive, he'd be eager to write for television. Vonnegut *is* alive, and *is* eager to write for television. And he's not joking when he calls TV an art.

In 1969, public television imported a lengthy BBC miniseries called *The Forsyte Saga*, based on nine novels by John Galsworthy. It was a major hit in England, and as major a hit as any program shown on public television in

1969 could have hoped to be. Its success in America led directly to the decision to launch *Masterpiece Theatre* in 1971, and the demand it generated—both for Galsworthy's books and for weekly doses of the long-running serial—was a tip-off of things to come with other TV adaptations of popular and classic novels. However, what I find most fascinating about *The Forsyte Saga* in retrospect is an after-the-fact salute by author James Michener—who, like Canby with *The Singing Detective,* was sufficiently taken by something he'd seen on television to become TV critic for a day.

Michener's 1970 review in *TV Guide* is nothing less than a clarion call to have the miniseries form—and all of TV—taken seriously. "The brilliance of this series does not stem from the books," Michener writes, mincing no words. "The early volumes were good, but the series was better." Later in the article, Michener adds,

> Many critics have asked, "Isn't the *Saga* really a soap opera?" That's easy. Of course it was soap opera—at its glowing best. . . .
>
> In *The Forsyte Saga* the characters are differentiated, well rounded and with universal application; the dialogue is literate; the problems dealt with are substantial; and over all there is a high seriousness. In the Bible the Book of Ruth is a soap opera saved by these same qualities. *Ethan Frome,* one of the best short novels ever written, is pure soap opera, but with what magnificent control and impact! I have never objected to soap opera if it attained the quality of *Romeo and Juliet,* and I am not ashamed to confess that I fell completely under the spell of this one.

Michener closed the article by suggesting other novels worthy of a lengthy serial ("Thackeray's *Vanity Fair* could be stunning"), and noting with some surprise that "at the moment I can think of no American novels that could be so used." After that, by coincidence or design, he went out and wrote some himself—and both *Centennial* and *Space,* in time, were given the lengthy miniseries treatment. "I'm very proud of the *Centennial* miniseries," Michener confessed to *Entertainment Weekly* in 1991. "It'll be around a long time in schools as a faithful picture of what happened out West."

Sometimes, life imitates art. Other times, TV instigates art. And at this point in time, TV deserves to be *recognized* as art.

13

TELEVISION DESERVES
SERIOUS STUDY

Thirty years ago, in a 1962 essay titled "Climates of Criticism," Moses Hadas advised that "all who take education seriously in its larger sense—and not the professed critics alone—should talk and write about television as they do about books." Needless to say, Hadas was ahead of his time. For that matter, the way things are going, he's ahead of *my* time. Yet according to film critic Stanley Kauffmann, my time—or, rather, my age—may explain why I'm willing and eager to step up and defend television.

Twenty years ago, in his 1972 book *American Film Criticism,* Kauffmann noted a significant pattern after collecting the work of film critics in the medium's first half-century or so of development. "One can discern three groups of critics, distinguishable by date of birth, in the short, forty-five-year period covered," Kauffmann wrote. "There are the critics who were adults when film was invented, those writing before 1910. Then there are the critics who were born about the same time as film and grew along with it. Third, there are the critics who came to consciousness when film was already a force in the cultural environment." Naming critics representative of each "generation," Kauffmann went on to say, "Frank E. Woods has some of the tone of a Cortez; Gilbert Seldes insists that popularity does not necessarily mean inferiority; Harry Alan Potamkin neither discovers nor demonstrates, he acts on common assumptions."

Overlay that same development curve of critical recognition onto television, starting about 1948, and the parallels work—so far. Jack Gould of the *New York Times,* enthusiastic champion of Rod Serling and Paddy Chayefsky, was a first-generation class act. I fit in the second-generation category—and, just as Seldes did with film, find myself insisting that TV's popularity "does not necessarily mean inferiority." If the schedule holds, *TV Critics: The Next Generation* should be right around the corner, accepting TV's artistic possibilities as a given. But will they? Or will the continued popularity of TV as *the* mass medium count against it when it comes to serious critical scrutiny and appreciation?

"What I think," says the *Baltimore Sun*'s David Zurawik, "is that nobody knows how to really cover TV. Our generation is in the eye of the storm. Television is still so new, and we're in the middle of this, so we just have to grab around and flail at it." Zurawik sees untapped value, though, in the observations and memories of TV critics who have been on the beat for a significant stretch of time:"We carry around an informal history of the last fifteen to twenty years of broadcast network television—the sort of history that hasn't been formalized anywhere."

Zurawik mentions a recent example, when he decided to write an article on the loss of virginity among teen characters in prime-time network TV series. With no textbook to refer to, Zurawik started his own list, picked the brains of some peers (including, coincidentally, Dawidziak, whose brain, like Zurawik's, *I'm* picking for this book)—and quickly managed, he says, "to piece together a history," starting with *James at 15* in 1979 and working back to recent episodes of *Roseanne, Life Goes On,* and *Beverly Hills, 90210.*

"We've been brainwashed not to think of it as serious cultural and historical information," Zurawik says. "When you say 'culture,' everybody thinks of the opera and the Museum of Modern Art—but the anthropologists' definition is 'shared information, beliefs and values.' And, in fact, television is the primary purveyor, and vehicle or deliverer, *of* shared information."

Zurawik makes a good point. It's true that, when I'm assembling a similar type of story and can't find the necessary information in books, I work the phones—calling Dawidziak, or Rich Heldenfels of the *Schenectady News Gazette,* or other walking TV reference books. More of that history needs to be collected, formalized, published, and analyzed, just as more of TV's past and present programs need to be studied exhaustively—not for their violence counts, but for what *really* counts. Their artistry.

That much, at least, seems to be happening. "Even when I was in graduate school in 1981," recalls Robert Thompson, "there was only half a shelf on the stuff." That very year, Levinson and Link noted in *Stay Tuned* (one of the new TV books Thompson would add to his shelf) that a change was coming. "More and more books and critical studies are being written," they wrote, "not only the expected ones about television's social, psychological, and/or political ramifications, but also investigations into its aesthetics, of all things." One such book, published seven years later, was written by Mark Dawidziak about the Levinson–Link *Columbo* series. Called *The Columbo Phile,* it analyzed every episode; interviewed its writers, producers, stars, and guest stars; and put the entire series in context, in terms of both the medium at the time and the careers of Levinson, Link, and star Peter Falk. "I think he did a very good job," Link says now. "I was amazed. Not only did he know the character extremely well, but the fact that he analyzed every single *Columbo* [episode] was amazing. I was very happy with the book."

"Film criticism exploded in the sixties," Dawidziak says, "and the same thing is happening with TV criticism right now. Over the last ten years, there's been an explosion of books about TV. A lot of them are good, a lot of them are very poor—they're all over the spectrum. But it's the building up of a *scholarship*."

Before the explosion, books about TV were few and far between. Harlan Ellison's *The Glass Teat*, a collection of his TV essays for the *Los Angeles Free Press*, was published in 1970. Les Brown's *Television: The Business behind the Box* was published in 1971. Annual books collecting TV production data were published for a few years in the midseventies, which was also when media studies professor Horace Newcomb began writing and editing collections of TV-related academic essays. Vincent Terrace's *Complete Encyclopedia of Television Programs* was published in 1976—the first mass-market reference book in its field. Another book by Brown, the *New York Times Encyclopedia of Television*, followed in 1977. These weren't the only books of that era, but they were among the first or best.

One of the most unusual critical studies of that decade came in 1979, when Christopher Wicking and Tise Vahimagi wrote *The American Vein*, an analysis of the careers and output of directors working in television. The book singled out not only directors exclusive to television, but directors who also worked in film—and their entry on Robert Altman makes a great argument for certain TV shows to be given a second look. That entry identifies and enumerates not only Altman's work on such experimentally attuned anthology series as *Alfred Hitchcock Presents* and *Kraft Suspense Theatre*, but also episodes of such weekly series as *Bonanza, Combat, Hawaiian Eye*, and *Route 66*. Faced with such a buried treasure of Altman-directed TV shows, Wicking and Vahimagi wrote:

> The existence of nearly fifty signed pieces of work which are virtually unknown, and, if discussed at all, occupy only a footling footnote or pedantic parenthesis, calls into question the whole rationale of what passes as academic criticism. Quite simply, we ask, how can more than thirty hours of film made by one of the most unique of modern directors be ignored in this way?

Similar studies ought to be done about TV's current gifted directors—the comedy work of James Burrows, the dramatic work of Robert Butler, and so many others. Burrows, in fact, *has* been studied, along with Brooks, Bochco, Bruce Paltrow, and others, as part of a detailed collection of essays called *MTM: Quality Television*. That one, too, was coauthored by Vahimagi—and, like *The American Vein*, was a singularly serious look at American television . . . by British film critics. It's yet another example of critics from abroad getting a head start on taking *our* popular entertainment seriously.

And while it's nice to focus on TV's directors and producers, why not also study, in more detail, the literature of television—not only scripts adapting the works of, or written by, the likes of Vonnegut, but examining the individual and collected TV works of such TV authors as Serling, Chayefsky, and Potter?

One recent, encouraging sign that TV is starting to get its due is Eric Lax's *Woody Allen* book, published in 1991. While covering Allen's film output and development, Lax also takes great care to retrace and analyze Allen's years and work in television, including discussion of one PBS special that was produced but never broadcast. It's not comprehensive (for some reason, Lax omits Allen's brilliant 1969 NBC *Woody Allen Special,* the one in which Allen's guests included Candice Bergen and the Reverend Billy Graham). What Lax succeeds in doing, though, is establishing the developmental role television played in Allen's artistry—just the sort of scholarship the authors of *The American Vein* hoped would happen with Altman.

Another way to get television taken more seriously in a critical sense is to get academia involved—which, again, is not exactly a new idea. In the early sixties, according to one published bibliography, PhD dissertations had already been written on such topics as "Television Theater as an Art Form," "The Stylization of the Dramatic Television Image," and, amazingly, "Television—Its Critics and Criticism (A Survey and Analysis)." In the early nineties, the same interest in TV is evident from certain individuals and circles. At the 1990 Popular Culture Association Convention, for example, Daniel A. Panici, an assistant professor of communication arts at Berry College in Rome, Georgia, presented a deeply detailed paper called "This Must Be Where Cherries Go When They Die: Vertical Intertextuality and *Twin Peaks.*" Certain professors have always cared passionately about television. However, transferring those passions to the classroom isn't always easy, or encouraged.

"Music professors are allowed (even expected) to love Mozart," Robert Thompson wrote in a 1988 essay for *The Chronicle of Higher Education,* "and literature professors to feel the same about Shakespeare. But as a television professor, I'm not supposed to love TV; I'm supposed to indict it." Funny—many TV critics, or TV-critic employers, work from the exact same job description.

American literature, modern literature, and modern poetry weren't always welcome topics of study on college campuses, and "film studies" didn't surface at universities until well into the sixties. Television—parts of it, anyway—faces the same prejudices and battles. "Sociological, political, and psychological studies of television have been accepted in academe for years," Thompson notes in his essay, "so why is it so difficult to perceive *the programs themselves* as worthy of academic scrutiny? It is not because they don't contain artistic merits, but because so few people have ever bothered to look at them carefully enough to find these merits and teach them to others."

This is where professors and magazine writers have the edge over daily TV critics, because the latter rarely have the time and outlets for analyzing programs and issues in true depth—except for theme and "think" pieces, which often break new ground and stake a fresh claim on an issue, but seldom dig deeply enough. What should happen—what I truly hope *does* happen—is that the critical and professorial worlds of TV criticism start to draw and depend on one another. There are things TV critics, like all other viewers, can learn from the thoughtful analyses of *The Dick Van Dyke Show* in David Marc's *Comic Visions* and Ella Taylor's *Prime-Time Families*, or from a detailed essay on the symbolism in the *St. Elsewhere* finale—an article enthusiastically written, in a scholarly journal, by Alexander Nehamas, the professor who so astutely linked television and Plato to begin with.

As an example of how TV's popular shows can be looked at differently but not disparagingly, here's how Taylor compares two characters from *The Dick Van Dyke Show:* Mary Tyler Moore's Laura Petrie and Rose Marie's Sally Rogers.

> The show proposed separate worlds populated by two types of women: the world of work, which contained career girls like Sally, who was talented, funny, and a good sport even though she was mannish and plain and could not get a date; and the domestic world, which housed wives like Laura, who was pretty but unthreatening, made charming but fruitless excursions into the world of achievement, had few creative talents, and was generally content with her role as a supportive and eminently sensible spouse and mother. . . . By the time Laura Petrie became Mary Richards in *The Mary Tyler Moore Show* in the 1970s, the assumptions that guided her earlier role had been deeply compromised.

David Marc, appearing on CBS's *60 Minutes* in 1989 with Newcomb and Thompson, also read a lot into *The Dick Van Dyke Show.* "One of the things I like about it very much is, it's a kind of artifact from the Kennedy era, from the New Frontier period," Marc told a smirking Morley Safer.

> Even Mary Tyler Moore's hairdo in the show—there's something so "Jackie" about it. There was a change going on in America. The paintings on the wall showed a certain level of sophistication that was not something you'd see in the Andersons' home on *Father Knows Best*. And so one, in a sense, can see the history of the situation comedy, which attempts to represent us in our living rooms, as a kind of para-history of America—a companion text for reading American history.

Confronted with such a serious discussion of a mere television program, Safer warned on *60 Minutes* that, in such university media courses around the nation, "Every sitcom ever made is examined and analyzed. Every commercial, every grain of dust in what someone called the 'vast wasteland' now joins the romantic poets, Shakespeare, and *The Iliad* on the shelves of academia." Richard Gehr, the *Village Voice* TV critic, reviewed that program a few weeks later. He characterized Safer's sarcastic comment as "hyperbole" and, countering with his own brand of sarcasm, added, "Let's hope *60 Minutes* never hears about film studies."

There's no small irony in the fact that, when analyzing *The Dick Van*

Dyke Show in *Comic Visions,* Marc spent a good deal of time on the episode "I'm No Henry Walden." In it, Dick Van Dyke's Rob Petrie is invited to a high-society charity party, where his occupation of TV comedy writer is sneered at by all in attendance: "Why, I don't even own a television machine!" one guest informs Rob. But Rob is vindicated when the revered guest of honor, poet "Henry Walden," is both familiar with and enamored of Rob's TV-comedy writing credits.

Finding a respected literary figure who's similarly enthusiastic in the real world may sound impossible, but it's not. In fact, such a case is found later in this very book—courtesy of Kurt Vonnegut.

14

TELELITERACY IS HERE . . . SO TELEFRIEND

"**L**ong after they proved themselves the twentieth century's most important form of mass entertainment," film critic Molly Haskell wrote in a 1991 cover story for *Entertainment Weekly*, "movies have become our common cultural touchstones. Even films and genres that were once dismissed as escapism—say, Disney movies such as *Pinocchio* and *Mary Poppins*—are now seen as revealing windows on our lives and times, without losing their charm as pop pastimes. Movies have given us a common language that unites people divided by nationality, geography, class, and age." If you don't want to be "out of it," she warns, "you'd better learn to become *cinema literate.*"

Nice sentiment, but a little outdated. Movies may have been the most important form of mass entertainment in the *first* half of the twentieth century, but television has the clear advantage as we approach the millennium. For every film like *The Terminator*, which added Arnold Schwarzenegger's "Owl be bock!" to the common language, there's a TV show like *The Simpsons*, offering Bart's equally familiar "Don't have a cow, man!" Television reaches more people, and a wider age group, than movies, and certainly reaches them more often. If the average family were to spend as much time in movie theaters as it did in front of the TV set, it'd have to watch four or five movies every *day*. In a way, it's almost quaint that Haskell would feel the need to define and defend *cinema literacy*, because the artistic worth of films has been accepted for decades—and certainly, Disney's classic children's films have been *called* classics for so long that, even in that respect, Haskell is preaching to the converted.

As I see it, the concept of *teleliteracy* is equally obvious and inarguable—except that, when it comes to television, a lot of otherwise logical and open-minded people *don't* see it. Again, it's a set of artificial barriers that have been erected, making it appear that television and literacy are mutually exclusive terms.

In what was commonly called preliterate society, stories were told verbally, stored in memory, and shared by repetition. With the development of the written word, reading and writing became more respected—and elitist—than talking and listening. One, however, complemented rather than replaced the other. In everyday speech as well as in written correspondence, people quoted the written word: inspirational addresses, romantic poems, bawdy lines from plays.

In the current century, with the development of film, radio, and television, people were introduced to mass media they didn't have to "read," in the accepted sense, to enjoy. With film and TV, the ears and eyes were equally important; with radio, it was back to the "preliterate" verbal days. When people quote from the movies, radio, or television, and quote with both accuracy and enthusiasm, they are demonstrating a fluency—a literacy—in that medium. This fluency doesn't demand or suggest a relative illiteracy in the print medium, nor does it mean the dramatized works performed on film, radio, and TV cannot themselves be considered literature.

Are Shakespeare's plays considered literature when performed, or only when read? Is *Death of a Salesman* a work of literature only in the printed playbook, or does Arthur Miller's play remain literature when the words are spoken aloud by performers? Is a poem any less artistic or meaningful when read aloud? And if people who are visually "literate" can immediately recognize the look of a Busby Berkeley dance number or a catch phrase from a *Bullwinkle* cartoon, isn't that widespread capability worth something? Isn't that fluency, in itself, a form of literacy? Of course it is—and when it comes to television, that's the primary definition of the term *teleliteracy*.

Think, for a moment, about some of the complex references you absorb, decode, and take for granted when watching TV, and you'll appreciate the scope and depth of teleliteracy. Take the seemingly simple Coor's Lite commercial in which Leslie Nielsen, wearing bunny ears and a powderpuff tail and banging a bass drum, interrupts another "commercial" in progress. To truly "get" this particular ad, viewers must first be familiar with the commercial it is lampooning: the Eveready Energizer "bunny" ads, in which a wind-up rabbit interrupts an ersatz commercial to literally beat its own drum. The Energizer commercials, in turn, spoof established short-form TV genres—the lathering-in-the-shower soap commercial, the women-in-jeopardy TV series promo—before shattering the illusion with the mechanical bunny. The success of the Energizer bunny ads depends on the viewer's familiarity with established TV conventions, just as the success of the Coor's commercial counts on a familiarity—a fluency—with the Energizer campaign, and with Nielsen's self-spoofing roles in TV and the movies. All that in thirty seconds or less.

And when the patriarch of *Dinosaurs* enters his humble abode, carrying a metal lunch box and complaining about his day, any similarities to similar characters on *Roseanne* and *The Honeymooners* and *The Life of Riley* are purely intentional. When Paula Abdul pays homage to *All That Jazz* in one video, or *West Side Story* in another, not everyone who watches MTV will get the references—but the "media literate" viewers will, and are likely to enjoy the videos more as a result. When such "real" TV newspeople as Walter Cronkite, Connie Chung, and Linda Ellerbee portray themselves in cameo roles on *Murphy Brown,* or when real presidential candidates travel the same campaign paths as the fictional politician of the Robert Altman– Garry Trudeau series *Tanner '88,* audiences not only understand that the lines between reality and fiction are being blurred intentionally, but their awareness of how TV is playing with, and against, its own conventions is what makes those scenes work. And when a cast member spouts a new catch phrase on *Saturday Night Live,* the people repeating that phrase on Monday morning are, in essence, "quoting" television.

Authors of written literature reveal their own enthusiasms and backgrounds when quoting from—or alluding to—previous written works. Why should TV's viewers, or its writers, behave any differently? When writing, or "reading," the visual *and* verbal language of television, why aren't we given credit for processing the often amazingly arcane and complex information and allusions TV throws at us constantly?

An ambitious half-hour *Second City TV* sketch in the early eighties, shot like a motion picture, starred *SCTV* regulars Dave Thomas and Rick Moranis as, respectively, Bob Hope and Woody Allen. Called "Play It Again, Bob," it revolved around Allen's attempt to write a film for Hope, his idol—a collaboration that the comics' differing styles made all but impossible.

Moranis, as Allen, was rebuffed in his attempts to write a "serious" part for Hope, and voiced his anguish by addressing the camera directly, *Annie Hall* style. Meanwhile, Thomas's Hope advised Allen to relax, do stand-up comedy again—and write funnier movies. The stalemate was broken after Allen was visited by the ghost of Bing Crosby (played by Joe Flaherty, now of *Maniac Mansion),* who offered sage advice. At the end, Allen and Hope walked off, in a visual echo of the "beautiful friendship" scene at the end of *Casablanca,* to make a "road picture" together.

The "prerequisites" for this one skit, to appreciate it fully, included a familiarity with Allen's *Annie Hall* and *Play It Again, Sam,* Hope's road pictures with Bing Crosby and his TV stand-up act, and key biographical information about both Allen and Hope, including their respective personal neuroses and critical reputations. "Play It Again, Bob" all but required an advanced degree in "cinema literacy," yet it was made not for the movies, but for television.

And consider the outrageously multilayered "MTM" episode of *St. Elsewhere,* in which a recurring character, an amnesiac named John Doe No. 6, decides after seeing the end of *The Mary Tyler Moore Show* on the psychiatric-ward TV set that his real identity is . . . Mary Richards. This one-hour 1985 show was an exercise in teleliteracy at its most advanced, with references to other TV shows and characters crammed in like passengers in a Marx Brothers stateroom.

One of the other psych ward patients in that episode, played by guest star Jack Riley, is Elliot Carlin—the same abrasive therapy-patient character played by Riley on *The Bob Newhart Show.* In John Doe's delusional state as Mary, he assigns to Mr. Carlin the identity of best friend "Rhoda," and matches other *Mary Tyler Moore* characters to the "real" characters of *St. Elsewhere.* The gruff psychologist becomes "Mr. Grant," the friendly and balding Dr. Auschlander becomes "Murray," and so on—and, alluding to a running gag from the famous sitcom, "Mary" decides to throw a party, which for the "real" Mary Richards always would end in disaster. When John Doe's party is a hit, he begins to question his "true" identity.

In an initially unrelated subplot, an astronaut patient at the hospital proves so seriously agitated that a special armed forces doctor is requested to appear—and does, in the person of Betty White, whose character of a navy doctor had appeared on a previous episode of *St. Elsewhere.* Naturally, when White's doctor walks down the halls of St. Eligius, she runs into John Doe's "Mary Richards," who immediately "recognizes" White from the part she played on *The Mary Tyler Moore Show.* "Sue Ann! The Happy Homemaker!" the amnesiac screams with delight. White stares at him blankly. "I am afraid," she replies, "you have me confused with someone else."

Alexander Nehamas used this example, among others, in his 1990 essay called "Serious Watching." Nehamas hones in on the show's most intriguing complexities, as when Norman Lloyd's Dr. Auschlander, a fictional TV character, complains about having to "play" the fictional TV character of "Murray" at the party held by "Mary." And when the psychiatrist asks which TV character Auschlander would choose to be if given the chance, Nehamas notes that Auschlander "unhesitatingly replies that he would like to be Trapper John, MD—a doctor with a reassuring manner who invariably saves his patients, the very kind of doctor *St. Elsewhere* will not allow to exist within its own fictional space and which, from within its own fiction, is thereby asserted to be more 'real' than its competitors."

Nehamas doesn't mention that Trapper John *himself* is an example of a TV reference (Pernell Roberts's title character in *Trapper John, M.D.* is intended as a modern-day, older version of the character played by Wayne Rogers on TV's *M*A*S*H)* or that the numeral in the name "John Doe No. 6" might be an oddball allusion to the unidentified hero of TV's classic *The Prisoner* series. (With the playful and inventive *St. Elsewhere* writers, no connection is too implausible a stretch.) Nehamas does, however, make a terrific point about the "MTM" *St. Elsewhere* episode's teleliterate climax. "Doe goes for a walk with Dr. Auschlander," Nehamas describes in his essay,

> who reassures him that his many friends will help him find out who he is. At the hospital's main entrance, Doe, calm, peaceful, and happy, says, "I'm gonna make it after all," and in an exact parallel to the final shot

of the title sequence of *The Mary Tyler Moore Show*, tosses his beret in the air, replicating Mary in word and deed in the very process of liberating himself from her. . . . Only a literate and active audience could ever appreciate or even get the point of this ingenious use of intertextuality.

Defining the "literate viewer" as "someone familiar with television," Nehamas—a philosophy professor, remember—writes in "Serious Watching": "The television audience is highly literate (more literate about its medium than many high-culture audiences are about theirs) and makes essential use of its literacy in its appreciation of individual episodes or whole series. Its enjoyment, therefore, is both active and comparative."

In an interview for *Teleliteracy*, Nehamas makes the point that our already impressive working knowledge of television has been enhanced by the growing accessibility of old and new shows on cable and syndicated TV. "Technologically," he says, "television is exposing its audience to a number of temporal stages of its own history. We have first-run shows in prime time, second-run shows in syndication, thirty-year-old shows on Nick at Nite and other cable channels—anyone, with the touch of a button, can watch forty years of TV history within a space of a few hours. . . . It's all there in front of you," he says, adding, "I would say the TV audience is *extraordinarily* literate about this medium of television."

Thompson agrees, and taps into that knowledge and enthusiasm for his "television studies" courses. In an argumentative essay of his own, Thompson boasted of the expertise his students displayed *before* enrolling in his class. "They see contemporary shows in prime time every night, and the rest of the history of television around the clock in reruns," he wrote.

They've followed the generic transformation of medical series from *Marcus Welby* to *Trapper John, M.D.* to *St. Elsewhere*. They've seen the presentation of the nuclear family go from integrated *(Father Knows Best)* to disintegrated *(One Day at a Time)* and back again *(The Cosby Show)*. They understand the self-referential in jokes on such shows as *Saturday Night Live, Late Night with David Letterman,* and *Moonlighting* better than most of their professors do, and almost any one of them could write an annotated commentary on each of the shows, explaining to the uninitiated what is meant by all the allusions.

Not everyone agrees, though, that teleliteracy—or its academic synonyms and offshoots, "reading television," "visual literacy" and "media literacy"—is a virtue, or even a reality. "The oft-used phrase 'visual literacy' . . . is a misnomer," announces Joshua Meyrowitz in *No Sense of Place*. "Understanding visual images has nothing to do with literacy." Meyrowitz argues that the skills necessary to decode and enjoy TV, as opposed to the skills necessary for reading, are almost nonexistent, putting young children on equal footing with well-educated adults. As proof, Meyrowitz writes: "In recent years, for example, children have enjoyed the adult soap opera *Dallas,* and adult viewers have found pleasure in a children's puppet show, *The Muppets.* Indeed, in 1980, both of these programs were among the most popular shows in *all* age-groups in America, including ages two to eleven."

Meyrowitz's assumption here equates exposure with comprehension, which hardly is the case. Young children might well *enjoy* watching *Dallas,* but it's highly unlikely they'd understand the character motivations and subtexts—and while *The Muppet Show,* even in reruns, remains one of TV's more valuable treasures for youngsters, there's no denying adult viewers can "read" more into some of the jokes and skits and satires. Watching *The Muppet Show,* though, is actually a great way for young viewers to *increase* their visual literacy levels—for, as a TV show about putting on a TV show, it plays up the medium's conventions even as it plays *with* them.

Although Meyrowitz is a hard-liner when it comes to accepting TV as a literary experience, he's better about crediting TV's reach and impact— in language I'd consider very close to a definition, much less an acceptance, of teleliteracy. "Many jokes, phrases, expressions, and events heard and seen on television provide a common set of 'experience' for people across the land," Meyrowitz writes elsewhere in *No Sense of Place,* citing, in a footnote, such examples as "But Noooooo!" from *Saturday Night Live* and "Good answer, good answer" from *Family Feud.* Good examples, good examples. Meyrowitz could be patting TV on the back here—but Nooooo! Instead, he adds, "Such phrases come and go quickly, their content being less important than their use as a common, and ever-changing, tradition." The authors of *The Dictionary of Cultural Literacy* also vote for the transitory nature of such things, arguing against their inclusion in the *Cultural Literacy* dictionary on the grounds that "our collective memory of most of the people and events in the fields of sports and entertainment is too ephemeral to take a permanent place in our cultural heritage."

Sorry about that, chief—but you're wrong.

One former FCC commissioner, Lee Lovinger, has referred to television as "the culture of the low-brow" and "the literature of the illiterate"— meaning it, of course, as the keenest of insults. And while there's so much more to television than that, there's no denying that the medium's vast popularity and easy accessibility makes it the primary carrier of information—*including* literature—to many Americans. Meyrowitz himself has noted,

> Even the biggest best-sellers reach only a fraction of the audience that will watch a similar program on television. It took forty years to sell 21 million copies of *Gone with the Wind,* but about 55 million people watched the first half of the movie on television in a *single evening. . . .* The television program *Roots* was watched, in part or whole, by approximately 130 million people in only eight days. Even with the help of the television-spurred sales, fewer than 5 million copies of *Roots* sold in eight years.

Before moving on, let's linger, just a moment, on that literature-friendly phrase: "television-spurred sales."

In *Cultural Literacy*, E. D. Hirsch, Jr., admits, "In the minds of literary specialists, a literary work is a text, but that is not the cultural reality. The information about literature that exists in the minds of literate people may have been derived from conversation, criticism, cinema, television, or student crib sheets like *Cliffs Notes*." (At least TV made the list ahead of *Cliffs Notes*.) And if TV and movies can be the source of some of our "literary" knowledge and quotes, is it really any wonder they can generate their *own* literature, and create and sustain their own memorable scenes and phrases?

It doesn't necessarily follow that the "literature" of film and TV will *replace* that of the printed word, but the tone in some people's voices suggests that's a fear they're harboring. Robert Geller says the once-traditional literary and conversational convention of quoting poetry—starting a line and having a companion finish it—still may show up in the movies now and then, but it's a rarity in real life.

"Most people aren't that familiar any more with the works of e. e. cummings, Wallace Stevens, and Elizabeth Barrett Browning, say," Geller notes. "And most of the very smart people I know, the ones who might *know* the quote, don't *talk* in quote."

"I find that very few people read out here," William Link says of Hollywood. "You go to writers' homes, there are no books. There's not a daily newspaper. In other words, what they're absorbing comes from the tube and from the motion picture screen. And I think to writers, this is a deadly diet. I think you've *got* to read." This helps explain, to Link, why so much of cinema and television is self-referential, but he offers another possible explanation as well.

"I guess it's a Jungian thing," Link says. "For people who were born after a certain date, there is a vast well of images that can be recalled—and you get into a 'tribal thing' here. I think that's possible. I think they do dip into that well, and bring back images, you know, and it *will* get clearcut responses from people now, who are watching the new shows. I don't know quite *why* that's done. Ask some psychologists."

Instead, I asked some sitcomologists—Burrows and Brooks—whether they accepted the concept of teleliteracy, and, if so, why they participated in advancing it. The Boston bar of Burrows's *Cheers*, for example, played host one episode to characters from another Boston TV institution, the doctors of *St. Elsewhere*. Why do TV writers enjoy playing with TV references in their own TV scripts?

"It's because, I think, the generations now have all been raised on television—*weaned* on television," Burrows says. "Back in the late sixties and early seventies, it was movies and books. And now, with the popularity of television and with all the homes it's in, I think they are weaned on that, and everybody assumes that everybody's up on what's the latest, and what went before. Because there are so many venues to *watch*. You can catch almost every show that's ever been on the air on some station at some point."

Brooks, whose *Mary Tyler Moore Show* inspired not only the *St. Else-where* "MTM" episode but a series of spin-offs *(Lou Grant, Rhoda, Phyllis)*, likes the fact that certain TV scenes, phrases, and characters have enough impact to be enjoyed, perpetuated, and referred to, by everyday viewers especially. "I think it's important. I think it's part of the common language," Brooks says. "I think it's true of *The Simpsons* right now. I always get a kick out of the fact that there are probably, on any given Saturday night, *x*-thousand first dates where they start to like each other because they can talk about *The Simpsons* a little."

The concept of teleliteracy extends beyond what's on the screen, to an understanding of the other factors involved in and affecting television. Just as movie audiences these days are informed about—and fascinated by—box-office grosses and star salaries, so do TV audiences follow, at least generally, which shows are popular, which are in danger of cancellation, and which stars are unhappy, pregnant, or coming to the end of their contracts—factors that could affect the content, or survival, of their favorite programs. Most viewers know about lead-ins and stunt casting and spin-offs, and have such a keen interest in the shows they enjoy that advance word about upcoming plot developments is considered newsworthy by many magazines and newspapers. Actually, this particular development, in which details about the demise of a regular character or the plot of an impending cliffhanger are "leaked" by TV studios or uncovered by media reporters, has gotten way out of hand. The phenomenon does indicate, however, just how interested people are in the entertainment they enjoy.

That enjoyment starts very early, and there's a school of thought that advocates setting up a school *for* thought when it comes to television, to help young students learn to watch TV critically and objectively. This means bringing TV sets into the classroom, which in itself is still controversial. Even very young students, though, can benefit from an understanding of such potentially manipulative production techniques as editing and special effects—and for older children, being "media literate" can mean watching and discussing news programs, documentaries, political commercials, music, stage plays, and almost anything else within reach of the dial.

History students might watch a docudrama, research the actual event on which it was based, and compare their own findings to what was—and wasn't—included in the television version. Peter B. Orlik, a media professor, defends such scholastic activities by asking, in his book *Critiquing Radio and Television Content:*

> How many book reports, for example, has the average student had to complete before leaving school? On the other hand, how many media listening or viewing reports have been assigned? That there are probably many times more of the former than the latter is in direct contradiction to the media use patterns those students will exhibit throughout the rest of their lives.

In many American classrooms, from kindergarten on, TV is now becoming part of the curriculum—and the United States is not, by any means, a pioneer in this regard. According to a 1990 article by Randall Rothenberg in the *New York Times,* media studies are now part of the British curriculum's national requirements. In Ontario, junior high and high school students have been studying TV's methods and messages in required courses since 1986. But America is learning, and teaching, fast. In New York, the Educational Resources Center at public TV station WNET has designed separate "media literacy" courses for both kindergarten students and adult-education classes. PBS, like many cable networks, offers special programming for relatively unrestricted classroom use. And even outside the classroom, in the home, TV sometimes—though rarely—takes the time to teach viewers about television.

A superb example of TV's "in-house teleliteracy course" was a 1989 HBO *Consumer Reports* special called *Buy Me That! (A Kids' Survival Guide to TV Advertising)*—a show that demonstrated, by example, that toys weren't always as reliable as commercials made them seem to be, treats weren't always as delicious, and games weren't always as easy. It showed how editing could turn a disastrous session with a new toy into what looked like nonstop fun. It taught kids to read the small print on ads and listen for such quickly spouted disclaimers as "each sold separately." It demonstrated how some TV ads suggested that toys could do things they weren't really capable of, and it interviewed a "food makeup" man, who revealed some of the tricks of his trade in the TV and magazine ad game.

He explained to kids how, to give hot cocoa a yummy-looking bubbly surface, he blew soap bubbles on top with a straw. To make cereal look tasty, he rummaged through several boxes of cereal to handpick a bowlful of perfect flakes—then poured glue, instead of milk, to make everything look and stay fresh. Premiering a few weeks before the Christmas holidays, *Buy Me That!* was almost a public service (and was so well received a sequel, the cleverly titled *Buy Me That Too!,* was mounted two years later, in December 1991). My kids saw the original *Buy Me That!* more than two years ago, and haven't looked at commercials the same way since. Their reaction, and the potential of such programs, should silence any critics of the "media literacy" concept. But, of course, it doesn't.

Walter Goodman, media critic of the *New York Times,* was so annoyed by his colleague Rothenberg's story on "media literacy" that he rushed into print less than three weeks later with a "Critic's Notebook" rebuttal. After explaining he had formerly—though reluctantly—supported the use of TVs in classrooms to provide newscasts for students, Goodman drew a line in the sand where "visual literacy" was concerned. "Using television to deliver information in an inviting way or to draw students into geography or chemistry," Goodman wrote, "is not the same as using television to teach about television. That smells of pandering. The best way to protect children from being misled by television or newspapers or politicians or corporations is to broaden their knowledge. As a start, they might be taught to read well enough to recognize the ignorance behind a phrase like 'visual literacy.' "

"You know what I say to people who say there's no place for television inside the public schools?" asks teacher Timothy Brittell. "If anything, it should be part of the job of public schools to *teach* students how to be discerning viewers."

Linda Ellerbee has written and produced a TV newscast for youngsters—a TV activity more or less endorsed by Goodman. However, she also produced a 1991 Nickelodeon children's special called *It's Only Television*, doing precisely the kind of teaching that Goodman calls "pandering." Meeting with TV critics the summer before that special was televised, Ellerbee explained her interest in, and thoughts on, the topic of children and television:

> It's clear that since we all know now they will spend so many more hours in front of a television set than they will in a classroom, that they need to know how to *watch* it. We're talking about media literacy. . . . Although there are no traditional means of teaching kids this type of literacy, there are skills you can teach, skills you can learn, in order to understand what you're watching. The show is designed to give those kids those tools— how to look at their TV and make their own decisions. And it starts with the premise that you're smarter than your television.

Ellerbee, one of the best wordsmiths on television, knows and uses the medium well. Her newsmagazine series with Lloyd Dobyns, NBC's *Weekend* (1978–79) and *NBC News Overnight* (1982–83), sparkled with well-crafted, highly original writing—hers *and* his. And when Ellerbee teamed with Ray Gandolf on ABC's *Our World* in 1986, they did in a network prime-time series what TV can also do in the classroom: they taught history in a way that made it come alive, and made you want to learn more. I, too, wanted to learn more—about Ellerbee's opinions. So she, too, was contacted for *Teleliteracy*, and, as expected, minced no words.

"It ought to be taught in elementary schools—how to watch television," Ellerbee says. "It always bothers the hell out of me that parents who would not censor what their children *read* feel it's perfectly OK to censor television, instead of teaching them how to watch it. Teaching them what a commercial is *really* selling them: 'This commercial is selling toothpaste.' 'No, it isn't, it's selling popularity, that's why it's getting to you.' "

Yet when it comes to the more mature TV viewers, Ellerbee feels they are much more savvy when it comes to television—much more teleliterate—than even most people *in* television believe. Ellerbee, for example, was comfortable enough with that notion to agree to be the very first "real" newscaster to appear on *Murphy Brown*, breaking the ice for what is now considered a harmless cameo. At the time, though, there was talk that to step onto a sitcom might somehow taint a TV journalist's reputation or unduly confuse viewers. Asked about that, Ellerbee laughs.

"My guess is that it gave them no problem at all," she says, then shifts to an even more controversial subject. "You know, when I did that Maxwell House commercial, the *New York Times* did an editorial damning me because, it said, I had tried to fool people into thinking it was a *newscast*. . . . You think the audience didn't know it was a commercial? I suspect the audience knew very *well* it was a commercial. I don't think they had any *trouble* with that." Asked if she believes the TV audience is indeed rather sophisticated, Ellerbee replies, "Yes, I do. I truly do," but she doesn't necessarily spread that praise to those who *make* TV.

"We have for years taken, and continue to take, the position that we must be smarter than they are, because we're making it and they're watching it," she says. "And the sad thing about that is that, invariably, the result . . . is that we give them what *we* think they will understand and what *we* think they want, rather than simply giving them our very best."

If all these preconceptions and misconceptions could be set aside or overcome, television, in turn, could rise to heights as yet unimagined, but even in the current "real world," it's doing better than most people think. For those willing to look past the "boob tube" reputation and seek out and sample the fine things currently available on television, the treasures are there. There ought to be a "required viewing" list for those who consider TV such an inferior art form. Send them off to watch *The Singing Detective* and *The Civil War,* and the best episodes of *Cheers* and *Twin Peaks,* before allowing them to make any more silly generalizations about television. Art is where you find it, but only if you look for it.

And just as reading more and better books is a way to increase literacy and cultural literacy, finding and sampling more and better programs is a way to increase teleliteracy. Children should be taught young, in and out of classrooms, what television can offer and how it works. Older viewers, in turn, should use their TV sets wisely, creatively . . . and unapologetically.

"If you're not aware of the fact that you can assemble a very healthy diet from television, for you *and* for your children, then you are misusing the appliance," Mark Dawidziak says, "just as you would misuse a refrigerator if you had nothing but junk in it. If you're not aware of the fact that there are good shows in prime time, and that there's PBS and the Discovery Channel and the Learning Channel and Bravo and Arts & Entertainment and all the wonderful things that cable has developed, and that you can put together a smart and educational and stimulating diet of TV, you're not using television properly.

"Look, you walk into a Walden bookstore, right? What's going to hit you immediately will be the mass-market paperbacks—essentially, your best-sellers. You have to *look* a little hard to find the classics, but they're *in* there. You know, they're not going to put Melville and Shakespeare out *front.* I'm sorry. You're not going to see it happen. Well, neither is television."

Teleliteracy is a concept that envelops the past, present, and future of television. In the present, it means using and treating TV properly—taking advantage of the best it has to offer, and giving it due credit for its triumphs and accomplishments. In the future, teleliteracy will involve accepting and absorbing newly developed and improved media as TV, computers, and communication systems collide and connect in the upcoming technological Rushin' Revolution.

As for TV's past, the true teleliterate is not merely aware of it, but awash in it. As television spreads out technologically, the inventory from television's recorded history is increasingly available, and enthusiastically viewed and reviewed. While moving forward, television also is looking back—retrieving, and often remaking, old TV shows.

In the nineties, Bill Cosby is adapting Groucho Marx's *You Bet Your Life* for a new generation, while Francis Coppola has announced plans to oversee a series of telemovie projects under the proposed umbrella title of *Playhouse 90's*—a teleliterate homage to the classic Golden Age anthology series, *Playhouse 90*. Some will charge that such remakes display a lack of invention and imagination, but what they really indicate is a growing willingness to acknowledge the cultural importance of TV's past. Like modern movie remakes of old films (and even modern movie remakes of such old TV series as *The Addams Family)*, these series suggest today's television artists are ready, and even eager, to reveal—and revel in—their own teleliteracy.

Alexander Nehamas says it's a clear sign of TV's growing development. "Film started doing remakes after the twenties and thirties," he notes, adding that "it takes a good generation for the people exposed to an art form when they were young to become so much older and more mature that they enjoy seeing the same stories over again, remade." Television, he says, is at that stage today, and is entertaining two generations simultaneously.

"The new generation sees the remake as the true representation of that story," Nehamas says, "while we oldsters sit around and decide which one is better—usually preferring the old one, but watching the new one so we can compare it and feel superior. Merely the comparison, engaging in it, is what we enjoy."

And finally, Nehamas defends TV's examination and celebration of its own past by pointing to examples from a much more distant past. "Once again, you can go all the way back to the time of Plato," he says. "The three great Greek tragedians *all* composed a play dealing with Elektra. Euripides went so far as to satirize the earlier Elektras, and could depend on the audience's familiarity with the earlier plays. The popular audience is generally *very* aware."

That was true in the time of Plato, and it's no less true today. For the most part, the awareness—the teleliteracy—is there. What we must do now is recognize, celebrate, develop, and utilize it. Otherwise, we'll remain mired in a pattern that has repeated itself through history, taking our most popular entertainment medium for granted until its place is taken by something else.

It's time to rise up and respond to the film snobs, the violence counters, the anti-TV absolutists, and the other elitist and narrow-minded attitudes that have persisted and fermented throughout the centuries. It's time, at long last, to put the screws to Plato—and to *The Republic,* for which he stands.

PART III

A MEDIA ROUNDTABLE

In the first part of this book, television was put into context—historically, culturally, and personally. In the second part, it was defended from all attackers, and discussed by some of its most impressive writers, directors, producers, actors, watchers, and users. In this third and final section, television will be looked at—"up close and personal"—regarding several general, and a few specific, topics of interest.

When the talk turns to the role-model effects of TV, or to TV's effectiveness and impact during the Gulf War, there is debate, and often direct disagreement, among some of the people interviewed—which is fine with me. When I assembled this ad hoc panel of TV experts, I expected neither solidarity nor timidity. What I wanted, and got, was a group of well-informed people willing and able to talk about television seriously.

When they disagree with one another, or I with them, we're all engaging in the sort of discussion that is outrageously uncommon, given the pervasiveness of television in our daily lives. Trashing TV is easy. Trashing *anything* is easy. I come not to bury television, but to praise it—or, at least, to analyze it without condescension.

The people joining me in discussing TV in this last part have been introduced and heard from already, but at this point in the book—just prior to launching into the final section—listing and identifying them all in one place seems a logical, or at least user-friendly, thing to do. I thank them all, once again, for their participation—and list them alphabetically, to avoid any distress over top billing. The *Teleliteracy* panel includes:

David Attenborough, writer–producer of *The Trials of Life, The Living Planet,* and *Life on Earth;* nature-documentary filmmaker, formerly a BBC-TV executive.

Linda Bloodworth-Thomason, creator and coexecutive producer of *Designing Women* and *Evening Shade;* a former English teacher.

Timothy Brittell, social studies teacher at Leota Junior High School in Woodinville, Washington.

James L. Brooks, writer–producer–director whose TV credits include *The Mary Tyler Moore Show, Taxi, Lou Grant* and *The Simpsons;* film credits, as writer, producer, and director, include *Terms of Endearment* and *Broadcast News.*

James Burke, a science documentarian whose TV works include *After the Warming,* the *Connections* series, and *The Day the Universe Changed.*

Ken Burns, documentarian; director, coproducer, and coauthor of *The Civil War.*

James Burrows, director and coexecutive producer of *Cheers;* directorial TV credits include *The Mary Tyler Moore Show* and *Taxi.*

Peggy Charren, president of Action for Children's Television and veteran TV advocate.

Bill Cosby, star and guiding rudder of *The Cosby Show* and the recipient of a doctorate in education; previous series include *I Spy.*

Mark Dawidziak, TV critic of the *Akron Beacon Journal* in Ohio.

Shelley Duvall, creator of *Shelley Duvall's Faerie Tale Theatre* and other family programming, actress, and president of Think Entertainment; film credits include *3 Women, Nashville,* and *Popeye.*

Linda Ellerbee, writer and cohost of *Weekend, NBC News Overnight,* and *Our World.*

Fred W. Friendly, executive producer and occasional moderator of televised Columbia University seminars on media issues; former CBS News president and, as producer, former partner to the late Edward R. Murrow.

Mark Frost, cocreator (with David Lynch) of *Twin Peaks* and a writer–producer on *Hill Street Blues.*

Robert Geller, creator and executive producer of *American Short Story* and president of Learning in Focus.

Don Hewitt, creator and executive producer of *60 Minutes.*

Peter Jennings, ABC News anchor, *ABC World News Tonight.*

Lindsay Law, executive producer of *American Playhouse.*

William Link, TV writer–producer and the cocreator (with his late partner, Richard Levinson) of *Columbo* and *Murder, She Wrote.*

Lorne Michaels, creator and executive producer of *Saturday Night Live.*

Bill Moyers, TV documentarian, interviewer, and political analyst.

Alexander Nehamas, Edmund Carpenter Professor of the Humanities at Princeton University, specialist in media and philosophy.

Carolyn Olivier, director of admissions at Landmark College, an educational facility in Putney, Vermont, specializing in learning disabilities.

Fred Rogers, creator and host of *Mister Rogers' Neighborhood;* an ordained minister of the United Presbyterian Church.

Donald Rosenberg, classical music and dance critic of the *Pittsburgh Press.*

Robert J. Thompson, associate professor at Syracuse University's Newhouse School, specialist in media studies.

Kurt Vonnegut, author of *Cat's Cradle, Slaughterhouse-Five,* and other novels, short stories, essays, and teleplays.

David Zurawik, TV critic of the *Baltimore Sun.*

Let the discussions begin . . .

15

A SERIOUS LOOK AT CHILDREN'S TELEVISION—NO KIDDING

More than thirty years ago, at the age of seven, I wrote my first words about television. They were written—printed, actually—in my diary on December 3, 1960, the day after the telecast of *Alice in Wonderland* on ABC's *Disneyland*. "Man, was Alice in Wonderland good," I wrote. Other entries that month included: "Was PETER PAN good today," "Today on 6 O'Clock Adventure I saw the first story of MISTER MAGOO," and "Today at 6:00 I saw THE WIZARD OF OZ." One entry the following month complained, "Today on TV they took off FUNDAY FUNNIES. I love that program, and I don't like it being taking off." My English needed a little work, but my enthusiasm was clear. (Is it any *wonder* I became a TV critic?) In my diary, I even counted down the days to *The Wizard of Oz*—which, like Christmas and my birthday, came but once a year. It was, as the capital letters indicated, a BIG EVENT, and my enthusiasm was shared by millions of annual wide-eyed viewers. As late as 1970, *The Wizard of Oz* accounted for half of the top-rated movies in television's all-time Top 10.

In 1985, when my daughter, Kristin, was two, I showed her *The Wizard of Oz* for the first time. She watched, quietly and spellbound, until the Wicked Witch of the West threatened Dorothy and disappeared in a puff of red smoke. At that point, Kristin said, "I want to see the witch again." Because we were watching on videotape, it was an easy thing to hit Rewind for a few seconds, press Play, and watch as, once again, Margaret Hamilton cackled and said, "I'll *get* you, my pretty . . . and your little *dog,* too!" As the witch vanished, Kristin told me, "One more time, and that's *all.*"

She didn't have to wait a year to see it again, as I had as a kid—and she not only had the power to stop and review the movie, but she *knew* she had that power. My daughter is now nine, and has a video library to match her library of books; she loves to read, but also loves television. And as I write these words, my son Mark, seven, is upstairs manipulating the video-disc player, running and rerunning through their brand-new widescreen copy of *Home Alone*. My kids treat TV the way they treat books: saving and savoring what they enjoy, choosing what they want and when they want it, and sharing their favorites with friends and each other. They see television a lot differently than I saw it when I was their age. And when *my* dad was their age, he didn't see television at all. He saw radio.

Virgil Bianculli, my father, was born in Pittsburgh in 1923, three years after KDKA began broadcasting there. Consequently, this new thing called radio was a big part of his childhood. His older brothers built crystal sets, and they all listened to boxing matches, to re-creations of baseball games—and, in the early thirties, some children's radio shows my dad remembers fondly and accurately to this day. My dad would have been seven, his grandson Mark's age today, when he first heard radio's *Sherlock Holmes,* yet he claims to still remember the show's sponsor: G. Washington Coffee. *The Shadow, The Tom Mix Ralston Straightshooters,* and *Jack Armstrong, the All-American Boy* were other shows he named when I asked him—and along with the names, he rattled off stars, plots, broadcast times, and even advertisers. In every case, he was absolutely right. "It's amazing how vivid it is," he says of his radio days. "That stuff's even clearer than what I did last month."

I have the same vivid memories of my own media childhood, and those memories are now as quaint to my kids as my dad's are to me. After all, I watched black-and-white TV on a tiny circular screen then, had only three or four stations from which to choose, and could watch only whatever was being shown at the time. My kids—the third generation to have a mass medium broadcast directly into the home—have it much better. And as parents governing what they watch and when they watch it, so do we.

When they were younger, the only "live" TV shows my children watched were *Mister Rogers' Neighborhood, Sesame Street,* and old *Looney Tunes* cartoon showcases. Otherwise, their TV came pretaped and prescreened. The quantity of TV they watched wasn't of concern to me, because we, as parents, controlled the quality. They worked their way through the complete set of *Shelley Duvall's Faerie Tale Theatre,* delighted in the songs and antics in *Mary Poppins,* and sat transfixed as *Reading Rainbow* "read" such storybooks as *Tight Times.* On those occasions, TV wasn't being used as a baby-sitter; it was serving the dual functions of entertainer and educator.

When they were toddlers, and our children's entire literary world was limited to the fairy tales and Mother Goose rhymes we read to them, the sight of a *Sesame Street* Little Bo Peep Muppet—or, for that matter, a Little Miss Muffet Muppet—was, to them, a surprise encounter with a familiar friend. More technically, it was their first exposure to the world of allusion—the first literary references they were able to comprehend and appreciate. When *The Bullwinkle Show* fractured those fairy tales all those years ago, the jokes were funnier to me, in *my* young childhood, because I knew the real stories and fables the show was lampooning. Watch *Sesame Street* today, or a *Muppet Show* rerun on cable, and you'll see how sophisticated the satire has become.

When Kermit the Frog dons his reporter's hat to interview the Little Old Woman Who Lived in a Shoe, TV news as well as Mother Goose is being made fun of, and many children's shows include levels of parody that presume a great deal of teleliteracy on the part of their young viewers. Or, like my beloved *Bullwinkle*, they presume to entertain older viewers as well. Youngsters watching *Sesame Street* may laugh at the silliness and repetitiveness of "Vincent Twice, Vincent Twice," the mustachioed host of "Mysterious Theater," but only elder viewers, familiar with Vincent Price's hosting chores on PBS's *Mystery!* series (a job subsequently handed over to Diana Rigg), will be aware of the source of the parody and know the Price is right. As Steven Spielberg has said of his earliest memories of *The Bullwinkle Show,* "It was the first time that I can recall my parents watching a cartoon show over my shoulder and laughing in places I couldn't comprehend."

In these days, the foundation of TV knowledge upon which young viewers build grows exponentially. Parents checking out the Weather Channel and the evening newscasts expose children to those forms early. Nickelodeon's Nick at Nite and local independent stations provide a menu of TV history from generations past—and while the promos on Nick at Nite poke gentle fun at these shows, young children take them seriously and are genuinely entertained by them. Television also exposes kids to music and musicians, sports and athletes, and so many other things that, though its potential for abuse is great, its potential for use is even greater.

Television can expose children to literature, it can be "read" as literature, and it can inspire them in countless and often surprising ways. I can remember going to the school or local library as a boy to check out the latest picture book shown, and read aloud, on *Captain Kangaroo*—only to learn that other watchful, book-hungry viewers had beaten me to the punch and checked out all the available copies of *Mike Mulligan and His Steam Shovel*. The cartoon version of Maurice Sendak's *Really Rosie*, Sendak has said, reached "more children than I could ever reach in twenty publishing lifetimes." And even if such TV shows as *Jim Henson's The Storyteller* and *Faerie Tale Theatre* don't send children scurrying off to the printed page, the fact the stories are being enjoyed at all is a cause for celebration.

Repeated viewing, a side effect of VCR and videodisc technology, is nothing to worry about, either. When my kids discovered *Dumbo*, they played the tape so many times that a visiting relative, hearing "Pink Elephants on Parade" for what seemed like the five-hundredth time, marched into the kitchen—in time to the music—and stuck his head in the oven. Right after seeing the *Faerie Tale Theatre* version of *Three Little Pigs* for the first time, our children saw it for a second, and a third, and kept going until my wife and I, in the event of a power failure, could recite the entire script verbatim. Yet the giddy performance of Billy Crystal as the smart pig, and Jeff Goldblum as the Big Bad Wolf, so delighted them that they watched it almost daily for more than a month. Waste of time? No more so than reading your child the same favorite bedtime story night after night.

"Parents who read to their children know that repetition is where it's at," says Peggy Charren. "The VCR gives kids a kind of control over the content. They can fast-forward over the parts they don't like, and go back to the parts they do." Shelley Duvall herself says, "They'll watch the program and be inspired. . . . Whether they read or watch, it doesn't matter, because they're hearing the words. They're still imagining." She loves books, but also loves the potential of visual media. "Good television shows or good movies," she says, "inspire you to learn more, to do more."

Sometimes TV can just inspire you, period. Maybe it's *not* so silly that my fascination with television, documented in my diary at age seven, led to a career spent watching, analyzing, and discussing TV. Or that Shelley Duvall, who as a youngster loved the humor of *Bullwinkle* and the scariness of *Alfred Hitchcock Presents*, grew up to produce an anthology series she hosted herself (a la Hitchcock), full of multilayered humor (a la *Bullwinkle*). "I loved *Rocky and Bullwinkle*," she says. "Everybody in this industry was inspired by *Rocky and Bullwinkle*, whether they'd admit it or not. They affected us all." She was also inspired by watching old movies on television, and foreign films, and lots of other things.

"I watched a lot of public broadcasting in Houston, Texas, when I was growing up," she says, "and it opened my eyes to films from all over the world. It opened up my eyes to other countries, other cultures. This is *very* important for a child. American kids, in either an urban or a rural location, have generally never been outside their cities. They don't have a clue about what people are like in other cities and countries. The only culture they're exposed to *without* television is the local one. I think television helps open their eyes to other worlds, and to the possibilities that lie ahead for them as they grow up."

Robert Geller, who hired Duvall for his adaptation of Fitzgerald's *Bernice Bobs Her Hair*, was inspired not only by the literary works he loved to read, but by the programs on TV and radio he loved to see and hear. "Red Barber really taught me what metaphor and simile were all about," Geller says, referring to the famed radio sportscaster (who, into the nineties, had a casual, wide-ranging weekly guest spot on National Public Radio's *Morning Edition*). "He made language more exciting." On television, Geller was drawn to anthology dramas—a form of TV he ended up producing himself eventually. "I cut my teeth on television in the days of *Playhouse 90*," Geller says fondly, "looking at a lot of good plays done for television." Duvall and Geller are anything but isolated cases. In fact, it's not farfetched to suggest that many of those who are working in TV by choice—and doing some of the medium's most inspirational work—were themselves inspired by programs broadcast when they were younger.

Fred Rogers, whose *Mister Rogers' Neighborhood* is populated by fanciful characters and gentle eccentrics, turns out to have been a loyal listener of the thirties' and forties' radio show *Vic and Sade,* which had a similarly imaginative feel. "I loved *Vic and Sade,*" Rogers says, speaking fondly of such characters as Uncle Fletcher and gentle jokes as "The Ohio Home for the Bland." "I just love whimsical stuff," says Rogers—and look where that love took him.

Lorne Michaels, who grew up in Canada, says, "I don't remember the year that television arrived, but I can tell you it was like a miracle. . . . I remember the early part of my childhood as being incredibly boring. I can remember sitting on the curb in front of my house *waiting* for something to happen . . . and then suddenly *this* thing happened." His early favorites? "I *loved* Jackie Gleason, and I *loved* Milton Berle," recalls Michaels, naming two of television's all-time reigning comedy-variety performers. Those shows, and that genre, had a significant impact on Michaels: when he grew up, he wrote for *Laugh-In* and launched *Saturday Night Live.*

When Linda Bloodworth-Thomason was young, she recalls, "We had the first TV in our town, and we only got one station." Her favorite show from her own youth? "I really liked *Lucy,*" she says, almost apologetically. "I thought she was fantastic." Yet it makes sense that a girl who loved *I Love Lucy* would grow up to write roles for *Designing Women,* just as it follows she would eventually end up writing for TV after pursuing other careers.

"Television was bigger than life for me," she says. "I guess, even then, TV was really exciting, because I was in a little town. I can remember my mother talking about Teddy Nadler, the contestant on *The $64,000 Question,* and whether or not he would go for the $64,000 that night. And she was out talking to some of the neighbors, and they were trying to decide if they thought Teddy would win. So television brought a certain element of excitement into our town, and I think I was excited by that. It made the world bigger for me. I'm not surprised I ended up in television, although I never calculated to do it."

"We were definitely a house hooked on television," says Lindsay Law, thinking back to his childhood in Westport, Connecticut. "We had the first color television in our town." His father was a salesman, which explains why Law was both transfixed and transformed when, as a high school kid, he "tripped across" the 1966 CBS broadcast of Arthur Miller's *Death of a Salesman,* starring Lee J. Cobb as Willy Loman.

"I was amazed at that," recalls Law. And, after seeing his first play on television, "I started definitely *looking* for them." So, in addition to his "normal" diet of *Perry Mason* and *Checkmate,* Law sought out TV versions of more theatrical fare. One such program he remembers vividly was an *ABC Stage '67* musical special called *Evening Primrose,* with music and lyrics by Stephen Sondheim and book by James Goldman. (Sondheim and Goldman would reteam in 1971 for *Follies.*) Much, much later, as executive producer of *American Playhouse* on PBS, Law would work with Miller on TV versions of two plays (Miller's own *All My Sons* and his adaptation of

Ibsen's *An Enemy of the People),* and mount TV versions of two musicals with scores written by Sondheim *(Sunday in the Park with George* and *Into the Woods).*

The connections between Law's childhood viewing and his adult producing go even deeper than that. Not only did Law, who loved television's drama specials, end up overseeing a dramatic anthology TV series, but when *American Playhouse* premiered in 1982 with *The Shady Hill Kidnapping,* the director was Paul Bogart, who had directed *Evening Primrose* all those years before.

I don't know if even Law is aware of *that* connection, but he's well aware of the power of TV to influence would-be writers. Law teaches screenwriting at Yale University, mostly to produced playwrights interested in adapting their techniques to a new medium. "I asked them all, 'How did you all get to be writers?' " Law says, "and every one of them in my class was introduced to the fact that they wanted to be a writer from *television.* It was their first experience of seeing a play."

Donald Rosenberg, like all children of the fifties, watched *The Wizard of Oz* faithfully "*every* year" as a kid, but also was an avid viewer of *The Ed Sullivan Show,* which fed his appetite for Broadway musicals. "I watched normal things, too," the music and dance critic says, laughing, citing such sitcoms as *The Dick Van Dyke Show* and *Car 54, Where Are You?* But Rosenberg's most significant early viewing pleasure may well have been CBS's *Young People's Concerts,* which predated, and perhaps helped spark, his serious interest in classical music. Premiering in 1958, these TV programs were conducted and hosted by the New York Philharmonic's Leonard Bernstein throughout the sixties, and Rosenberg, looking back, gives Bernstein the TV teacher a lot of credit.

"I think most people of my generation learned about classical music from Leonard Bernstein—not going to it, but watching him on television," Rosenberg says. "He was a *master* at that kind of stuff. Natural showman, brilliant mind, a great conductor, a great composer, a great pianist—really. He made it live. Nobody's ever done anything like it, and nobody will. Nobody has the qualities that Bernstein had." Rosenberg's precritical opinion of those *Young People's Concerts* at the time? "Loved them," he says. "I was *mesmerized* by them."

Rosenberg wasn't the only one. Fred Rogers tells this story: "This young boy—he told me this himself, as a grown-up—had nobody in his family who was musically gifted. Yet he was so entranced with those *Young People's Concerts* that one day he said to his father, 'I'm going to grow up and do that.' Well, that young man is now John Mauceri, who grew up to become a conductor. I met him one night at the Kennedy Center, after he had conducted Bernstein's *Mass.* He became a protégé of Bernstein's, and his son is named for Leonard." Ironically, Rosenberg played under Mauceri while a student at Yale University. When I mention to Rogers that Rosenberg, too, was entranced by Bernstein's TV appearances, Rogers says he considers both cases to be examples of "a tie that I think is so significant" between television and inspiration. "And ... Rosenberg, he is a very thoughtful critic, that man," adds Rogers. "We have two very thoughtful music critics in Pittsburgh." When Rogers is told his praise probably will mean a lot to Rosenberg, Rogers's reply is pure, quintessential *Mister Rogers:* "I hope he knows it inside."

Something Rosenberg *does* know, for sure, is that children's television continues to use classical music with abandon—and sometimes, but not always, with imagination. Rosenberg, like me, has two small children and logs a fair amount of family-viewing TV time. I asked him to take notes (and *listen* to the notes) on a typical cartoon show, then report back. He did.

"I was watching *The Smurfs* one Saturday morning with the kids," Rosenberg says. "This is what I heard within five minutes: themes from Tchaikovsky's *Nutcracker*, Rimsky-Korsakov's *Scheherazade*, the first movement of Schubert's *Unfinished* symphony, Strauss's *Till Eulenspiegel's Merry Pranks*, Stravinsky's *Firebird*, Mussorgsky's *Pictures at an Exhibition*, Berlioz's *Symphonie Fantastique*, Liszt's Piano Concerto No. 1, and the Storm from Beethoven's *Pastorale* symphony." And what were the Smurfs doing during all this? "Just Smurfing around," Rosenberg says.

Kids are not watching cartoons, or most other television programs, to become musically sophisticated, but when action is linked cleverly and memorably to a piece of music, the results can stay with them for life. Most children, and many adults, will receive their first exposure to classical music not from radio or recordings or concert halls, where the works are presented in their entirety and without distraction, but in small snatches on television and in the movies.

Fantasia is the clearest and purest example, but probably not the most effective. (Among Walt Disney's revered full-length animated classics, *Fantasia* is the one that, more than any other, makes many children restless in spots.) Compare that to the radio and TV theme for *The Lone Ranger*— lifted from Rossini's *William Tell Overture*, and still a perfect, instantly identifiable example of musical teleliteracy. Or the catchy theme to *The Huntley– Brinkley Report*—lifted outright, of course, from the opening bars of the second movement of Beethoven's Ninth Symphony. People who know their television also know music from Gounod's *Funeral March of a Marionette,* Sousa's *Liberty Bell March* and Mouret's *Rondeau*—though not necessarily by those names. (Substitute, instead, the respective themes to *Alfred Hitchcock Presents, Monty Python's Flying Circus,* and *Masterpiece Theatre.*)

"There are literally hundreds of examples," says Rosenberg. "United Airlines has been using a lot of Gershwin lately, for instance. And I don't think it's all bad. What better music can you use than classical music? It's proven, durable music." He also sees it as potentially educational, especially for young viewers, but with lots of disclaimers attached. "All that old *Merrie Melodies* stuff, those guys were great at it. They used all the classical themes very cleverly—much more wittily than *The Smurfs.* In *The Smurfs,* the music is kind of awkwardly stitched together. With *Merrie Melodies,* those guys knew the repertoire."

On TV, Rosenberg says, the same themes seem to get tapped over and over. "Most of the classical music you hear on television is from the nineteenth century," he says, "and it's the stuff most people know. It's exactly what John Williams does in his film scores. He imitates composers exactly so that the audience recognizes the style instantly. . . . I won't say he gets away with murder, but it's one of the reasons he's very successful. And Danny Elfman—he imitates Prokofiev, and it's very clear he knows the literature very well. It's not that they're *stealing,* but they want to set a mood immediately. Elfman's music from *Beetlejuice,* or even some from *Batman,* that's vintage Prokofiev." Both Elfman and Williams, incidentally, have added to one repertoire while borrowing from another: their musical themes for television series include Elfman's *The Simpsons* and *Tales from the Crypt,* and Williams's vintage *Lost in Space* and *The Time Tunnel.*

As for the use of actual selections from classical music in TV themes, Rosenberg does have some complaints. "Basically, they're reducing it to its most simplistic form, and it does give you an unrealistic and exaggerated view of the piece," he says. "On *The Lone Ranger,* all you ever hear is the last section of the *William Tell Overture.* The first three sections contain some really fabulous music, and it's not really a whole piece until you hear everything. It's not an isolated event. All this use of classical music, in some sense, is perverse. . . . It's better than not hearing it at all, but it really doesn't serve a sure purpose." Finally, Rosenberg says, "There's a cynical reason why I think television and film use classical music so much. It's public domain. They don't have to pay anything for it. They can rearrange and distort it any way they like, and nobody's going to say a word. That's not just a cynical view. That's a realistic view."

But even when money *is* a factor, and the songs more recent, music is a major part of the television experience. Television themes and commercial jingles are some of the most persistent, catchy, and unforgettable elements of our popular culture. As children, we absorb them like sponges. As adults, we never seem to be willing or able to wring out the old. And Madison Avenue, eager to rekindle aging Baby Boomer memories while playing to their children, are recycling rock songs with a cynical, feverish passion. Pay attention to the commercials in one night of prime time, and you'll hear enough adaptations of rock songs to fill a Top 10. For the most part, this is a harmless exercise, and, arguably, borders on teaching teleliteracy to a new generation. Does it really matter if my son identifies the Rivieras song "California Sun" as "The Pepsi Chill-out Challenge," so long as he can enjoy the tune and I can steer him to the original version from my CD collection? I draw the line when it comes to the Beatles: the idea that "Revolution" could be used by Nike to sell sneakers was an insult to my entire generation, and was rightly yanked after a storm of protest from unhappy viewers. However, I'm merely protecting the best memories, and musical group, of my own youth. My g-g-generation won't be in charge much longer—and reclaiming and recycling old rock standards in TV ads, and on children's shows, is a sneaky, almost subliminal way of passing the music on to the next generation.

Sometimes, in television, the links between generations are constant and comforting. *Sesame Street* and *Mister Rogers' Neighborhood* are such durable favorites that some who watched the early shows as children now watch with children of their own. Don Herbert, who started as TV's Mr. Wizard in 1951, is still going strong on Nickelodeon forty years later with his *Ask Mr. Wizard* series, and puppeteer Shari Lewis just returned to TV with a new PBS series, *Lamb Chop's Play Along.* And on reruns and videocassette, the cross-generational delights are almost infinite. Watching *Looney Tunes* or *Bullwinkle* cartoons with my kids is a way to not only enrich their childhood, but to temporarily reclaim my own. And whenever an opportunity arises to take advantage of my children's TV-generated enthusiasm and expand on it, I leap at it—often without knowing, until we get there, just how big a leap we're taking.

Both Mark and Kristin were enthralled by Michael Jackson's MTV videos, and delighted when musical satirist "Weird Al" Yankovic poked fun at Jackson's "Beat It" with his spoof video, "Eat It." (Satire, allusion, direct references—all there, and all clearly received.) Then, going back to the source of the original gang-war imagery of "Beat It," I showed the kids a videodisc of the 1961 film version of *West Side Story,* thus introducing them to some artists already mentioned in this chapter: Leonard Bernstein (composer) and Stephen Sondheim (lyricist). My children adored the movie, and the music, so we moved on to other musicals, including the recently rereleased Mary Martin TV version of *Peter Pan* (the one I had raved about in my 1960 diary) and the 1956 film version of *The King and I.* (Had the children been a little older, *Romeo and Juliet* would have been another obvious selection.)

When those shows all passed the "interest" test, we took the kids to a *real* show: *Jerome Robbins' Broadway,* which included selections from three musicals they were, by then, thoroughly familiar with. Not bad: from "Beat It" to Broadway in a few easy lessons, and with TV as the tour guide.

Since then, the kids have responded to stuff I would have thought was above them, including the Broadway cast recording and TV adaptation of Sondheim's *Sweeney Todd.* But if *I've* learned one thing from television, it's never to underestimate the intelligence of a child watching it.

That goes for music, entertainment—and certainly for news, perhaps the most underrepresented TV genre where children are concerned. "We have all this news for *adults* now on television," says Peggy Charren, "but we still have almost no news for children. That's not only outrageous, it's also disturbingly sad." Commercial TV's rare but laudable efforts, such as CBS's *30 Minutes* and NBC's *Main Street,* fell victim to budget cuts; when news for adults was being hit hard, news for children was viewed by many as an unnecessary luxury. Yet just as news coverage of the Americans held hostage in Iran led to the development of *ABC News Nightline,* coverage of the Gulf War in 1991 sparked measurable interest in initiating news-related programming to young viewers. Peter Jennings anchored a Saturday-morning news special explaining the Gulf crisis, one that won the 1991 Television Critics Association award as children's program of the year—and also won an award from Charren's Action for Children's Television. Fred Rogers appeared in public service announcements addressing kids' wartime concerns and fears, and Linda Ellerbee anchored news briefs for children on Nickelodeon—which led to her series of nonfiction news specials in 1991 and her weekly *Nick News* series in 1992. All three of these people, it turns out, have the same secret recipe when it comes to relating to children via television.

"To be perfectly frank," Jennings says, asked to give his own opinion after his *War in the Gulf: Answering Children's Questions* Saturday-morning special, "I went away feeling confirmed that if you talk to children as if they were adults, that's precisely how *to* talk to them. . . . I certainly felt that way, and I felt that we should do it again." (Which he did, in shows devoted to other topics.)

Linda Ellerbee agrees: "I really don't think that, in order to do a kids' show, you must 'lower' your sights." Instead, she says, you simplify. "And when I say 'simplify,' I don't mean you boil it down to 'Dick and Jane News.' " As an example, she mentions a piece from her Nickelodeon news special on the environment. "We were talking about a certain kind of pollution, and . . . I wanted to explain that we got to this point in pollution because it was considered progress to have factories to make goods, because more people could have goods then, and people's wages would be better—and to explain how a good could lead to a bad. If that's simplifying it, so be it. To me, that merely means putting it into context. . . .

"Using Greenpeace, I want to get the kids involved in debating when or if it's right to break a law in order to point out a wrong law. By leading them in almost a Socratic manner of questioning, you'll get them to see both sides, and they'll have to *think.* It's good to leave something for the audience to do. That applies to kids' television, and it ought to apply to adult television. I really don't believe we ought to be in the business of supplying answers. We ought to be in the business of supplying the right questions."

And Fred Rogers feels that children—like adults—recognize, respect, and are hungry for the truth. "Every one of us longs to be in touch with honesty," Rogers says. "I think we're really attracted to people who will share some of their real self with us."

So here is some honesty from my real self: when it comes to letting my children watch television, I am fairly flexible. As they've gotten older, they've inherited certain TV freedoms—not the least of which is to make their own viewing choices, at least within reason. Saturday morning, for example, is theirs to do with what they will. I may not approve of every selection they make, but I remember how much I loved sneaking downstairs early on Saturday mornings, turning the TV dial, and enjoying a giddy sense of video independence. Dinnertime TV viewing is out, as a rule. But on weekdays, they can watch after-school shows of their choosing—if and when their homework is complete—and are allowed to request that tapes be made of shows broadcast after their bedtime. (This particular technological innovation serves two wonderful parental functions. First, it obliterates the basis for any frantic pleas of "just-one-more-TV-show-before-bed." Second, it allows us, as parents, to prescreen those particular programs and decide whether they're appropriate for the kids to watch. With some series, it's a case-by-case toss-up.)

One thing I've found is that, even with so many broadcast and cable channels from which to choose, the kids often will opt to watch a tape or videodisc from their own collection—or, just as often, elect not to watch at all. Another thing I've found is this: The best way to ensure my kids are getting the most, and the best, from television is, whenever possible, to watch it with them.

This doesn't mean parents have to sit there, like prison guards, forcing their children to watch quality family programs in which they have no interest. But if parents choose their opportunities wisely, watching TV as a family can be a rewarding and enriching experience for all involved. The *Anne of Green Gables* miniseries is one such example; another is the more recent PBS special *Math . . . Who Needs It?!*, showcasing the teaching style of Jaime Escalante, the teacher played by Edward James Olmos in *Stand and Deliver*. At one point in the special, Escalante showed his students— and the viewers—a shortcut method for multiplying double-digit numbers by eleven. Escalante's trick was so amazingly easy that my daughter caught on immediately and spent much of that night's dinnertime begging for more questions and solving problems like "What's sixty-three times eleven?" in her head, almost as fast as I could ask them.

Had I not steered her toward that show, and watched it with her, I wouldn't have known the trick—*or* that she was intrigued by it. Conversely, if we're watching a TV show together and it contains words or actions we as parents don't like, we can discuss those things as a family—as they are happening on TV, or after the show is over. This goes for special effects (explaining the difference between pretend and reality), violence, language, and all sorts of questionable behavior.

Bill Cosby, who hosted the *Math . . . Who Needs It?!* special, has some very definite ideas about television's potential to influence, and about parents being an important part of the equation. "These shows, when parents are watching with their children, *can* teach," Cosby says, referring to such educational programs as *Sesame Street* and *Electric Company*, "just as I believe that kids are influenced by guys with guns on TV, and by people who show no respect or appreciation for the rules and laws of society."

Writing in *Parents* magazine in 1991, Cosby noted, "One of the biggest complaints parents have about television is that current moral standards on TV often conflict with traditional family criteria. . . . Parents should not be passive. For example, if you find that your kids are exposed to cusswords on television that you ordinarily ban from your household, you should see this as an opportunity to talk with your children about the meaning and use of these words. When these unsavory sounds suddenly became audible in the Cosby household, Camille and I were able to explain to that child that cussing and the repetitive use of curse words clearly demonstrate a very limited vocabulary."

Cosby has been singularly sensitive to the messages *The Cosby Show* sends out each week, and runs them past psychologists and other experts to ensure that his programs present positive themes and role models. "If you treat old people in a negative fashion," Cosby says, "and have them always seen as people who can't remember, and are knocked back by the younger ones, and see kids who are putting the parents down just for a joke, you've giving kids the wrong picture. . . . If one kid out of a million is watching a program and decides that it's great to go out and do some drugs or whatever because some favorite program says it's okay, then clearly, it is the fault of the media for allowing that to come about."

This gets into a touchy area of argument: the differing philosophies of *The Cosby Show* and *The Simpsons*, two series immensely popular with viewers of all ages. Not only do these two programs fight between themselves to attract viewers on Thursday nights (a battle usually won by *The Cosby Show*), but they fight with almost totally different weapons. *The Cosby Show* champions family unity; *The Simpsons* favors general anarchy. The makers of *The Cosby Show* acknowledge and embrace the responsibility of shaping young minds; the makers of *The Simpsons* deny and reject it. Yet as a TV critic and a parent, I enjoy and defend both shows, and feel both shows demonstrated artistry and uniqueness from the very start.

In the very first episode of *The Cosby Show* in 1984, Cosby's Cliff Huxtable had a heart-to-heart talk with son Theo, played by Malcolm-Jamal Warner. Theo had brought home a poor report card, but defended himself on the grounds that he did not need good grades to work in a service station or at some other "regular job," and that his father should love and accept him no matter *what* grades he got in school. It was a heartfelt, liberal speech, echoing the style and sentiments of such Norman Lear sitcoms as *One Day at a Time*. The studio audience, accustomed to similar speeches and "Son Knows Best" attitudes from other sitcoms of the time, warmly applauded Theo's remark.

Then Cosby, with impeccable delivery, said, "That's the dumbest thing I've ever heard in my *life!* It's no *wonder* you get D's in everything!" The response from the crowd, and from viewers at home, was almost cathartic. It was an adult taking charge on the tube again, going against the grain of the previous few years of TV comedies and dramas. *The Cosby Show* not only revived the sitcom, but restored respect to TV's authority figures.

Five years later, when Matt Groening's animated Simpsons characters were spun off from *The Tracey Ullman Show* into their own 1989 Christmas special, *Simpsons Roasting on an Open Fire*, that show, too, went against the

grain. Like *The Cosby Show*, it revived a genre—in this case, animation—
that had been pronounced dead in prime time. Unlike *The Cosby Show*, it
didn't respect authority figures, but openly ridiculed them. From the moment in that holiday special when Bart Simpson shattered the uniformity
of the school choir's rendition of "Jingle Bells"—by substituting the lyrics
"Jingle bells, Batman smells, Robin lays an egg"—he was speaking, if not
singing, to a new TV generation. Bart was such a troublemaker that the
principal's office had an entire file drawer marked "Simpson, Bart," and
such a scholastic slacker that his motto, quickly immortalized on T-shirts,
was "Underachiever . . . and proud of it."

"When I read that critics laud Bart and *The Simpsons* because the show
has a certain edge to it," Cosby says, "my belief is, there's an irresponsibility
to lauding something that—," and Cosby stops for a moment to focus his
argument.

"When I looked at Bart spitting, and telling his father and mother
things that are really antisocial things, people said, 'Now *this* is a real family,
let us watch *this.*' . . . What really was happening, which is what the critics
should have noticed, is: here is a show with an antisocial character.

"This is not a negative—I'm not saying, 'Don't watch the show.' But
when you look at Bart, and the questions that went out about why so
many lower socioeconomic kids were watching, and wearing Bart Simpson
T-shirts, clearly it was because kids saw Bart as a person who had no
control over what he was going to become, or who he is in relation to his
community and to his family. He was a fellow who wasn't doing well. And
in not doing well, Bart's behavior became something where he *attacked*. He
clearly had given up."

According to Cosby, Bart Simpson exhibits the classic classroom problems and hostile behaviors of a child with a disability, what Cosby calls "a
learning difference." *The Simpsons*, in Cosby's view, should be showing the
system trying to help him, rather than showing him continuing to oppose
the system.

Cosby explored this exact territory several seasons into *The Cosby Show*,
when Theo, the perpetually struggling student, was diagnosed as having
dyslexia. Instead of reacting with horror, the Huxtable parents cheered,
because the source of their son's scholastic difficulties had been identified,
and they and Theo could begin to combat it. According to NBC, that
episode prompted more reaction from scholastic and public-interest
groups than any program in *The Cosby Show*'s history—and Cosby wasn't
through yet.

By 1991, Theo had dealt with his difficulty to the point where he was
now working his way through college, interning as a counselor at a local
community center. This not only allowed *The Cosby Show* to present a positive example of working for the local community, but also allowed Theo,
in his new role as authority figure, to identify a problem child at the center
as a possible dyslexic. The character of that youngster was partly inspired,

Cosby says, by a real-life backstage meeting he'd had with a thirteen-year-old boy one day at the urging of a concerned parent.

By asking the right questions—some of the ones Theo asks in the show—Cosby began to suspect the boy's antisocial attitudes might stem in part from a learning disability, and suggested he be tested. According to Cosby, the reluctant student in the final *Cosby Show* script was based partly on that boy, and partly on Bart Simpson. The goal of the show, Cosby says, was to show how informed and caring teachers could begin to help those whom he calls "Bart-inized kids."

Cosby charges many public school systems, even in major cities, with continuing to treat learning disabilities as "some sort of smallpox epidemic," separating the students into "special" classes. "They still refer to people as slow, medium—they treat them like hot sauce," Cosby says. Some universities and teachers, he says, are "very, very proud to deal with people who are dyslexic," while others "feel they don't have the time to stop their train and go back and figure, 'Yes, this is something that I should know about.' " Even Cosby's writers had to be educated, he said, and prevented from making easy or uninformed jokes about the subject—a battle he wages on many different episode topics. "Something can go awry if the person writing the comedy only cares about the joke," Cosby says. "They don't want to do the research. It's like, 'Don't bother me with the facts, because you're going to ruin my jokes.' I've had so many problems with writers who refused to call an agency to get the facts."

One of the agencies Cosby instructed his writers to call for that dyslexia episode of *The Cosby Show* was Landmark College, where Carolyn Olivier is director of admissions. "I had a lot to do with helping the writers figure out how that kid was going to behave in that classroom," she says of the youngster in Theo's class. Scripts were faxed back and forth, changes were suggested, and alterations were made in the child's behavior to make it more consistent with the behavior of actual learning-disabled children.

"In one early script, they had him reading a passage out loud in front of the class," Olivier says, calling it a classic mistake. "Never in the world would a dyslexic kid agree to read out loud in front of his schoolmates. There's nothing a dyslexic kid hates more than to read out loud in front of his peers." The effort put into the final two-part episode, incorporating many of the suggestions from Olivier and other experts, impressed her immensely. "Dr. Cosby's incredible passion for the truth—you have to respect it," she says. She also respects the power of television.

"We have the largest collection of specialized materials on learning disabilities and dyslexia," Olivier says of Landmark College, "and it's 98 percent inaccessible to the entire learning-disabled population because it's in *books*. We have the most learned writers and thinkers on the subject writing in a medium that's inaccessible to the people who *need* access to it. So when someone like Bill Cosby takes those ideas and communicates them in a visual, multisensory way, it's the most universal way of communicating with them. I have had students say to me, when Theo was diagnosed as dyslexic, they and their family realized *they* were dyslexic. It wasn't until they saw it on television, and felt its truth, that they recognized it in their own family."

A final note on the subject—one that might surprise even Cosby: when the thirteen-year-old boy Cosby met that day finally *was* tested for learning disabilities, it was at Landmark, a few months after the two-part *Cosby Show* episode had been broadcast. He had not seen or heard about the show, but Landmark had a copy and showed it to the youngster, without comment, before his tests had been analyzed.

"He sat glued to the TV," Olivier says, "and he said, 'I'm dyslexic. That is *me* on the show. I *know* that is my problem. I am *dyslexic!*' He had no problem saying it," Olivier adds, "and he wanted to watch it a second time." Such reactions have convinced her of TV's power—and what she sees as its calling. "If I were speaking to these people who write TV shows," she says, "I would want to just say this: you have the most wonderful tool at your fingertips, an audience in every family in the United States. . . . That gift, to me, imposes a sense of responsibility to be deliberate and careful about everything you put on television. . . . TV is a far more impressionable teacher than many teachers in the classroom are."

So how does James L. Brooks, executive producer of *The Simpsons,* react to all of this? Informed of Cosby's genuine and specific concerns about Bart Simpson's antisocial attitude and the messages it sends, Brooks replied in kind—that is to say, very seriously and specifically.

"I think it's very dangerous," Brooks says, "to focus on television characters as role models. You know, it's so nakedly anti-art and pro-propaganda. My role model may not be somebody else's role model, so to say I'm doing a series to create role models for the society that will witness it is, to me, very dangerous terrain. I guess I'd rather risk irresponsibility more than smugness. . . .

"I think *my* idea of Bart Simpson is—it depends on which episode you're watching. I mean, the kid has good weeks and he has bad weeks. To me, that's the *truth* of it, if we get into that."

To Brooks, the pressure to make Bart "behave" is something like the pressure he felt, and fought, when he wrote *Room 222,* a 1969–74 drama series set in an inner-city high school. *Room 222* was one of the first weekly dramas (after, ironically, Cosby's *I Spy*) to feature black actors in starring roles, and the relative rarity of other leading roles for blacks on television put added pressure on the show's writers to ennoble those characters.

"I felt then, too," Brooks says, "if you have a sense of responsibility, and you care about your work, you're writing *your* characters. . . . I remember, back *then,* I resisted the tendency for every character in the show to be a superperson." It was the same, Brooks says, when feminists attacked *The Mary Tyler Moore Show* because Mary Richards addressed Lou Grant as *Mr.* Grant—which, he argues, was totally true to her character:

"I thought it was preposterous that they missed the point. . . . We had no responsibility to womankind. You can't write a character that represents womankind. I've felt it was so obvious that I didn't understand the argument from any other side—except to think of entertainment television as propaganda, which I refuse to do. What *I* think is, the job, when you have some control over a television show, is to use that control to make sure that the *show* controls itself, and that you slap all the other hands off the wheel."

The idea of a TV character as role model is something Brooks either laughs at or rejects outright. Yet Linda Ellerbee, when serving as guest host on *Later with Bob Costas* and interviewing *Murphy Brown* creator Diane English, told English that, in some way, the fictional Murphy's stay at the Betty Ford Center helped Ellerbee face and seek treatment for her own problems with alcohol. "It gave me courage," Ellerbee told English, "in the way that, years ago, when Mary Tyler Moore slept with a man on *her* TV series, you knew at that moment that if Mary did it, it was okay for unmarried people to have sex in America." When that comment is repeated to him, Brooks laughs and says, "I've got a hunch Linda Ellerbee might have had sex before *The Mary Tyler Moore Show.*"

To observe how strongly Brooks believes "role model" concerns and outside intervention are improper when it comes to television, you need only look at the second-season episode of *The Simpsons,* in which Marge Simpson launches a one-woman campaign against her children's favorite cartoon program, "The Itchy and Scratchy Show." Itchy and Scratchy, like the "real" cartoon adversaries Tom and Jerry, engage in violent games of cat and mouse, and Bart, Lisa, and baby Maggie watch their animated adventures with wide-eyed delight. One day, when Homer is down in the basement trying gamely to build a spice rack for Marge, baby Maggie sneaks up behind him, grabs a giant hammer, and strikes him repeatedly with it. (In a terrific example of a teleliterate reference, the entire sequence is presented as in Alfred Hitchcock's *Psycho,* complete with Bernard Herrmann's screeching violins, a can of red paint spilling down the basement drain, and a camera zoom-out starting with a close-up of Homer's eye and ending with an overhead view of Maggie's "victim.")

"Where would an innocent child get the idea to attack her father with a mallet?" Marge asks, then looks at the TV and sees Itchy and Scratchy going at each other with giant hammers. In the next scene, she's watching "Itchy and Scratchy" with pencil in hand—"I'm cataloging the violence in these cartoons," she tells Homer, who's lying on the couch with his head bandaged. Before long, she's sending off admonishing letters to the show's creators and sponsors, beginning with the salutation, "Dear Purveyors of Senseless Violence."

Marge soon finds herself a media sensation—like the real-life Terry Rakolta, a housewife who became nationally known after writing letters of protest regarding the raw humor in *Married . . . with Children* (like *The Simpsons,* a series from the upstart Fox network). Marge agrees to be a guest on "Smartline," a local version (and cartoon spoof) of *Nightline,* where anchor Kent Brockman opens the show by saying, "Are cartoons too violent for children? Most people would say, 'No, of course not, what kind of *stupid* question is that?' But one woman would say yes, and she's with us tonight. . . ."

Marge loses the TV battle that night, but wins the war: her protest gains steam and supporters, and the producers of "Itchy and Scratchy" finally enlist her input in writing the cartoon's storyline. Following Marge's guidelines, the "new" Itchy and Scratchy get along, share a pitcher of lemonade, and proclaim their friendship for one another. "Itchy and Scratchy seem to have lost their edge," Lisa notes sadly, so the Simpson children switch off their TVs in disgust and head outside—as do, in unison, all other children in the neighborhood. To the sounds of Beethoven's Symphony No. 6 (the *Pastorale*), they play and interact in an idyllic manner outside, and use good manners and clear their dinner plates at home.

All seems well with the world—at least until Michelangelo's David is scheduled to be exhibited at the local museum, and the town mothers come to Marge and ask her to spearhead a campaign against that work of "filth." Marge, though, thinks the statue is a beautiful work of art, and refuses to take part ("I *told* you she was soft on full frontal nudity," one woman scowls). This puts Marge back in the "Smartline" hot seat, where she's asked, "How can you be for *one* form of freedom of expression and against *another*?" She agrees that she can't—which is too bad, she adds, because she really *hates* those cartoons.

The idea of a cartoon character protesting against *other* cartoon characters is as wickedly warped as the episode's tongue-in-cheek utopian display of a world without television. Yet everything Marge, Bart, and everyone else did in that episode of *The Simpsons* was totally true to his or her character—just as another episode, in which Bart has to pass a Colonial history exam or repeat the fourth grade, remains true to its characters and sensibilities. It also presents evidence that *The Simpsons* and *The Cosby Show* may have more in common than Cosby and Brooks suspect.

In this "Bart Gets an F" episode, Bart does everything he can to avoid studying (including, at one point, taking a break to watch some "Itchy and Scratchy" cartoons), but finally bears down and studies all night. "The little tiger tries so hard," Marge whispers to Homer, peeking in at their son. "Why does he keep failing?" Homer replies, "Just a little dim, I guess." At a family conference at the school, Bart is described as being an "underachiever" and "proud of it"—yet Bart's reply, when asked why he does so poorly in class, hints at a less secure level of self-esteem.

"I am *dumb*, okay?" he blurts out. "Dumb as a post. Think I'm *happy* about it?" Bart works hard, takes the history test, waits eagerly for his grade—and when his teacher says casually, "It's a 59; that's another F," Bart Simpson bursts into tears right there in the classroom. "I'd think you'd be used to failing by now," his teacher says, but Bart continues to sob. "You don't understand," he tells her. "I really tried. It's as good as I can do, and I *still* failed." Bart's teacher is surprised by his emotional outburst, and stunned when she hears him moan, "Now I know how

George Washington felt when he surrendered Fort Necessity to the French in 1754." Impressed, the teacher tells Bart his comment demonstrates "applied knowledge," so she adds one point to his grade—passing him with a D.

Because Bart's character has been so credible and consistent for so long, and because his failure at the end is so unexpected, his tears are truly touching. This episode of *The Simpsons*, like the very first episode of *The Cosby Show*, was well-written enough to play against expectations—one thing the two series have in common.

And if you look closely at Bart's actions and comments in the "Bart Gets an F" episode, Cosby's analysis of Bart Simpson as an antisocial kid with a learning disability looks right on the money. Cosby feels Bart's family and teachers should recognize this, get help, and turn Bart's life and attitude around, so Bart could serve as a positive role model. Brooks, on the other hand, doesn't believe in character alteration for the sake of a role model, and may well feel that if that particular plot line were pursued, Bart Simpson, like Itchy and Scratchy, would lose his edge.

I appreciate both sides of the argument—and, thank goodness, have neither the need nor desire to choose between them. I can, and do, enjoy and support *The Cosby Show* because its values and plots are so positive and responsible, just as I can, and do, enjoy and support *The Simpsons* because its values and plots are so skewed and irreverent. I agree with Cosby that television can serve a higher purpose and help to influence viewers—but also agree with Brooks that it doesn't always *have* to. I'm comfortable letting my children watch *The Cosby Show* unaccompanied, but I make a point to be with them the first time they see each *Simpsons* episode, so I can let them know I disapprove of certain actions, attitudes, and lines of dialog, while approving of the series as a whole. Does this make *The Cosby Show* better than *The Simpsons*? No—just different. And one of the wonderful things about television is that it need not—make that *must* not—be monolithic.

"Let's stop this right here for a second," says Mark Dawidziak. "We're at a point where criticism of television—and I mean criticism with a capital 'C,' including the greater social context—has gotten a little ridiculous. It's at a point where characters and writers and plots, and everything that's on television, has to meet some kind of 'social acceptability' level."

He refers, once again, to the idea of Dickens and Twain writing for TV. Would Fagin be objected to because he abuses and exploits young men? Would Huck Finn have to display a willingness to advance his education? "Literature's allowed to be reflective of society. . . . *Oliver Twist* presents a reality—a very gritty, ugly reality—of the Victorian times. Now, would people up and say, 'Listen, you can't show that on television because you have to show another side' or 'There has to be balance'? Yet we see this done on television all the time, particularly in shows about minorities. . . .

"Cosby *himself* came under this fire, that *The Cosby Show* had to be reflective of *all* black experience," Dawidziak notes. "Now who could live up to *that*? Do we ask that white shows be reflective of all *white* experience? We never have. And the rap against *Cosby* from the start was, 'Well, this isn't realistic. It's not the way a black family lives.' There are two easy answers to that. Number one, it's not reflective of how *many* people live. Neither was *The Danny Thomas Show.* And the second answer is, Cosby was basing that show on his comedy routines, which were drawn from his own life. So it was reflective of at least *one* black American, and that was Cosby, and that's all it *needed* to be. . . . Now apply that to *The Simpsons.* All of a sudden, Bart has to be a role model for every child out there. Why? Why can't Bart be reflective of children out there? To say that Bart doesn't represent the reality that's out there is just closing your eyes."

Cosby, though, thinks TV is selective in what it reflects—and, for adults as well as children, not concerned enough about the messages it relays.

"If we go and put these messages out, like the one about the dyslexic kid," Cosby says, "we are put down because we're doing Don Quixote, and being self-righteous and idealistic, and society is not like this. Well, that's exactly *why* we're doing it, because society is *not* like this. And if *The Cosby Show* is idealistic, my defense is, what is more idealistic than looking at *Murphy Brown* and looking at a newsroom where they're not dealing with African-American issues and Asian-American issues? And *this* is a great show?"

Cosby points with pride to the many ethnic groups represented as regulars and guests on *The Cosby Show*—and points with anger to *All in the Family,* which he feels squandered a great opportunity to improve race relations through television. "Archie never said he was sorry," Cosby says flatly. And though Cosby is fully aware of the satiric side of Archie Bunker's character, he's also aware some viewers failed to get the joke—laughing with Archie's racial epithets, not at them. "What can you say?" Cosby says of Archie Bunker as role model. "If you don't tell people that this guy needed some *help!* . . . And year after year, the jokes continued to flow. Yes, there was another viewpoint on the show, but that kind of flip-flopped so my man could get on with what he was doing."

Others have a different, higher opinion of that series, its messages, and its effectiveness. "I thought *All in the Family* was very high art, and more," says Ellerbee. "There was a series that used words as a mirror on ourselves, one that made us look at our attitudes. That was as educational a series as I've ever seen in comedy on television. You know, when you want to change someone's mind, you don't do it by bullying them, you don't do it by yelling at them, and you don't do it by telling them they're wrong and you're right. You do it by walking across over to where *they* are, standing there, looking around, and saying, 'Yeah, now I see it from where you are.' That's what that show did. And in the course of doing it, it took us there. It gave us 'liberals' a much-needed walk inside the head of the Archie Bunkers of this world, to begin to see some understanding. And it gave the *Archie Bunkers* of this world a much-needed walk *outside* the head of Archie Bunker."

Lindsay Law credits *All in the Family* as a rare example of a TV show that altered "people's perception of things." And Brooks, once again, finds himself on the opposite side of the issue fence from Cosby. Brooks calls *All in the Family* more uniting than divisive, and even considers it optimistic.

"There were very literate observations about the life of anybody who's grown up in a lower-middle class background, as I did and a lot of other people did," Brooks says. "And you know, Archie's chair was an observation that nobody made in any other place—and I don't know *any* home of my class that didn't have that one reserved seat that was for the leader of the household. And it was so enormously hopeful, too, *All in the Family*, because you had sort of a narrow, bigoted, hardworking guy at the core, and you couldn't help loving him, and so it was unifying in that way, too."

My children haven't yet encountered *All in the Family* on reruns—but when they do, or shortly thereafter, I'll be there to talk seriously and pointedly to them about the show's language, undercurrents, and messages. I agree with Cosby that the wrong messages can be gleaned from Archie Bunker's rantings and racial slurs, but I also agree—again, with Cosby—that with proper guidance from parents, a lot of "questionable" TV can actually raise valuable questions.

"Parents must use television's positive *and* negative dimensions as a device to educate and uphold the best in social and family traditions," Cosby wrote in *Parents*. "Take an extra moment in the car, at the dinner table, or just sitting around the house to talk with your children—to share your values, to teach, and even to have some fun laughing and complaining together about the worst and best on TV." Great advice. And at my house, according to our values, both *The Cosby Show* and *The Simpsons* rank among TV's best.

The final word on this subject comes from one of family television's biggest stars and advocates, Fred Rogers. "There are certain things that I feel that television can do that other things can't," he says, "because of the widespread nature of it. But television doesn't bring only positive images. It also brings distorted, sordid images, and shows super-selfish ways of solving problems, and that bothers me. . . .

"I would much rather read a book than watch television, but I don't want to appear highfalutin about it. There's something superb about it, but no medium is going to be perfect, just like no person or family is going to be perfect—whatever 'perfect' means anyway."

16

TELEVISION AS A TEACHER

Having discussed the kinds of lessons television can and should teach when it strives to entertain, I would like to shift the focus to the effectiveness of television when it's *overtly* trying to teach. I'm talking about educational TV—a phrase usually conjuring images of talking heads and boring discussions.

That's an unfair stereotype in several regards, not the least of which is that even when a TV show *is* a "talking heads" affair, it can be anything but boring: Fred Friendly's *The Other Side of the News* seminars and Bill Moyers's *World of Ideas* programs are proof enough of that. However, educational TV is not relegated merely to "talking heads," or to PBS, or even to broadcast TV. For children and young adults, educational TV exists in *and* out of the classroom. For adults, educational TV—in the truest sense of the word—is a way for those who are long out of college, or who never got that far, to keep learning. Television can be, and often is, the most effective and important "adult-education class" in the nation. People talk all the time about television's reach—about the scores of millions of viewers it attracts—but seldom mention its touch.

Yet TV, by informing and elucidating as well as entertaining, is "touching" viewers all the time. All those who moan and groan about the national decline in our high school students' scores on the Scholastic Aptitude Test are quick to point to television as part of the problem—if not the outright, evil cause. Our society puts so little value on the quality of our children's education that school resources and teacher salaries are woefully underfunded, classrooms are overcrowded, and schools have as little true accountability as politicians—maybe even less. Yet these are seen as incidental factors, not root causes, to those who would rather blame the "boob tube" for America's educational ills. (Perhaps anyone looking at standardized college entrance exam scores ought to look less closely at the overall score than at those students who score in the bottom twenty percent. Why? Because forty percent of *them* end up as education majors.) The truth is, if America really wants to shape up its educational system, a proper use of television and its new technologies may be the best and fastest means to that end.

The "politically correct" stance on this issue is an unstable and often unfathomable one. In 1991, Donald Stewart, president of the National College Board, blamed the SAT score decline on "too much TV, too many videos, a decreased amount of time spent reading." George Bush, our self-appointed Education President, visited two Maine schools the same year, accompanied by First Lady Barbara Bush. To reporters chronicling that visit, the president said he was convinced "the excesses" of television "are having a bad effect on our children and family stability and learning." His own grandchildren, he complained, "watch stuff that has no redeeming social value," and he advised parents, "Don't make the mistake of thinking your kids only learn from 9 a.m. to 3 p.m."

Looking at it from the opposite side, that's *my* point, too. Thanks to television, children can and *do* learn from TV, in and out of class. What they learn depends upon what they watch, and how the TV is used. It's just as true for adults—and it's a truth that, on occasion, is even admitted. Barbara Bush, for whom literacy is a pet cause, has said, "When a good TV show makes you want to find out more, find it in a book. TV and books work together to really take you places." Paradoxically, George Bush, three months before making that anti-TV speech in Maine, made a pro-TV speech saluting public television for its regular and in-classroom broadcasts. "You push everyone in the industry to do more, to do better," Bush told the PBS broadcasters. "For years your efforts . . . have promoted respect for learning and an appetite for education." As part of a presentation honoring Rae Ellen McKee, 1991's Teacher of the Year, Bush announced the donation of . . . a satellite dish, so that McKee's West Virginia remedial-reading class, and her school, could have access to public television's offerings during the day.

Some people are hard-liners, seeing any use of television in—or by—the classroom as a bad thing. "For most teachers," Marie Winn wrote in *The Plug-in Drug*, "assigning TV viewing for homework is not a maneuver taken lightly to slough off on their duties; it is an act of true desperation." (Assigning *The Civil War*, as did many teachers across America, was an act of desperation?) As for TV *inside* the classroom, Winn wrote, "With school remaining the last bastion of the printed word and the last chance of ensuring its survival, any movement of the education establishment away from this single, all-important goal must be seen as unprofitable and even dangerous."

Shelley Duvall disagrees strongly—very strongly—with that assessment. "Television, combined with the computer, is the most powerful educational tool that we have," she says. "It's a matter of the people in the industry utilizing it. Schools should be wired with cable, they should be armed with television sets and computers and VCRs that all should be integrated—and all of this is occurring right now, as we speak. . . . You can watch what you want to watch when you want to watch it." Responding to the charge that teachers who use TV are lazy or desperate, Duvall says, "I don't think so at all. I think that's totally wrong. I think they're enlightening their students—depending on what they show them. It all depends on the programs. As Shakespeare said, the play's the thing."

Linda Bloodworth-Thomason, true to her roots as a high school English teacher, phoned her brother to unofficially "assign" *The Civil War* to her nieces and nephews (who ranged in age from ten to fourteen). "I knew they would love it, and they did. They knew nothing about the Civil War, and they came away with a real feeling about it. It's a feeling I don't think they could have gotten from a book."

Timothy Brittell, who still *is* a high school teacher, *officially* assigned *The Civil War* to his social studies students—and, instead of just using the study guides provided by the series' underwriter (General Motors), Brittell wrote his own, adapting the information provided in and by the program for his own classroom purposes. For his students, *The Civil War* was used as a supplement to the text—but Brittell beams about such TV intangibles as the infectious enthusiasm of author Shelby Foote, a prominent expert showcased in *The Civil War*. "He's got to be one of the best historians there is," Brittell says.

When using TV in the classroom, Brittell is resourceful, but hardly indiscriminate. He used some of the concentration-camp scenes from ABC's *War and Remembrance* miniseries because they were such powerful reenactments, yet "got rid of all the hokey love-story crap." And after watching a teacher divide his students into arbitrary prejudicial groups in an old ABC drama called *The Wave*, Brittell adapted the idea for his own purposes—and taught constitutional rights by turning his classroom into a rigid totalitarian state.

In the nineties, teachers need not work that hard to bring TV into the school. Broadcasters, cable companies, and independent contractors are lining up, and elbowing one another, to work their way inside. Public television has the overwhelming and well-deserved edge in this department, with classroom programming and services reaching, at the start of 1992, nearly ten-thousand schools. Compare that to the approximately six-thousand schools participating in Whittle Communications' controversial Channel One service, which provides free video equipment if its daily newscast is relayed to students. If it sounds too good to be true, it is. The catch? The Channel One newscast, which was launched in 1990, is advertiser-supported, which means ads are being channeled—literally—to a captive and vulnerable audience.

"It's a twelve-minute program, and one-quarter of that is commercials," complains Brittell, whose school is receiving Whittle's newscast (actually, the ratio is slightly less: two minutes of ads in each twelve-minute show). "My students hate it." The exchange for free video equipment is contingent upon the school's broadcasting Channel One for a minimum of three years, but Brittell tells stories—without placing them for certain at his own school or state—of teachers who have disconnected the sets regardless, or switched to PBS and CNN during the Gulf War or any other period of breaking news. "I can tell you," he says, "Channel One is not being turned on in many classrooms. There are teachers who flat-out don't turn it on."

Not everyone is as opposed to the conditions attached by Channel One. *NBC Nightly News* anchor Tom Brokaw, for example, defended the service in 1991 by saying:

> The idea that somehow we're going to corrupt these children by showing them commercials in the classroom astonishes me. They're bombarded by these commercials in all other parts of their lives. They're hip. They know how to sort it out. . . . Almost anything that can stimulate kids' interest in public affairs and raise their consciousness about news is a good idea."

Yet Brittell's biggest complaint is that the Channel One newscast, with its forced entry into many classrooms, has an unwelcome monopoly of sorts. "Part of the honesty of the media comes from the competition," he says. "What do they have to keep them honest?"

There is, however, an awful lot of competition when it comes to TV in the classroom. It is by no means a totally altruistic endeavor: every program supplier, including PBS, has hopes of fostering audience awareness and viewer loyalty at a young age, and can see potential profit in the widespread rights fees attached to duplication or dissemination of specific products. The wealth of opportunity exists, however, for the teacher as well.

A consortium called Cable in the Classroom, providing curriculum-based support materials and special copyright clearances for classroom duplication and replay, presents programs without commercials—appropriate offerings from such participating networks as Arts & Entertainment, Black Entertainment Television, Bravo, C-SPAN, CNN, The Discovery Channel, HBO, The Learning Channel, Showtime, and nearly a dozen others. PBS provides teacher guides, student worksheets, and/or posters for classroom use with *National Geographic Specials, Nova, Reading Rainbow, Square One TV, The American Experience,* and many others—and recently joined forces officially with Cable in the Classroom. Arts & Entertainment goes so far as to hold national competitions, awarding teachers who most creatively integrate A&E programs into their lesson plans. The 1991 first-prize winner, Richard N. Lord, Jr., of Maine's Presque Isle High School, revolved his lesson plan around A&E's docudrama *The Race for the Double Helix,* a detailed and captivating story about DNA research. Students built their own double helix models and held a mock community meeting to vote on whether or not a genetic laboratory would be welcome in their own neighborhood.

The real advances in classroom TV, however, are in the mind-boggling possibilities provided by interactive multimedia—televisions, computers, and videodiscs all working to save, store, and retrieve related information upon demand. The format descriptions and acronyms alone are enough to lead to sensory overload (this is where I could, but won't, launch into definitions of such terms as CD-I, CDTV, DVI, CD-ROM, and NeXT), but the results are astounding. The current generation of TV users, armed with VCRs and videodisc players, is lucky enough to entertain and educate itself by watching, renting, or buying whatever programs it desires. The next generation—the one starting now—inherits even more power and control, and gets to blaze its own trail through an information bank more accessible and voluminous than ever before.

Imagine a student sitting down at a computer to study American history, assigned to learn more about a specific subject or period. By entering his or her requests into the computer, the student can blaze a trail through the available information. Want to hear the popular songs of the time, or get a list or printout of the most popular literature? No problem. Encounter an unfamiliar name, and want to read a biography of that person? Here it is, with cross-indexed suggestions for further study. Want to see photographs of a particular general or battle, and compare them to paintings of the same subjects? Go ahead. Want to hear Harry S Truman's voice, or see Neil Armstrong walk on the moon? Do it. With the right equipment, nothing's stopping you.

One such interactive multimedia program, created for Apple's Macintosh computer, is devoted to Pablo Picasso's epic canvas *Guernica*. The painting itself is shown on the screen, and the computer user can either call up supplementary materials related to the painting or hone in on portions of the painting itself. A quintet of art critics can be heard—and seen—providing analysis of Picasso's work. The history of the Spanish Civil War is available to be tapped into by curious students, as is a representative roster of paintings from Picasso's contemporaries. Isolating a portion of the *Guernica* canvas leads to suggested interpretations of each element, as well as other related information. "The point is to find your own paths within," Robert Abel, the program's codeveloper, told *Newsweek*. "You get turned on to different ways of learning. We're trying to create giant superhighways to education, because right now, the roads look pretty washed out."

It's an almost endlessly digressive exercise, and is only as thorough and intriguing as the programmers are capable of making it. In fact, what is most crucial at this early stage in the development of interactive multimedia is the establishment of strong alliances between the programmers designing the software and the educators and experts most adept at illuminating and condensing their chosen subjects. Teachers will never be replaced by the new media, but the new media ought to make strong use of the best teachers. Think of what Shelby Foote did in the TV documentary *The Civil War*, or Jaime Escalante did in *Futures*, and imagine how their enthusiasm and knowledge could translate into a sprawling, challenging, and rewarding road map of possibilities. With the right programmers and educators working in tandem, multimedia packages could work wonders.

As a way to tap into a student's natural inclinations and interests, and allow his or her curiosities to be sparked and rewarded, interactive multimedia isn't just the wave of the future. It's the tsunami.

Interactive multimedia technology is something teachers should cheer, not fear. It's not a threat, merely another classroom tool. Yet as tools go, it's anything but cheap, and many of the school systems convinced of the potential of this new technology simply cannot afford it. Indeed, though the technology seems twenty years ahead, the level of funding for most school audiovisual departments is where it was twenty years ago—back when an audiovisual "department" often consisted of nothing more than an overhead projector and a slide carousel. And even if funding can be amassed from public or private sources, other considerations and obstacles exist. Many schools do (and should) place a higher priority on reducing class size, improving classroom conditions, and funneling more funds toward teachers and textbooks.

Once those needs are met, however, interactive multimedia should be high on the agenda. Students are ready and eager to work with and learn from them, even if some of their teachers are not. Brittell tells a story about students in his school who have access to a new, ten-thousand-dollar set of thirty-two videodiscs from CBS, allowing rapid perusal of decades' worth of *CBS Evening News* reports. The index could be better, Brittell says, but the students maneuver through it freely and eagerly—more so, he says, than most of the librarians and teachers.

Ernest L. Boyer wrote in 1988, "Today, self-study can be more enjoyable and materials more accessible, and learning can proceed at a far more rapid pace. Educators would be naive to ignore these influences, which have become, in effect, a new curriculum." Boyer's "today" is already yesterday: he was discussing instructional classroom television and videocassettes, which have started to be complemented, if not displaced, by today's "today" of interactive multimedia. Schools with sophisticated computer and video technology enjoy an edge over those without, just as children in homes with VCRs and/or computers enjoy additional avenues in which to bring knowledge resources into the home.

Let's not kid ourselves here. Much of the time, kids with access to home computers are enjoying games, not *Guernica,* and a motivated child can learn and excel without any technologies more recent than the printing press. The point is to never underestimate the power of television—or computers or interactive multimedia—as a prime motivator. Charren is right when she surveys the current media landscape, in and out of the classroom, and says, "What we have today is a system that works much better if you have some money than for kids whose families don't. The advantages pile up for kids with money." But there's a flip side of that coin. Even at the poverty level, most families own and use a TV set, and have access, at least, to an entire world of information.

Small children can begin to learn the alphabet from *Sesame Street* and self-worth from *Mister Rogers' Neighborhood,* while youngsters can pick up math concepts from *Square One TV* and geography concepts from *Where in the World Is Carmen Sandiego?* Adults, even those who cannot read, can gain a workable general knowledge of current events by watching the national news. They can entertain more than one side of an issue by listening to the dialog on certain segments of *Donahue* and *The Oprah Winfrey Show*— or, in a slightly more sophisticated setting, on *The MacNeil/Lehrer NewsHour* or *Nightline*. And if they actively strive to educate themselves by seeking out the best TV has to offer, the rewards are limitless. All work and no play would make TV a dull medium, but when television sets out to inform and educate, and succeeds mightily at that task, its true impact can be neither minimized nor measured.

Bill Moyers likes to quote Saul Bellow, who wrote: "The people who come to evening class are only ostensibly after culture. Their great need, their hunger, is for good sense, clarity, truth—even an atom of it. People are dying—it is no metaphor—for lack of something real when day is done." Moyers sees TV as a medium that can feed that hunger, and is convinced of "the role that television plays for those people who regard life itself as a continuing course in adult education." Moyers adds, "My ambition always was to be a teacher, and I think that is what, essentially, television has enabled me to do. It is the largest classroom in America."

James Burke, who has a teaching background as well as an educator's appetite for exhaustive research, intentionally tailors the content and narration of his science series to appeal to a mass audience. In England, Burke says, fewer people attend universities than in America, yet a large percentage of British TV viewers are eager to tune in programs that might teach them something.

"There's this bunch of interested people out there with no formal training in how to find things out," Burke says, "and those are my red meat. Those are the people that my mandate has been tailored to talk to. If the guys with degrees also happen to enjoy it, well, that's nice. . . . But above all, I think, the programs are made for people who have a natural curiosity for formal education." In such shows as *Connections* and *The Day the Universe Changed*, Burke hops from concept to concept like a one-man interactive-media machine, relying on the originality of his ideas, and the naturalness and enthusiasm of his narration, to keep viewers interested.

"I know my own speech patterns, and so I write in my own patterns," Burke says, revealing the simple secret of his on-camera ease. His years in front of the classroom trained him early in "trying to be articulate while being casual," and he's well aware of the importance of his narrative style and personal presence in getting, and keeping, people tuned to his programs. His idol in this regard, coincidentally, is another British documentarian: Sir David Attenborough.

"I wish I were like him. I think Attenborough is *the* supreme communicator on television worldwide today," Burke says. "He just comes through the camera. You sit down and he simply rivets you. I think it has something to do with what I take to be a sort of slightly diffident nature in which he does it. He doesn't talk to you as if he knows you are going to love it—he talks to you almost with a certain shyness, and I find that quite riveting. . . . He is my hero."

Of his own style of delivery, Attenborough says, "It would be dishonest of me to say, 'Oh, no, I don't do any acting.' You have to. . . ." But when he thumps on the ground to communicate with an underground mole rat, or picks up a hillside rock and shatters it in two to reveal the fossil within, Attenborough is acting as the world's most prominent and well-traveled nature guide. Whether speaking to us from deep within a termite mound or high above a rain forest, Attenborough brings nature—and an appreciation of it—into our living rooms.

It is my belief that television is largely responsible for the rise and strength of the environmental movement, animal-rights concerns, and improved zoo conditions. It used to be that the average American's contact with wild animals was limited largely to *National Geographic* magazine photos, visits to the local prisonlike zoo, and perhaps Walt Disney's highly staged nature films (which, shortly after the premiere of *Disneyland* in 1954, became TV staples as well). Then television moved in, taking millions of viewers on voyages to the bottom of the sea—courtesy of Jacques Cousteau, not Irwin Allen—and everywhere else, thanks to TV's *National Geographic Specials* and the efforts of Attenborough, *Nova, Nature,* and others. Thoreau's *Walden* and Rachel Carson's *The Silent Spring* deserve credit, of course, but so do documentary specials and even network newscasts that have brought us closer to endangered species, to natural beauty and disasters, and to a greater understanding of our world's creatures and ecosystems.

"There isn't any question," Attenborough says, "but that the public is now better informed about nature than it has been for centuries, and that the dangers that face the natural world have naturally been reflected far better." Attenborough, too, gives TV a good deal of credit for that, as well as for a change in the content of most modern zoos. "One hundred, even fifty years ago, 'zoos' meant the equivalent of elephants, a rhinoceros, a giraffe—preferably big, hairy stuff," Attenborough says, laughing. "But now we go to see butterflies, crabs, and colonies of ants. . . . The public is more sophisticated and more sensitive to perceived ecological requirements."

Attenborough's enthusiasm for educational TV has remained unabated for decades. As a BBC administrator, in fact, Attenborough commissioned 1970's *Civilisation,* the thirteen-part Kenneth Clark series examining Western art, architecture, and music from the seventh through nineteenth centuries. The ambitious, wide-ranging series not only predated (and led to) several similarly epic documentary series, but also proved so successful in America that a book based on the *Civilisation* scripts remained on the best-seller lists for the better part of a year.

"The BBC had an ethos and a drive," Attenborough says, almost wistfully. "We were not there to make money, and we *didn't* make money. We were there to use this new device, this new technology which had unparalleled access to the homes of a vast population, to convey all the ideas you thought society might want to hear or be interested in. It was our responsibility to say, 'What haven't we done and why aren't we doing it?' "

British documentaries continue, on average, to get more respect and viewers than their American counterparts, yet such programs as *The Civil War* are proud exceptions. Besides, before anyone falls into the trap of believing British viewers are so much more teleliterate and sophisticated than Americans, it should be noted that the three most popular programs in England, week in and week out, are not documentary specials or period costume dramas, but soap operas: *EastEnders, Coronation Street,* and *Neighbors,* in that order.

In America, as in England, well-intentioned and well-made educational television may not be the most popular form of TV, but it exists. And with a larger overall audience from which to draw, American documentaries deemed ratings "failures" often draw as many viewers as their "successful" British cousins. A case in point: ABC's *Our World,* the 1986–87 series thrown against NBC's top-rated *The Cosby Show.* Coanchored and cowritten by Linda Ellerbee and Ray Gandolf, each *Our World* segment looked at a particular period in time (usually a season) and analyzed it—relying on interviews, music, news, film clips, and anything else applicable to gain perspective about what it was like in the summer of 1969 or the fall of 1938. It was entertainment TV because it was entertaining TV. It was educational TV because it was loaded with facts, history, and commentary. And it was a "failure" because only six or seven million people watched it each week.

"In the best sense," Ellerbee says, "what you were able to do with *Our World* was to do quite a bit of teaching without people feeling as if they'd been taught. That was what was remarkable about that. That show you could enjoy on a number of different levels. It could be a memory show for you, if you had lived through that time and remembered it well—then you were touching the 'nostalgia' points inside you. . . . If you had not lived through that time, it was a first-class education, because it does what history books do not. It was a slice *through* the tree. 'This is what we were watching on television, these were the movies we were watching, here's the music we were listening to.' It was everything but what it *smells* like."

The impact of *Our World,* and of any educational or inspirational series on commercial or public television, should not be measured only in terms of audience size. Education and enlightenment, inspiration and change, seldom happens as a mass movement. Teachers reach students one at a time, at different points and for different reasons, and educational TV is the same. To measure the potential impact of TV as a teaching tool, don't read the Nielsen ratings. Listen to the viewers affected and inspired by specific television programs. The wide range of people reached, and the depth of their gratitude, is perhaps the truest test.

"If I could do a book on the number of men and women who came up to me over the years and said their lives had been empowered by something they had heard on public broadcasting," Moyers wrote in 1988, "it would be a very large volume. Ideas matter." Today, Moyers agrees that the audience for his programs is relatively small "compared to what the networks deliver," but adds that reaching two million viewers with an interview or a documentary is accomplishing something, and reaching some people, in a way that simply cannot be duplicated in print.

"That is why I used to get angry," Moyers says. "I got a reputation as a nag and a scold at CBS and elsewhere, but it is only because I know television's potential. How do I know its potential? It is not from speculating from afar. It is from reading, over the years, these thousands upon thousands of letters." The letters, he says, come from an encouragingly wide cross-section of society: "In fact," he says, "one of the great myths of our time is that public broadcasting only reaches the elite."

Moyers's 1980 series based on Dr. Mortimer Adler's *Six Great Ideas* prompted a letter to Adler that began:

> I am writing on behalf of a group of construction workers (mostly, believe it or not, plumbers!) who have finally found a teacher worth listening to. While we cannot all agree whether or not we would hire you as an apprentice, we can all agree that we would love to listen to you during our lunch breaks.
>
> I am sure it is just due to our well-known ignorance as tradesmen that not a single one of us had ever heard of you until one Sunday afternoon we were watching public television and Bill Moyers came on with *Six Great Ideas*. We listened intently and soon became addicted and have been ever since. We never knew a world of ideas existed.

It was no coincidence years later that Moyers, seeking a title for a new interview series, settled on the phrase *The World of Ideas*. He had seen a copy of that plumber's letter.

"I am aware that I lack eloquence to express the measure of my heart's gratitude," a housewife in Utah wrote Moyers after watching his *In Search of the Constitution* series. "I can say, however, that these programs are a landmark among my life's experiences. Among all the things I must teach my children, a healthy interest in understanding the Constitution now figures prominently." After *Joseph Campbell and the Power of Myth*, Moyers got a letter from a sheep farmer in Vermont, describing how the locals planned their evenings around the series. "Every Thursday night they would meet to discuss Campbell," Moyers says, "except on the fifth Thursday night they couldn't, because they had to shear their sheep."

A forty-six-year-old mother from Florida wrote Moyers to thank him for helping inspire her to change her life:

> Years ago your programs and interviews gave me insights and directions that I might never have discovered otherwise, being busy with growing children and the exigencies of daily life. I still have the printed transcripts of your interviews with Joseph Campbell and George Steiner.

Reading one source and subject always seemed to lead me on to others, and others beyond that. I began reading philosophy and history and literary theory. . . .

Yesterday I received the news that I had been accepted by Cambridge University to enter the doctoral program in art history in October. You can not imagine the euphoria I feel; I can barely breathe.

High school English teachers write him, telling him of their students' reactions to the poets on his *Power of the Word* programs. Even a prisoner from Illinois wrote Moyers, after watching the *Six Great Ideas* series, to say "what a truly joyous opportunity that program was for an institutionalized intellectual. After several months in a cell, with nothing but a TV, it was salvation."

Robert Geller, too, remembers a letter he got from a prisoner—a maximum-security inmate who, as a reward for good behavior, was given access to an eleven-inch TV set. He saw Geller's *American Short Story* adaptation of Richard Wright's "Almos' a Man," starring Le Var Burton, and wrote to tell Geller he would not soon forget the show's final image of Burton brandishing the weapon on his lap. It spoke prophetically, and almost too personally, to his own sense of manhood.

And so far as reaching a literally captive audience, the record may well go to Bloodworth-Thomason. Her *Designing Women* episode on battered women so impressed the head of the domestic violence unit for Los Angeles County that he took a copy of it to the district attorney's office, which ruled that any batterer brought into the country on domestic violence charges has to watch the show as part of his rehabilitation. "That," she says, "just made me feel great. That was very empowering to me, and that's an example of the power of television."

Other quick examples:

Lindsay Law says of *American Playhouse*, "I can just tell by the letters we get in terms of how people's minds have been altered, or something has been introduced to them that previously they never thought of." He mentions as an example *El Norte*, the *Playhouse* film about a brother and sister who leave Guatemala in hopes of finding a better life in America, only to encounter unexpectedly harsh difficulties and prejudices. "An amazingly large number of people" who saw *El Norte*, Law says, have told him after seeing it that "from that moment on, literally, the maitre d', the busboy, the taxicab driver, the bellhop became 'people' to them for the first time."

Bill Cosby tells a story about Troy Brown, a young man in Mississippi who met Cosby and thanked him for doing his first dyslexia show. Brown was in graduate school and doing well, but had struggled all through school, and into college, before learning of his problem, getting help, and developing a healthier self-image. *The Cosby Show*, Brown said, was part of that realization process. "This young man said to me, 'I was known as Troy Brown, Dumbest Kid in Town.' You get stuck with something like that," Cosby says, "and what's a kid's choice?"

Fred Rogers's mailbox is an eclectic exhibit of TV's reach and influence. He hears from viewers young and old, from a youngster who began taking violin lessons after watching a musician visit the *Neighborhood* to a grown woman who had been abused as a child—and who used Rogers's on-screen words of encouragement and friendliness as both a role model and an escape valve. "Your words," she wrote, "planted and nurtured the seed that there could be a better life and that my experience was not what I deserved."

One mother wrote on behalf of her seven-year-old son, who has been blind since birth and also suffers from hearing loss and epilepsy. "Because of the fact that he cannot see anything, television means very little to him," the mother wrote Rogers, explaining that *Mister Rogers' Neighborhood* was an exception because of his deliberate, explanatory manner of speaking. "I truly believe," she added, "that you have helped this child to learn how to deal with his anger and frustration with the lot that life has dealt him. . . . Even though the two of you have never met, you truly are his friend."

David Attenborough says, "The wonderful thing about making natural history documentaries is that there is something, in *any* sequence, for everybody at every conceivable level of age, education, and interest. . . . I have a letter from a child who writes, 'Dear David, I loved your show,' and I have a letter from a professional biologist of sixty-five, asking specific questions and saying *he* loved to watch the show." Same show.

"There isn't any simple panacea or formula that works for everybody," Bill Moyers says, putting the whole idea of "educational TV" in perspective.

"The best teachers in the classroom don't do it except for those students in that classroom. Right down the hall there might be a class that's talking about dogs, so that class misses it. You only can do what you can do, where you can do it, when you can do it, for whom you can do it, and one can't be messianic about this. Because you are not going to save the world with either classroom instruction or this kind of television. But for those who are there, who have arrived and are ready to be touched, it is unmistakably a redeeming experience."

To end this serious discussion on a slightly lighter note: Linda Bloodworth-Thomason, (remember, a former English teacher), decided to do her bit for literacy again. She inaugurated a reading program in her hometown of Poplar Bluffs, Missouri, partly by promising high school students such attention-getting prizes as a Mazda Miata. The goal was to have students work their way through a supplied list of "the hundred greatest books ever written"—twenty-five each year, beginning as a freshman.

"We've just been doing it one year," Bloodworth-Thomason says. "One kid read thirty-nine books last year, and there were at least twenty-five others who read at least fifteen." Princeton's Educational Testing Service has expressed interest in getting the voluntary, extracurricular program standardized and certified, so the student's efforts could be recognized and credited on his or her transcript. Bloodworth-Thomason hopes the idea will spread to other schools across the country, and it's already spread to at least one other location—the fictional TV town of Bloodworth-Thomason's *Evening Shade*.

"Everybody in the town on *Evening Shade* is going to be reading the 'hundred greatest books ever written,' and they will be talking about them," she says, anticipating the start of the 1991 fall season. "And what has happened in *my* hometown is, you have mentors in the community, and each mentor is responsible for one book. Like there's a clerk at JC Penney, for example, and this woman has become an expert on *Moby-Dick*. And she never went to college herself, but that is *her* book, and she is so proud of that. . . .

"A mentor can make the book more exciting. And now people pull into the filling station in Poplar Bluffs, Missouri, and they go, 'Hey, Virgil, how'd you like that *Pride and Prejudice?*' And they're talking about literature. And so everybody on *Evening Shade* is going to be talking about these books. . . . In almost every show, it'll just be a little reference, it'll have nothing to do with the story we're doing."

Bloodworth-Thomason made good on her promise. The "great books" idea became a running theme on *Evening Shade* during the 1991–92 season, with typical tossaway scenes like the one where Fontana, the town stripper, opened one show by remarking, "Well, the main thing I noticed about Heathcliff in *Wuthering Heights* is that he really didn't have a very good sense of humor."

When those shows were still in the planning stages, though, the former English teacher was relishing the prospect of slipping literary references into a Top 20 TV series. "Wouldn't that be fun," Bloodworth-Thomason asks, contemplating the possibilities, "if we got the whole country reading?"

Then, after a burst of unbridled optimism, comes a dose of bridled reality. "Here's the sad thing I don't want to tell anybody," Bloodworth-Thomason says, almost whispering. "We're having to go out and buy Monarch Notes, because the writers have not—and neither have I—read *all* of the hundred greatest books ever written. We're doing just what we *don't* want anybody to do."

17

THE CIVIL WAR
TO THE GULF WAR

They were two major TV events that took place in a single television season, yet were separated by more than a century. One was the PBS documentary series *The Civil War*, which riveted viewers with its humanistic examination of the War Between the States. The other was the Gulf War, which riveted viewers with its mechanistic view of America's war with Iraq.

The Civil War was a tale told mostly from the bottom up, with letters and pictures of soldiers providing much of the information and emotion; the Gulf War was a tale told mostly from the top down, with TV news organizations reliant largely upon military generals and briefers for their information and visuals. *The Civil War* relayed images of one bloody battle after another; the Gulf War, as filtered through the carefully controlled lens of television, was largely bloodless. *The Civil War* presented battles more than 130 years old; despite censorial restrictions on both sides, the Gulf War telecasts presented occasional live video and/or audio of bomb and missile attacks. *The Civil War* was television taking its time, sifting through written and visual records to shape an account, and provide a perspective, on a crucial event that happened a long time ago. The Gulf War was television on the fly, making instant decisions while providing information and perspective on crucial events that were happening at that very moment. One was pure history; the other was not yet history at all. Even so, *The Civil War* and the Gulf War, despite their many differences, were events with certain things in common—not the least of which was the manner in which they transfixed American TV viewers.

The eleven-hour *The Civil War* unspooled on PBS over five successive nights in late September 1990—one of the most competitive weeks of the year in prime-time television. The documentary series, which had been assembled by writer-producer-director Ken Burns, writer-producer Ric Burns, and writer Geoffrey C. Ward over a five-year period, was anything but action-packed. In fact, as a matter of pride and taste, there were no recreations of battles at all. Instead, *The Civil War* told its tale by more subtle means.

It relied on the contemporaneous letters of soldiers and witnesses, as well as the subsequent perspectives of historians, to set the stage for each confrontation. The voices of such contributors as Jason Robards, Morgan Freeman, Julie Harris, Colleen Dewhurst, Arthur Miller, and Kurt Vonnegut were used on the soundtrack, reading letters, speeches, and other quotes. A panel of Civil War experts served as advisors to the project, and a few even appeared onscreen. Shelby Foote, the most prominent of them, emerged from *The Civil War* with as much instant fame as Ken Burns: Foote's drawl, enthusiasm, knowledge, and rugged good looks made him an overnight TV star. Sounds of birds, cicadas, gunfire, wagon wheels, and other effects were used throughout the series to create and recreate the proper atmosphere, and authentic period music complemented the voices and sound effects beautifully. The only piece of modern music used in the series was its theme: a 1982 composition called "Ashokan Farewell," written by Jay Ungar (a friend of Ken Burns's) and released, virtually unnoticed, by Ungar's Fiddle Fever group on a Flying Fish record album, *Waltz of the Wind,* in 1984. Used often and evocatively in *The Civil War,* "Ashokan Farewell" became one of its most instantly recognizable components.

Finally, there was the element of *The Civil War* no less important than the script, and even more important than the voices, music, and sound effects: the photography.

The Civil War was the first at which photography was present, and the thousands of photographs shown in the documentary reduced—and, at the same time, elevated—each battle to human terms. Ken Burns, as director, employed those still photographs as if filming on a movie set, using close-ups, pans, tracking shots, and slow zooms in and out to make them moving pictures in every sense of the word. We saw the faces of the victorious and the vanquished, the survivors and the slain. We heard their inner thoughts and fears, confided to wives and families in letters sent from the battlefield. We heard from both sides equally, coming to understand the scope of their respective causes, concerns, and casualties. And in the midst of battles in which thousands were slain, we were moved not only by the overall carnage, but by individual deaths. Narrator David McCullough, in just one example of his incomparable work throughout, injected just the right note of sadness and loneliness while recounting the last words in a blood-stained diary found on the body of a soldier who, injured on the battlefield and surrounded by his slain comrades, had survived long enough to make one final entry. "June 4, 1864," he had written. "I was killed."

If, however, there was one moment in the entire eleven hours exemplifying *The Civil War*—a moment, in fact, cementing its reputation and guaranteeing its success—it was the three-minute, twenty-three-second segment that climaxed the series' opening installment. In it, McCullough tells of

Sullivan Ballou, a Northern soldier writing to his wife, Sarah, after hearing rumors of an impending battle in which he expects to take part. At this point in the documentary, photographs of young and old soldiers, and the loved ones they left behind, are slowly and affectionately presented and examined, and enhanced by sound effects of soldiers in camp and on the move. Then actor Paul Roebling, as Ballou, reads the husband's words with a heartbreaking tenderness and sincerity.

"Lest I should not be able to write you again, I feel impelled to write a few lines that may fall under your eye when I am no more," Roebling-as-Ballou says. At that moment, Ungar's "Ashokan Farewell" violin music appears, quietly and poignantly making the mood even more reverent as the letter continues.

> I have no misgivings about, or lack of confidence in, the cause in which I am engaged, and my courage does not halt or falter. I know how American civilization now leans upon the triumph of the Government, and how great a debt we owe to those who went before us through the blood and suffering of the Revolution. And I am willing—perfectly willing—to lay down all my joys in this life to help maintain this Government, and to pay that debt. . . .
>
> Sarah, my love for you is deathless. It seems to bind me with mightly cables that nothing but Omnipotence can break. And yet my love of Country comes over me like a strong wind, and bears me irresistibly with all those chains to the battlefield.
>
> The memory of all the blissful moments I have enjoyed with you come crowding over me, and I feel most deeply grateful to God, and you, that I have enjoyed them for so long. And how hard it is for me to give them up and burn to ashes the hopes of future years, when, God willing, we might still have lived and loved together, and see our sons grown up into honorable manhood around us. If I do not return, my dear Sarah, never forget how much I loved you, nor that when my last breath escapes me on the battlefield, it will whisper your name. . . .
>
> But, O Sarah! If the dead can come back to this earth and flit unseen around those they love, I shall always be with you, in the brightest day and the darkest night. Always. Always. And when the soft breeze fans your cheek, it shall be my breath. . . .
>
> Sarah, do not mourn me dead. Think I am gone and wait for me, for we shall meet again. . . .

Roebling stops reading, and narrator McCullough returns to add a one-sentence postscript. "Sullivan Ballou," he says, "was killed a week later at the first Battle of Bull Run." The "Ashokan Farewell" theme concludes, and so does the first, unforgettable installment of *The Civil War*.

"The series is incredibly literate," Ken Burns says, speaking of the documentary's verbiage in general and the Ballou letter in particular. "It owes its great strength to the word. Television is supposed to be a medium that is unkind to the word, and it's not true." It was no accident that Ballou's letter ended the keynote episode of *The Civil War*, just as it was no surprise to Burns when most print and broadcast reviews of the documentary series independently singled it out for praise.

"It's a letter that transcends even the extraordinary story of the Civil War," Burns says. "It's about the tension and the love that exists between a man and a woman. Every man in this country wishes he could say those things to a woman, just as every woman in this country wishes the man she was with could say those things to her. . . . It was my favorite letter, and I knew where it should go. But, in fact, I didn't go for the jugular with it." His original plan was to cross-fade the soundtrack so that the voice of Roebling's Sullivan Ballou would be replaced partway through by that of an actress playing Sarah, who would read the remainder of the letter. "It was so emotional, it was just too much," Burns says, "so we toned it down." To this day, the letter carries such resonance with Burns that he carries a copy of it in his back pocket.

The week *The Civil War* aired, Burns seemed to have most of America's TV critics, and many of its viewers, in his back pocket as well—an appreciation generated not by bribery, but by quality. Individually, critics from both sides of the Mason-Dixon line were effusive in their praise. Marc Gunther of the *Detroit Free Press* advised readers that *The Civil War* "has everything it takes to make great television: an epic story, intense drama and unforgettable characters." Tim Funk of the *Charlotte Observer* wrote, "Forget all the hype from the networks about the fall TV season. This is the show to see." R. D. Heldenfels of the *Daily Gazette* in Schenectady, New York, wrote, "Often on documentaries, and dramas based on real events, filmmakers come armed with a poetic vision, then bend the story to suit the vision. Burns has done the opposite, going to the events and unearthing the poetry within them. You will not find better television this year." Hal Boedeker of the *Miami Herald* called it "an epic likely to be this TV season's grandest achievement," and recommended it "for everyone."

Collectively, TV critics presented a virtually unified front, sounding the enthusiastic alarms that something remarkable was about to hit the small screen. That unanimity was reflected later in an end-of-season *Electronic Media* poll of TV critics, where *The Civil War* was honored as the best of all miniseries, specials, or telemovies in 1990 – 91, and in the annual Television Critics Association awards, where *The Civil War* was honored as both Best Special and Program of the Year. In the history of the TCA Awards, the only previous documentaries to have won awards in two different categories were the 1987 – 88 HBO special *Dear America: Letters Home from Vietnam* (which shared many of the same production techniques as the subsequent *Civil War*) and the 1986–87 PBS series *Eyes on the Prize* (which told of a different kind of civil war, the early history of the American civil rights movement).

The media attention played a giant part in getting viewers to sample *The Civil War* when it premiered on September 23, 1990, but it was the quality of the work itself that kept people tuned, and kept them coming back for more. Word of mouth built quickly, and, like a major miniseries,

The Civil War gathered notice and momentum with each additional install-ment. By Tuesday night, Johnny Carson was praising its virtues on *The Tonight Show.* By the time it was over five nights later, *The Civil War* had gathered the largest audience for a single event in PBS history, with 38.9 million people sampling part of the series. The loyalists—the ones watching from start to finish—numbered about 14 million. The documentary's over-all national share of the nightly viewing audience averaged 13 percent, taking a sizable bite out of the available TV viewership just at the time when the commercial networks were doing everything in their power to lure people back for premiere week.

The result: the five nights of *The Civil War* averaged a national rating of nine, making it the highest-rated series in PBS history. "It's the most important thing to come to public TV since *Sesame Street,*" Ward Chamber-lin, vice-chairman of WETA-TV (which coproduced the series), told a re-porter once the reviews and ratings for *The Civil War* were in. "You can't overestimate the impact of this series."

Basically, *The Civil War* gave PBS programmers the courage to compete more directly with commercial network fare, as well as to schedule certain high-profile series in nightly, rather than weekly, installments. It was a fund-raising gold mine on the local station level, and certainly helped public television's supporters argue their case the next time a funding bill came up in Congress. Those, however, were unintended bonuses. *The Civil War* succeeded in its declared task as well, which was to ignite and reignite interest in the Civil War itself. Within a few weeks of the documentary's broadcast, the Civil War became the cover story of both *Entertainment Weekly* and *Newsweek.* The latter magazine even devoted its "Conventional Wis-dom" feature to Civil War generals, ranking them with up, down, or side-ways arrows in what was billed as "CW on the CW." Attendance at Civil War battlefield sites increased significantly, and in many different respects, *The Civil War* created such a splash that ripples could be felt the rest of the year. For a while, it seemed the appetite for anything related to the Civil War was insatiable.

The documentary itself was repeated once by local stations, then again in a nationally scheduled encore presentation, within ten months of its initial telecast. The fifty-dollar companion volume to *The Civil War* resided for months on the *New York Times* best-seller list, selling more than 700,000 copies. An audiocassette version of the companion book was also produced, with Ken Burns reading the text. The diary entries and letters of Union soldier Elisha Hunt Rhodes, who survived twenty Civil War battles and whose writings were a seminal ingredient of *The Civil War,* were edited by his great-grandson, Robert Hunt Rhodes, into a well-received 1991 book.

A *Civil War* soundtrack album, including the "Ashokan Farewell" theme and the dramatic reading of the Sullivan Ballou letter, was released, while Fiddle Fever's *Waltz of the Wind* album, the original source of "Asho-kan Farewell," was rereleased. Ken Burns, working with them and many other musicians, collaborated on a 1991 spinoff PBS special, *Songs of the*

Civil War, and several of Burns's previous documentaries—including *Brooklyn Bridge, The Statue of Liberty,* and *Huey Long*—were resurrected and repeated by PBS in a season-long retrospective. Foote's massive, three-volume *The Civil War: A Narrative,* begun in 1954 and completed twenty years later, had sold a total of 11,000 copies in paperback during the five years preceding the TV documentary in which he was featured. After *The Civil War* was broadcast, the publisher sold that amount in as many months.

"The book will always be where you go after the television has gotten you interested," Foote had told TV critics at a press conference the summer before *The Civil War* premiered. "That's not to underrate for an instant the enormous value of this thing to people who won't read books, or don't want to."

Its value was recognized, all right, and not just by viewers and TV critics. *The Civil War* received, among other honors, a Peabody Award, a $50,000 Lincoln Prize from Gettysburg College, a Christopher Award, a Parents' Choice Award and a D. W. Griffith Award from the National Film Board Review. Burns, who rankles at the racism and historical inaccuracies present in Griffith's *Birth of a Nation,* makes a point of repeating what he said to the National Film Board when accepting that last award. "I told them," Burns says, "I accepted it on behalf of D. W. Griffith the great filmmaker, not on behalf of D. W. Griffith the lousy historian."

Not that Burns could be mistaken for anything resembling a lousy historian or a lousy filmmaker. "He turned television into art," Bill Moyers says of Ken Burns and *The Civil War,* "and it's art that has the power to move you, to touch you. I thought it was an unparalleled accomplishment, and I am jealous of it."

"Television," Kurt Vonnegut says, "has produced something that's on a par with Beethoven's Third Symphony, and on a par with Picasso's *Guernica*—and that's a documentary on *The Civil War,* by the Burns brothers."

Vonnegut notes he contributed his voice to the soundtracks of both *The Civil War* and *Brooklyn Bridge,* but insists that's not why he, or anyone else, responded to *The Civil War* so strongly. "Everybody's so grateful for the truth," he says, "and it had the ring of truth."

"Best television show I ever saw in my life," gushes Don Hewitt, who credits its success to Burns's methodology of "starting with words, and then finding the pictures that complement the words." And though those pictures didn't move, *The Civil War* imbued them with movement—slowly exposing more of a particular photograph, or moving in to examine a small but telling detail, or even standing still. "In film, we regulate the time in which you see something," Burns explains. "Automatically, that's a kind of movement. It's like music, where you hold a note, and the amount of time you hold that note affects the entire composition."

Moyers underscores the importance of the documentary's visuals by recalling an interview he conducted for TV with filmmaker Frank Capra, who had been "drafted" by Franklin Delano Roosevelt during World War II to counter Nazi propaganda and help explain to young boys from foothills and factory towns and ranches why the war was so important. Capra, Moyers paraphrases, said they tried lectures, but the young men didn't listen, and pamphlets, but they wouldn't read them. Then it suddenly dawned on Capra that all these kids in boot camp had been spending twenty-five cents each Saturday to go to the movies, and that the Nazis were ahead of the game in recognizing the value of motion pictures in capturing attention and persuading audiences.

Capra got hold of Hitler's already produced propaganda films and re-edited them, adding narration from an American perspective and calling the resultant documentary series *Why We Fight*. It was astoundingly successful in terms of bringing abstract ideas and distant conflicts to life, and Moyers feels *The Civil War* accomplished the same thing, especially when used in scholastic settings.

"That is what teachers tell me," Moyers says, "that they could get kids interested in the Civil War somewhat before this series came along, but now, just being able to say 'We are going to watch a film first' makes the kids think, 'We are going to be entertained before we have to work.' And then they discover that the *work* is entertaining. That is what a well-done film or television show or video can do. It can hold out to people the prospect of being entertained, and therefore spending time more pleasurably, but it can then reveal to them that *learning* is pleasurable."

One such example: Even before Timothy Brittell's school purchased a copy of *The Civil War* series for classroom use, the social studies teacher was showing a personally taped copy to his students, and remembers the effect the Sullivan Ballou letter had on them.

"They had read some about the Civil War by that point," Brittell says, "but frankly, what they had read about was a faceless war, with 600,000 people who died. And all of a sudden there was a person—one person—in front of them. That's a beautiful letter, and I have a very sensitive group of kids. They reacted strongly to the sensitivity of that letter, and for that to be the closer of part one—well, that was the hook for all the other parts."

Burns, for his part, thinks there was another reason why so many millions of viewers became hooked on *The Civil War*. "I think I figured out why right away," he says. "We touched a nerve that really changed the country. If you see the sense of your country in the same sympathetic way you see the life of a human being, the Civil War is *the* great traumatic event."

Not quite everyone was hooked, or touched, by *The Civil War* with equal force. In fact, both Linda Ellerbee and Lindsay Law, speaking independently, cited Henry Hampton's civil-rights documentary series *Eyes on the Prize*—which examined the movement's early heroes, villains, victims, and triumphs—as a work deserving of equal or greater acclaim. "I enjoyed it," Ellerbee says of *The Civil War*. "And I was certainly, like most of us who produce for public television, glad to see it get so much attention. That only helps all of us. But I didn't think it was the greatest thing ever to come down the pike. . . . It was not great television. It *was* good. But possibly, my lack of entire enchantment with it has to do with the fact that I am not, as so many people in this country are, that particularly obsessed with or overcome by the Civil War.

"On the other hand, I thought *Eyes on the Prize* was better. *Eyes on the Prize* does what television does best, which is the transference of experience, the transfer of emotion. *The Civil War* transferred information, but not the emotion of *Eyes on the Prize*. It did not transfer that *experience* to you."

Law, asked about *The Civil War*, says, "I thought it was splendid. But I also thought *Eyes on the Prize* was splendid, and equally deserving of having gotten an audience of that size and scope. And frankly, I think it would have had an even greater impact on the country than *The Civil War*." About the latter documentary series' record audience, Law says, "It was the first time that public television actually, finally kind of did what everyone else has known how to do for twenty years. You know—how do you get everybody to watch the first episode of *Twin Peaks*? Well, you start six months ahead of time, and you write a million articles, and you buy some advertising, and you get everyone excited about it. Oh, I found it maddening. Conceivably, it may even end up being suddenly dangerous, because now everyone calls that successful because it reached all those people. The reverse of that is, anything less than that is a failure.

"But I liked that a great deal, and I think Ken is a remarkably talented fellow. I just think that there have definitely been other things that were every bit as good. I find it frustrating that there weren't 14 shares for *Eyes on the Prize*. . . . But it was still much more comforting watching *The Civil War* because you could say, 'Ooh, here's our history,' as opposed to, 'Here's our recent history that we've lived through, which is not so pleasing what it says about us.' "

There were, however, very modern—and not very comfortable—lessons to be learned in the Burns documentary at the time of its premiere. One month before, Iraqi troops and tanks had invaded Kuwait, prompting President Bush to announce economic sanctions against Baghdad and call up the US Reserves. My own *New York Post* review urging viewers to watch *The Civil War* that September noted, "The modern-day parallels and tactics in *The Civil War*—naval blockades, lengthy sieges of fortified cities, outrageously overpriced contracts for the manufacture of military equipment—are not stressed in the documentary, but are not lost, either." Certainly, they were not lost on one of the most important and powerful viewers of the documentary, General H. Norman Schwarzkopf.

"I bumped into Schwarzkopf over the weekend," Burns told me in May 1991, "and he told me he watched the film constantly, especially in December when the [Gulf] war was being planned. He said it was an incredibly moving experience for him to see the film."

One of the lessons Schwarzkopf may have drawn from *The Civil War* was to do everything in his power to avoid, in press coverage of the Gulf War, the eyewitness battle accounts and corpse-strewn photographs that gave the Civil War documentary such power and emotion. Then again, it's not exactly news that media coverage of war is a risky business. In American history, each new conflict has presented a different set of dilemmas for military planners and the news media alike. How, and how quickly, is news from the war gathered and relayed, and what impact does that have on the campaign itself? What events, if any, should news organizations be prevented from reporting? And how does the public's response to media coverage of a war affect the course and outcome of the war itself?

These and other questions regarding the reporting, impact, and censorship of the news arose slowly in America. In fact, with freedom of the press a key issue in the fight for independence, there was virtually no thought of censorship during that entire war—nor, for that matter, during the War of 1812 and the Mexican War. The first records of military censorship in War Department files occurred during the Civil War, and were a direct result of the invention and widespread use of the telegraph.

When Samuel B. Morse opened the country's first telegraph line in 1844, a connection stretching from Baltimore, Maryland, to Washington, DC, he envisioned it as the start of a communications system that would make "one neighborhood of the whole country"—a nineteenth-century nationalistic precursor to McLuhan's "global village." Before the decade was out, the Associated Press had been formed, and the mechanisms were in place to transmit news reports from far-flung locations almost instantly. The Civil War generals and news organizations faced, in the invention of the telegraph, the same kinds of possibilities and problems posed by satellite TV technology during the Gulf War: the delivery of wartime news at an unprecedented speed and volume, reporting on conflicts as they occurred. There was even the capability to send information overseas: William Howard Russell, who covered the Civil War for the London *Times,* made an international reputation for both himself and his newspaper with his informative and dramatic dispatches.

During the Civil War, changes initiated by the telegraph affected the style of news stories, the demand for them, and the military reaction to them. The cost of sending lengthy stories by telegraph, for example, gave reporters and editors a pragmatic reason to be more concise and objective. "One way to compress stories," notes media historian Edwin Emery in *The Press and America,* "was to omit opinion and coloration. By modern standards, Civil War reporting was rambling and colored, but compared with the journalism of an earlier day it was much more readable." It was also a great way to sell papers. Most publications, North and South, devoted a sizable percentage of each edition to the latest news from the various battlefields, and relied on competitively fresh stories to sustain and increase their readership. "Telegraph fully all news you can get," one *Chicago Times* editor wired a war correspondent, "and when there is no news send rumours."

From the very beginning, dispatches from the Civil War had a sense of immediacy previously absent from wartime journalism. In 1861, *New*

York World reporter B. S. Osbon, witnessing the bombardment of Fort Sumter from the deck of a naval cutter, dispatched this terse and timely report: "CHARLESTON, April 12—*The ball is opened. War is inaugurated.* The batteries of Sullivan's Island, Morris Island, and other points were opened on Fort Sumter at four o'clock this morning. Fort Sumter has returned the fire, and a brisk cannonading has been kept up."

When war correspondents were present at key battles, both the reporters and their editors recognized them as such, and assigned newspaper space accordingly. Whitelaw Reid, writing under the pen name of "Agate," was an eyewitness at the Battle of Gettysburg, and his story took up almost thirty percent of the next edition of the *Cincinnati Gazette.* And no wonder, because his as-it-happened details of death and devastation were astounding. "The rebels—three lines deep—came steadily up," Reid wrote. "They were in pointblank range. At last the order came! From thrice six-thousand guns there came a sheet of smoky flame, a crash of leaden death. The line literally melted away; but there came a second, resistless still. . . . Right on came the rebels. They were above the guns, were bayoneting the gunners, were waving their flags above our pieces."

Southern papers, too, were prepared and eager to cover the war, and were impressively resourceful in two important respects. When the onset of war severed their connections with the Associated Press, they established a pool of reporters to furnish dispatches for all the affiliated papers in the South. And in order to gain and maintain access to military telegraph lines, that service, called the Press Association of the Confederate States of America, mandated an objective tone for all its news reports—thus sidestepping many of the censorial problems that would arise in the North. And the South, like the North, had some resourceful and memorable war correspondents. Felix Gregory de Fontaine, who wrote for the *Charleston Courier* under the alias "Personne," witnessed the 1862 battle at Antietam, which claimed more casualties in a single day (more than 25,000) than any other battle in American history. "Before us were the enemy," he wrote in a dispatch filed at noon that day. "A regiment or two had crossed the river, and, running in squads from the woods along its banks, were trying to form a line. Suddenly a shell falls among them, and another and another, until thousands scatter like a swarm of flies, and disappear in the woods."

Civil War generals on both sides of the war were fighting with new types of equipment (everything from Gatling guns and submarines to multiple-shot rifles and ironclad ships), facing or employing new tactics (the rebels, for the most part, rejected Napoleonic formations of marching soldiers in favor of establishing positions behind safe cover and firing from a distance until ready to charge), and sometimes using railroads to transport troops and telegraphs to maintain communications among them. Everything was new, and everything was news.

But what to one side was an encouraging rumor about an impending attack, to the other was potentially crucial information about whether and where to establish a defensive front. The speed at which news could be delivered by telegraph meant that details of ongoing battles potentially could be intercepted or received by the enemy in time to send reinforcements or alter strategies. Three months after the attack on Fort Sumter, General Winfield Scott, commander of the Union armies, took the decisive (though illegal) action of forbidding telegraph companies from sending any information of a military nature. Congress legally gave the President that control six months later, but until then, telegraph censorship was exercised often, and hardly objectively.

The first blatant example of such censorship occurred after the first Battle of Bull Run on July 21, 1861—the battle at which Sullivan Ballou and thousands of other soldiers were slain in a lengthy, grisly confrontation eventually and decisively won by the Confederacy. Henry J. Raymond, a *New York Times* reporter, sent an early story claiming a Union victory, then corrected that account in a follow-up story—which, unlike the first, was blocked by Northern censors.

After the Battle of Bull Run, Washington correspondents were invited to a meeting with General George B. McClellan, commander of the Army of the Potomac, who proposed voluntary censorship guides to help avoid similar journalistic confrontations in the future. When that failed to produce the desired results, an even harsher set of guidelines was established by the government, forbidding any telegraph dispatches describing civil, not just military, government operations. Congress overturned the restrictions on nonmilitary transmissions in 1862; for the rest of the war, rules became clearer, reporters more responsible, and military officers more tolerant of the press—well, most of them, anyway. Ambrose Burnside and William T. Sherman were just some of the Northern generals who made a point of keeping reporters sequestered far away from actual military action, or of forbidding their presence entirely.

Sherman had little but disdain for the press, even though Northern papers cooperated so fully with Sherman that he was able to lead his famous march to the sea, behind enemy lines, without his plans being leaked by the press. But that was late in the war, and, so far as Sherman was concerned, the damage already had been done.

"No matter how rapidly we move," Sherman complained, "our enemy has notice in advance. To them more than any other cause do I trace the many failures that attend our army. . . . Never had an enemy a better corps of spies than our army carries along, paid, transported, and fed by the United States." Reporters, he said, "come into camp, poke about among the lazy shirks and pick up their camp rumors, and publish them as facts. They are a pest, and I treat them as spies—which, in truth, they are." Sherman dismissed war correspondents as "dirty newspaper scribblers who have the impudence of Satan," and made similarly devilish remarks on other occasions, as when he said that if he killed them all, "there'd be news from hell before breakfast."

As for Burnside, he was the author, and chief enforcer, of the so-called Burnside Decrees, which claimed the right of a commander to squelch the public expression of information and ideas deemed harmful to the government's military effort. Burnside's command included military districts in Illinois, so when the *Chicago Times* ran an especially hostile diatribe attacking President Abraham Lincoln for issuing the Emancipation Proclamation, Burnside ordered the newspaper offices padlocked, and suspended its publication by military decree.

Such antipress sentiments were not universal throughout the Union, however. Although Lincoln surely appreciated the gesture by one of his loyal generals, he appreciated the concept of press freedom even more. Three days later, the President himself rescinded the order. Lincoln, in fact, was perhaps the greatest champion of media access in American history. As President, he gave Mathew Brady and his crew permission to travel from city to city, battlefield to battlefield, following the path and course of the war—and protected, every step of the way, by Secret Service agents. Brady's weapon was a camera equipped with the recently developed "wet-plate" process, and his job was to provide a photographic record of the war.

The pictures credited to Brady would have as big an impact on the war as Morse's telegraph (an ironic development, since Brady once served as Morse's understudy in the science of optics). Newspapers, during and even after the Civil War, were incapable of reproducing photographs effectively, because the half-tone process wasn't introduced until 1877; instead, newspaper illustrations consisted of painstakingly drawn maps and woodcuts. Photographers, too, were limited technologically, for the process at the time was not sophisticated enough to capture subjects or objects in motion. But with Brady's "portable" darkroom—a large wagon equipped with cameras, lenses, chemicals, glass plates, and other necessary paraphernalia—he and his colleagues were unsurpassed at providing haunting and revealing photographs of what Daniel Boorstin called "the war's architectural and human debris." Oliver Wendell Holmes, seeing Brady's Civil War photographs, called the camera "the mirror with a memory," and Brady took that mirror and displayed its images almost everywhere.

Wherever newspaper correspondents descended to paint their word pictures of battles and soldiers, Brady and/or his colleagues were there to produce pictures of their own—in a literal rather than literary sense. Brady and company were there at Fort Sumter, recording the devastation of that early battle, and they became a familiar presence throughout the war: photographing soldiers, officers and the aftermaths of armed conflicts, then distributing and displaying the results as quickly and widely as possible.

Within days of the horrifying Battle of Antietam, Brady's New York gallery unveiled an exhibit called "The Dead of Antietam," a collection of clear and evocative pictures of lifeless bodies and seemingly endless carnage. A *New York Times* report of the exhibit summed up how the new medium of photography forced those who saw it to look at war differently, or at least more closely, than before. "The dead of the battlefield come up to us very rarely, even in dreams," the reporter wrote, then noted that this new exhibit changed all that. "Mr. Mathew Brady has done something to bring to us the terrible reality and earnestness of the war. If he has not brought bodies and laid them in our dooryards and along our streets, he has done something very like it."

Yet just because a photograph could reflect reality, that did not mean it always did so. Brady was not the only one armed with a camera during the Civil War. For that matter, Brady was nearly (though secretly) blind, and entrusted the actual photographing of most exposures to his able and loyal assistants. In any event, there were scores of cameramen throughout the war, on either side of it, only too happy to cooperate with the army in staging a particularly dramatic picture—or even to instigate such photographs for their own purposes.

"There are some pretty outrageous examples," Burns says, adding that a typical trick was for Union soldiers to gather the bodies of Confederates killed in battle, rearranging them into a more compelling photographic composition—more compelling to Northern eyes, that is, and more frightening to Southerners. Consider them early versions of what TV now calls "recreations," or even "docudramas"—accounts of factual events, but with certain elements altered, added, or deleted.

In *The Civil War*, Burns had originally intended to have a longer segment focusing on battlefield photography, including the occasional intentional fakery, but decided it would undercut the sense of reality he was working so hard to achieve with the pictures used in his own documentary. His compromise was to reject photos he knew or suspected to be staged—except in the case of a fairly famous photograph of a Confederate sharpshooter at Gettysburg, where the photo was so familiar, and the image so striking, that poetic license was invoked.

Poetic license, though, was as much a part of early war coverage as were, say, censorial restrictions or technological innovations. Consider the following:

The Civil War was the first war in which still photographs were brought back from the battlefield, yet it was only a generation later—thirty-two years after the Civil War ended, to be precise—that battlefield action was captured, for the first time, on motion picture film. The subject was the Greco-Turkish War of 1897, and the pioneering cinematographer was British war correspondent Frederick Villiers. Even though filmmaking had developed only a decade before, Villiers thought there was enough demand for such dramatic footage to justify the risks of daily filming; after all, the previous year's *May Irwin Kiss*, with its single close-up smooch, had caused a sensation and made a small fortune, and the audience's appetite for film fare seemed inexhaustible.

Day after day, commuting by bicycle from the British consulate to the front, Villiers filmed the Battle of Volo in Thessaly, Greece, and returned to London with what he thought was the photojournalistic coup of the century. Ironically, though, he found no buyers for his actual battle footage, because an enterprising film outfit in Paris had already filmed dramatized reconstructions of the battle and saturated the market with them. It didn't matter that Villiers had the genuine article on film; audiences had already seen that battle. Or, at least, thought they had.

A year later, in 1898, Vitagraph—one of several American companies staking out territory in the fledgling film business—sent a cameraman to cover the Spanish-American War. Teddy Roosevelt, not yet president, was a major subject of those "topicals," and apparently an eager one as well: several accounts have him personally welcoming and ushering the Vitagraph crew on board before leaving for Cuba. And according to Vitagraph cameraman and cofounder Albert E. Smith, Roosevelt was not above playing to the camera, and even showed "a willingness to halt his march up San Juan Hill and strike a pose."

However, portions of that account must be questioned as to their veracity. The famous charge actually took place on Kettle Hill, then up the San Juan Heights—not on San Juan Hill, as is widely thought. (Technically, the conflict is known not as the Battle of San Juan Hill, but as the Battle of San Juan.) And if the fierce actions that day, as vividly described by historian Edmund Morris in his Pulitzer Prize-winning biography *The Rise of Theodore Roosevelt*, are to be accepted as truth, Roosevelt would have had no time for such foolishness as playing for the camera. It is much more likely that Smith subsequently persuaded a cooperative Roosevelt to go through some motions that would appease audiences hungry for film footage containing news, action, and heroes.

Incidentally, Smith himself was more than willing to play with perceptions and stage a thing or two. When he returned from Cuba with the Roosevelt footage, his reception in New York was no better than the one Villiers had experienced upon returning to Paris. Smith's partner at Biograph, expecting an exciting "charge up San Juan Hill" sequence to match the exciting (if inaccurate) newspaper headlines, instead saw a slow uphill trudge by an obviously posing Roosevelt. Rather than trash the footage, though, Smith and his partner built and filmed a tabletop scale model version of Santiago Bay, replete with cigar-smoke "fog," cardboard "ships," and an inch-deep "bay." Spliced with the self-conscious performance by Roosevelt, it fooled, and wowed, the moviegoing public. Ironically, at the same time Smith was moving around his scale-model ships, the US Navy was cracking down on press reports of ship movements and battle plans by establishing "censorship units" whose orders were to read and clear all cables.

Newsreels, as we remember them today, began in 1910 and spread quickly around the globe. Within a few years, they had amassed the kind of clout that TV news currently enjoys, and were even more willing to exercise it. In 1914, Mexican General Pancho Villa signed a contract with the Mutual Film Corporation giving that company the film rights to all battle coverage, and promising, whenever possible, to fight during the day so that cameras could capture the action. In one instance, Villa postponed his army's attack on the city of Ojinaga until the Mutual cameraman arrived.

In the twentieth century, technology entered the action as well as recorded and reshaped it. Each military action brought new types of equipment to the soldiers and reporters alike; there were differences, in each major conflict, about the manner in which the fighting was conducted, as well as in the way news of it was distributed. Weapons got deadlier and more accurate; news reports got faster and, one would hope, no less accurate. And, in every conflict, press freedom and censorship was a major issue.

In terms of technology, World War I not only introduced tanks into the theater of war, but introduced radio as well. Years before radio was introduced as an entertainment medium in America, it was used by the Armed Forces as a means of transmitting intelligence, and "ham" operators in the United States relayed messages intended for naval stations and shipping companies. World War I proved that radio had a future; by the time that future had arrived, and World War II with it, the promise and problems of broadcast news had opened a Pandora's Box that still cannot be shut.

World War I also proved that, if the government and the media were going to work together, it was not destined to be a happy marriage. America's 1917 entry into that war led directly to the formation of the country's first formal censorship agency, the Committee on Public Information. Even before Congress had declared war, the State, Navy, and War Departments had drawn up a set of regulations and restrictions; afterward, with the Committee on Public Information overseeing things, the press voluntarily accepted them. After all, the guidelines seemed clear and reasonable enough: no specific troop or ship movements could be revealed, and units sent overseas could not be fully identified. However, Congress soon threw even more power in the government's direction, and basically went overboard. The Espionage Act of 1917 prohibited the publication of any information that could be remotely construed as aiding the enemy or interfering with American military efforts, and the Sedition Act of 1918 made it illegal to criticize the government or its military in any manner, or even to make disparaging remarks about military uniforms or the flag.

Between the two world wars, there was much discussion between the media and the military about whether those restrictions, though deemed constitutional, were nonetheless much too severe. By the time World War II erupted in Europe, radio was the dominant mass medium, and the networks rushed to establish internal guidelines regarding breaking news coverage, in hopes of preempting any sort of governmental intervention by the FCC or the military. Network radio listeners in 1939 could tune in and hear complete speeches by Benito Mussolini, Adolf Hitler, and others, accompanied by simultaneous translations and subsequent commentary for American listeners. News from abroad ran often and at length, and such CBS correspondents as William L. Shirer and Murrow set a high industry standard with the quality of their reporting.

As for more formalized standards, CBS and its competitors pledged voluntarily to avoid descriptions of "hypothetical horrors which have not actually occurred," and to "try to distinguish between fact, official statement, news obtained from responsible official or unofficial sources, rumor, and matter taken from or contained in the foreign press." The networks, through the National Association of Broadcasters (NAB), also promised that "if broadcasts become available from scenes of battle, bombed areas, air-raid shelters, refugee camps" and other such locations, correspondents would "use taste and judgment to prevent such broadcasts from being unduly harrowing." Good guidelines, and with good reason—only the year before, Orson Welles's realistic-sounding "news coverage" in his adaptation of H. G. Wells's *The War of the Worlds* had proven quite harrowing indeed. The fear generated by that program made broadcasters fearful, in turn, of being denied freedoms and access just as the medium's potential in wartime was within reach of being realized.

Potential became fact in September 1940, when Murrow, after arguing, pleading, and even auditioning, finally received permission from the British government to broadcast live from the rooftops of London during the German bombing raids. Within days, *London after Dark* featured Murrow giving a thrilling yet calm account of the bombing raids he was witnessing, his words punctuated by the steady sound of antiaircraft fire and the louder, more random explosions of bombs impacting nearby. One of Murrow's own broadcasting edicts, that "the reporter must never sound excited, even if bombs are falling outside," literally was tested under fire during those raids, and Murrow passed his own test magnificently. Antiaircraft barrages, Murrow described, "seemed to splash blobs of daylight down the streets." The exhaust trail from a night bomber, Murrow said, was "a pale ribbon stretched straight across the sky." As high explosives fell, Murrow compared the image to what it might look like if "some giant had thrown a huge basket of flaming golden oranges high in the air."

Biographer A. M. Sperber, in *Murrow: His Life and Times*, writes: "It was *The War of the Worlds* come to life, the fantasy of 1938 became the reality of 1940, the rooftop observer, reporting on the life and death of cities, no longer an actor in a studio. This was the real thing, broadcasting's first living-room war." Once Murrow broke the ice, reporters at rival networks soon made their way to the rooftops, and the battle was on . . . on live radio, that is. But Murrow was there first—and with him, though it is not generally known, was a British censor, who stood next to him as Murrow filed his live rooftop broadcasts. When Murrow introduced a topic the censor thought was too sensitive, the censor would tap Murrow on the wrist, and Murrow would quickly shift subjects.

As war activity increased, so did press restrictions and censorial concerns. In December 1940, a full year before Pearl Harbor, Navy Secretary

Frank Knox asked the media to refrain from reporting any details about shipyard construction or troop movements without authorization—a voluntary system that was deemed sufficient until Pearl Harbor was attacked on December 7, 1941. Less than two weeks later, Congress had established an official Office of Censorship and passed the War Powers Act, making the unofficial guidelines extremely official. Significantly, though, the Code of Wartime Practices, as the media guidelines were called, stopped short of perpetuating the controversial Espionage and Sedition Acts of World War I.

Even so, questions of patriotism and media content were in the air, even as Murrow and company were on the air. One Congressman, establishing a position that has been echoed ever since, rose to attack the broadcasting medium, accusing its dire commentaries from abroad of eroding patriotism at home. "Do their predictions aid the enemy?" Emanuel Celler of New York asked. "If disheartening predictions prove false, have they unnecessarily hurt home-front morale?" On the other side of the spectrum, Professor Max Lerner wondered if there wasn't "something a little hypochondriac in our preoccupation with our own patriotic temperature." Right in the middle was the NAB, which tightened its own industry guidelines by banning "livid news dramatizations," discontinuing weather forecasts (for fear of giving information to an enemy planning a bombing raid on the United States), and even discontinuing man-on-the-street interviews, out of fear that workers in defense plants might inadvertently let something slip.

Not even those restrictions were enough to appease all members of the military. In the Pacific, General Douglas MacArthur and Naval Chief of Operations Admiral Ernest J. King, acting with a dislike for reporters rivaling that of General Sherman during the Civil War, imposed tough review boards, pushed for stories that portrayed the Navy positively, and delayed or rejected stories with too negative a slant. Even in the continental United States, censors ordered reporters not to write any stories about race riots at army camps, for fear that the enemy would seize upon the news items as further grist for their bigoted propaganda mill. In fact, controls on the news media grew so stringent that as late as 1943, American newspapers and magazines were forbidden to publish any photographs of dead US soldiers. And all the way to the end of the war, MacArthur stood firm in his antimedia stance, going so far as to declare all of Nagasaki off limits to the press after the A-bomb was dropped.

Regardless, the media made their presence known. Radio's coverage of Roosevelt's "day that will live in infamy" Pearl Harbor speech was one of the century's most galvanizing events; Murrow's reports from London and elsewhere made history even as they reported it; and Joe Rosenthal's photo of troops raising the American flag at Iwo Jima became so cherished an image that it won a Pulitzer and became the model for a beloved memorial, even though the photo was staged.

According to rival war correspondents, Rosenthal had arrived hours late, heard about the soldiers who had raised a small flag as a patriotic gesture, and had them recreate it using a larger flag. And while the news media was not above using the military, the reverse was no less true. When it suited the military to have reporters in place, they were there: in Western Europe, 558 journalists were accredited to accompany invasion forces on D-Day, and Robert Capa's dramatic photographs of soldiers landing at Omaha Beach proved to be among the most famous and memorable of the entire war. The Office of War Information transmitted the D-Day story in twenty-eight languages, while American networks pre-empted all regular programs to present twenty-four-hour coverage. When the news broke, the number of radio sets in use rose 78 percent above normal, and stayed nearly 20 percent above normal for the rest of the week. "The biggest spot news story in history," *Broadcasting* magazine exulted, "was handled as expertly as if it were a routine occurrence."

It took days, even weeks, for film footage shot by news crews to be shipped or flown to the United States, where it was developed, edited, printed, distributed, and finally shown in movie theaters. Radio, not newsreels, owned World War II. The movies had the pictures, but radio had the immediacy. In fact, network radio's insistence on using only live reports actually proved a hindrance in covering many battles and stories. The technology existed to make recordings of distant battles or remote bombing raids, and bring them back for later transmission, but American radio stubbornly rejected to do anything of the sort.

"It was an idiotic ruling," Shirer later wrote, "that prevented American radio from doing the job it should have done during World War II." A few wars later, television would have both pictures *and* immediacy, and no reservations about using delayed reports from the field. Even at the end of World War II, TV began testing the waters, thanks to the February 1944 debut of NBC's *The War as It Happens*. Begun in New York and soon broadcast to Philadelphia and Schenectady as well, the ten-to-fifteen-minute weekly show did not quite live up to its title (most of the film was supplied, on a less than immediate basis, by the US Army Signal Corps), but it was the first television newscast seen regularly, and simultaneously, in different cities.

By 1950, when hostilities erupted in the Korean War, NBC had John Cameron Swayze and the *Camel News Caravan*, and CBS, ABC, and DuMont all had similar fifteen-minute newscasts in place. More than a hundred hours of United Nations debate on the Korean crisis had been televised, and film reports of hostilities were provided whenever possible. These black-and-white film reports, though, were transported and produced almost as slowly as newsreels had been during World War II. As for censorship of stories from Korea, both film crews and print journalists began the war working under an entirely voluntary system, but one in which military authorities "suggested" arbitrary and sometimes conflicting areas of sensitivity. Before too long, the Overseas Press Club formally requested specific guidelines to help them decide what stories and angles to pursue and avoid. By the time the war ended, five different censorship schemes had been implemented—some as stringent as MacArthur's multiple-censors approach, others much more lax, but none deemed totally successful by both the media and the military. Censors blocked transmission of certain stories for no justifiable reason, and reporters spent a lot of time trying to avoid or evade censorship.

On television, correspondents found documentaries, not fifteen-minute newscasts, the best forum for reporting and analyzing the Korean War. Even the best of them, though, had to learn to adapt to, and not abuse, this new medium. Murrow, the most popular and trusted reporter on radio during World War II, included a report from the Korean War on the 1951 premiere broadcast of *See It Now*, the weekly documentary series produced by Fred Friendly. It was part of the same, famous opening show in which live views of the Atlantic and Pacific Oceans were shown simultaneously, and the footage from Korea shown that day—*See It Now*, like *60 Minutes*, started out in a low-risk slot on Sunday afternoons—was remarkable in its own right.

Its natural sounds were recorded on site, rather than dubbed afterward in a studio, and the slogging of boots in the mud gave even a simple march a heightened sense of drama and reality. You heard the joking of soldiers as they moved equipment and dug foxholes, and, in the segment's concluding sequence, heard each member of the Second Platoon of Fox Company identify himself by name and hometown. Those literally moving snapshots were followed by Murrow, back in the studio, who announced soberly that in the short time since those scenes were shot, half of the young men just introduced to viewers had been wounded, killed, or reported missing in action. One critic wrote the next day that it was "the first Korea report that actually brought the war home to us," and *Variety* noted, "Where it had been generally accepted that video could never equal radio's job of reporting, Murrow and Friendly exploited to the full . . . the drama and excitement inherent in the news."

An ironic and noteworthy footnote to this story is that CBS News reporter Robert Pierpoint, who was the correspondent for the *See It Now* piece from Korea, had done a similar story for CBS radio earlier that same year. He had been with Fox Company at night, on the front lines, when artillery fire exploded close to their position and sent everyone diving into trenches. Pierpoint's tape recorder caught the whole thing, and Murrow and Friendly so liked the results they asked Pierpoint to do the same sort of story again, this time for their brand-new television show. But as Joseph E. Persico recounts in *Edward R. Murrow: An American Original*, Pierpoint knew he could not take TV cameras and lights to the front lines at night ("The minute we turned those lights on, I didn't know who would shoot me first, our GIs or the Chinese"). And besides, Fox Company had taken heavy casualties and been reassigned to the rear. So Pierpoint filmed the company at its rest area, which is where most of the footage for that first *See It Now* was taken. Murrow's *See It Now* narration never claimed the images were from the front lines; then again, it never made it clear they were not. In any case, the scenes were more human and touching than those shown in newsreels, and *See It Now,* like other fine TV nonfiction shows, would learn to recognize and utilize television's particular strengths quickly and impressively.

Thirteen months later, in December 1952, *See It Now* returned to that war with a one-hour special called *Christmas in Korea.* Murrow and his correspondents visited the front lines (for real, this time) and supply lines, the hospital patients and the fighter pilots, and relayed the faces and thoughts of the American soldiers back to audiences in the United States. *Christmas in Korea,* assembled skillfully by Friendly, put the war in starkly human terms, and included the types of sentiment that would have been declared criminal during World War I.

When correspondent Pierpoint, still on duty for *See It Now,* asks a private from Cedar Rapids, Iowa, what he thinks of the war, the soldier pauses and says, "Can't see the sense of it." Ed Scott, interviewing soldiers very close to the front lines, asks them the same question, and one replies, "It is pretty hard for me to figure out. I tried to think of it in different ways, but I come up with the same answer—that I think it's a bunch of nonsense." Murrow taped his closing sequence on Christmas morning in Korea, and the entire special was broadcast three days later. Murrow's final words on the program were damning in their intentional lack of finality: "There is no conclusion to this report from Korea," he said, "because there is no end to the war."

The response, from critics and viewers, was emotional and enthusiastic. The show had provided a much closer look at war, at its lowest and ultimately most important level, than the newsreels or newscasts had yet provided. Instead of "shots of bombers tearing great holes in the Korean real estate," TV critic John Crosby wrote in the *New York Herald Tribune,* the cameras focused on the soldiers of Fox Company "as they ate and slept and gambled and groaned and joked," capturing "the humanity of an essentially inhuman profession." Ben Gross of the *New York Daily News* wrote that the show provided "the most graphic and yet sensitive pictures of war we have ever seen." In the *New York Times,* Jack Gould praised *Christmas in Korea* as "a visual poem, one of the finest programs ever seen on television."

Here, one conflict earlier than commonly thought, was the first true "living-room war." Television, at that moment, reflected a different image of war than newsreels or most newscasts. Viewers heard—and, even more unusually, saw—expressions of skepticism and disapproval from American fighting men. For many watching at home, it was a first-time experience, but would not be the last. Vietnam was just around the corner.

Even though the Vietnam War generated some outstanding wartime reporting from print journalists (David Halberstam and Peter Arnett, just to name two), it came to be known as "the living-room war," a phrase popularized by Michael Arlen, TV critic of the *New Yorker.* Part of the reason was that technology and television had made some rather giant strides in the intervening decade.

Network newscasts, by then, were thirty minutes long, and reports from the field came on videotape as well as film—saving, in the former case, precious time otherwise spent in the developing room. Faster transportation and communication systems also reduced the lag time in getting a news story from the fields of Vietnam to the TV screens of America, and the relatively unrestricted movement of civilian aircraft and vehicles in and out of war zones made it comparatively easy for reporters to get their crews in and their stories out.

Because the military had no official control over civilian movement, and because it was thought in the early years of Vietnam that a greater press presence would increase interest and support in the war from those back home, Vietnam war correspondents worked under no compulsory censorship rules. Only the minimal voluntary guidelines, established in previous wars, applied. This allowed print and TV reporters to pursue and file their own stories, as well as attend the daily military briefings known derisively as "The Five O'Clock Follies." These briefings rarely generated much news, but certain TV reports from the field certainly did.

One of the most famous reports from the Vietnam War came early, when CBS correspondent Morley Safer followed marines in 1965 as they retaliated against villagers suspected of aiding the Vietcong. Safer and the CBS camera captured the action as soldiers, using cigarette lighters, set fire to more than a hundred thatched huts, leveling an entire community and making its men, women, and children temporarily homeless. It became known as the "Zippo lighter" report, and, like certain photographs from previous wars, became an indelible part of our American historical consciousness.

Later in the war, both Eddie Adams's print photograph and the as-it-happened film account of the execution by a South Vietnamese police chief of a Vietcong officer would prove equally memorable. In the print photo, published in newspapers and magazines everywhere, the right arm of General Loan (the police chief) is outstretched, his pistol aimed at the bound captive's head, and the captive's face frozen in a painful grimace as the bullet penetrates his skull. On film, the drama continues, swiftly and silently, as the prisoner's body slumps to the ground, blood spurting from the bullet hole in his head. Those images—individual, almost incidental examples of wartime hostility, frustration, and brutality—stuck, and came to exemplify the war itself. And on the evening news, other battle pictures, statistics, and commentary piled up—night after night, month after month, year after year, adding up to what Arlen called "those almost helplessly routinizing film clips of combat." Even when television had nothing new to report, it was there as a presence and a force, reminding viewers that nothing was new, and adding to the perception that the war effort was not proceeding swiftly, if at all. Vietnam was seldom out of mind, because television would not let it be out of sight.

While the nightly newscasts during the Vietnam War were infinitely more important a factor than during the Korean War, documentaries related to Vietnam sometimes carried significant clout as well. Just to name three, each of which made an impact at a different stage of the conflict, consider the 1967 public television documentary *Inside North Vietnam* (originally commissioned by CBS), the 1968 Walter Cronkite CBS special, and the 1971 *The Selling of the Pentagon,* also on CBS.

The first documentary, showing behind-enemy-lines footage of bomb craters in civilian areas and depicting what life was like for the citizens of North Vietnam, ended up on public television in 1967 after CBS declined its option on the Felix Greene film. *Inside North Vietnam* so enraged war supporters that thirty-three congressmen signed a letter of protest to National Educational Television without having seen the film. Nevertheless, *Saturday Review* critic Cleveland Amory called it "superb," and its objective look behind enemy lines would have echoes in coverage of a future war.

In February 1968, a month after the Tet Offensive, Cronkite returned from Saigon to write and present a half-hour special in which he shed the mantle of objective anchorman and gave his own opinion about what he had just witnessed and heard in Vietnam.

"It seems now more certain than ever," the veteran newscaster—the Most Trusted Man in America—told his viewers that night, "that the bloody experience of Vietnam is to end in a stalemate." As David Halberstam noted in *The Powers That Be,* "it was the first time in American history a war had been declared over by an anchorman." Halberstam quoted President Johnson as saying if he had lost Walter Cronkite, he had lost Mr. Average Citizen. It was a broadcast that marked a shift in tone throughout CBS; even though its correspondents had pushed hard-hitting stories through the pipeline before, CBS after the Cronkite special was more likely to question the official body counts and optimistic pronouncements. So, for that matter, were the other networks, and even the print press: Cronkite's stature was such that his opinion mattered even to the editors of the nation's leading newspapers.

And in February 1971, the CBS broadcast of the Peter Davis documentary *The Selling of the Pentagon,* with Roger Mudd as correspondent, attacked the public-relations and lobbying arms of the American military complex itself. The program thought the unthinkable, mentioned the unmentionable: it suggested the American military industry was as interested in protecting its budget appropriations and fat-cat contracts as in protecting the global peace.

"Pentagon propaganda insists on America's role as the cop on every beat in the world," Mudd said. "Not only the public, but the press as well, has been beguiled—including, at times, ourselves at CBS News. This propaganda barrage is the creation of a runaway bureaucracy that frustrates attempts to control it."

The documentary was itself slightly propagandistic: in at least one case, it was proven that an interview subject's responses to certain questions were edited to appear they actually were replies to other questions entirely. The controversy about the program's production and journalistic techniques undercut the credibility of the message somewhat, and CBS found itself facing a Congressional subcommittee—yet the network television attack on the military in *The Selling of the Pentagon* would not be forgotten by either the viewers who saw it or the administration and Pentagon officials who endured it.

Those and other documentaries, coupled with the often literally colorful coverage on nightly newscasts (the dead and dying in Vietnam, by the late sixties, were filmed and televised in "living color"), made their mark and, in terms of Pentagon public relations, took their toll. By the time Saigon fell in 1975, with Peter Arnett one of three reporters staying behind to report the action for the Associated Press, the media and the government had been polarized by the Vietnam War—and even more so by Watergate—to the point where neither seemed to trust the other at all.

In retrospect, some in the government and the military blamed the media for all that went wrong in Vietnam, and became determined not to make the same mistakes twice. That meant, in future wars, limiting media access and doing everything in their power to prevent reporters from telling their stories in emotional, human terms. Almost as important as not losing another war to an enemy, it appeared, was not losing another battle to the news media.

In the eighties, satellite technology and sophisticated portable video equipment appeared to favor the media enormously. Stories could be sent from any location with access to a satellite transponder, and, in cases of breaking news coverage, could be sent live and relayed to viewers instantaneously. Infrared filters could permit photography at night without the use of additional illumination, so even live reports from the battlefield after dark were a technical reality and a definite possibility. More like a probability, actually, because the appetite and avenues for TV news had mushroomed with the growth of cable television. Instead of a fifteen-minute network newscast during the Korean War, or a thirty-minute newscast and occasional documentaries during the Vietnam War, there were twenty-four-hour news services like Cable News Network, and aggressive network news programs like ABC's *Nightline*. In the Civil War, photographers could not shoot anything that moved. In whatever war came next in the eighties, television could shoot anything that moved, day or night, and bring it back live.

The next military action involving US forces came in 1983, with the invasion of Grenada. It was then that the government, faced with the realization there was no longer any way to prevent independent reporters in the field from getting their stories out, decided to circumvent the problem by not letting reporters in. During the Grenada campaign, American military planners instituted and enforced a total ban on media access to the war zone, which, from the administration's standpoint, worked only too well. News organizations thought otherwise, and thus were in a weak bargaining position when a Joint Chiefs of Staff panel set out to draft a new, workable set of censorship guidelines.

Formalized, somewhat fittingly, in 1984, the panel's report essentially returned to the sensible guidelines from World War II, but with several additional recommendations. Among them were a suggestion that pool reporters be used if that was the most feasible method of providing access during the early stage of a military operation, and a polite threat that if any reporters violated the principles of voluntary censorship, their credentials should be revoked for the duration of the war. For the military, the official guidelines and unofficial suggestions returned a lot of the media control that had eroded during the Vietnam War. For the media, they at least appeared to prevent another total press lockout, as had happened in Grenada.

The December 1989 invasion of Panama was the first test of these new rules, but it was over too quickly to provide a proper test. It did, however, provide clear hints of things to come. When the attack was launched, it was a sudden and massive operation. Reporters eventually gained access to report from Panama, but only in organized pools, and these proved both cumbersome and overly controlled—kept out of harm's way, and out of the news's way as well. The press was frustrated. The government was jubilant.

The Gulf War was next.

When US forces first were sent to the Persian Gulf, on August 8, 1990, reporters were denied permission to accompany them. Within a week, a seventeen-member press pool was allowed to set up shop in Dhahran, Saudi Arabia, but they were accompanied by six press officers assigned by Assistant Secretary of Defense for Public Affairs Louis A. (Pete) Williams—who, by the time the war was over, would become a very familiar face to millions of viewers. Those six officers established the Joint Information Bureau (JIB), the wartime censorship unit through which those (and subsequent) reporters cleared their stories. Williams and his staff worked on many drafts of what would be the official guidelines, which were finalized and announced on January 7, 1991.

Those guidelines specified a dozen categories of information the military considered restricted, and introduced procedures that effectively hampered both the gathering and dissemination of news. On the news-gathering side, access was restricted to pool reporters, whose daily movements were tightly controlled—and who were forced to accept, if assigned, the presence of a military escort whose job was to stand by and listen in during interviews with soldiers.

Though technology made it easy to get stories out quickly, the military's security review system made it difficult. The new rules required all stories, pictures, and photographs from pool journalists to be approved by military public affairs officers, which slowed the news flow considerably. An appeals process was built into the procedure, allowing reporters some official recourse if they disagreed with the ruling of the public affairs officer in the field. Reporters could take their case, and the questionable material, to the JIB—then, in another step in the appeals process, to Williams's office in Washington. Then and only then, if the material was still ruled improper after all those reviews, could news organizations choose to publish or broadcast the material in question and risk the consequences.

On its surface, the guidelines sounded fair. Beneath the surface, they served as a way of freezing "unwanted" stories and images in a holding pattern until their news value was reduced or even eliminated. Pool reporters could be steered in the direction of some stories and denied access to others, while other reporters could be denied access to almost anything and anywhere, and could even be denied inclusion in the pool itself. These were the restrictions and guidelines in place on January 7. Nine days later, when the Allied bombing of Iraq began, they were the guidelines under which television set out with the capability to broadcast yet another first: the first "live" living-room war.

In the months leading up to the bombing, TV informed viewers fairly well, and not only on the nightly news shows. Shortly after American troops were dispatched in August, ABC News presented a prime-time special called *A Line in the Sand*, explaining the history and possible consequences of the Middle East conflict (a second special, updating the situation, was presented January 14, two days before the war began). CNN's nightly *Crisis in the Gulf* specials were up and running by mid-August. In September, *Frontline* broadcast a special called *The Arming of Iraq*, tracing the rise, and measuring the might, of that country's military power. And so on, with those and other networks escalating their efforts, matching the Gulf conflict's escalating tensions.

A lot was background, a lot was conjecture and analysis, but some of it was spellbinding and important—and the closer it got to midnight January 15, the United Nations' deadline for Iraqi withdrawal from Kuwait, the more valuable television became. The debates in Congress about whether to authorize the use of military force, broadcast live the weekend before the deadline by C-SPAN, public broadcasting, and other sources, provided gripping coverage of democracy in action. And when the deadline came and went, the network news organizations were prepared—some more than others—to cover the possible onset of hostilities.

From the other side of the tube, as a viewer, it was not hard to see what was coming: the media, print and broadcast, had offered and elicited plenty of opinion about the optimum dates, hours and methods of attack should America and its allies want to launch an air strike. That was why, on the afternoon of January 16, I had six television sets and VCRs running, a babysitter hired to watch the kids all evening, and space held open for the later editions of the *New York Post* late Wednesday afternoon. In the event hostilities erupted during the evening news or prime time, I'd be ready and waiting. I wasn't a mind reader—just a news reader, and a TV viewer. The media, in setting the stage for the Gulf conflict, had performed rather well. Strategically, there was talk of when weather conditions, tides, and cycles of the moon offered the most opportunistic "windows" for an air strike. Emotionally, there was talk of the heightened tensions at home and abroad—talk that often carried great weight and resonance.

One resonant moment came less than three hours before the first bombs dropped. Cronkite, a guest on CNN's *International Hour*, was talking by telephone to the network's staff in Baghdad, urging them to pack up and come home because of the impending danger. "I think you guys are really under the gun, all right," Cronkite warned Bernard Shaw. And when Peter Arnett, an old friend, got on the line, Cronkite's tone turned more casual, but no less concerned.

"Peter," Cronkite said, "you're a very valuable asset to courageous reporting throughout the world." Then he added, in a pleading, almost paternal voice, "Don't grandstand this one. Save your skin, boy." Within hours, the special cellular phone lines on which Arnett and Shaw had talked to Cronkite would become the chief media link between Baghdad and the American people, and bombs would be falling all around them.

Less than an hour before war broke out, viewers with home satellite dishes could hone in and eavesdrop on a particular CNN news feed—a not-for-broadcast internal communication between the Middle East and CNN headquarters—and watch, live, the actual launch of Operation Desert Storm, though it was never identified as such. As *Satellite Orbit* columnist Jay Hylsky later described:

> At 6 P.M. ET, nearly an hour before the first official reports of war . . . dish owners could see CNN correspondent Charles Jaco and a CNN camera crew in Saudi Arabia rushing about a lot more anxiously than usual to get ready for live reports. Jet fighters could be heard roaring into the sky every few minutes. The CNN crew was discussing the likelihood that the fighters were off to bomb Iraq and Kuwait. Even before any confirmation, viewers got an eerie feeling that the war was unfolding.

I did not have a satellite dish, but I watched that night, and for weeks thereafter, with TV screens and VCRs tuned to CBS, NBC, ABC, PBS, CNN, and C-SPAN simultaneously—watching a war unfold from six perspectives at once, and reporting and analyzing the results. Here, as the only personal "war story" I'll include here, is a sample from my *New York Post* column for Thursday, January 17, 1990, written on deadline for the final edition:

> Operation Desert Storm, the American code name for the air strike against Iraq, was launched last night without warning, but with unprecedented exposure. It began during the networks' early evening newscasts, and the start of it was broadcast live—by ABC and CNN, at least—thereby making history even as it reported it.
>
> CBS, NBC, and ABC had all just begun their 6:30 P.M. national newscasts with updates on the Persian Gulf crisis, and CNN was midway through its news hour. Just before 6:40 P.M., ABC's Gary Shepard began to describe to Peter Jennings what CNN's John Holliman, based in the same Baghdad hotel as Shepard, was simultaneously describing on CNN:

a sighting of tracer fire, explosive flashes in the sky, and the sounds of gunfire and antiaircraft fire.

There were no pictures, but the sound from CNN and ABC made it clear—frighteningly, incredibly clear—that Baghdad was under attack. 'I can feel the building shaking underneath me,' Shepard said. . . .

ABC and CNN had the momentum in that initial hour of coverage, and CNN had the bulk of the drama. By keeping its phone line open from the point at which the air strike began, CNN presented an almost uninterrupted stream of reports from its CNN crew in Baghdad—led by the brave and brilliant reporting of John Holliman, Peter Arnett, and CNN anchor Bernard Shaw.

Shortly after the first air strike, Shaw left the room to do some legwork inside the hotel, leaving the open mike—which the Baghdad crew wasn't even certain was operational—in the hands of Arnett, the veteran reporter who had covered Vietnam from ground level, and the descriptive, informative Holliman. . . .

There's no sense cowering from the comparison. It was the most riveting eyewitness account of a war strike since Edward R. Murrow intoned those famous words, "This is London."

Later, even reporters in Saudi Arabia were dragged into the drama as sirens on military bases in Saudi Arabia sounded, warning of the possibility of a missile attack. Reporters fled for cover, donned gas masks and protective gear, and viewers were left feeling, voyeuristically, some small sense of the panic, uncertainty and mortality of wartime.

The night of the attack, President Bush explained his motives behind the air strike in an unscheduled TV address carried by all the major commercial and news networks. That address was seen in an estimated 71.5 million households, which means it was watched by more Americans than any single broadcast in television history—with the exception of John F. Kennedy's funeral. CNN's coverage that first night was seen in nearly 11 million cable households, the largest audience in the history of cable.

And the following night, with viewers riveted to the networks' expanded evening newscasts, bombs fell once again, but this time, Iraq was the aggressor, not the target. And this time, on live TV, they fell on Israel. Tom Fenton of CBS, reporting live from Tel Aviv, told Dan Rather there'd just been an explosion in that city. "I'm putting on my gas mask right now," he said, reporting and repeating the fear that Saddam Hussein may have unleashed chemical weapons. The next few hours were, almost without argument, the most frightening and important of the entire Gulf War. Was nerve gas used in any of the warheads? And whether it was or not, would Israel retaliate?

Watching all those channels at once led to two unforgettable viewing experiences that second night of Operation Desert Storm. One was watching simultaneous reports from three different network correspondents— NBC's Martin Fletcher in Tel Aviv; CNN's Larry Register and ABC's Dean Reynolds in Jerusalem—all of whom were wearing gas masks. General Sherman's phrase about "news from hell" seemed to take on a whole new meaning. And later that same night, as the networks scurried to chase down the truth about the nerve gas rumors, there was a moment when what you heard depended upon which network you watched.

NBC confirmed that nerve gas agents had been dropped, while, at the same time on rival networks, ABC cited two independent sources saying the same thing, CBS said it had insufficient information to confirm or deny it, and CNN denied it. NBC and ABC quickly, and somewhat sheepishly, retracted their stories and pressed onward. By 10 P.M., ABC recouped with a coup, showing the first images from Baghdad under siege. Taken by a free-lance British cameraman under contract to ABC, the green-tinged pictures were taken using a special night scope, and provided the visual fireworks that matched the images Arnett and company had described by telephone the previous evening. Those pictures became an indelible part of the national memory of the Gulf War—a war, in the end, that offered several unforgettable visuals without really showing a lot.

In previous wars, soldiers figured prominently in the most durable photographs and films. Because of pool restrictions during the Gulf War, however, reporters were kept far away from most of the action, and most of the ground-level fighting men and women as well. From the "official" coverage, the only members of the military to surface as stars were generals who already wore them—predominantly General Norman Schwarzkopf. Pictures that defined the war were provided, for the most part, by the high command, and they were carefully selected to be both ruthless and bloodless, showing "smart bombs" that could be guided into the ventilation chimneys and other weak points of enemy buildings, and showing the resultant demolition without any signs of human casualties.

Sometimes when releasing these photos to the media during a televised briefing, Schwarzkopf would even joke about them. When an aerial view from a bomber's scope showed a truck passing through the crosshairs, driving safely off a bridge just before it was blown up, Schwarzkopf called the driver "the luckiest man in Iraq on this particular day." (It was the sort of footage that prompted comparisons to a modern video game, although, incredibly, the smart bomb point-of-view image actually goes back to the earliest days of television. In 1928, experimental New York station W2XAD, in one of its earliest telecasts, mounted a science-fiction production dramatizing a guided missile attack on New York City, from the point of view of the missile itself. All the TV director did was zoom slowly in on an aerial photograph of the city and end with an explosion, yet it was an eerie forerunner of the "high-tech" Gulf War bombing footage.)

So, what televised moments from the Gulf War appear destined to stick, to become that conflict's equivalent of Safer's Zippo lighter? The contenders for this dubious honor say a lot about the manner in which the Gulf War was managed by the military.

Leaders, not soldiers or pilots, dominate the spotlight. Weapons, not people, take precedence. Officially released military photos stress accuracy and avoid bloodshed. The closest glimpse of actual carnage comes at the end of the war, hours before the liberation of Kuwait City, when an impromptu convoy of hundreds of Iraqi military and civilian vehicles is pummeled by coalition bombers—and even then, all we see is the aftermath, the smoking hulls, the long-distance remnants of lives and limbs. Not once do we see bombsight footage of such a sortie in progress, where death, as well as destruction, would be clearly visible. Consider, instead, what makes the list in this admittedly subjective compilation of what might be called "The Gulf War's Greatest Hits":

The initial air strike on Iraq. Our perspective was limited to Baghdad, but that was enough. Shaw, Holliman, and especially Arnett provided a spellbinding audio-only commentary that lasted through the first night. Night-scope pictures of the strike, eventually smuggled out and broadcast, added memorable visuals, but the CNN reporters already had painted an indelible portrait with words. It was TV as radio, and it was historic.

The initial air strike on Israel. Gas masks and overall panic. Scuds rained over Israel. Confusion reigned over American television.

Subsequent Scud scares. NBC's Arthur Kent and CNN's Charles Jaco became instant celebrities because of their seeming inability to seek out bomb shelters. From the rooftop of the Dhahran International Hotel, Kent offered instant play-by-play of a Patriot missile intercepting and destroying an incoming Scud, pointing out the aerial confrontation with the coolness of an astronomy professor—and brandishing his gas mask like an L. L. Bean accessory. "This is not a drill, New York," he snapped, lobbying to go live as a Patriot was launched nearby with a frightening roar. "Let's go, let's go!" *Entertainment Weekly* ran a fan-magazine-style story about Kent, dubbing him "Arthur of Arabia" in the headline, and adding to the previously coined, equally ridiculous nickname "Scud Stud." Jaco, meanwhile, stood on an outdoor platform during Scud attacks and earned points for both bravery and unpredictability. When he mistook exhaust fumes from a Patriot missile for what he feared was poison gas, he demonstrated abject fear while fumbling for and donning his gas mask. Not a proud moment, but definitely not a dull one, either. On another occasion, he screamed "Break it down!" to his CNN crew, instructing them to scurry for the bomb shelters. These scenes with Kent and Jaco had the tension and flavor of instant war movies, which, in a way, was exactly what they were. Meanwhile, the footage of Patriot missiles seeking and destroying incoming Scuds became, in that war, the most instantly recognizable shots heard round the world.

The Schwarzkopf briefings. There weren't many of these, but each one had its durable highlights—high-tech bomb footage, wise-guy wisecracks, tough-guy posturing, tender-guy emoting. Though Schwarzkopf has admitted that one of his own military heroes is famed reporter-hater William T. Sherman, the modern major general handled the media as effectively as he handled the Iraqi forces, and could be joking or menacing, depending upon the question. When asked his opinion of Saddam Hussein's leadership, Schwarzkopf replied dryly that the leader of Iraq was "neither a strategist, nor is he schooled in the operational art, nor is he a tactician, nor is he a general, nor is he a soldier. Other than that, he is a great military man." On the other hand, when asked to comment on a newspaper article painting an unflattering portrait of one military operation, Schwarzkopf snarled, "I would describe that report as bovine scatology—B.S." Shortly before the official end of the ground war, Schwarzkopf's one-hour briefing on the operation's success, in which he displayed maps, strategic details, and a wide range of emotions, enhanced his reputation even more. When one reporter asked whether the breached Iraqi minefields were "not as intense" as the military had expected, Schwarzkopf angrily fired off a question of his own. "Have you ever been in a minefield?" When the reporter quietly replied that he had not, the general—who earned his third Silver Star by leading a company across one in Vietnam—continued coldly, "Because all there's got to be is one mine, and that's intense." End of exchange. And when settling on an analogy for the surprise flanking maneuver that sent forces deep into Iraq, Schwarzkopf, forsaking military doublespeak, said, "We did what could best be described as the Hail Mary play in football." Standing next to his map, pointer in hand, clothed in his four-star camouflage uniform, Schwarzkopf virtually personified American military involvement in the Gulf war.

Smart bombs. The smart bombs made war look sterile and easy, even though the majority of bombs dropped on Iraq were of a more conventional, less accurate design. By withholding footage of those types of hits (and misses), the military created and perpetuated an illusion of exactitude that did not exist. Yet television was so starved for images, footage of smart bombs seeking and hitting their targets became memorable not only because of their technical proficiency and visual majesty, but because TV news shows repeated them endlessly.

"Dumb" reporters. It wasn't really that the reporters in the various military press briefings were stupid—just that they were made to appear so by the surroundings. When they pressed for specifics, their questions often were deflected as jeopardizing national security. If reporters pressed further, they generally were seen as rude. The newsgathering process was no different from the "Five O'Clock Follies" of Vietnam, but those were not televised at all, much less broadcast live. The public at large resented what they perceived as a rude and stupid press corps, and even *Saturday Night Live* came down on the side of the military: when *SNL* mounted a sketch about the military briefings, the reporters, not the generals, were the butt of the jokes.

The POWs. The American military was reluctant to zero in on human faces and human suffering during the Gulf War, but Iraqi commanders had no such reservations. Within a week of the start of Operation Desert Storm, Iraq released audiotapes, then the accompanying video, of allied prisoners of war. Most of the thirteen captured pilots (eight of whom were American) displayed bruised and bloody faces, and slurred or robotic voices, as they identified themselves and repeated antiwar statements that few viewers doubted had been thrust and forced upon them. Each television network had to decide what its viewers would see and hear, and sometimes reached different conclusions. By dint of an unofficial consensus—and a harrowing *Newsweek* cover photo—the one POW who came to represent all the rest was Navy Lieutenant Jeffrey Zaun, who was finally released March 4. That cover photo, shot directly from a TV screen, prompted so much negative and emotional mail that the editors of *Newsweek* defended their decision in print a few weeks later. It was a defense that bears repeating: "Throughout the opening days of the war, there was an inclination among military briefers, the press and much of the American public to view the war as a remote and somehow antiseptic conflict. *Newsweek* genuinely believes it was the images of the anguished and battered faces of the captured pilots that brought the war home to many Americans."

Peter Arnett in Baghdad. Indisputably, Arnett was the most valuable and controversial correspondent during the Gulf War. He was the only reporter stationed in Baghdad from start to finish, and many of the most lasting moments of TV coverage from the war were reports in which Arnett could be seen or heard: the first-night sixteen-hour audio coverage, with Arnett expertly distinguishing between antiaircraft fire and incoming explosions. Arnett's video tour, cleared by Iraqi censors and with handlers standing nearby, of what Iraq claimed were the bombed remains of a baby-milk factory. Arnett's unexpected, exclusive January 28 interview with Saddam Hussein, face-to-face and with no restrictions on the types of questions asked. Arnett's bleak photographic report of the Baghdad building in which hundreds of Iraqi civilians had died, even though the American government insisted the shelter was actually a military target. When reporting other wars, Arnett amassed awards (including a 1966 Pulitzer Prize while in Vietnam), and proved no stranger to relaying things that would exemplify and outlast the conflict he was witnessing. Arnett was the reporter who got that famous quote from an American adviser after a particularly nasty Mekong Delta operation—the quote that "It was necessary to destroy the village in order to save it." Yet armed with a television camera crew and an uplink satellite dish, Arnett walked away with not only the story, but with stardom.

Iraqi soldiers surrendering. The instances of such behavior were plentiful, but two images stand out among the rest. One was the oft-repeated scene of a small, isolated group of soldiers who had dropped to their knees to surrender peacefully, and what appeared to be gratefully, to a cameraman from an Italian TV news crew. The other image was of an astoundingly long line of Iraqi prisoners of war, being marched single file across the desert, hands on their heads. Thanks, for the most part, to careful media handling by the military, TV viewers saw countless more live prisoners than Iraqi corpses, even though the latter far outnumbered the former. Allies stopped counting enemy prisoners when the count topped 26,000, and Schwarzkopf—who participated in, yet privately hated, the "body count" exercises in Vietnam—deflected similar questions about the Gulf war by saying only that "There were very, very large numbers of dead."

Burning oil fields. Saddam Hussein accused American military leaders of rupturing oil wells and starting a devastating series of fires in Kuwait. The American military, on the other hand, accused the Iraqi leader of intentionally sabotaging the oil fields himself. While sorting out the truth, reporters scrambled—in some cases, away from the protective cocoons of the pool restrictions—to photograph the fires and oil spills and measure the extent of air and water pollution in the Persian Gulf. Once footage became available, raging fires—always a reliable staple of TV newscasts— became a lasting image of the Gulf War. So did close-up pictures of dying, oil-covered corcorans, which were all over the news in those days when the environmental angle was vigorously pursued. The irony there, naturally, was that showing the ornithological victims of hostilities in the Gulf was something TV was allowed to do, while showing the human victims was another matter entirely.

The ride into Kuwait City. In the last days of the Gulf conflict, the promise of live TV war coverage became a reality. CBS correspondent Bob McKeown and three colleagues, breaking from the press pool and heading out on their own with the capability to transmit live video and audio, broadcast an exclusive "Road to Kuwait City" daylight drive, allowing viewers to see what was left of the landscape as they made the long, unauthorized trip to the embattled capital. When McKeown reached Kuwait City, broadcasting live in pitch darkness as jubilant Kuwaitis scurried from the shadows to welcome him, CBS had quite a scoop—and viewers had a rare look at what reporting could have been like with less severe military restrictions. ABC's Forrest Sawyer, who followed McKeown into Kuwait City, accompanied Saudi and Egyptian forces with his own satellite uplink, and confirmed with his own dramatic nighttime reports that the technology worked—and that reporters, in similar wartime situations, should be allowed to do likewise. It makes a certain amount of sense, though, that such live reports of troops on the move are safe to show only when no resistance is expected—when, for all intents and purposes, the war is over.

Walter Cronkite, while arguing for greater press freedoms in a *Newsweek* opinion piece published the last week of the war, granted that the concept of live battlefield coverage was "nothing but science fiction, despite our early experience of seeing Baghdad, Tel Aviv and Dhahran under attack, live in our living rooms." Imagine, he asked, "the Iraqi commander monitoring American troop movements via CNN!" The military should, and would, not allow that, of course, but in the Gulf War, the military did not allow much of anything.

When President Bush addressed the nation the first night of Operation Desert Storm and vowed, "This will *not* be another Vietnam," he was talking about the duration and casualty count of that war, but could just as easily be referring to the government's handling of the media. Controls were enforced so tightly that pool reporters had few places to go and even fewer genuine news items to report when they got there—and even then, stories and TV reports were delayed and edited while the layers of censors reviewed the content and language of each one. The week before the war began, with the finalized Pentagon guidelines going into effect, wartime censorship was one of the only stories the media could pursue aggressively. *The MacNeil/Lehrer NewsHour* devoted the bulk of two entire shows to military censorship and the proper role of the press; Phil Donahue held a sober, informative two-part roundtable with media correspondents on his syndicated *Donahue* show; Ted Koppel moderated a debate on the issue for *Nightline;* and several reporters in the Middle East filed stories, or were quoted in stories by colleagues, and went on the record to complain about the severity of the Gulf War press restrictions.

Significantly, two of the TV reporters who voiced objections early, Forrest Sawyer and CBS reporter Bob Simon, later broke away from the pool system in search of independent, unauthorized stories. "There is a beast of war out there, an elephant we're trying to describe," Forrest Sawyer said on *Nightline.* "Based on the information we're given, we're about at the toenail range." At the end of the war, Sawyer dove out of the pool and made his way to Kuwait City in time to record that city's liberation. Bob Simon, on the January 11 edition of *CBS This Morning,* complained to host Paula Zahn about the chilling effects the Defense Department's new rules would have on press coverage. One such effect was the elimination of the type of candid and casual comments Murrow elicited from soldiers in the groundbreaking *Christmas in Korea.* During the Gulf War, "escort officers" were to be present during interviews with soldiers and officers, which Simon said would inhibit and intimidate them. "It affects the very intimacy of the kinds of conversations you can have with people," he complained, adding, "Not only do we have to be with an escort officer, but we are traveling in what are known as 'pools,' which means that at least seven of us are together at the same time. It is enforced pack journalism."

The day before Operation Desert Storm began, Simon linked the stringent media guidelines in the Gulf to military memories of another war. "The [military] brass is still convinced that the press had a lot to do with the political fallout from the war, so they are trying to do what they can to prevent those things from happening again," Simon told *USA Today.* During the next few days, Simon not only provided one of the best TV stories about the press restrictions, but he and his team broke away from the pool on January 18, without authorization, to find, tape, and report a minor skirmish in "the no-man's-land between Saudi Arabia and Kuwait." Two days later, Simon and company (producer Peter Bluff, cameraman Roberto Alvarez, and sound man Juan Caldera) went out alone again— and were captured by Iraqi soldiers and held as POWs until after the war.

The first POWs taken by Iraq, the thirteen pilots captured during the early days of Operation Desert Storm, prompted several levels of media censorship and self-censorship. The most absurd example was a military spokesman who, days after the American pilots had been paraded on Iraqi TV, refused to confirm their status as POWs. The most introspective, perhaps, was ABC's internal decision to refrain from broadcasting certain audio portions of the recorded statements of prisoners—a sensitivity acquired after ABC correspondent Charles Glass's hostage ordeal in Lebanon in 1987, during which he was coerced into making certain remarks at gunpoint. All the network news organizations showed the Iraqi television footage, however, because their capture and survival were newsworthy, and all networks added caveats about the probability that the prisoners were tortured and threatened into making antiwar statements. It was one case where military concerns were fully warranted: after a story or two circulated in which relatives of certain POWs described their loved ones' tones as robotic or exaggeratedly different from normal, the word went out quickly, and convincingly, that any such information could be harmful to the hostages if it found its way back to Iraq.

Other restrictions, imposed as the war went on, made gathering and broadcasting the news increasingly difficult, and TV correspondents based in other countries had to adhere to their rules as well. When NBC correspondent Martin Fletcher reported, without getting prior approval from the Israelis, that a Scud attack in Tel Aviv had claimed casualties, Israel cut off NBC's satellite capabilities, and refused to restore them until Tom Brokaw apologized on television for violating the Israeli censorship agreements. (Which he did, quickly.) The lack of access to real action turned TV correspondents like Jaco and Kent into field soldiers by proxy: theirs was the only danger in sight, so they attracted the attention, worry, and glory that, under a less restrictive newsgathering system, should have been aimed at the pilots—and, later, the ground soldiers—themselves. The correspondents also benefited from the fact that, for the most part, it was a story distant and dangerous enough to keep the anchors from descending and taking over. In part, some TV correspondents' reputations were made during the Gulf War because they were permitted to do so.

Their dramatic exploits, seen nightly on national and sometimes international television, gave TV correspondents the edge in terms of visibility as well as technology. Print reporters, in and out of the pool system, filed some excellent stories during the war, but not one was met with the kind of celebrity accorded the likes of Arnett and Kent—and when reporters saw things the TV cameras did not, their stories often received too little attention.

Reporter John Balzar of the *Los Angeles Times* was assigned as a pool reporter to cover a helicopter aviation brigade in the Eighteenth Army Corps, which was running night raids into Iraq shortly before the start of the ground war. Balzar was shown infrared gun-camera footage of one of those raids, and wrote graphically about what he saw:

> Through the powerful night-vision gunsights they looked like ghostly sheep, flushed from a pen—Iraqi infantry soldiers bewildered and terri-

fied, jarred from sleep and fleeing their bunkers under a hellstorm of fire.

One by one they were cut down by attackers they couldn't see or understand. Some were literally blown to bits by bursts of 30mm exploding cannon shells. One man dropped, writhed on the ground, and struggled to his feet. Another burst tore him apart.

It was just the sort of thing the military wanted to prevent the press, and the public, from seeing. Incredibly, Balzar's story made it through the Defense Department restrictions relatively unscathed, but after it was filed Balzar and the other members of his pool were steered away from combat, and helpful contacts, for the rest of the war. The story saw print, but TV viewers never saw the sort of bloodshed Balzar's story described.

As at the end of World War II, restrictions at the very end of the Gulf War were eased to get reporters in place to witness and record the final victory. Up to that point, though, the American military both used the media (feeding it detailed disinformation about the intentions of its off-shore amphibious force, with hopes that Iraq would pick up the news reports and react accordingly) and kept tightening its reins.

When the ground offensive was launched on February 23, Secretary of Defense Dick Cheney imposed the strictest censorship policy of the entire war, suspending all pool reports and press briefings indefinitely. A fresh set of regulations from the JIB took care of rogue reporters, too. Print and TV reporters who had broken away from the pools had gathered stories by hiding in civilian homes, making friends with soldiers and officers in the field, filing stories by cellular phones, and looking as much as possible like soldiers in order to breeze through checkpoints and escape detection. By the time the ground attack was initiated, new rules forbid reporters from wearing military dress or using cellular phones to send stories. The ground war went so well, though, the military had neither the time nor the inclination to do much enforcing of those particular guidelines.

On February 25, two days into the ground war, a Scud missile penetrated coalition defenses and hit a barracks near Dhahran, where twenty-eight American soldiers died. Pictures of the devastation were tightly controlled, photographs of body bags were forbidden, and the absence of military briefings closed that avenue of journalistic inquiry. However, except for that tragic surprise Scud hit (on February 25), ground troops fared so well that, by the next morning, the Saudis arrived in Kuwait City, with McKeown as an unauthorized but not unwelcome witness. The military eased press restrictions, and briefings were resumed February 27 when Schwarzkopf delivered his famous account of the ground war. Within days, Dan Rather and other high-profile newspeople were reporting from abandoned bunkers and foreboding alleyways in and around Kuwait City, finally free to conduct interviews and take pictures.

Throughout the war, the only network that felt censorship pressure from both sides was CNN. Its correspondents based in Saudi Arabia and

Israel were under the same constraints as everyone else, and even the commentators, anchors, and weathercasters in CNN's Atlanta headquarters had to exercise care. The global reach of CNN, which made it the only American network whose reports could be—and were—monitored locally in Iraq, gave it a special responsibility. As in World War II, when weather forecasts were stopped so that the enemy could be denied the opportunity of intercepting that information, CNN stopped providing weather forecasts—not of America or England this time, but the Middle East. The assumption, after the first days of bombing, was that the Iraqis may have been incapable of generating their own meteorological information, and providing them with news of storm movements that might affect air or ground assaults was considered an unacceptable risk.

Of course, it was the global reach of CNN that made it such a major player in the Gulf War in the first place. Baghdad officials had been importing the CNN signal since 1989, and were much more familiar with CNN's mandate and content than they were with those of CBS, NBC, or ABC. CNN also offered communication as a two-way street: whatever went out to America also came back instantly to Iraq. Understandably, the Iraqis gave CNN preferential treatment, approving a special four-wire phone line (which CNN had requested months before the war began) while denying it to other networks, and letting CNN's Arnett remain in Baghdad after all other Western journalists were removed. The four-wire line was destroyed by coalition bombing about a week into the war, but Arnett was allowed to transmit sporadically using a portable satellite uplink. Some of the media competitors put a sinister spin on CNN's arrangements with Iraq, but it was merely a reversal of CNN's underdog salad days, when it was handicapped trying to elbow its way onto beats where the competing networks enjoyed long-standing and advantageous relationships with newsmakers and power brokers.

Arnett's presence in Iraq was also considered sinister to some—and here, too, there was a parallel to World War II, when many members of Congress raised their voices in anger, questioning the loyalty of war correspondents who spread bad news or potentially hurt morale at home. This time there were dozens of politicians who came forward to protest, and the charge against the media was led by Republican Alan Simpson of Wyoming, who had himself traveled to Baghdad to praise Saddam Hussein a mere four months before Iraq invaded Kuwait. Seeing Arnett interview the Iraqi leader on CNN, though, infuriated Simpson even more than had Arnett's "baby-milk factory" reports, which seemed to question the Pentagon's assertion that the factory's true purpose was the manufacture of biological weapons. Simpson called Arnett "a sympathizer" who "won a Pulitzer Prize largely because of his antigovernment material," and accused him of being "married to a Vietnamese whose brother was active in the Vietcong." The final charge was unfounded (Arnett's ex-wife had two brothers, but the one who participated in the war was, according to Arnett, a colonel in the South Vietnamese Army), and the others were ludicrous.

The *New York Times* editorialized that Alan Simpson's comments were "too snide even for Bart Simpson," and, despite dozens of other Congressmen who went on the record in opposition, many of Arnett's peers rallied to his defense.

"If you're a media person, how can you possibly not support Peter Arnett's presence in Iraq?" asked Phil Donahue in *Columbia Journalism Review.* "Are his reports going to be homogenized? Certainly! But we know that. Celebrate his presence there. Hope he doesn't get killed. Divide everything he says by ten, but keep him there." CNN made sure to label every report of Arnett's as "Cleared by Iraqi censors," and the anchors who introduced those reports added their own disclaimers—so much so that ABC's Peter Jennings called up a CNN executive in the middle of the war and asked him to "tell your anchor people to lay off Peter Arnett." Jennings calls Arnett "an accomplished, competent reporter" who deserved better treatment from his own network. And when Arnett returned from the war and was interviewed by Linda Ellerbee on *Later with Bob Costas,* she prefaced her interview by saying, "If there is one reporter I admire more than any other in this business—I hate to gush, but I tell you the truth—Peter Arnett is as good as it gets."

Asked why she came out so strongly for Arnett from the very start, Ellerbee says, "Every once in a while we have to stop by the road and review some of those little truths we hold, or say we hold, to be self-evident—not just our belief in a free press, but what that *means.* And for the record, it means reporting the facts freely as best you can. It means trying to tell all sides of a story as accurately and fairly as possible, and it means railing at censorship whenever and wherever you find it—and that includes when you find it in your own government.

"Nothing Arnett said did, or could have done, as much damage to this country as could have been done by people who thought you had no right to hear what he said. . . . One of the reasons I felt so strongly about Arnett is that if we learned anything from Hitler, it should be that it never pays to ignore a madman. And if we learned anything from Vietnam, it should be that what you don't know *can* hurt you."

Both examples, in fact, have direct applications to Arnett's situation in Iraq. In 1966, the same year Arnett earned his Pulitzer for his reporting from South Vietnam, Harrison E. Salisbury of the *New York Times* crossed into North Vietnam and wrote about civilian casualties from American bombing missions—filing some excellent stories, but generating a resentful reaction from many readers and politicians back in the States. Arnett himself reported from North Vietnam in 1972, where he had "handlers" similar to the ones assigned to him in Baghdad. Yet those who sneer at the fact that Arnett did the bulk of his reporting from Iraq with censors standing by to steer him away from any topic too sensitive in nature should be reminded that, as has been pointed out, Murrow's live broadcasts from the rooftops of London during World War II were broadcast with a British censor standing by his side; Murrow would get a gentle tap on the wrist, a cue to switch subjects, if objection was found to his remarks or observations. Similarly, when Murrow broadcast from Studio B-4 in London, there was always a censor nearby with one hand on the switch.

An even more exact parallel from that era existed in the CBS Radio reports from William L. Shirer, who worked under Nazi censorship while following (often literally) the rise of Hitler and witnessing the events that ultimately led to World War II. Shirer worked under several types and levels of censorship, from local handlers to Hitler's own propaganda machine, but remained in Germany as long as he felt he "could fairly depict what was going on." As for getting facts and observations past the censors, Shirer later wrote, "I had learned what all correspondents became aware of after working in the totalitarian lands: that you could say a great deal if you were not too careless in how you said it."

Certainly, Arnett managed to convey a great deal, especially in the unscripted conversations with CNN anchors that followed the majority of Arnett's sixty-nine live segments over the course of the Gulf War. Once, when asked a Catch-22 question about identifying the types of things he was being prevented from discussing, Arnett replied—carefully and cannily—that one thing he was not allowed to mention was anything having to do with the changing skyline of Baghdad. Without saying anything, Arnett had just said a lot. Viewers knew Arnett was providing a heavily censored viewpoint from behind enemy lines, but that did not make it any less valuable. Arnett's trustworthy background, and his insistence on reporting only what he could personally witness and verify, made his reports as important as they were exclusive. And certainly, in shifting from print to television in order to experience a greater amount of feedback, Arnett proved himself quite a video visionary. "The reason I really joined television," Arnett confessed to Ellerbee during their interview, "is I felt that print had sort of pooped out."

Fred Friendly says that wars and crises have a way of enhancing careers, news organizations, and even a young medium. He cites William Howard Russell, whose Civil War dispatches "made the London *Times* famous"; Murrow and company before and during World War II, whose reports from abroad "made CBS a landmark"; and the rise of *Nightline*, Ted Koppel "and all of ABC" as a result of the hostage situation in Iran. "Now," Friendly adds, "you have CNN. Why CNN? Because they had the one central thing television needs: air time." Friendly is of the opinion, however, that CNN offered "more breadth than depth," and that, as at the other networks, "nobody asked the hard questions." That was true, Friendly says, even at the daily military briefings during the Gulf War, when reporters badgered briefers with mostly technical and tactical questions. "They still haven't asked the right questions," Friendly says.

It appears the questions, the answers, and the tone of the briefings themselves have all infuriated or embarrassed viewers to some degree. Live televised press conferences have been a somewhat familiar sight since the Kennedy administration, but usually with the President of the United

States as the subject. The sight of reporters pressing military generals and spokespeople during wartime, trying to get them to reveal specifics and clarify inconsistencies, didn't sit well with the general public, even though it was part of the regular routine for both the media and the military.

"Those kinds of questions have always been asked," Friendly says. "They've just never been on television before." Don Hewitt, thinking back to the daily Vietnam briefings that reporters called "the Five O'Clock Follies" (because of their relative worthlessness as sources of genuine information), says, "There were no satellite capabilities out of Vietnam, so there's a fascination in watching all this happen in real time in the Gulf. But had you been able to go to the 'Five O'Clock Follies' live, my feeling is they would have been canceled. They didn't need that. . . . Not with the body counts which nobody ever believed." The Gulf War briefings didn't impress Hewitt, either: "I think they ought to cancel them," he said midway through the war.

Peter Jennings, too, is no fan of televising live briefings, even though ABC broadcast its share. "It's a bit like televising surgery," Jennings said a month into the war. "What you see in those news conferences are a lot of inexperienced reporters asking a lot of dumb questions. I think to expose the process—to expose that part of the process to the general public—is confusing. . . . I'd like to see that disappear."

"The Gulf briefings are ridiculously inadequate," Cronkite complained in his February *Newsweek* essay, but his barbs were aimed more at the briefers than the reporters. "Why should we not be told what bridges have been hit? Don't the Iraqis know?" Most of the public opinion, though, came down squarely on the side of Schwarzkopf and company. "The single biggest blow to the media's reputation," media critic Jonathan Alter countered in a *Newsweek* essay printed two weeks after Cronkite's, "was the televising of badly framed and occasionally idiotic questions at the Riyadh and Pentagon briefings." Overall, the best measure of public sentiment at the time may have come from *Saturday Night Live*, where a sketch a few weeks into the war poked fun at the military briefings, ridiculing not the officers evading the questions, but the reporters asking them.

"We were dealing with what we saw," Lorne Michaels recalls, "which was these press conferences in which people were asking for details like when we'll be invading—knowing that everybody else in the world can see the same show. The army, for once, looked sympathetic."

Saturday Night Live also deserves credit for providing the first widely disseminated (as in televised) media criticism of the Gulf War coverage, courtesy of the Wayne and Garth characters in a last-minute "Wayne's World" skit. Three days after the war began, *Saturday Night Live* evaluated and poked fun at the TV coverage in a brilliant, extended sketch written, Michaels says, after midnight the previous night. Mike Myers's Wayne and Dana Carvey's Garth ridiculed CNN's drum-beat "Crisis in the Gulf" theme, dismissed CBS's early coverage as "Dan Rather—not!," had fun with the name of CNN Pentagon correspondent Wolf Blitzer, and made other sweeping or specific comments, knowing full well the *Saturday Night Live* audience would get, and love, every reference. "You can tell when you connect," says Michaels, who knew in the war's early days that "everybody in the country was watching one thing again."

It was amazing, in a way, how quickly TV viewers absorbed what they were watching—how rapidly the geography, weaponry, lingo, and major figures of the Gulf War became common knowledge. Riyadh and Dhahran, Scuds and Patriots, sorties and smart bombs, Schwarzkopf and Arnett, strategies and worst-case scenarios entered the national lexicon and dominated conversations. When television could not advance the story, which was most of the time, it whiled away the hours explaining what was and was not happening, like football broadcasters caught in an interminable time out. (The analogy isn't all that extreme: one network military analyst actually used a Telestrator, the machine John Madden uses to draw his instant-replay squiggles for football games on CBS, to diagram possible ground-war attack plans.)

Television imparted a great deal of necessary information during the Gulf War, but, except for such standout examples as CNN's first-night, all-night scoop, rarely got credit for doing so. Instead, TV attracted blame—for its relative inability to provide live news of substance, for its often undue fascination with air-raid sirens, for broadcasting some briefings and not broadcasting others, for cutting back on air time devoted to stories of antiwar protesters, and for providing few images or stories, other than that first night in Baghdad, truly worth treasuring. A lot of that had to do with the Pentagon pool and censorship restrictions, but it didn't make the criticisms any less valid. The military outflanked and dominated the media as effectively as it did the Iraqi forces, and most people watching, or even appearing on, television were aware of it.

Ken Burns, in his January 27, 1991, *New York Times* essay on war and its images, suggested, "In recent years, as we have grown more and more dependent on visual signs and language, less and less a country and society of letter writers and diary keepers, television has become more and more the way we are connected to the making of history." He added that "these visual connections have become a kind of emotional glue that makes our new histories stick in our minds and hearts," and questioned whether media coverage of the Gulf War had produced, or would produce, any intensely memorable visual records: "For the time being, there are just too few, too painfully overused or overhyped, too censored, or too remote to make the kind of lasting impression on our visual history [that] other wars and images have."

Months later, Burns was quoted as calling the Gulf War "the perfect war for Antonioni," which the author of the article interpreted as a reference to the Italian film director's penchant for themes of "alienation from real events." (I'd argue the analogy works better if one agrees that, in Antonioni movies, everything looks staged and hardly anything interesting ever happens on camera.) And in our interview, Burns suggests the lack of powerful war images, despite the enhanced technology of all types of photography and video, may have a lot to do with the enhanced power and technology of war itself. "The whole nature of war, now, is so different," Burns says. "It's a war in which the GI, the regular grunt, never saw action. We were killing things that were out of sight. We were shooting at tanks two miles away; it wasn't a guy aiming through his sights at the other guy."

"It was like watching a Western," Hewitt says of the Gulf War coverage. "That missile going through the front door of a bunker—it's like the sheriff plugging the guy on the main street of a Western town. Wham! We drew first, and we shot the gun out of his hand. It's a great parallel. . . . It was a bloodless war, and you don't see blood in Westerns, either."

"Given the constraints imposed by the government, they did a good job," Ellerbee says of TV's Gulf War coverage, but she, too, has a complaint. "When you watched the war, it was confusing because you got the distinct, disturbing feeling that everything you watched was more or less than real. Is it a videogame? Is it an old movie? Is it a miniseries? Is it a *sporting event?* There was some of *that* to it. . . . In the end, you forever had to remind yourself that what you were watching was not war. What you were watching was television."

Jennings disagrees. "It wasn't even a television war," he insists. "The whole point is, we didn't *see* the war on television." To critics and viewers who accuse ABC, in Jennings's words, of "letting us see too much" and "letting the *enemy* see too much," the anchorman replies, with apparent frustration, "You're not seeing *anything*—only [ABC military analyst] Tony Cordesman."

Reuven Frank, in a *Columbia Journalism Review* article, expressed equal skepticism about the newsworthiness of much of what the networks were televising. "All this 'liveness' is bull[expletive deleted]!" Frank said bluntly. "There isn't anything happening live except for some Scud attacks. What we're getting 'live' is briefings about events that are from twelve to forty-eight hours old. And reporters talking to each other 'live.' "

"The Kennedy assassination never became a television show," Don Hewitt says. "It was news about what was happening. Desert Storm became a television show. You know, *Showdown in the Gulf.* It sounded like *High Noon.* I find a lot of that ridiculous—everybody had his own titles. It kind of cheapened us." Hewitt, like Ellerbee, also likens the Gulf War coverage to that of a sporting event. "It was a Super Bowl," he says, "but we were playing a bush league team."

Kurt Vonnegut concurs, and adds some opinions of his own. "It was history as entertainment," he says. "The whole country agrees on the same story. We all saw the same story. It's like we all saw the same Super Bowl game, and it's frightening, because it makes it almost impossible to change opinions in this country, with everybody considering the same evidence.

"When I lecture now, the first goddam thing I have to say, because of television, is, 'Our troops behaved magnificently.' There's some question how they would have behaved if somebody had shot back. One thing I say in speeches: I'm sixty-eight-years old. When I went to war, and when relatives of mine went to war in World War I, and even in the Korean War, the young citizen soldier going in to defend his country, to serve his country, dreaded two things, not one, and he dreaded them equally. One was that he would be killed, and the other was that he might have to kill somebody. And television has so hardened us now that killing is a sport."

Vonnegut's World War II experiences, which he drew upon to write *Slaughterhouse-Five*, included being captured by the Nazis and sent to Dresden, where he survived a bombing raid by American and British pilots that created a firestorm, killing an estimated 135,000 people—nearly twice as many as were killed at Hiroshima by the atom bomb. Not too surprisingly, this gives him a special perspective when watching televised scenes of precision bombing and surrendering soldiers.

"I myself have been in this position," Vonnegut says, locking the fingers of his hands together and putting them on top of his head, "with American soldiers as far as you can see—all stripped of their weapons, often with their uniforms in rags, without anything to eat for a long time. Because the Germans beat the [expletive deleted] out of my division, with a regiment on either flank. So when I saw those Iraqis, I knew exactly what they were feeling, and what they'd been through. And they did not show us," Vonnegut adds, referring to the American military, "the shooting up of that bumper-to-bumper convoy, that pitiful traffic jam of all these people trying to get out of Kuwait. They did not show it, but I'm sure they've got footage of it."

Vonnegut pauses for a long, mournful moment. "There's something to be said," he says, "about sportsmanship."

There is also something to be said about the way in which the media sometimes were used as propaganda tools by the American administration—not only unwillingly, as when false plans of an amphibious assault were leaked as a decoy, but as both a disseminator and an originator of less than objective attitudes. "The demonization of Saddam Hussein by George Bush was brilliant," Jennings says, his voice betraying a mixture of admiration and irritation. Jennings feels the media—print as well as broadcast—helped in that respect, perhaps even a bit too eagerly.

"I think we as institutions were, and are, a bit frightened about our role in this society," Jennings says, choosing his words carefully. "I think that since the public climbed on the media in general during the Reagan years, in the sort of post-Vietnam, post-Watergate era, I think they made us self-conscious—not all of us, but most of us. I think that when you get to situations like the Gulf War, there is an unspoken belief that we are in a popularity contest with the American public—us versus the Administration, versus the military establishment, versus the Congress. We are one of the big, important branches of society, but somehow we have gotten nervous about becoming unpopular. . . .

"Reagan was very good on television, but I quite think that George

Bush is in many ways better than Ronald Reagan. And I had this feeling during the war that we were a bit like those people who said, 'Listen, we are against the war, but we are not against the boys.' You know, early instruments of policy, you see. I don't know how we are going to deal with it." Commenting on the press restrictions during the war, Jennings adds, "We allowed ourselves to get into, I thought, the most appalling pool arrangement in the Persian Gulf, and paid a price for it. And I think the military paid a price for it, because they were victorious and nobody saw it."

"I don't think it was so much control as it was our willingness to play our part in America's moment of glory," Hewitt says, adding, "Let's face it. During the Gulf War, Jennings, Rather, and Brokaw were American cheerleaders." Hewitt thinks the shift in attitude is traceable to the period after McCarthyism, when the networks first were accused of being unpatriotic. Partly to make amends (and friends) in Washington and elsewhere, Hewitt suggests, the networks provided voluminous and largely uncritical coverage of the fledgling space race. "This was a chance," Hewitt claims, "to go, 'Hey, listen, we're on the team, we're just as patriotic as anyone else.' There never was a piece of paper, but there was an unwritten agreement then in effect: 'You help us get our appropriation from Congress, and we'll give you the goddamnest television shows you ever saw. We'll give you the moon.' "

"Are we nervous, apprehensive, afraid, to take on popular presidents?" Jennings asks. Jennings confesses to being concerned about viewer reaction "if we suddenly turned on the dime" and steered attention from Bush's foreign policy to his domestic problems ("OK, that's it, guys, he's done the war, now how about education?"). "We will get to it," Jennings said at the time—and has since made good on that promise. As for giving any thought at all to public perceptions of the media, Jennings says, "I may be dead wrong. There may be no other journalists who think this, or are foolish enough to admit it. But that does enter into it."

"The root word of television is 'vision from afar,' so it can take us to where we can't go," Bill Moyers says. "It can show us the earthquake victims, the victims of famine. It can generate an enormous response to the *20/20* or the *PrimeTime Live* piece about the children in Romania. It can do that. But if, on the other hand, it shows us only what the authorities want us to see, as in the case of the Persian Gulf [War], then it becomes an instrument of mass manipulation or social control for breeding conformity, for instilling propaganda, and I am troubled by that part of it.

"I mean, George Bush got away with defrauding us in the Persian Gulf War because we could only see what they wanted us to see. He used in his speech to Congress the story of the Iraqi soldiers coming up with their hands above their heads, and the American soldiers saying, 'That's all right, you're all right now.' And George Bush said we are a caring, generous people. But what you didn't see was the hundreds of thousands of Iraqis whose bodies were bulldozed into mass graves by American bulldozers. That disappeared before we got there."

Moyers does not take much comfort in the fact that the truth eventually has a way of surfacing. "You can correct the record," he says, "but the record never reaches the people watching instantaneously during the crisis. The truth never catches up with the lie, except slowly—and then, maybe, too late."

Yet television, over the long haul, can prove very persistent, and those who use or view TV properly will find it has a great appetite for providing additional perspective and revisiting old stories and newsmakers. *Frontline* hustled quickly enough to serve up an in-depth biographical and psychological profile, called *The Mind of Hussein,* two days before the war ended. "Saddam surviving a war—coming out alive after the West's rhetoric and ammunition are spent—has been described as the nightmare scenario," the documentary said. "But if Saddam survives all that, he may actually gain more of the one thing that ever really mattered to him: power for its own sake."

After the war, television brought the suffering of Kurdish refugees into American living rooms, reminding viewers that, though the war had been declared over, suffering and problems in the region remained. In May 1991, the PBS series *The 90's* showed "Inside Iraq" footage from the war, taken by a free-lance NBC producer whose piece was rejected by *Today.* In October 1991, *Frontline* returned to Iraq to do a story called *The War We Left Behind*—a terrific report that interviewed American military commanders and Iraqi civilians to assess the scope of the war and its long-term effects. *The War We Left Behind* revealed that only 10 percent of the weapons dropped on Iraq were precision bombs, and that the country's inability to rebuild its power plants has crippled sewage treatment plants as well, with the result that a single damaged plant pumps 15 million gallons of raw sewage into the nearby river each hour. Many Iraqis drink straight from the rivers, which is why cases of typhoid are averaging 2,000 a day in one of the few health centers still operating. Moyers is right: these programs are seen by far fewer viewers than tuned in to the Gulf War itself, but each program counts.

Sure, there are some gung-ho missteps along the way. Arts & Entertainment's four-part *Desert Storm* documentary, shown in June (the same month New York's Desert Storm Victory Parade was held), was little more than a commercial for a larger defense budget. And without question, the worst offender of all was *Heroes of the Desert Storm,* an ABC docudrama presented in October 1991, nine months after the war. Dramatizing the true stories of a handful of well-chosen members of America's Armed Forces, *Heroes of the Desert Storm* mixed actual combat footage (of flying Scuds and driving jeeps, mostly) with "recreations" to present the most blatantly political and one-sided war story since John Wayne starred in *The Green Berets.* The Persian Gulf docudrama was introduced by President Bush and produced "with the full cooperation of the Department of Defense," which sort of sums up its point of view right there. But if you wanted television to provide a slightly different viewpoint in its dramatic programming, that too could be found, and the most startling example was on a May 1991 episode of another ABC offering—*thirtysomething.*

In the series, Ken Olin portrayed Michael Steadman, an earnest young advertising campaign designer who worked for the powerful and enigmatic Miles Drentell (played by David Clennon). The war-related episode, written by producer Joseph Dougherty, involved a beer manufacturer who was upset because the actor the agency had hired to represent his beer in TV and magazine ads had been photographed at a peace demonstration protesting military intervention in the Persian Gulf. The beer manufacturer wanted the actor replaced, no matter the expense to remount the ad campaign. Michael protested the demand, but Miles acceded to it, and lectured his junior colleague for expressing shock that the media would intentionally embrace patriotism as a way to sell products, or treat as pariahs those whose ideas differed from the mainstream.

"He expressed an unpopular opinion," Miles said of the actor. "No one wants to be unpopular. That's why we're here. That's the dance of advertising. We help people become popular. . . . We calm and reassure. We embrace people with the message that we're all in it together, that our leaders are infallible, and that there is nothing, absolutely nothing wrong. That is what we do. It's what we've always done." In the same speech, Miles also tells Michael, "Do you know what I love about this country? Its amazingly short memory. We're a nation of amnesiacs. We forget everything—where we came from, what we did to get here. History is last week's *People* magazine, Michael."

But with television characters making speeches like that, the dangers of the process, and the media, are pointed out in ways that just might stick. Moreover, television actually has a good history of appreciating history, even if the best efforts take years to develop. Look at *Vietnam: A Television History,* or *The Civil War,* or the very recent *Pearl Harbor: Two Hours That Changed the World.* Each one of those documentary series looked at war in a way that was necessary to understand war: from both sides at once. The "as it happened" telecasts of the Gulf War didn't allow full coverage of one side, much less two, but give it time. America will remain interested in the story, and in history, just as it has remained interested in the lives and works of some of the people who gained fame from their connection to *The Civil War* or the Gulf War.

After *The Civil War,* Shelby Foote has enjoyed a resurgence of interest in his three-volume history of that war, and filmmaker Ken Burns has seen his earlier films scheduled in a retrospective by PBS; he's also gone on to make a documentary about pioneer broadcast inventors, and start work on another about the history of baseball.

The Gulf War, as presented on television, was almost like a major miniseries: it had a definite beginning and end (with room left for a possible sequel), and even created some of its own stars. It is no wonder that, when the war ended, the people and things associated with it kept going.

The conflict spawned so many instant, uniformly tacky home-video retrospectives—including CNN's *Desert Storm: The War Begins,* CBS's *Desert Triumph,* and ABC's *Gulf War*—that author James Gorman cracked, "Never have so many fought so fast and been marketed so quickly." Fittingly, none of these pasted-together overviews have approached the popularity of MPI's home-video release of *Schwarzkopf: How the War Was Won,* a snazzy title for what's essentially a copy of the one-hour briefing the general held at the end of the ground war. Despite (or because of) its familiarity with viewers, *How the War Was Won* quickly went platinum. Next to Whitney Houston's midwar rendition of *The Star-Spangled Banner* at Super Bowl XXV, which was rushed out as a single by popular demand and quickly raised $500,000 for the American Red Cross Gulf Crisis Fund, Schwarzkopf's home-video briefing tape was the "sleeper hit" of the entire conflict.

Peter Arnett struck gold, not platinum, by signing a lucrative book deal, taking some time off, and getting and accepting a public apology from Alan Simpson—who, for his next high-profile badgering job, took on Anita Hill during the Clarence Thomas confirmation hearings. Arthur Kent parlayed his Gulf War fame into a guest-hosting stint on *Today,* which probably would not have been available to him before—and which, by confining him to a studio and script, played to his weaknesses rather than his reportorial strengths; by the fall, he was back reporting in Europe for NBC.

Bob Simon, upon his release from captivity, dropped his objectivity long enough to be quoted on CNN that he hoped his Iraqi interrogators would "die soon and painfully"—then, with a cooler head and a keener perspective, went back to Iraq in July 1991 for a strong CBS News special, *Bob Simon: Back to Baghdad.* Jeffrey Zaun returned to Cherry Hill, New Jersey, for a hometown parade, and with an admirably introspective attitude: "The Vietnam POWs stared down death for seven years," he was quoted as saying, with obvious discomfort. "I was there for two months. And I get all this hero's welcome." Forrest Sawyer and Bob McKeown enjoyed slightly more air time at ABC and CBS, respectively, as a result of their war-end high-profile scoops. Charles Jaco, instead of standing in Saudi Arabia at night, could be seen in December 1991 in broad daylight in Palm Beach, anchoring CNN's inexplicably exhaustive coverage of the William Kennedy Smith trial. And in August 1991, Wolf Blitzer appeared in the *New York Times Book Review,* reviewing a book called *In the Eye of the Storm: The Life of General H. Norman Schwarzkopf.*

Finally, as for Schwarzkopf himself, he made a highly viewed appearance on PBS's *Talking with David Frost* exactly one month after holding his "platinum" briefing, retired from the military in August, signed a book deal worth a reported five million dollars, and came out of the conflict with the clout and following to do almost anything he wants: a *Newsweek* story headlined "Schwarzkopf for President?" was no laughing matter, even if it was published April 1.

The retired general refused many offers for appearances, endorsements, and merchandizing deals. However, one of the things he chose to do, it is worth noting, was to return to the Civil War era—by narrating Aaron Copland's *A Lincoln Portrait* for a recording with the St. Louis Symphony. Another was to revisit World War II, and serve as cohost with Charles Kuralt, for the CBS News special *Remember Pearl Harbor,* broadcast on the fiftieth anniversary of the attack.

In that show, Schwarzkopf also served as a historical commentator, analyzing both the leaders and actions of the American and Japanese officers. He noted weaknesses and strengths, put himself in the position of the generals on both sides, and ended up admiring the boldness and effectiveness of Japanese fleet commander Isoroku Yamamoto. "It was a masterpiece of planning and execution," Schwarzkopf said, in an authoritative TV appearance that made the most of his expertise and charisma and vaulted him above all other contributors to the documentary. In essence, Norman Schwarzkopf was to *Remember Pearl Harbor* what Shelby Foote was to *The Civil War*—which sort of brings everything full circle.

The moral to all this? The careful, probing history of *The Civil War* and the instantaneous, incomplete history-as-it-happens of the Gulf War are two sides of the same TV coin. Each complements the other, and viewers can be enriched by both, so long as they do not expect more than each type of television can give them.

ABC's Jeff Greenfield, a serious student of TV who happens to do most of his work *on* TV, wrote near the end of the Gulf War:

"There has never been anything like the way that television has colored, shadowed, illuminated, and distorted the Persian Gulf [War]. . . . And this, perhaps, is the most significant, most troublesome aspect of television's first 'real-time' war: the uneasy blend of instant, immediate, round-the-world, round-the-clock access to information that is inherently incomplete, fragmentary, or downright wrong."

That's one way of looking at it. Another way is Arnett's, who was asked by Larry King to name the major difference between reporting for print and live broadcast journalism.

"The immediacy, Larry, the immediacy," Arnett replied. "Being able to talk about cruise missiles coming near you and having that information going out instantly to the world—I mean, not just to the United States, to the whole world! . . . It is just tremendously thrilling to communicate in this way." The circumstances around that very interview supported Arnett's point: it was the night of March 8, 1991, and Arnett was talking to King from Amman, Jordan. Arnett was appearing on *Larry King Live* sixteen hours after he had left Baghdad, for the first time since war broke out.

The real way to look at live television, though, is responsibly. The best way for the networks and the military to deal with the question of live war coverage may be to delay the live element—give the reporters and camera crews access, but delay anything of a sensitive nature until its broadcast would no longer endanger lives. Meanwhile, viewers can take matters into their own hands by taking their TV remote controls in those same hands.

If you favor a particular broadcast news organization or newscaster, turn there first in times of crisis, but sample others as news breaks to compare the flow of information on other networks. Switching back and forth is not being disloyal: when news and rumors are flying fast and furious, it is being sensible. Also, be aware that, when news is happening before your very eyes, you become not just a viewer, but an editor. Just as you should graze from network to network in search of corroborative or conflicting reports, you should question the veracity and weight of each report until more information comes in. The more you watch, the more you know—and, an obvious observation that's equally true of such "dated" history as *The Civil War*, watching is seldom a substitute for reading. To be well informed, do both.

Finally, do not discount the importance of certain fictional shows in the context of what they say, overtly or accidentally, about war. The innocence that allowed television to make a hit of *Hogan's Heroes* and *Combat* is gone now. In drama series, where Vietnam was a forbidden subject in the early eighties, the end of the decade saw such intelligent and emotional efforts as *China Beach* and *Tour of Duty*. In comedy, the classic example remains *M*A*S*H*, which used Vietnam-era attitudes in a show about the Korean War. Sometimes, though, actual Korean War history played an important part. One of the series' best episodes, "The Interview," starred Clete Roberts as a journalist who visits the *M*A*S*H* outfit and interviews them as part of a TV documentary. The idea was inspired by Murrow's *Christmas in Korea* special—which the makers of *M*A*S*H*, at least, had not forgotten.

TV is more aware of history than most people realize. What is unfortunate is that more people are not aware of TV's own history, and how, in presenting fiction as well as fact, it has matured so steadily and impressively over the years.

18

TELEVISION AS
A MATURING MEDIUM

The date: 1972. The place: poolside at the home of June Foray, who provided the cartoon voices of, among others, Natasha Fatale and Rocky the Flying Squirrel on *The Bullwinkle Show*. As she's done for a few years, Foray is raising money for the Hollywood chapter of an international animation society by selling cels—individually drawn scenes and frames from TV cartoons and film shorts. She's obtained them from the animation studios, most of which consider the cels worthless. Foray, though, thinks kids might like a Woody Woodpecker or a Bullwinkle J. Moose to tack up on their bedroom walls, and sells them in her backyard for five to thirty dollars each. She is one of the first to recognize the wide appeal of animation as art, and the way it can generate—from *adults*, not kids—both enthusiasm and money. "I made five-thousand dollars in one afternoon, selling them very cheaply," she recalls. Most of the studios curbed their generosity after that particular 1972 fund-raiser was such a cel-out.

The date: 1991. The place: Christie's East, an august New York auction house on Park Avenue. For the first time, original production cels from *The Simpsons* (and the characters' original showcase, *The Tracey Ullman Show*) are put up for sale—twenty-seven of them, each signed by series creator Matt Groening, along with a special cel drawn by Groening for the Christie's East catalog cover. "Usually, estimates are set in relation to similar pieces that have sold before," explains Christie's representative Susan Britman. "In this case, there was no precedent." So without knowing the market value, Christie's publishes in its catalog some supposedly optimistic estimates: seven-hundred dollars for the most simple cels, eighteen-hundred for the most elaborate, and seven-to-nine hundred for Groening's specially commissioned drawing of Bart Simpson auctioning his sister Maggie. On the day of the auction, one of the prospective buyers is James L. Brooks, the executive producer who brought the Simpson family to TV in the first place.

"I was going to bid on the one that Matt did," Brooks says, "and I was on the phone to be a phone bidder, and I was prepared to go up to two thousand." Brooks laughs. "And I was so embarrassed, because there was somebody whose time I was tying up on the floor, and the *first* bid knocked me out." After each successive bid the Christie's representative asks Brooks, "Are you bidding now? Do you want to bid now?"—but Brooks's only response, listening to the price escalate wildly, is "Oh, my God." Groening's drawing, officially titled *Bart Auctions His Sister Maggie,* ultimately sells for $24,200. Actual production cels from the TV shows go for up to $7,920, and the biggest bargain of the day is auctioned for a mere $1,540.

"It says a lot about the popularity of the characters and the overwhelming popularity of the show," a pleasantly surprised Britman says the next day. "I think we're talking about a new generation of collectors, ones who are perhaps more involved with characters from television animation than from film animation—looking at Bart Simpson rather than Snow White." Simple economics may have something to do with it: at the same auction, a cel from Disney's 1937 *Snow White and the Seven Dwarfs,* showing the heroine running through the foreboding forest, sold for $71,500. Yet it's also another sign of TV audiences willing and eager to acknowledge their emotional connection to television shows past and, in some cases, present. Brooks says, with a chuckle, "Matt's beginning to figure out what his signature is worth."

This connection between past and present, between Jay Ward's Bullwinkle and Matt Groening's Bart, is just as strong for TV's creators as for its viewers.

"Rocky and Bullwinkle and George of the Jungle were brilliant, in my opinion," Groening told *Emmy* magazine in 1990. "Jay Ward, an absolute hero of mine, was very important to me as a kid because his shows were the only cartoons, other than *The Road Runner* and *Bugs Bunny,* that I could watch with my parents. And that's one of the goals of *The Simpsons*: to do a show that each member of the family can get into on his or her own level." Not everyone has gotten into *The Simpsons,* of course. Bill Cosby's reservations about the Bart Simpson character have been covered already, and Hal Erickson, in his 1989 encyclopedia *Syndicated Television,* thought so little of Groening's cartoon contributions to *The Tracey Ullman Show* that Erickson dismissed them without mentioning Groening or the Simpsons by name, saying simply that "the only detraction" in Ullman's show "was the dreadfully unfunny animated sequences used as buffers between the sketches."

To others, though, *The Simpsons* has struck a very responsive chord. The show's popularity is reflected not only in the ratings, and the caliber of stars eager to supply guest voices (Dustin Hoffman, Michael Jackson), but in the supply of, and demand for, Simpsons mass-market merchandise. Clothing, dolls, toys, games, video games, books, magazines, postcards, and even record albums have flooded the market, selling for the same reason those high-priced cels did. People, young and old, have responded to a program they enjoy; owning something related to it reflects that enjoyment.

Children have responded that way to television from the start. Howdy Doody distributed 100,000 campaign buttons to eager youngsters when he ran for president "of all the boys and girls" in 1948—the first puppet politician to own up to that description. The *Davy Crockett* adventures on *Disneyland* made coonskin caps all the rage in the midfifties. The TV version of *Batman* in the sixties captured as much interest, and spawned as many merchandising offshoots, as the movie version of *Batman* in the eighties, and *The Monkees* manufactured a pop group that, for a while, rivaled The Beatles in sales. Most recently, *Teenage Mutant Ninja Turtles* have worked their way into the pop-culture mainstream, starting as underground comic books, then striking gold as a syndicated and network cartoon TV series—leading the way for live-action movies and, incredibly, pay-per-view concerts. (When *these* Turtles sing, though, they're not singing "Happy Together.")

Merchandisers in the modern era have been much quicker, and greedier, to make such TV-to-toy connections. Ira H. Gallen, a video archivist and toy expert who runs Video Resources in New York City, is of the opinion that manufacturers in the fifties didn't produce much TV-related material, except for the occasional *Howdy Doody* board game and *Maverick* vest and derringer set. "It was totally the opposite of today," Gallen says, even though there was never a shortage of children's TV stars willing and able to hawk toys, games, cereals, and other trinkets on and between their programs.

In every era, these TV-related toys, clothes, and artifacts have been consumed, forgotten, and discarded quickly, only to resurface years later as valued collectibles. A mint seventy-two-card set of *Star Trek* trading cards from 1967 was valued twenty years later at seven-hundred dollars, while an eighty-eight-card *Brady Bunch* set, not released until 1971, was valued at two-hundred dollars within seven years. What we respond to as kids stays within us, dormant but very much alive, and can trigger fond memories as we get older. It's why oldies stations have such appeal on radio, why nostalgia will never get old, and why being a lifelong packrat can pay big dividends. A generation from now, some of that Simpsons paraphernalia might well command hundreds of dollars on the nostalgia market—and who knows what the going rate will be, in the year 2025, for a "vintage" *Simpsons* cel?

The paradox is that items attached to television are being accorded value faster than television itself. Toys and trading cards are hot commodities. Cels are art, available in fine galleries and sold at respected auctions. Archie Bunker's living-room chair from *All in the Family* sits snugly in the Smithsonian Institution's American History Museum, not too far from Fonzie's leather jacket from *Happy Days*. An exhibit called "From Receiver to Remote Control: The TV Set," held in 1990 at Manhattan's New Museum of Contemporary Art, examined and celebrated the evolution of the television as a piece of furniture. (Perhaps the exhibit can find a permanent home next door to the National Video Game and Coin-Op Museum in St. Louis, which opened in 1991 with such technological hands-on relics as Pong and the original Donkey Kong.) In Washington, DC, the National Museum of American History recently presented an exhibition called "This is Your Childhood, Charlie Brown: Children and American Culture, 1945–1968," collecting coonskin caps from *Davy Crockett* fame, Mr. Moose and Bunny Rabbit puppets from *Captain Kangaroo,* and other formative Baby Boomer playthings. In February 1992 the Smithsonian's Air and Space Museum acknowledged the silver anniversary of *Star Trek* by displaying uniforms and scale models of the Starship Enterprise. By private collectors and public institutions, this former "junk" is being taken very seriously indeed.

"Many people feel uneasy when serious attention is paid to objects and subjects that they are accustomed to classify as 'trash,'" wrote the always quotable Marshall McLuhan, adding that such people "have little heeded the lessons of history and archaeology which reveal how the midden-heaps of the ages provide the wisdom and riches of the present." In 1978, arguably decades overdue, the Library of Congress established a Motion Picture, Broadcasting, and Recorded Sound Division, saving for posterity films and tapes as well as the written word. Broadcast historian Erik Barnouw was hired to oversee the creation of the collection, and his concept of what was considered "valuable" was as liberal as McLuhan's—and backed up by lessons learned from overseeing other divisions of the Library of Congress. Barnouw wrote:

> Among the diverse treasures of its rare-book room one finds surviving copies of dime novels—now considered an important link in our social and political history, but once regarded as so ephemeral in value that most people felt they could be thrown on the trash heap. Who can tell what information historians will glean from our broadcasting ephemera as well as from our more "important" programming?

New York's Museum of Television & Radio, which began in more cramped quarters in 1976 as the Museum of Broadcasting, was established by William S. Paley as a means to collect, preserve, and appreciate broadcasting's past achievements. The operation was moved in 1991 to a larger, more "serious" building designed by noted architects Philip Johnson and John Burgee. "Here, in this limestone building with its classical arch," wrote Paul Goldberger, architecture critic of the *New York Times*, "will television show that it is Serious Culture." The capital letters are intended Rather Insultingly, but the elevation of TV and radio programming to museum status is a concept way behind its time. The point is not that it's Serious, but that it's Culture. The fondness many people demonstrate for things attached to TV, from *Simpsons* cels to *Andy Griffith Show* and *Twin Peaks* card sets, is so strong because our attachment to television itself is so strong.

"If there were no TV," Don Hewitt says, "I figure there'd be underground Broadway revivals of *Brady Bunch* episodes." Hewitt was joking at the time, unaware that such a phenomenon existed as he spoke. The Annoyance Theater of Chicago's production of *The Real Live Brady Bunch,* in which actors took on the roles of the Bradys in staged performances of twenty different scripts from the actual TV series, proved so popular it was "sometimes turning away as many as a hundred people a night," according to one account. Robert Thompson, who took a class to experience the Chicago production firsthand, was amazed by the uncritical, howlingly approving reception the dialogue received from the entire audience. "It was like every single line was a 'boffo' one-liner," Thompson says. By the fall of 1991, the show had moved to New York for an Off-Broadway run, where the nicest words it received from *New York Times* drama critic Mel Gussow were that "a live *Brady Bunch* may be defensible as cultural trivia preservation."

That interpretation would make more sense if *The Brady Bunch* were a "lost" television series, but it's so readily available in syndication that "preservation" isn't the point. Enjoyment is the point. Whether audiences are attending *The Real Live Brady Bunch* to laugh at it as a camp event or laugh with it as an artifact from their more innocent past, what's really significant about the stage show's success is that people are gathering in groups to experience publicly what was formerly an individual and private form of entertainment. Without putting too fine a motivational point on it, the popularity of the Annoyance Theater production should be seen not solely as an appreciation of *The Brady Bunch,* but also as a celebration of the impact of television.

One of the remarkable things about television is that it has matured without making its own past obsolete. Instead of new product pushing old product off the shelves, television keeps building new shelves to house the old product, and many times makes room for the old shows right alongside the new. Nickelodeon's Nick at Nite lineup has made brilliant use of such sixties mainstays as *Get Smart, Bewitched, The Dick Van Dyke Show,* and *Mr. Ed,* and other cable networks, such as Comedy Central, have reached even farther back, showing the classic old programs starring Ernie Kovacs, Steve Allen, and Sid Caesar. In 1950, the average TV household received four channels; in 1990, the average number was twenty-seven, and many relied strongly on old TV shows and movies to fill their schedules.

It may sound like nothing more than cost-effective filler material, but it turns out to be much more than that. In fact, in the winter of 1991, off-network reruns or cartoons were the highest-rated of *all* regular series on WTBS (*The Andy Griffith Show*), The USA Network (*MacGyver*), Lifetime (*L.A. Law*), The Family Channel (*Gunsmoke*), Nickelodeon (*Looney Tunes*), and TNT (*Bugs and Pals*). Even in prime time on the major broadcast networks, such TV specials as tribute shows, remakes, and reunions are considered potent weapons—and enticing bait—in the battle for the increasingly elusive viewer. With TV, as we've seen, it isn't a case of forgetting our past and being condemned to repeat it. It's a case of remembering our TV past and being eager to watch it in repeats.

Everywhere you look, "old" TV shows are bubbling to the surface and being treated with new respect. Cable television networks, long aware of the value of such series, now mount marathons, tributes, and specials with regularity, and lots of accompanying promotion. *The Outer Limits, The Dick Van Dyke Show, Perry Mason, Police Squad!,* and *Get Smart* were just a few marathon collections launched by cable networks in 1991, and other showcased reruns were given the reverent treatment of exhibits from an over-the-air TV museum. The "lost episodes" of *The Honeymooners,* taken from Jackie Gleason's variety shows, "discovered" by the Museum of Radio & Television, and displayed initially on Showtime, led the way, and other shows and networks followed quickly.

Early black-and-white episodes of *The Avengers,* starring Honor Black-man and never seen in America, were presented as "lost episodes" by Arts & Entertainment. TBS, which found the advertising revenues from reruns of *The Andy Griffith Show* so lucrative, nevertheless made a big deal out of replacing approximately three minutes of scenes cut from each show by the original syndicators, and presenting the "restored" episodes as part of a major promotion. Even the Learning Channel saw enough educational value in such early TV productions as Paddy Chayefsky's *Marty* and Rod Serling's *Patterns* to televise them, and others, in a retrospective series called *The Golden Age of Television*—which, ironically, is *itself* a repeat, having been presented originally in the late seventies.

Broadcast TV, as well as cable, is well aware of the appeal of the ghost of television past. In syndication, a twenty-fifth-anniversary marathon of *Star Trek* episodes and an accompanying tribute special did very well for local stations in 1991. On the network level that same year, CBS's dusty prime-time reruns of Norman Lear's *All in the Family* drew larger audiences than *Sunday Dinner,* the brand-new Lear comedy with which it was paired. CBS also repeated, in prime time, long-shelved episodes of *Police Squad!* and *The Bullwinkle Show* that year, and played prime-time archivist by presenting the original pilot for *I Love Lucy* as a one-hour "TV history" special. NBC, in a similarly nostalgic vein in 1989, repeated the delightful 1960 TV version of *Peter Pan* starring Mary Martin, after letting the show sit on the shelf for sixteen long years. Viewers, young and old, were Hooked all over again.

Anniversary shows and tributes have proven even more popular than marathons and reruns. CBS, the network with the most impressive past and the most current scheduling holes to fill, loaded a January weekend in 1991 with a trilogy of nostalgic specials: *All in the Family's 20th Anniversary Special, The Very Best of Ed Sullivan,* and *Mary Tyler Moore: The 20th Anniversary Show.* The *All in the Family* tribute did well enough to persuade CBS to place twenty-year-old reruns of the series in prime time; Moore's program wound up in the Top 10 of the season's most popular specials; and *The Very Best of Ed Sullivan* placed second, drawing more viewers that season than any TV special except for the Academy Awards. All three specials performed so strongly that CBS assembled a similar "Classic Weekend II" package that November, featuring more clips from *The Ed Sullivan Show* and tributes to *M*A*S*H* and *The Bob Newhart Show*. NBC mounted a prime-time fifteenth-anniversary *Saturday Night Live* special in 1990, and PBS celebrated the twentieth anniversary of *Masterpiece Theatre* with specials and reruns in 1991, repeating 1977's *I, Claudius* in its entirety to especially strong acclaim. In October 1991, the over-the-air TV museum concept became official when the Museum of Television & Radio presented its first prime-time special, an NBC tribute to *Funny Women of Television,* covering the gamut from Gertrude Berg of *The Goldbergs* to Roseanne Arnold of *Roseanne.*

The appetite for old television shows is actually twofold. For those too young to remember them firsthand, TV provides a second chance to experience them—and though such media-savvy outlets as Nick at Nite poke fun at the vintage offerings on their schedules, children often respond enthusiastically and without smugness, laughing at the exaggerated adventures of *Dennis the Menace* and getting caught up in the formulaic adventures of *Lassie.* The old movie musicals and *Muppet Show* reruns on TNT, too, are a big hit, whether young viewers are experiencing them for the first time or older viewers are enjoying a repeat visit. With grown-ups, some reruns do more than provide programming blasts from the pasts. Like certain songs on the radio, they trigger long-dormant memories and fond associations.

We also, on occasion, want to pass on that past to the next generation. Reading Mother Goose rhymes and fairy tales to children is a wonderful way to recall your own childhood while enriching theirs, but so is sitting with them and watching Rocky and Bullwinkle and Mister Rogers and Mister Wizard and *Looney Tunes.*

By unearthing and repeating old movies, and eventually doing the same for old TV series, television gave—and continues to give—viewers the opportunity to revisit the past. Moreover, because of home-video technology, no one even need wait for the networks to provide these kinds of viewing experiences. In the eighties, advanced television technology made entertainment history accessible and repeatable, and has triggered an appetite, and a revolution, comparable to the one sparked by the introduction of the phonograph record. As television has gotten older, access to its past productions has gotten easier. The technology of VCRs and videodiscs has allowed many of us to become not just viewers but collectors, building our own individualized film and TV libraries—personalized "museums" full of things that, for whatever reasons, are important or enjoyable to us.

Judy Garland once discounted television as "the hell where all little movies go when they're bad." Actually, television and the home-video industry have helped save and revive many movies, genres, and reputations in recent decades—decades in which the number of revival houses and film societies has dropped substantially. In 1949, just as television was coming into its own, James Agee regretted the relative unavailability of certain movies made only twenty-five or so years earlier. "At the moment, as for many years past, the chances to see silent comedy are rare," Agee wrote. Except for some two-hundred long and short comedies available on home movie projection, he noted, nothing was being distributed for sale or revived in the movie theaters.

A generation later Pauline Kael, while applauding the fact that television made old movies available to viewers at the flick of a dial, actually complained that TV was providing for public consumption *too many* old movies: "What does not deserve to last lasts," she complained in 1968, "and so it all begins to seem one big pile of junk." And that was before cable TV, before the exponential explosion of the home-video market.

Home video, of course, has changed everything. The concept of "narrowcasting"—of providing specific programming for a small but appreciative audience—has reached its zenith not in cable TV, where many networks seek to please most of the people most of the time, but in the video rental and sales market. Anything and everything is out there on the market now, and the demand for video product, even in small quantities, has rescued thousands of film and TV productions from near-total obscurity and unavailability. In the near future, when high-definition television and digital technology will combine to make collecting films and TV shows an even richer viewing experience, the sky's the limit. Even now, at a little above ground level, the video marketplace offers a tantalizing and historically significant mass-media history lesson to those willing and able to probe past the "latest releases" shelf. The operative motto ought to be: "Seek hard enough, and ye shall find."

To name one example, Gallen's Video Resources company sells many of the D. W. Griffith and comedy shorts Agee feared would be lost to the ages (not to mention the Agees), and also lists in its catalog such "broadcasting ephemera," to borrow Barnouw's description, as more than twenty one-hour collections of classic commercials. To name another example, the catalog for Movies Unlimited, boasting one of the country's best video inventories, includes an almost bottomless repository of videos preserving television's past. These include perennial cult shows widely available in syndication (such series as *The Honeymooners, Star Trek,* and *The Prisoner),* the vast majority of the worthwhile telemovies produced since the late sixties, and tapes of vintage series and specials rarely if ever seen on television. From the forties, episodes of *The Ed Wynn Show* and a *Studio One* production featuring Charlton Heston in *Of Human Bondage.* From the fifties, everything from *The Goldbergs* and *Mr. Peepers* and Milton Berle's *Texaco Star Theater* to *Rocky Jones, Space Ranger* and *Lights Out* and Edward R. Murrow's *Person to Person.* From the sixties, everything from the pop potpourri of *Shindig!* and *Hullabaloo* to the action of *The Rebel* and *Danger Man.* From the seventies, sets of *Roots* and Michael Palin's *Ripping Yarns.* From the eighties, the complete series of Shelley Duvall's *Faerie Tale Theatre* and *Tall Tales & Fables* programs. And, already representing the nostalgic nineties, handsomely packaged collectors' editions of *Twin Peaks*. From Moyers to Madonna, a well-stocked video store has most of what any customer could hope to find. Most, but not all.

Television, as well as movies, nevertheless has gaping holes in its history, caused by either carelessness in preserving and storing early productions or an unwillingness to make the effort. According to the American Film Institute, less than half of the 21,000 films made in America before 1951 have survived the ravages of time, bad film stock, and worse judgment. American Film Institute archivist Susan Dalton notes that with the advent of the talkies, silent movies were thought to be essentially valueless. "Motion pictures were considered mere entertainment, without any long-lasting historical or cultural value," she told one reporter. "They never considered that fifty years down the line, you could be selling videotapes to a whole new market." Nor, for that matter, was there an awareness of a potential television afterlife by people who produced and performed on TV in the fifties and sixties.

In 1961, Dick Van Dyke met his boyhood idol, Stan Laurel, who confessed amazement that his silent films with Oliver Hardy were still remembered. "Nobody thought too much of them at the time," Laurel told Van Dyke, adding incredulously, "We didn't put too much importance on it. We loved what we were doing, but it's thirty years now, Dick, and people are still watching our shows." Van Dyke told that story to critics in the summer of 1991, at a press conference announcing the Nick at Nite scheduling of the complete *The Dick Van Dyke Show* series. "Driving here this morning," Van Dyke said, "I thought, 'It's thirty years for me, too, now. Thirty years. . . . And now I can say, thirty years later, that people are still looking at it just surprises all of us."

Norman Lear says, "You look at all of the great comedy of the two-reelers—Charlie Chaplin, Buster Keaton, W. C. Fields. They all stand up. If it evokes laughter, it'll always stand up. Jokes don't stand up because jokes require context; they suggest a particular time. Behavior is eternal. Foolish human behavior is eternal." Lear, however, says he never thought when making *All in the Family* that the show would survive a season, much less be remembered and celebrated a generation later. "Nothing is made for posterity," he says flatly. "That's a consummation devoutly to be wished." James Burrows, who directed a few episodes of *The Mary Tyler Moore Show*, remembers, "I knew *The Mary Tyler Moore Show* was a good show with good characters, but I had no idea it would be revered the way it is now."

William Link, whose telemovies with the late Richard Levinson are available both on home video and in TV syndication, says producers of one-shot television dramas accepted the "ephemeral quality" of what they did, and expected their work to be unveiled one day and obsolete the next.

"Years ago we got so used to that," Link says, "we didn't think in terms of longevity." Lindsay Law still echoes that particular work ethic, and considers his *American Playhouse* films to be more lasting than the productions he premieres first on television. "What happens to television is that it's done with in one night," Law says. "It's all done with. If you didn't see it, you didn't see it. . . . A movie is out there for three, four, five months, and people keep reading about it. It's an event that lasts for three months instead of one night."

And Robert Geller, though enough of a visionary to imagine a post-PBS marketplace for his *American Short Story* productions in the seventies, hoped only that libraries and certain schools might purchase 16-mm copies for instructional use. "I thought that was really the be-all and end-all," he says. "But then *American Short Story* had its life on Showtime, then on Bravo, and now, in the video world, it can exist for home consumption. Never in my wildest dreams did I imagine anything like this."

Attitudes are different now that video sales can make the difference between profit and loss on most movie titles, and many parents are actively "programming" their family's viewing time by buying or renting videotapes and discs for themselves and their children. The formats in which movies and TV shows are preserved and collected will change in the future, but never again will the productions themselves be undervalued or neglected. Since the early eighties, there's a new, widespread awareness of the value of what's known as the "software" of the video business. Ted Turner's purchase of the MGM archives to launch his very successful TNT Network is ample proof of that, as is the continued demand for vintage and recent animated classics released on various formats by the Disney studios, up to and including the unprecedentedly high sales figures for *Fantasia*. So, for that matter, are the videotape and videodisc offerings by Shelley Duvall, who cannily foresaw a home-video demand for her *Faerie Tale Theatre* productions and negotiated her ownership rights accordingly.

"I knew that from the beginning," she says of their potential durability as family classics for home consumption. "I wanted to make little jewels—shows that would become classics, and wouldn't be worn away by time." She pushed for the best performers, scenic designs, scripts, and directors she could find, and also relied on the longevity of the source material itself. "Fairy tales have survived centuries of retelling," Duvall notes, "and all of them had some meaning to them as well. They were the psychiatrists before Freud and Jung, and they dealt with our hopes and fears and dreams. The psychiatrists' offices today," she adds, "are packed with adults still trying to deal with their childhood hopes and fears and dreams."

Lorne Michaels, instead of expressing surprise that *Saturday Night Live* would eventually be regarded as a milestone in TV history, says simply, "I knew that then." Though some of the jokes and satirical sketches are quite dated, Michaels feels the old *Saturday Night Live* series, available on video and in reruns on Comedy Central, "has a whole other value to it now," given that some of its cast members and featured guests "have been stars for seventeen years." In other words, such skits as Steve Martin's "King Tut," Bill Murray's lounge lizard, and John Belushi's Joe Cocker imitation are not only hysterical, they're historical. And, thanks to cable and home video, they're readily available.

The buildup of such history, combined with the audience's familiarity with and appreciation of it, makes television the unquestionably dominant force in today's culture. In 1951, Milton Berle noted with delight that the television audience was refreshingly sophisticated when it came to understanding and appreciating the medium. "You don't have to tell an audience you're going to ad-lib," he told an interviewer at the time, "and then explain that it means you're going to add lines that aren't in the script—and then explain what a script is." In the nineties, viewers are not only well-versed in the intricacies and importance of ratings and time slots and back-door pilots, they're nearly as familiar with TV's past as they are with its present. As a result, there's been a shift in attitude and direction regarding the entertainment industry's inspirational food chain.

When TV began, it drew from radio, film, literature, and the stage for its major stars, stories, and inspirations, just as film had initially drawn from literature and the stage for its more fanciful concepts. Film remakes were common practice from the very beginning; worldwide variations on Shakespeare's *Romeo and Juliet*, Cervantes's *Don Quixote*, and Defoe's *Robinson Crusoe* now number in the dozens. However, it wasn't until 1929, at the end of the silent era, that Hollywood took its own contributions seriously enough to mount the first cinematic sequel: *Cockeyed Glory*, Raoul Walsh's return visit to the Marines introduced in 1926's *What Price Glory?*

A bit later, Hollywood got to the point where it presented sequels, prequels, and remakes with regularity, accepting both the durability of the original stories and the audience's potential affection for anything connected with them. (Even the cinema's best directors, if drawn to the material by their own strong responses to it, are willing to attempt remaking film classics on their own terms: witness Martin Scorsese's 1991 remake of 1962's *Cape Fear.*) Today, television has undergone a similar maturation process, and is becoming just as aware of the potential of its own history. Ironically, the cinema, too, is taking note of TV's growth.

Until the midfifties, the TV and movie industries had a pure love–hate relationship: TV did the loving, movies the hating. The movie industry so despised television that almost nothing was shared by the two media. Studio head Jack Warner took the rivalry so seriously that he actually had a rule banning televisions from appearing, even as furniture, in any Warner Brothers movie, and all major studios refused to sell broadcast rights to their film libraries.

TV made do, at first, by borrowing heavily from radio and the stage for its talent and ideas, but by the early fifties, TV was having great success adapting popular film series into even more popular television series. *Topper*, a 1937 fantasy film sparking several sequels, was spun off into a TV series in 1953, and a TV version of *Lassie*, inspired by the 1943 film *Lassie Come Home*, premiered in 1954 and ran, with many cast and format changes, for twenty years. In both cases, TV producers got around Hollywood's lack of cooperation by getting television rights to the original source novels that had inspired the movie versions.

Hollywood's reluctance to get involved with television, though, was overcome with a speed that matched the rise of TV itself. Most of the barriers fell quickly and almost simultaneously, like dominoes. Two early TV shows that had come from radio, *The Goldbergs* and *Dragnet*, inspired movie versions in 1950 and 1954 respectively. In 1955, as we've seen, *Marty* became the first teleplay to be remade as a movie—a movie that won four Oscars, including Best Picture. Also in 1955, Jack Warner reversed course and allowed Warner Brothers to be the first major Hollywood film studio to produce programs for television (one of the very first, *Cheyenne*, was an instant hit). Finally, at the end of that year, RKO owner Howard Hughes broke the unofficial Hollywood boycott by becoming the first major studio head to sell TV rights to his film inventory, with *King Kong* one of the major treasures in that collection. The one barrier that didn't fall is still in place today: the inferiority factor.

Slowly, though, TV is building, and building upon, its own rich history. Remakes of weekly series began as early as 1953, when William Bendix and an entirely new cast was assembled for a new version of *The Life of Riley*, which had run for a single season in 1949–50 with Jackie Gleason in the lead. Reunion shows, celebrating past TV series by reassembling cast members for a telemovie special, began in 1967 with *Make More Room for Daddy*, and have continued unabated ever since. Television continues to mount modern remakes of movies from prior generations (ABC's *A Streetcar Named Desire* and *What Ever Happened to Baby Jane?*, Fox's *Robin Hood*), and to remake old series, either as full-blown revivals or sporadic specials. Recent revivals include new series versions of *Dark Shadows*, *The Smothers Brothers Comedy Hour*, *The Twilight Zone*, *Alfred Hitchcock Presents*, *Columbo*, *Zorro*, *WKRP in Cincinnati*, and *The Carol Burnett Show*. And as previously noted, Bill Cosby, in search of just the right TV vehicle in which to star after the supersuccessful *Cosby Show*, settled on producing a faithful remake of Groucho Marx's classic quiz-show series, *You Bet Your Life*.

Sequels or prequels include such popular series as *Tiny Toon Adventures* and *Star Trek: The Next Generation*, and the list of telemovie reunion specials is, sometimes unfortunately, endless. Holding it to the most recent examples still allows for the inclusion of such memory-jogging (and often mind-boggling) efforts as NBC's *I Still Dream of Jeannie* (with Barbara Eden) and *The Return of Elliot Ness* (with Robert Stack of TV's *The Untouchables*), CBS's *Gunsmoke III: To the Last Man*, and ABC's *Dynasty: The Reunion*. Hollywood has tapped into TV's past, too, with the 1991 big-screen remake of *The Addams Family* and the 1992 cinematic prequel to *Twin Peaks*, reuniting most of the TV cast for a movie set in the days leading up to Laura Palmer's murder, and has mined its present by mounting a film version of the *Saturday Night Live* skit *Wayne's World*.

Though the movies are no longer above remaking certain TV dramas, television has yet to take itself seriously enough in this regard to follow suit. There has yet to be a single made-for-TV remake of a classic telemovie, even though such showcase vehicles as *The Execution of Private Slovik*, *Trilogy of Terror,* and *Duel* would seem to be prime contenders for such an honor. It could be argued that it's partly a function of age, that even those early telemovies are still too widely circulated and relatively recent to be reinterpreted for a new generation. But if Alfred Hitchcock could go back after twenty-two years and be intrigued enough by the challenge to film a new version of his own *The Man Who Knew Too Much,* why couldn't Steven Spielberg do the same thing with 1971's *Duel?* And since censorial restrictions and special-effects limitations worked slightly against Karen Black's four-character showcase in 1975's *Trilogy of Terror,* why not remake it for the nineties, giving another actress a shot at that terrific piece of material and allowing new adapters to realize the sexual undercurrents and spooky possibilities of Richard Matheson's original stories?

Before long, something like this is bound to happen. Already, television is taking the intermediate step of staging dramas about celebrities from TV's past—biographical, behind-the-scenes telemovies like *Ernie Kovacs: Between the Laughter,* which was very good, and the similarly titled *Lucy and Desi: Before the Laughter,* which was very bad.

"Television has been cannibalizing itself all along," agrees Alexander Nehamas. "Now it's doing it much more self-consciously and explicitly than before." Nehamas sees this as a natural and positive step in TV's development, though there is a partial trade-off. Much of this activity is calculated and unimaginative, like that of the sequel-obsessed film industry, which often prefers to invest in a *Police Academy 6: City under Siege* than try something new. Little is to be gained, except financially, when a network spins off an *America's Funniest People* from an *America's Funniest Home Videos.* Moreover, some of television's references to other TV shows and movies are nothing but quick and easy attempts to gain recognition and laughs. Yet there's something more complex at work than a mere trashing of popular culture, about which Johns Hopkins University media professor Mark Crispin Miller complains in a 1986 essay called "Deride and Conquer":

> Whatever was a source of pleasure in the past is now derided by and for the knowing, whether it's . . . *The Towering Inferno* as parodied on *Saturday Night Live,* or *Dragnet* as parodied to sell the Yellow Pages, or *Mr. Ed* as excerpted to sell tortilla chips, or the *Mona Lisa* as ridiculed to sell Peter Pan peanut butter. Through such compulsive trashing, the spectacle makes eye contact with the spectator, offering, in exchange for the enjoyment that TV cannot permit, a flattering wink of shared superiority.

Nonsense. Miller seems incapable of accepting the fact that many of the people who make television, like many of those who watch it, actually have an *affection* for it.

TV's current references to the popular arts of yesteryear, or the TV shows and commercials of the day before yesterday, are no more an exercise in "constant trashing" than Andy Warhol's soup can paintings or rap music's sampling techniques (slipping snippets of old songs into new ones).

Yes, there's always an attitude of "shared superiority" with satire, but poking deliberate fun is what satire is all about, and much of that fun is affectionate. "Most of the people on the writing and acting staff of *SCTV* were TV watchers growing up," Martin Short told me once in an interview, explaining why their skits lampooning television were so precisely and wittily detailed. *Saturday Night Live* and *In Living Color* could not skewer their chosen targets so thoroughly and knowingly without being acutely aware of them in the first place.

In most cases, what TV is really doing with its satires, salutes, and references is engaging in a friendly dialogue with the viewer, speaking what it knows is a common language. The explosive initial popularity of the board game Trivial Pursuit was traceable to the fact that it rewarded people for retaining what some considered "trivial" facts—giving many players, for the first time, positive reinforcement for things learned long ago and thereafter relegated to the recesses of memory. Television constantly reinforces viewers in a similar manner, rewarding them by alluding to current and previous touchstones of popular entertainment. Most of these allusions are affectionate, not disdainful, and their success and frequency are indications that television, more than anything else, is our society's common language. And as television matures, the language becomes more complex, the vocabulary more voluminous. To put it another way: Television isn't just getting older. It's getting better.

Yet as TV has grown, it has neither forgotten nor abandoned its early strengths. Today's numerous homages to the past, as when *Perfect Strangers* stars Bronson Pinchot and Mark Linn-Baker do delightful impersonations of Ed Norton and Ralph Kramden, elicit recognition and laughter precisely because the actors and viewers are equally well versed in the original performances and premises of *The Honeymooners*. Those original shows, in turn, worked so well because of their *own* familiarity: Jackie Gleason and Art Carney, along with the program's writers, crafted characters so distinctive and delightful that audiences knew them very well, and could anticipate and savor certain actions, comments, and situations.

Jeff Greenfield, now a *Nightline* correspondent, noted in his book called *Television* that audience familiarity, in this case, bred anything *but* contempt:

> They know that whenever Norton will write something, he will prepare for the task with an elaborate series of hand gestures, which will provoke Kramden to fury (*"Will you cut that out, Norton!?!"*). . . . The utter predictability of what a character will do, given his habits, quirks, and foibles, far from boring the listening or viewing audience enriches the humor, because it brings to any one joke or dilemma a knowledge of that character's response.

Some critics, Greenfield among them, charge that such predictability of characters and situations is a pervasive weakness of television. Actually, it is neither pervasive nor a weakness.

It is no longer pervasive because TV series, since Greenfield wrote that in 1977, have matured to the point where the better programs no longer follow such an interchangeable, predictable recipe. Such series as *The White Shadow, M*A*S*H,* and *St. Elsewhere* introduced sudden twists, and even sudden deaths of main characters, into their plots, and unexpected events and departures are now fairly common on the better written comedies and dramas (the final episode of *Twin Peaks*, in fact, left almost as many characters dead as alive). In fact, each twist and turn in prime time's more popular series is now considered fair grist for the gossip columns, and even some TV columns. The summer-long media fixation on "Who shot J.R.?" reflected the nation's own guilty-pleasure fascination with the doings on *Dallas* in 1980, and the resolution's remarkable ratings— higher than any Super Bowl game—led many news outlets to rethink their definitions of show-business "scoops." The years since then have seen the media slip into overdrive—and overkill—as reporters and gossip columnists scurry and compete to break the latest fictional "news" of a death on *L.A. Law*, a betrayal on *Knots Landing*, or a cliffhanger resolution on *Cheers*. The makers of *thirtysomething* were so frustrated by plot "leaks," they intentionally concocted misleading dummy scripts and kept the actual ones under much tighter scrutiny. It shows, again, how seriously some people take TV and how much interest it generates—but what's next? Breaking a story identifying the killer on an upcoming *Murder, She Wrote?*

In any case, this familiarity with and hunger for characters is TV's greatest strength, not its biggest weakness. Repeated exposure to a beloved character has done wonders in other media: literature with its Sherlock Holmes, film with its Marx Brothers and Laurel and Hardy, radio with its Edgar Bergen and Charlie McCarthy, and countless other examples. However, the exposure television gives to its biggest stars and characters, and the ability it gives audiences to observe them at close range, week after week and year after year, affords a frequency, and type of understanding and appreciation, no other medium can rival.

"Apparently," James L. Brooks says, "Francis Coppola has put all the *Godfather*s together. And I just think it's going to put down one of the amazing acting challenges we've ever seen anybody meet, where Al Pacino took a character over twenty years. Now that's an extraordinary movie; I don't know what to compare it with. But in television, seeing somebody portray a character over five, six, seven years is nothing unusual—and it's damned interesting, when you let them grow and you let them change."

Television has grown and changed, too, though it remembers and often retains its traditions. *60 Minutes*, which after twenty-four years is the longest-running series on prime-time television, has replaced several correspondents, but never its format, which has been retained intentionally by creator Don Hewitt. "*60 Minutes* is one of the few things that looks the same as it did when you were a kid," he says. "The gas stations look different, the supermarkets look different, the cars look different. Everything looks different, except *60 Minutes* still looks the way it did when a lot of the viewers sat on their fathers' laps and watched it. And over the years people have said to me, 'You know, you ought to change that stopwatch.' I said, 'You've got to be crazy!' I wouldn't change that stopwatch. You know why? That stopwatch is like the squeaky screen door to grandpa's house."

Bill Cosby, when asked to identify the TV shows and comedians he found most memorable, instantly rattles off a list that includes *The Dick Van Dyke Show,* Jackie Gleason, Ernie Kovacs, Sid Caesar and Imogene Coca, Steve Allen, Lucille Ball, and Carol Burnett. "And don't forget," Cosby says, "you're talking to a person who *studied* comedy. This is in my ballpark."

Saturday Night Live carries on the broad mass-media satirical tradition of Allen, Kovacs, *Your Show of Shows,* and *That Was the Week That Was*—and *SNL* creator Lorne Michaels is aware that his own show, while spoofing TV stars, traditions and institutions, has introduced more than its share of all three. "I recently met some people in their midforties, the same age I am, who would have been in the core audience seventeen years ago," he says. "Now they've got children, in the twelve-to-fifteen area, and they're watching the show with their kids."

And Fred Rogers, who has been lampooned by everyone from Johnny Carson to Eddie Murphy, remembers visiting the *Saturday Night Live* offices one day in search of Murphy, whose "Mr. Robinson's Neighborhood" skit presented a less positive role model—one who broadcast from the ghetto, advocating drugs and robbery, and sang such lyrics as "It's one hell of a day in the neighborhood" and "I've always wanted to live in a house like yours, my friend. Maybe when there's nobody home, I'll break in." Neither the spoofer nor the spoofee was at all uncomfortable with meeting the other. "He came out of one of the offices," Rogers recalls, "threw his arms around me and said, 'The *real* Mister Rogers!' "

Carson, who also poked fun at Rogers's deliberate delivery on more than one occasion, once defended the skits to Rogers by making two points already raised here. According to Rogers, Carson told him, "Fred, first of all, we'd never do these if people didn't know who we were talking about. And second of all, it's done with a certain affection." And watched with a certain affection as well, as TV continues to play an increasingly important part in our lives, and on our sets.

One measure of television's increased popularity is its rather recent presence *on* television itself. It used to be that televisions were as rare a sight on a TV series as in a Warner Brothers movie. Most living rooms were without them, most conversations ignored them, and the only time a TV set was visible in a TV show was when it had a news bulletin or other bit of business that advanced the plot, such as Ralph Kramden trying to win a TV set on an episode of *The Honeymooners.* The chief exception was *The Dick Van Dyke Show,* a TV show about people who *worked* on a TV show, but when Rob and his cohorts watched boss Alan Brady on television, it was mostly for business, not pleasure. (A few years later, the same was true for Van Dyke's costar, Mary Tyler Moore, when *she* starred in a TV show about people who worked on a TV show.) Television sets were spotted, and used, more often in such fantasy shows as *The Flintstones* and *The Munsters* than in sitcoms with "real people." In those days, the TV character who most often watched television for pleasure was Mr. Ed, who had his own set outside his stall. But he was just horsing around.

Times changed, however, and television slowly worked its way into and up through its own system. In the seventies, Archie Bunker's famous armchair was aimed straight at the TV set, reflecting its central role in the homes of working-class families. In the eighties, even such upper-class, well-to-do families as the Huxtables on *The Cosby Show* spent a lot of time watching TV, snugly nestled on their couch. And to kick off the nineties, *The Simpsons* began each episode by having the family members scamper home to dive on *their* couch and watch TV.

In the current generation of TV shows, a television set is an almost common sight. *Cheers* features and often uses a TV set in its bar, *Twin Peaks* had its characters addicted to a soap opera whose intricate plots mirrored those of *Twin Peaks* itself, and the family on *Married . . . with Children* fights over the right to remotely control the remote control. Even today's nostalgia shows give to yesterday's television a place in the home it was denied by TV shows at the time: the father on *The Wonder Years*, set in the sixties, focuses intently on his TV set as a way to unwind after work, and the kids of *Brooklyn Bridge*, set in the fifties, gyrate the antenna on their tiny TV set to try and lock onto a discernible image. Television rarely flatters itself with these inclusions, and often makes the same banal generalities about viewing habits as those who denounce the entire medium. Even so, it's a grudging and growing acknowledgment of TV's place and appeal in the home.

Concurrent with TV's rising pervasiveness as a visible TV-show object is its increased status as a TV-show subject. From simple name-dropping to elaborate fantasy sequences, TV is throwing out allusions with Joycean glee. The prime-time soap opera *Knots Landing* refers to its Thursday-night competitor, *L.A. Law*, by having one character tell another, "I forgot to set my VCR. I've got to see what Corbin Bernsen's wearing tonight." Meanwhile, a court-appointed temporary leader on *L.A. Law* finishes his morning briefing by telling the staff, "Let's be careful out there"—alluding to the weekly warning given by Sergeant Esterhaus on another Steven Bochco drama series, *Hill Street Blues*. On *Anything But Love* and *Maniac Mansion*, the entire cast joins in on a series of imaginative sequences imitating such shows as *Twin Peaks* and *Married . . . with Children*.

Twin Peaks, in fact, introduces such a distinct style that it is aped, or alluded to, by a dizzying number and range of programs, from the mysterious owls in the clever *Northern Exposure* to the foreboding ceiling fans in the insipid *Dynasty: The Reunion*. On *Dinosaurs*, a show in which the prehistoric TV set has almost a costarring role, the kids delight in watching the news on "DNN" and the scientific experiments on "Ask Mr. Lizard." Entire programs, such as Comedy Central's *National Lampoon* parody of MTV or CBS's couch-potato unsold pilot *What's Alan Watching?*, are devoted to spoofing popular TV forms in painstaking detail. Then there's HBO's *Dream On*, whose protagonist is a Baby Boomer overflowing with memories of TV shows from the fifties—memories presented, almost subliminally, in vintage TV clips that punctuate the sitcom's action and reactions.

Of course, shows need not rely on old clips to evoke nostalgic TV memories, not when old stars are eager to play along. In *The Gambler Returns*, a 1991 *Gambler* telemovie starring Kenny Rogers, room is made for cameo appearances by veteran stars reprising their characters from vintage TV Westerns: Clint Walker as Cheyenne Bodie, Chuck Connors as Lucas McCain (a.k.a. *The Rifleman*), Gene Barry's Bat Masterson, and Hugh O'Brien's Wyatt Earp. *The Torkelsons*, a new sitcom costarring William Schallert as a friendly boarder, alludes to one of his many previous series roles by giving the guest role of his daughter-in-law to Patty Duke, who played Schallert's daughter (and niece) on *The Patty Duke Show*. In what may go down as one of the most famous actor-as-character return appearances in TV history, Leonard Nimoy of *Star Trek* guest stars in an episode of *Star Trek: The Next Generation*, playing a 150-year-old Mr. Spock.

In 1991, one entire new series, the ABC-Nickelodeon coventure *Hi Honey, I'm Home*, was based on the premise that a fifties-style nuclear TV family (in the style of the Nelsons, but called the Nielsens) would move in next door to an "actual" nineties-style family: single mom, bratty kids. Each week would feature a guest appearance by a former TV star, usually in the role of the character that had brought fame to him or her: Audrey Meadows and Joyce Randolph as Alice and Trixie from *The Honeymooners*, and, as themselves, Jim Nabors of *Gomer Pyle, U.S.M.C.* and Ann B. Davis of *The Brady Bunch*. Great premise. Unfortunately, lousy show.

The former stars of *Leave It to Beaver* have parlayed the appetite for TV nostalgia into a lucrative second career, reprising the roles not only in a sequel TV series, but making in-character appearances elsewhere on television. Barbara Billingsley's June Cleaver and Ken Osmond's Eddie Haskell recently lunched together in a McDonald's TV commercial ("My," Eddie tells her unctuously, "that's a lovely double cheeseburger you're eating"), Billingsley and Jerry Mather's Beaver teamed for an appearance on the sitcom *Parker Lewis Can't Lose!*, and Mathers portrayed himself in a coldly sarcastic appearance on *Married . . . with Children*.

In that show, Mathers complained to the Bundys that, once again, "I have donned the lowly cap of 'the Beaver' in order to eke out a pathetic living." It was one of the harshest comedic indictments of TV fandom since William Shatner, in that famous *Saturday Night Live* skit, told a *Star Trek*–obsessed group of Trekkies to "get a life." Yet the TV-on-TV rules are so prismatic that, by saying those things *on* TV, those TV stars could seek refuge by claiming their remarks were made "only for television," even if they contained a measure of truth.

At its most cynical, television blurs the line between reality and fantasy by cranking out irresponsible docudramas and so-called reality shows, replete with lurid reenactments. At its most inventive, television blurs those same lines to great advantage, as when Garry Trudeau and Robert Altman invent a prototypical liberal politician (Michael Murphy as the Kennedy-esque Jack Tanner) and send him on the actual campaign trail, where he mingles with the likes of pundit Hodding Carter III and 1988 presidential hopeful Bruce Babbitt, or shares screen time with Gary Hart, Pat Robertson, and Robert Dole.

The result, HBO's *Tanner '88* series, made telling points about the unseen machinations involved in America's political process. Though ostensibly a comedy, it did a great job of explaining and exploring the symbiotic relationship between politicians and the media. "There's really no other form in the entertainment world," Trudeau told me at the time, "where I can do what I do in the *(Doonesbury)* strip. I write on the wing, and have the spontaneity of the work reflected in the final piece. . . . I think the stuff is fresh. It's alive. I don't ever expect to find anything like this again." Unless, that is, HBO antes up for a *Tanner '92* sequel, which, at this writing, seems highly unlikely. However, Altman did employ similar methods when mixing fictional characters and real Hollywood stars, writers, and other people in his 1992 movie *The Player*. (How many movie critics, I wonder, cited *Tanner '88* as an obvious precursor?)

Another reality-bending, headline-chasing series is *Murphy Brown*, with its parade of actual TV newspeople, from Walter Cronkite to Connie Chung, who treat Candice Bergen's fictional Murphy as an equal. The fictional "F.Y.I." newsmagazine of *Murphy Brown* mines for comedy the concepts and conflicts facing TV's real prime-time newsmagazines: ratings pressure, competition with other shows to book certain guests, the dangers of interviewing live, pressure groups, focus groups, good reviews, dirt-digging tabloids, interoffice rivalry, and so on. The audience isn't shocked by any of this, but accepts it all as part of TV's "real" reality.

The backstage bickering of *Murphy Brown*, in many ways, is easier to accept as truth than the on-camera "happy family" atmosphere of certain morning talk shows today. Or, during the Deborah Norville era, *Today*. And both *Tanner '88* and *Murphy Brown* owe a debt to such early reality-warping shows as 1978's syndicated *America 2-Night*, in which Martin Mull, as ersatz talk-show host Barth Gimble, interviewed such "real" celebrities as Charlton Heston and Robin Williams, who were only too happy to participate in a show sincerely poking fun at talk-show insincerity.

Finally, there's the development of finales, yet another indication of TV's maturation. In the first generation of television, the vast majority of series never really ended; like old soldiers, they just faded away. Things changed in 1967 with the telecast of the two-part finale of *The Fugitive*, which provided a conclusion to the four-year mystery of "Who killed Mrs. Kimble?" The finale drew an astonishing 72 percent share of all viewers watching TV that night, and ranked at the time as the most popular single TV episode in the history of television.

The popularity of that final hour of *The Fugitive* was instant, irrefutable proof that viewers, having invested years getting to know and love a show's characters, would respond emotionally—and perhaps in great (and profitable) numbers—if given a chance to bid a proper good-bye to those characters. Yet except for 1968's *The Prisoner,* conceived all along as a finite series with a definite (and definitely memorable) conclusion, it took a long time for other TV series to follow suit. The clincher came in 1983, when TV's *M*A*S*H* folded its tent after eleven successful years. Its movie-length finale episode—wrapping up the Korean War as well as one of the decade's most popular series—became, and at this writing remains, the most-watched TV series episode of all time (even though the *National Enquirer* had leaked key details of the final script).

Finales then became more commonplace throughout the eighties and into the nineties, as established but departing series said farewell to viewers with final installments good *(Hill Street Blues),* bad *(Magnum, P.I.),* and ugly *(Miami Vice).* Financially, series finales give the networks one last chance to milk a successful or once-successful show. Artistically, they give TV producers a chance to provide a sense of closure. Brooks, asked how important it was to provide a finale episode after seven years of *The Mary Tyler Moore Show,* replies passionately, "How important is it to complete an experience?"

In some cases, very—and very lasting. The moment in the *Mary Tyler Moore Show* finale when the entire cast hugged was restaged, knowingly and fondly, during the finale episode of *St. Elsewhere,* which then shattered conventions and undercut expectations with a climax suggesting that all the events dramatized on the series were nothing more than the idle imaginings of an autistic child. It was a way to end the series not only with a final, playful statement about TV's "reality," but also with an oblique laugh at the expense of *Dallas,* which had resolved one particularly stupid season in 1986—and erased the death of Patrick Duffy's Bobby Ewing—by claiming it had all been a bad dream by his wife Pam (played by Victoria Principal).

In 1990, *Newhart* matched the inventive impishness of *St. Elsewhere* and then some, ending its own lengthy run with a surprise ending in which all eight seasons of *Newhart* were explained away as a bad dream—a dream by Bob Hartley, whom the star of *Newhart* had portrayed from 1972–78 on *The Bob Newhart Show.* As the studio audience screamed with delight, Hartley described his "nightmare" to his wife Emily, played, as before, by Suzanne Pleshette. Those last seconds of *Newhart* built upon TV's past to provide one final twist and treat, one its producers knew *Newhart* fans would comprehend, revere, and remember. And, as happens with so many things related to television, people *did* understand and respond—and will *not* forget.

Final footnote: in the fall of 1991, there was yet another allusion to the infamous *Dallas* dream, but one created more by tragic necessity than playful creativity. The producers of *Married . . . with Children* had accommodated the real-life pregnancy of actress Katey Sagal by having her character, Peg Bundy, announce her own pregnancy at the start of the new season. When Sagal suffered a miscarriage, the show's producers—disinclined either to continue the story line for the actress's sake or to betray the program's nothing-serious approach—searched for a way out, and came up with a dream-sequence, *Dallas*-like reversal.

And so it goes . . . which leads right into the next chapter's discussion of TV as art, which begins with an emphatic statement from Kurt Vonnegut.

19

TELEVISION AT ITS BEST

"**I** would say that television has produced one comic masterpiece, which is *Cheers*," Kurt Vonnegut says. "I wish I'd written that instead of everything I *had* written. Every time anybody opens his or her mouth on that show, it's significant. It's *funny*."

Vonnegut's remark came early enough, and seemed controversial enough, for me to repeat it to several other interviewees. Linda Ellerbee, who has adopted Vonnegut's "So it goes" phrase from *Slaughterhouse-Five* as her own unofficial trademark, says, "I can understand that. Absolutely. But I would have thought he would have said *M*A*S*H*. That seems to be more Vonnegutesque." James Burrows, one of the creators of *Cheers*, re-layed the author's praise to partners Les and Glen Charles, then reported back to say, "We were all blown away, because we're all big fans of his. We're very impressed, and we would love to *meet* Mr. Vonnegut to tell him what fans we are of *his*." (Months later, they contacted Vonnegut by mail to tell him precisely that.) Other responses cut all across the spectrum.

Robert Geller: "I think he could write a hell of a *Cheers*. TV scenes like the talking frozen head on *Cheers*, and the death of Chuckles the clown on *The Mary Tyler Moore Show*, and the best of *Barney Miller* are close to what short stories in a comedic form are all about to me. They're like the best of Chekhov."

Linda Bloodworth-Thomason: "That's interesting. I'm a Kurt Von-negut fan *and* a *Cheers* fan, so I think they both have something to crow about. I agree with him that it's literature, and I think that *Cheers* deserves to be right up there with some of the things that Mark Twain has written. Absolutely. I think if Mark Twain were around today, like I said, I think he'd be working in television. I think Mark Twain would have a big deal at CBS."

David Zurawik: "I'm stunned. Really surprised."

Mark Dawidziak: "Part of me wishes he hadn't said it. The other part understands what he's saying. You hate to hear anybody who's done as much wonderful writing as Vonnegut has belittle that work that you have come to love so much, but I understand what he means. Here's a show that, each week, finds a moment of truth and reaches millions of people, and does what is the toughest thing to do in show business, literature, or anything else—to make them laugh."

James L. Brooks: "He must have seen their profit statement. . . . Look, really, there's something extraordinary about television when it works. You become part of people's lives. Not something that they witness, but something that is part of them. And I just think if you're talking about comedy writing that distinguishes itself, certainly a large percentage of it originates on television. I don't think there's a question about that."

Robert Thompson: "Coming from Kurt Vonnegut, that's pretty interesting. You can get Kurt Vonnegut, one of America's great intellectuals and users of the English language, and get an eight-year-old kid off the street, and the chances of the two of them agreeing on anything is pretty slim. Yet when you mention television, everybody has an opinion—and on *Cheers*, those two would probably agree, for different reasons, about how funny it is."

Yet Vonnegut not only raves about *Cheers* and rants about the Gulf War, but speaks enthusiastically about the *American Playhouse* production of Terrence McNally's *Andre's Mother,* a little-known but potent drama about the surviving mother and lover of an AIDS victim ("It was just deeply moving, and I started to cry"). And, warming up to the subject of TV excellence, says, "I think *Hill Street Blues* was very important, and no doubt mind-bending, to a lot of people—mind-bending in a good way. And so was *M*A*S*H,*" he adds, partly supporting Ellerbee's opinion of his tastes.

Vonnegut then talks unapologetically, almost proudly, of watching and enjoying "a lot of stuff that nobody else seems to notice"—including two of Dennis Potter's miniseries. "Let me tell you about two of the greatest things I've ever seen on television," Vonnegut says. "The first was *Pennies from Heaven,* which was ripped off by Hollywood and not done nearly as well. And then, by the same author, there was *The Singing Detective.* Nobody else saw it!"

Well, not exactly nobody. I saw it and loved it—and so did many of the people I interviewed, who mentioned it unprompted as a perfect example of TV as literature, as pure art.

The Singing Detective is actually many stories in one, stories weaving in and out of one another in a challenging and meaningful tapestry. The central character, played by Michael Gambon, is a man named Philip Marlow, an author of pulp detective novels who has been hospitalized with a crippling and disfiguring skin condition. The main story line takes place in the hospital, as Marlow insults and is insulted by doctors, jousts verbally with a staff psychologist, and endures the various stages of his horrible disease.

To keep himself from going crazy from the fever and the drugs, Marlow spends some of the time reworking an old novel, "The Singing Detective," which is enacted on the screen with a healthy Marlow as the dapper hero. But the fever, the drugs, and the persistent psychologist all take their toll, forcing to the surface long-repressed memories of Philip's boyhood—and feeding the bedridden author's paranoid imaginings about a plot by his wife and her lover to find and profit from Marlow's "Singing Detective" manuscript.

Through it all, period music from the forties erupts on the soundtrack and from the mouths of characters, as reality and fantasy become indistinguishable—and the various story lines, at first distinct and disconnected, coil around one another like snakes, finally becoming one in a powerful psychological climax. The images, captured by director Jon Amiel, are as deep and delicious as Potter's story.

It is, to this day, the single best television drama I have ever seen, and I would throw it down as a gauntlet, as Exhibits A to Z, to anyone ignorant enough to dismiss television as inferior to any other storytelling art form.

William Link calls it wonderful, praises the "brilliant performance" by Gambon, and says Potter "stretched the limits of what you could do on television." Shelley Duvall calls it "brilliant, incredible television," and says "the humor, and the sheer ingenuity of the writing," impressed her the most. "I thought it was magnificent," Linda Ellerbee says, adding, "I would love to have been in the meeting where they sold it, just to hear how they described it to the executives." (Presumably, it was *not* summarized, in ten words or less, as "the heartbreak of psoriasis.") Vonnegut calls it "pure television," likening it to James Joyce's *Dubliners* as a sublime work of art, and The Museum of Television & Radio mounted an exhaustive, impressive 1992 exhibition built around Potter's TV work.

Cheers, one of the most popular TV shows in America, and *The Singing Detective,* a much more esoteric and obscure production, are at opposite ends of the spectrum in many respects, yet both are excellent examples of TV at its best. Somewhere between those two shows on that same spectrum is *Twin Peaks,* the most talked-about series of 1990. On television, *Twin Peaks* rose and fell with astonishing speed, and both its ascent and descent were due to several significant factors.

Phase one, the prelaunch hype, involved getting the word out early about the wonderful weirdness of the David Lynch–Mark Frost telemovie. One of the earliest raves came from the September 1989 issue of *Connoisseur* magazine, in which Howard A. Rodman's article was headlined "The Series That Will Change TV." Once the national TV press got a look, it too responded with lavish and unusually widespread praise. When the series premiered in April 1990, Tom Shales of the *Washington Post* wrote, "For the adventurous explorer in the normally tame wilds of television, *Twin Peaks* is just this side of a godsend." As happened later that year with *The Civil War,* a general and vocal consensus of TV critics actually, though rarely, can make a difference. It happened with *Twin Peaks,* and the two-hour opener drew enough viewers to rank as the highest-rated telemovie of the 1989 – 90 season. The rest was up to Lynch, Frost, and the others involved with making *Twin Peaks.*

Phase two, a viewer and media response to the plots and characters in the early episodes, led to and fed a *Twin Peaks* mania. The "Who Killed Laura Palmer?" mystery story line dominated conversations, and the increasingly paranormal subplots kept viewers involved and guessing in different ways. After a couple of episodes, the audience leveled off. The viewers who remained, though, were a loyal core audience, delighting in Lynch's otherworldly dream sequences and playing along at trying to unravel, or at least follow, the various plot threads. The national media, enjoying and propelling the ride, geared up to "Who Shot J.R.?" levels all over again. *Newsweek* and *People* ran elaborate flow charts tracing the characters' intricate relationships, establishing a symbiotic bond between *Twin Peaks* and magazines that would continue throughout 1990: by the end of the year, *Time* had run a cover story on Lynch, and actresses from *Twin Peaks* had graced the covers of *Playboy, Rolling Stone, TV Guide,* and, fittingly, a photography magazine titled *Exposure.*

After the two-hour premiere and seven one-hour installments, *Twin Peaks* ended its first season with the Palmer murder mystery still unresolved, and with a cliff-hanger ending of Kyle MacLachlan's Dale Cooper being shot by an unseen assailant. It was, of course, an allusion to the way *Dallas* had ended its season a decade earlier, leading into the summer that begat the "Who Shot J.R.?" silliness. Like *Dallas, Twin Peaks* was a hot media topic that summer, and was given lots of credit for changing the rules of television. "Tried and true," one network executive said, "is dead and buried."

Phase three, the inevitable backlash, was accelerated by several factors. First, the show's "media darling" momentum was derailed at the Emmy awards in September, where *Twin Peaks,* nominated for fourteen awards, was snubbed in all but two minor categories, winning only for editing and costume design. Second, the merchandizing offshoots went from intriguing to overkill. The demand for cherry pies and *Twin Peaks* memorabilia at the Mar-T Cafe in North Bend, Washington (the model for the series' Double R Diner) was one thing, and compact disc releases by *Peaks* composer Angelo Badalamenti and featured singer Julee Cruise were welcome projects. However, the various authorized *Twin Peaks* offshoots mounted up too high, and may have amounted to distractions that kept the show's staff from focusing more energy on the series itself.

The stack of stuff generated by, and with the cooperation of, *Twin Peaks* ultimately included an audiotape of Cooper's messages to Diane, a *Twin Peaks* collectible card art set by Star Pics, and such books as *The Secret Diary of Laura Palmer* (written by Jennifer Lynch, the director's daughter), *The Autobiography of F.B.I. Special Agent Dale Cooper* (written by Scott Frost, the cocreator's brother), and even a *Twin Peaks Access Guide* (written by David Lynch, Mark Frost, and regular *Access* author Richard Saul Wurman). Unauthorized books were also crowding the shelves, including a quickie guide called *Welcome to Twin Peaks* and a more in-depth history and analysis, by Mark Altman, called *Twin Peaks behind the Scenes*. While this was going on, parodies on other TV shows occurred regularly, in everything from *Sesame Street* (where Big Bird and others participated in "Twin Beaks") to *Saturday Night Live*, where guest host MacLachlan participated in a dead-on parody tweaking fun at the show for dragging on the Laura Palmer murder mystery for so long.

The backlash against *Twin Peaks* was spurred most severely, though, by the very folks who had conspired to broadcast the series in the first place: ABC and Lynch-Frost Productions. ABC blew it by moving the series to Saturday night, where it hoped *Twin Peaks* and its lead-in, *China Beach*, would lure audiences back to Saturday-night TV and capture the attention of the weekend home-video crowd. Instead, both shows suffered. Many audience members were active on weekends and unable to be loyal viewers, ultimately frustrating formerly loyal fans who could no longer keep up with the serialized and complicated story lines. Also, the writers of *Twin Peaks* frustrated many viewers by stringing out the Laura Palmer story: the killer was revealed eight hours into the show's second season, and the subsequent wrapping up of loose ends turned it into a twenty-hour mystery. Members of the creative team of *Twin Peaks* would later plead guilty of losing steam and direction as the realities of weekly TV production made it tougher to match their prior efforts and generate a similarly entrancing story.

By the time *Twin Peaks* finally was pulled from the ABC schedule in the middle of the competitive February sweeps, its audience had shrunk to only 10 percent of the homes watching TV at that hour.

Phase four, the attempted comeback, was a big publicity push generated by the network and production company when *Twin Peaks* returned at the end of March. The episode relaunching the series was even available for preview, the first such case since the initial appearance of the series. Unfortunately, it was one of the very weakest offerings. The next week's episode, ironically, was excellent, but by then all hope of revival had been dashed. *Twin Peaks* limped along through April, then disappeared again until mid-June, when the final two installments were combined into one big finale. It ended with a brilliant, extended sequence directed by Lynch, but most of the audience had moved on.

In fourteen short months, *Twin Peaks* had washed across the nation's consciousness, then receded like an ebb tide. "Moving it to Saturday night didn't help," ABC Entertainment President Robert A. Iger said the summer after canceling *Twin Peaks*, but also suggested it may have been more effective as a self-contained, seven-episode special. "We tried it as a multiple-season series," he said, "and it just couldn't sustain itself."

The following season, at all the commercial networks, "tried and true" was alive and . . . well, let's just say it was alive. "I don't think," Frost told the *New York Times* just before the series' cancelation, "it changed television one iota."

But it did. *Twin Peaks* was not for everybody (William Link calls it "incredibly overrated" and sneers, "If this is revolutionary television, I'll take vanilla"), and the rapid acceptance of its unconventional images and dialogue made it difficult for it to escape its *own* conventions ("How," asks Robert Thompson, "do you parody irony?").

Yet never before, in the history of television, had a program inspired so many millions of people to debate and analyze it so deeply and excitedly for so prolonged a period. Other mass-media mysteries, such as the finale of *The Fugitive* and the "Who Shot J.R.?" cliff-hanger of *Dallas,* crested in a few weeks and were relatively superficial. *Twin Peaks* generated the kinds of annotated scrutiny usually associated with scholarly journals and literary monographs—or with *The Prisoner,* where a much smaller cult audience continues, decades later, to discuss and debate that series' possible interpretations in fan-club magazines and newsletters.

When it came to *Twin Peaks,* character names and plot details were traced to previous movies and TV shows, the meanings of owls, spotlights, and ceiling fans were argued endlessly, and the series spawned more one-liners and catch phrases than any series this side of *Saturday Night Live.* In casual conversations and detailed articles, elements of the series were dissected with a fervor that literature professors can both appreciate and envy. Just to pull one suitably obscure example at random: Tim Lucas, writing in a little-known journal called *Video Watchdog,* notes that "the first four shots in the pilot episode are all twin images," citing the twin waterfalls blending into one, two ducks gliding along the lake, a table ornament of two identical dogs, and Josie Packard admiring herself in a mirror. Lucas then makes a lengthy case for the importance of twin imagery in *Twin Peaks*—which, given the importance of the doppelgänger concept in the series's subsequent final episode, seems positively prescient.

Despite finding certain failings with its plot resolutions and internal inconsistencies, I defended *Twin Peaks* to the death—its, not mine—on the grounds that it tried harder, and did more, than most weekly series in prime time. It gave as much emphasis to visual images and lighting, and to the musical score and sound effects, as it did to the scripts and performances. Some sequences consisted of long, unbroken camera takes; others were subliminal montages, cut together a frame at a time. Several core scenes, such as the rock-throwing experiment from Tibet and the "dancing midget" dream, stretched from one commercial break to the next without changing scenes. Conversely, in the series' final episode, as a doppelgänger Laura Palmer ran screaming toward a frightened Cooper, Lynch increased the tension of the scene by inserting single-frame images of the villainous Windom Earle as she ran forward—close-ups alternating from a black-and-white negative image of Earle to a full-color positive image, then to a blending of the two, all shown too briefly for the naked eye to detect. Subliminal spookiness, Lynch style.

Twin Peaks, like *The Singing Detective,* was fascinating to watch, fun to try to figure out, and especially interesting when set in the context of the creators' previous work.

With Potter, it was a thrill seeing how the musical inventiveness of

Pennies from Heaven was used to even greater effect in *The Singing Detective.* With Lynch, it was exciting tracing threads that ran to *Peaks* through his other work, from the early *Eraserhead* to the subsequent *Wild at Heart.* I wonder, though, whether most film critics are as interested in acknowledging, much less tracing, the TV threads running through the latest big-screen efforts by Lynch and Potter, respectively.

How many of them stayed with *Twin Peaks* to the end, and are thereby fully qualified to judge the fidelity with which Lynch and company present their prequel film project, *Twin Peaks: Fire Walk with Me?* And when analyzing Potter's large-screen directorial debut in *Secret Friends,* which Potter also wrote, how many film critics can say with authority how much he picked up from Piers Haggard and Jon Amiel, who directed his two most ambitious miniseries seen in America? Or can compare the movie's themes to similar ones in Potter's early teleplay for *Double Dare?* How many, for that matter, will note that Alan Bates, the star of *Secret Friends,* had the title role in a 1978 *Masterpiece Theatre* adaptation of Thomas Hardy's *The Mayor of Casterbridge*—a novel adapted for television by Potter himself?

The three examples of quality television examined at length in this chapter—*Cheers, Twin Peaks,* and *The Singing Detective*—represent different genres of television, accounting for a sitcom, a drama series, and a miniseries, respectively. Looking at these specific works lends weight to the argument supporting TV's excellence and development, but so does a quick look at these and other television genres in general. If the fifties were the Golden Age of Television, the quantity and quality of today's TV offerings make the modern era worthy of the appellation "The Platinum Age of Television." To quote Red Serling for a moment: "Consider, if you will. . . ."

The situation comedy. It didn't take long at all for TV to crank out wonderful works in this genre. Some episodes of *I Love Lucy* belong right up there with the classic shorts of W. C. Fields and Laurel and Hardy, and everything about *The Honeymooners* will be just as fresh and funny to future generations as it already has been for more than thirty-five years. In the seventies, *All in the Family, M*A*S*H,* and *The Mary Tyler Moore Show* led the way with more sophisticated issues and humor, opening the doors for ideas as well as humor. David Marc calls them "literate sitcoms" and "lit-coms," but suggests their very aspirations doomed them to ultimate failure. Quite the contrary: each of those series had a lengthy, popular run, and their sophisticated emphasis on concepts and characters is reflected today in shows ranging from *The Cosby Show* and *Cheers* to *Brooklyn Bridge* and *Seinfeld.* When *The Brady Bunch* is performed on Broadway, it is done as camp—but someday, if someone mounts stage versions of, say, *Fawlty Towers* with a talented cast, those John Cleese–Connie Booth scripts will be recognized as the tightly written classics they are. (It's worth noting that the creators of *Cheers* have cited *Fawlty Towers* as the chief inspiration for their own series.) Sitcoms have stretched in other ways as well: doing without laugh tracks as in *The Days and Nights of Molly Dodd,* devoting themselves to parody as in *Mary Hartman, Mary Hartman,* and opening themselves up to wholly dramatic moments. As years go by, sitcoms from the past may be reevaluated in an even more appreciative light, as James L. Brooks has experienced when watching old installments of what he now considers his own personal best effort. Not *The Mary Tyler Moore Show.* Not *The Simpsons.* Not *The Tracey Ullman Show.* But, instead . . .

"I'm amazed now," he says, "that I revere *Taxi* as much as I do. I'm not comfortable saying it, but it's the truth. *Taxi* was an enormously well-received show, but I don't think it's ever gotten its due, because when I look at it, I just marvel at it. I guess that's the television series I revere most. . . . I don't think anyone connected with *Taxi* ever did better work. Judd [Hirsch] has won Tony Awards, and I think he was brilliant, Danny [De Vito] has distinguished himself, Tony [Danza] has gone on—everybody's gone on and done things. But I think it's certainly part of the best of any of us that were working on it. I mean, just the things we took for granted— we invented religions, we exempted moral and ethical codes, there was a place for Andy Kaufman, there were two characters who spoke a language that we made up. That was just thrilling stuff to be working on. . . . There was a great group of writers. Glen and Les Charles, some of their best work is on *Taxi.* Nobody who was on *Taxi* would deny that it was among their finest work."

The weekly drama. The evolution in this genre has come not in terms of seriousness or topicality, which were present in (and even before) such series as *East Side/West Side* and *The Defenders,* but in terms of story lines, which in many of today's prime-time dramas are both more complex and more linear. Subplots and multiepisode stories, a soap opera staple, became utilized in more ambitious drama series, so that episodes in a series could no longer be shuffled into any order, season after season, and still make sense out of context. *Lou Grant* brought the comedy and drama genres closer together. *Hill Street Blues* broke old rules and set new standards for cop shows, just as *St. Elsewhere* did for medical shows. On *St. Elsewhere,* not only were regular characters no longer impervious to pain and death, but it seemed they were placed in life-threatening situations more often than their patients: male and female staffers were raped, one doctor got AIDS, one resident died, another committed suicide, and, in one killer episode, a doctor was shot and killed by a staff nurse. Death, which in the old days of TV seldom visited series regulars, showed up suddenly, and sometimes without warning, on *The White Shadow, thirtysomething, L.A. Law, Tour of Duty, China Beach,* and other series—including, most certainly, *Twin Peaks,* where characters could die and *still* remain on the show. And characters who escaped death on such series seldom escaped change, as more and more series writers took advantage of the form and explored their characters more fully. Some fine examples: *Northern Exposure* and the late, lamented *Shannon's Deal* and *China Beach.*

The miniseries. Here is a form indigenous to television, one combining the "event" potential of a feature film with the length and exposure most films cannot provide. "There are many stories with extended time spans," Larry McMurtry wrote in an essay published in the late seventies, "that simply cannot be told adequately within the roughly three-hour duration of a movie. Obviously, the miniseries is ideal for such books. The five- or six-episode format allows writers to keep rhythms and textural details that are usually lost in the cuttings and budgetings of movie scripts." A decade later, a superb adaptation of McMurtry's own *Lonesome Dove* was perfect proof of his own thesis. Carved down to movie length (even to the generous three-hour length of *Dances with Wolves,* which it predated), *Lonesome Dove* would have been denied the full richness of its characterizations and vastness of its scope. "To get that many great performances and marvelous characters into a miniseries was astounding," Robert Geller says of *Lonesome Dove,* and Linda Bloodworth-Thomason adds, "*Lonesome Dove* is a perfect example of audiovisual literature. If that had not been a book first, it really wouldn't have mattered. It was so alive, and it was every bit as compelling on television."

Television's willingness to experiment with long-form drama came much earlier than most media historians realize. The first efforts were performed live, with casts returning to the TV studios to enact each subsequent installment. Probably the first (and certainly the first to be reviewed) was a 1945 production of Robert E. Sherwood's play *Abe Lincoln in Illinois,* broadcast in three installments over a two-month period by NBC's WNBT-TV in New York. After the first installment was televised, *Variety* called it "undoubtedly one of the most ambitious shows since the advent of video." In 1952, NBC's *Cameo Theatre* presented a three-part TV version of another stage play—Henrik Ibsen's *Peer Gynt*—in weekly installments. England's first effort was the 1953 science-fiction miniseries *Quatermass Experiment,* which generated two popular sequels.

Back in America, similar success greeted the trio of *Davy Crockett* adventures shown in 1954 on ABC's *Disneyland.* Not a miniseries? Think again. There were three installments, presented individually. The final installment, "Davy Crockett at the Alamo," showed how Fess Parker's Davy died, giving the saga a very finite ending. (The series' popularity, though, prompted Walt Disney to cast Parker in some "earlier" Davy Crockett adventures, thus popularizing the concept of the prequel.)

Once miniseries really caught on with *The Forsyte Saga* in the late sixties, public and commercial TV wasted no time in recognizing and taking advantage of the potential of the form. *The Six Wives of Henry VIII* and *Elizabeth R* were wonderfully made and acted costume dramas; *Upstairs, Downstairs* was a two-tiered soap opera with class and wit; and ABC's *QB VII, Eleanor and Franklin,* and especially *Rich Man, Poor Man* brought clout and mass audiences to long-form drama. The continuing story of *Rich Man, Poor Man* made overnight stars of its leading players in 1976, and that same year the other networks triumphed with such long-form dramas as CBS's *Helter Skelter* and NBC's *Sybil.* Then, in 1977, came *Roots,* whose impact was as large as its still-unmatched miniseries audience.

Since then, there's no better case for the status of miniseries as an art form than a list of some of its most impressive efforts. If you haven't seen the following, you should. If you have, it's likely you have not forgotten them: *Scenes from a Marriage. I, Claudius. Holocaust. Pennies from Heaven. Shogun. Tinker, Tailor, Soldier, Spy. Masada. Brideshead Revisited. The Life and Adventures of Nicholas Nickleby. Concealed Enemies. The Jewel in the Crown. Das Boot. Berlin Alexanderplatz. Anne of Green Gables. Edge of Darkness.* And, of course, *The Singing Detective* and *Lonesome Dove.*

Drama specials and telemovies. "When I watch these black-and-white *Golden Age of Television* episodes on cable," James L. Brooks says, "it's so clearly literature, it's so clearly theater. It's so clearly about excellence, and about the condition of America at a certain time and place. *The Days of Wine and Roses*—it's amazing. The style of that time was so extraordinary. We were dignified by it, we were enlarged by it, we were more literate because of it."

These days, live drama is done mostly as a gimmick, and rarely done even at that. But production techniques have opened up whole new worlds of possibilities, changing most TV drama specials from stagebound productions to small-screen films. Even so, many television dramas continue to do their best work by telling small personal stories, honing in on a subject and a few characters in a manner naturally suited to the intimate TV screen. *Promise,* starring James Woods as a schizophrenic and James Garner as the older brother suddenly and reluctantly entrusted with his care, is one such powerful example. However, when it comes to discussing the development and content of TV dramas and telemovies, the only safe generalization is that it is not safe to generalize. The genre encompasses everything from *The Shakespeare Plays* to *Friendly Fire,* from exploitive docudramas to explosive originals. When it comes to adapting literature, television's drama specials have fared as well, on occasion, as the very best miniseries. The *American Playhouse* production of Philip Roth's *The Ghost Writer,* coadapted by the author himself, is witty and beautiful, as are the Peter H. Hunt adaptation of Mark Twain's *Life on the Mississippi* and virtually all the TV adaptations of works by Vonnegut.

But where the telemovie has matured the most is in its willingness, sometimes even eagerness, to explore serious issues in a serious manner. Levinson and Link were pioneers in that respect, thanks to their exploration of an interracial relationship in 1970's *My Sweet Charlie* and a homosexual relationship in 1972's *That Certain Summer.* Other writers and producers presented thoughtful and meaningful telemovies on racial pride and prejudice *(The Autobiography of Miss Jane Pittman)*, wife-battering *(The Burning Bed)*, AIDS *(An Early Frost)*, Alzheimer's *(Do You Remember Love?)*, incest *(Something About Amelia)*, and other topics. I won't argue that there aren't as many bad telemovies as there are bad *theatrical* movies. But I will argue, and do, that there are also as many good ones, and that television often has the courage to hit certain issues first.

The variety show. Certainly, this is one genre, like the Western, that has all but disappeared from the current TV scene—and the newest version of *The Carol Burnett Show* didn't help things much. Where the old variety showcases, exemplified by *The Ed Sullivan Show,* used to be the major outlets for many branches of show business, today's proliferation of cable services and syndicated programs has given those branches much more room to grow. Stand-up comics, today, can aim for appearances on HBO, Showtime, Comedy Central, or any of a dozen syndicated comedy-club shows. Pop musicians have VH-1; rock and rap artists have MTV and ABC's *In Concert* series; and classical musicians have Bravo and Arts & Entertainment. Vegas-style magicians such as David Copperfield, and maverick magicians such as Penn & Teller, get their own respective network shows, and animal acts have moved on to *America's Funniest Home Videos, Fantastic Pets,* and David Letterman's "Stupid Pet Tricks." The components that used to make up a variety show have left the roost and established their own nests, which makes it tougher these days for a variety show to attract and hold an audience. Satire, at least, is alive and well, thanks to *Saturday Night Live* and *In Living Color,* both of which are fully capable of turning around a topical social issue and skewering it cleverly and enthusiastically.

The talk show. The appeal of *The Tonight Show* when Jack Paar was at the helm was that he talked naturally—conversationally—with celebrities, authors, politicians, artists, and others who were generally not seen in such a casual setting. Under Johnny Carson, who inherited the *Tonight Show* chair from Paar (who, in turn, had inherited it from Steve Allen), the conversation became more structured, the quid pro quo more obvious: most guests had a book to plug, a clip to show, a tour to announce. Today, the seemingly insatiable demand for celebrity news and appearances, and the endlessly multiplying number of talk shows competing to snare guests and viewers, put such power in the hands of certain publicists that many talk shows barter terms to get the hottest stars: if *Today* offers three days of short features on a new movie, a rival show may counter with a theme week. All of it has turned many talk shows into show business with the emphasis on business, and the ones relying more on issues than celebrities, or a mixture of both, are competing in that arena as well, constantly upping the ante on sensationalism and weirdness. Besides, there simply are so many talk shows out there that the quantity of conversation makes the lack of quality that much more noticeable.

But the quality is there. David Frost and Dick Cavett are still around, effectively plying their trades with shows and specials allowing them to spend blocks of time with a single guest. Bob Costas uses the same technique, relying on lots of research to frame his questions, and Larry King does too, relying on virtually no research to frame his. Though I prefer the former technique, there are times when King's conversational approach pays off, and even emulates Paar's unpredictable digressions. Former *Saturday Night Live* cast member Dennis Miller, whose talk show premiered in 1992, brought with him a refreshing intelligence and unpredictability. On the hard-news side, Ted Koppel remains the best interviewer on television, usually making *Nightline* required viewing. *The MacNeil/Lehrer NewsHour,* whose format inspired that of *Nightline,* continues to link questioners and newsmakers from various parts of the country, employing satellite technology to conquer distance while tackling topics. The roundtable, freewheeling discussions on ABC's *This Week with David Brinkley* and on Fred Friendly's PBS specials are both informative and entertaining, as are the no-nonsense conversations between Bill Moyers and his thoughtful guests on his own PBS series and specials. Also, it takes little imagination to see how important Phil Donahue and Oprah Winfrey have been in bringing issues and ideas before the public. Yes, both their shows, like so many others, are guilty of sensationalism (especially during ratings sweeps), but Donahue and Winfrey, especially, have been instrumental in easing certain topics into the national consciousness. They are one way to take America's pulse—just as the best way of all for a generation, better even than public-opinion polls, had been to listen to Johnny Carson's nightly monologues on *The Tonight Show.*

Through his frequency of exposure, Carson long ago supplanted Bob Hope (who had in turn supplanted Will Rogers) as the national comedian of record. The country's take on any issue, from the Clarence Thomas confirmation hearings to the latest marriage of Elizabeth Taylor, could be measured by the amount and type of one-liners served up by Carson on *The Tonight Show,* and by the audience's reaction to them. Finally, there are TV's "anti-hosts," Regis Philbin of *Regis & Kathie Lee* and David Letterman of *Late Night with David Letterman.* Both project the oddly endearing attitude that they're stuck in a job they don't quite love, or at least certainly don't take very seriously. Philbin has the affectionately grouchy demeanor of Arthur Godfrey, while Letterman has traits of both Jack Paar and Steve Allen. *Regis & Kathie Lee* is a "family atmosphere" TV show where the atmosphere appears genuine, and *Late Night with David Letterman,* which uses TV more inventively than any show since Ernie Kovacs, has that rebellious feeling to it—as though *Late Night* were beamed from some offshore pirate TV station, rather than straight from Rockefeller Center. Letterman's is a new generation of talk show, but one that knowingly builds upon the best of the old.

News and documentaries. This is an area where, despite all the talk of the downsizing and bastardizing of network news divisions, television continues to thrive and shine—though not necessarily in the same places. CBS, NBC, and ABC rarely engage in the single-topic news documentary business any more, unless someone like Peter Jennings or Ted Koppel pushes the network to devote and clear the time. But on PBS, *Frontline* and *The American Experience* provide weekly, often provocative documentaries on timely and historical subjects, while lengthy multiepisode specials include works of the scope and impact of *The Civil War, Eyes on the Prize,* and *Vietnam: A Television History.* For documentaries on the cultural arts, PBS's *American Masters* does an often superb job of analysis, and PBS's *Edge* of cultural reporting and commentary. For science and nature reporting, there are the fine PBS contributions by David Attenborough, James Burke, *National Geographic, Nature,* and *Nova,* as well as all the offerings by The Discovery Channel, The Learning Channel, and TBS.

When news breaks today, its pieces can be found all over the place—from CBS to CNN, from C-SPAN to Court TV, twenty-four hours a day. Network newscasts are immeasurably more advanced, technologically, than they were a generation ago, and the fact that news is gathered and disseminated so quickly today is both a liability and an asset.

It's a liability because the filtering system doesn't always work, causing rumors and unverified information to slip through the cracks and get on the air. However, errors are uncovered and corrected with the same speed, so viewers who stay tuned, or hop back and forth among various news outlets, are likely to be well informed as a crisis or major news event unfolds. Most viewers have learned to judge for themselves the rawness and veracity of the data relayed to them by television. The fact that twenty-four-hour news outlets exist on cable, and that the broadcasting networks are getting back into the overnight news business, suggests that Americans can seek out and receive news on demand—which, in itself, is quite a change from a generation ago.

Yet here, too, links to the past remain, and the news organizations of today have built upon the reputations and ideas of yesterday. When Peter Arnett made his pictureless reports from Baghdad the night the bombing began, the legacy of Edward R. Murrow was resonating almost as clearly as another voice. And if one person personified the best of TV news through its first generation, that person was Murrow.

"When I first started in television news, which is when television news began," David Brinkley told TV critics in the summer of 1991, "everybody was trying to imitate Ed Murrow, who was a great figure at the time." Fred Friendly, Murrow's producer, says, "I had Ed as a teacher, and half the things I do, even now, are because those are the things Ed would have me do. He got a lot of stuff on the air. That was what Ed was best at—getting stuff on the air."

There is, however, at least one prominent newsperson unwilling to jump on the Ed Murrow bandwagon.

"Oh, boy, don't get me started on the subject of Murrow," Peter Jennings says. (But apparently he already was, so he continued.) "I think there have been occasions when at least one of the television networks has used Murrow contemporaneously to convince people it is still the news organization it was in Murrow's day," Jennings says, showing just enough restraint not to mention CBS by name.

"If they had looked more carefully, I think they would have found they were a better organization than they were in Murrow's day. I don't mean to denigrate Murrow, but it was far less crowded then. I mean, there was Murrow, and then there was Murrow, and there was Murrow. . . ." For a modern comparison, Jennings turns to NBC, and cites John Chancellor and Garrick Utley as well-traveled intellectuals, "clearly of the Murrow mold." Then he adds, "I could put together from all three networks now, it seems to me, a worldwide team of electronic journalists that would knock your socks off."

The trouble, Jennings acknowledges, is that he is not sure he could assemble a similar team for each network—though he is more certain that the network newscasts of today compare favorably to those of the distant past. "We get more news on," Jennings says, "the technology is better, the cameras are better, the camera people are more sophisticated." Viewers are still underinformed if they rely only on TV for their news, he says, but they're nonetheless better informed by television than they were a decade ago. "It sounds like a little bit of a contradiction to what I've been saying," Jennings admits, "but viewers are better informed because I think we have mastered the primary aspects of the technology better."

It's the technology, after all, that has linked the nation via TV the way it was once linked by radio. The events that wash across television, preempting regular network programming or relayed live by cable, instantly sweep across the nation and into the national consciousness. The Gulf War, the failed Soviet coup, the Clarence Thomas hearings, even the Magic Johnson press conference—all were relayed live, then examined energetically, by television.

The same medium can bind the nation together in other ways, and with other types of programming—*The Civil War, Twin Peaks,* the 1991 World Series, even *Cheers.* People watch. People care. And as television continues to change and grow, it also continues to entertain and inform.

Only idiots continue to think of it as an idiot box.

20

TELEVISION
AS A SERIOUS SUBJECT

"When I show the opening of *The Beverly Hillbillies* in class, my students all sing along; when I read 'Ode to a Grecian Urn,' they don't," wrote Robert Thompson in his intentionally inflammatory 1988 article for *The Chronicle of Higher Education.* "They whistle the song on *The Andy Griffith Show,* they snap their fingers after the first four notes of the introduction to *The Addams Family,* and they recite the opening narration of *Star Trek.* But no one chimes in when I read a soliloquy from *King Lear.* In fact, when I mention Lear, most of them think I mean Norman, the guy who created *All in the Family.*"

Thompson is well aware, when writing such pro-TV pronouncements in scholarly magazines, of fanning the flames of intolerance in some of his more conservative professorial peers.

"Allan Bloom was one of my teachers. That sort of says it all," Thompson says, laughingly recalling his student days at the University of Chicago. "I'm sure he'd be ashamed to know he turned the likes of me out." Yet when he suggests that college freshmen take courses devoted to the likes of *The Brady Bunch* before moving on to Shakespeare, he's not just being scholastically irreverent. He's suggesting a way to tap into the students' accumulated knowledge and enthusiasm and steer it in new directions, rather than starting from scratch. Bombarding first-year students with *King Lear,* Thompson writes, demands they read the play at least once, try to become comfortable with its unfamiliar language and Elizabethan context, and read some other works by Shakespeare before analyzing its style and meaning. "Unfortunately, by the time they've done all that," Thompson adds, "the semester's over. Students rarely get a chance to really jump in and enjoy the plays themselves."

His courses in TV programming, Thompson says, present a completely different classroom attitude and experience. "It's a professor's dream. It's unlike any other subject matter. They've done all the reading already." Thompson sees this not as an abomination, but as an opportunity. "Because students are already experts of sorts on television, my class can begin on the first day at a level of sophistication usually reserved in other fields for graduate school," Thompson told (or tried to tell) his colleagues in that controversial article. "Exercises in close textual analysis can be undertaken immediately. Freshmen in a television class have the capacity to do real criticism right from the start—criticism of a kind they can go on to practice on *King Lear* in subsequent semesters."

Professors disagreeing with Thompson's approach do not deny the spread of teleliteracy. They merely abhor it. Teaching students more about what they already know seems a waste to those instructors, who feel that so much other ground needs to be covered and *re*covered. At Johns Hopkins University, Mark Crispin Miller traces the shift in student attitudes and knowledge to the midsixties, and complains in his book *Boxed In,* "No longer, certainly, could you assume that your lit class would recognize, say, Donne's Holy Sonnet XIII, or the Houyhnhnms, or the first sentence of *Pride and Prejudice,* or any of the other fragments that had once been common knowledge among English majors." By the midseventies, Miller goes on to say, things had gotten so bad that only a few of his undergraduates could be expected to "catch broad allusions to *Citizen Kane* or *Dr. Strangelove,* or to recall the last scene of *Sunset Boulevard,* or to know who Frank Capra was"—yet they were totally conversant in TV's advertising slogans and jingles.

The irony is that Miller not only bemoans a drop in "cultural literacy," but regrets a perceived decrease in what Molly Haskell called "cinema literacy"—while, not too long ago, "film studies" courses on campus were generally as rare, and suspiciously regarded, as "TV studies" courses are today. (It's not too much of a stretch to imagine a professor, twenty or thirty years hence, longing for the good old days when his students could catch broad allusions to *The Mary Tyler Moore Show* or *Hill Street Blues,* or recall the last scene of *The Fugitive,* or know who Jack Webb was.)

Thompson sees still another irony: the historical reticence of the academic community to make room for new art forms, evidenced as far back as when Latin and Greek works were the only legitimate courses of study in many literature programs. When American literature and modern novels were brought into the college classrooms for study, it was not without several rounds of institutional in-fighting.

"English professors used to be what TV professors are now," Thompson says of those avant-garde teachers who first brought Fitzgerald and Hemingway into their literature courses. "Later, film went through the same problems. There have always been complaints about making room for the next tier of popular entertainment."

"In our age of fluid art forms and rapidly changing techniques of art and dramatic reproduction, the customs of the academic community have a more insulating effect than ever before," Daniel J. Boorstin wrote in *The Image*.

> These customs inevitably lead us to ignore the profound implications of great current changes in our forms of art, literature, and drama. I do not know of a regular course on the art of the movies in a department of literature in a single major university, although there may be such. A result is that many of our scholars who are best equipped to judge contemporary dramatic forms against those of earlier ages ostracize the leading forms of our own age.

Boorstin wrote that in 1961. Very shortly thereafter, film indeed stormed the gates of academia, as teachers began analyzing movies both on their own merits and in comparison with other art forms. Robert Geller, who taught high school English in the midsixties, remembers being considered "fairly progressive" for encouraging his students to compare the novel and film versions of *Moby-Dick* and *Lord Jim*. "It was around the time of McLuhan," Geller recalls, "and I was always kind of hung up on the immeasurable possibility of the word, yet the excitement of taking those words and giving them a kind of visual relative."

With Thompson and television, the excitement comes not only from screening and discussing the accepted TV "classics," but from analyzing some of the most popular programs from society's most popular medium. Instead of just studying *Harvest of Shame* and *Marty*, Thompson also "required" his students to watch *Charlie's Angels* and *Leave It to Beaver*, prompting immediate and outraged protests from certain intellectuals at his own university, and even from some of his students' parents. "They would call and complain," Thompson says, "saying, 'The reason I sent my kids to college was to get them *away* from television.' " Even the students, he says, often sign up with the assumption it's a "gut course" (no brains required), and initially are resistant to lectures where you *really* talked about *Leave It to Beaver*.

"Students, by this time, have the very strong opinion that television is garbage," Thompson explains. "It's a very rough sell, at first, to get students to take it seriously. But you can really watch the scales fall from their eyes as you're talking about it." Feeling that professors, of all people, should be equipped to handle pop quizzes, I asked Thompson to give a quick example of his classroom technique by offering his instant analysis of *Cheers*. Here's his quick version of what might be called "*Cheers* 101."

"*Cheers* falls right in that tradition of *The Andy Griffith Show* and *The Beverly Hillbillies*—that sort of anti-intellectual, just-plain-folks show." The simple-minded bartender Woody, Thompson says, is a "lovable dunce" in the tradition of Jethro, Gomer, and Goober, and he notes that while Diane Chambers was "the first person ever in the history of TV" to be a graduate student who made Schopenhauer jokes, the writers of *Cheers* made sure she was the butt of every joke. According to Thompson, bartender Sam, an ex-Red Sox pitcher, and bar potato Norm represent one Boston. Diane, the cultured intellectual, represents the other.

Thompson even finds meanings in the show's character names. Sam Malone's biggest character flaw since the beginning of *Cheers*, Thompson says, is his inability to commit to a one-woman relationship. Despite all his flings, "Sam's really all by himself. He's Sam Malone—Sam alone." And Norm, described by Thompson as "this fat, beer-chugging chunk of cholesterol," is "the show's everyman, the norm. So he's named Norm." Thompson's students, he says, are "almost amazed you can find those kinds of literary riches" by applying critical analysis to a TV sitcom.

No less amazed, perhaps, than the creators of *Cheers*, who find some people are reading much more into their show than they wrote into it. With someone like Shakespeare, there's wide disagreement among scholars as to whether he even wrote the works attributed to him, much less what he meant by them. But when dealing with something as modern as *Cheers*, a critical analyst can find his or her scholarly interpretations graded by the creators themselves. Enter *Cheers* cocreator James Burrows.

"All I can tell you is," Burrows says, "after the first year that we did this show, we were at a conference at San Francisco State. It was actually a seminar on the show, and a woman handed the three of us a forty-page treatise she wrote on the meaning of *Cheers*. I can tell you, not only for myself but my two partners, all we did was try to make the most funny show and characters you could identify with."

As for the supposedly symbolic character names of Sam Malone and Norm, both were actually a function of the casting process. Burrows says the character of Norm was named "George" originally, but Burrows, as the show's director, asked for a name change after George Wendt was cast in the role, to minimize confusion on the set between the actor and his character. That's how Norm got his name. "Sam Malone used to be Sam Harrison," Burrows adds. "He was a wide receiver for the Patriots originally. Then when Teddy [Danson] was cast, we decided to go relief pitcher, and he didn't look like a Harrison, and we wanted kind of a semi-Irish name, so it was Sam Malone. So they are reading a lot more into it, but that goes on in the world of art and criticism, and that's what it's about."

No television series in recent years has been scrutinized and analyzed more energetically than *Twin Peaks*, each episode of which was sprinkled with references to film, television, literature, mythology, photography and other such inspirational influences. Cocreator Mark Frost says, as does Burrows, that people found things in his series that the writers didn't intend. Frost, however, doesn't necessarily dismiss those enterprising discoveries.

"It's that weird thing," he says, "of how do you know when something's in your work and when it isn't? If someone sees it there—I mean, if they *see* it there, it must *be* there. Because for them it *is* there. It gets into a strange kind of gray area, then, where creativity becomes something that is shared, and the audience is using its own creativity in interpreting the material. I think that's kind of the magic of it."

With *Twin Peaks,* Frost admits a lot *was* injected into the series for the benefit of those who would look for and catch the references—to *Vertigo* and *The Fugitive, Double Indemnity* and *Laura, The Scarlet Letter* and *Dallas.* "I have always loved things like James Joyce's work," Frost says, "and other things that had hidden layers and hidden meanings that were open to interpretation. I think it's fun to layer those things in. They will reward people's scrutiny."

From the academic community, the scrutiny can indeed be illuminating. When University of Texas professor Horace Newcomb told Morley Safer on *60 Minutes* he considered *Gunsmoke* "one of the important shows in the history of television," he backed his praise by explaining that *"Gunsmoke* was teaching us about race relations, and showing us how to defend human rights, at a time when nobody was doing that overtly." David Marc, in his *Comic Visions* book, provided details and insights relating to such topics as the rare TV appearances of Lenny Bruce and Jack Kerouac.

You can take anything too far, though, as when John Fiske, in the book *Television Culture,* analyzes *Hart to Hart* as a "contemporary urban myth." (Unless, by dismissing *Hart to Hart* as escapist romantic nonsense, I've completely myth-ed the point.) Even Thompson, when insisting that Aaron Spelling's *The Love Boat* is "very good art," pushes his enthusiasm for television to the point where I have to bail out and part company. Yet grudgingly, I admit he and coauthor Marc, in *Architects of the Air: The Makers of American Television,* make a case for at least one "artistic" contribution by that shallow series: the introductory boarding scene, which introduced the week's plots and subplots in a quick, efficient manner.

"Though *The Love Boat* is rarely credited for its ingenuity," Marc and Thompson write, "this ritual introductory sequence that Spelling developed for the show can be seen as a formal source for organizational conventions employed by some of the finest multiplot dramatic series of the eighties. Examples include the squad room roll call that opened *Hill Street Blues* each week and the partners' meeting similarly placed in *L.A. Law.*"

Others are more critical, however, when it comes to assessing and accepting the work of professors who teach TV in the classroom and analyze it at such lengths. "Thompson may be at the vanguard of a new aesthetics," one book reviewer wrote of Thompson's TV auteur theory as delineated in *Adventures on Prime Time: The Television Programs of Stephen J. Cannell.* "He may also just be blowing smoke." Brandon Tartikoff, the former NBC Entertainment President who had ordered and televised series from Cannell, Bochco, Spelling, Cosby, Brooks, Burrows, and literally hundreds of others, told a *New York Times* reporter in 1990, "When I hear about college professors writing books about people who do prime-time shows, my natural cynicism says there's got to be courses for all these athletes to make them academically eligible to play football." And even though Don Hewitt showcased Thompson, Newcomb, and Marc, among others, in a *60 Minutes* piece about TV's professorial champions, his opinion of *their* opinion is even more cynical than Tartikoff's.

"They're full of [expletive deleted]," Hewitt says, waving his hand as if waving them away. "It's pop art. It's the popular culture. . . . If we woke up tomorrow morning and there had been some sort of electrical storm during the night, and no television ever worked again, I don't think America would be culturally poor. It would be culturally richer. But it's fun."

Here, of course, is where I part company with Hewitt, and any other powerful TV participants who downplay the effects and content of their chosen medium. Television has developed to the point where it deserves respect, and serious examination as an art form. When David Zurawik says he would like to do his doctoral dissertation on the notion of the hero in prime time—taking Joseph Campbell's ideas of the mythic journey and applying them to such shows as *The Fugitive, Kung Fu,* and *Star Trek*—he's not "blowing smoke." He's interested in trying to track how television has done its part, like fairy tales and classic literature, to satisfy certain needs and explore certain themes. He's not only looking at television, but looking at it seriously, and wants others to do the same.

"The more traditional 'book culture' intellectual community in this country," Zurawik says, "is very reluctant to accept certain truths about television as a cultural force. *Doogie Howser, M.D.* and *The Wonder Years*—those sorts of shows are what the coming-of-age novels like *Catcher in the Rye* and *Huckleberry Finn* used to be for the book culture. . . . The first episode of *Doogie Howser* ends with him sitting down at that computer, writing in his diary something like, 'Lost my first patient today. Kissed my first girl. Life will never be the same.' Life and death, juxtaposed sort of in the same sentence—that's exactly what John Donne and the metaphysical poets did, but because a guy named Doogie wrote it on TV, a professor might mock it."

But if more high school and college classes opened their doors and minds to television, those teachers might discover a threefold benefit in talking about TV with their students.

First, as Thompson has suggested, teaching television is a way to develop students' critical skills in other subject areas, a tactic that can be used at the high-school level as well. John Merrow, host of The Learning Channel's *Learning Matters* and former education correspondent for *The MacNeil/Lehrer NewsHour,* writes, "Students assigned to watch and analyze *The Cosby Show, thirtysomething,* and other series can easily transfer those skills and interest to *To Kill a Mockingbird* and *Our Town.*" It's not a case of "If you can't beat 'em, join 'em," but a case of allowing students to build on their self-motivated knowledge and passions.

Second, students should study TV, scholastically as well as at home, to appreciate more fully its nuances and deceptions, its worth, and its frequent unworthiness. Advertising techniques, political propagandizing, distortion of fact in so-called docudramas—all of these should be examined closely, as should television's more commendable activities and achievements.

"To say that the communications media are central to the functioning of our society is to state the obvious," says Everette E. Dennis of the Gannett Foundation Media Center. "However, American undergraduate education almost completely ignores the study of mass communications." As Peter Orlik notes in *Critiquing,* "Recently, print literacy has grudgingly had to share the spotlight with computer literacy, but media literacy remains an unrecognized and unmet need despite the fact that the graduates of our school systems collectively will spend much more time with the software of radio/television than with that of computers."

Finally, and this is the most surprising and valuable benefit, discussing television in the classroom can be an immense aid in helping teachers learn about their students. When Horace Newcomb launches each new semester of media classes, he begins by instructing his students to write a "media autobiography," an essay on what TV has meant to them, what moments from it are most memorable, and how it may have shaped their personalities and beliefs. I provided my own version in the opening chapter of this book, and conducted a small experiment by throwing out the question while appearing as a guest lecturer at Northwestern University's National High School Institute. The summer course, attended by media-major high school seniors from across the country, provided a fascinating sample study from which to elicit responses. William Link, who had lectured there two years previously, remembers the students as "definitely a cut above average"—my assessment as well.

What struck me most was how deeply the majority of them felt about TV, and how vivid their memories and emotions were. For many of those young adults, television coverage of the *Challenger* explosion was to them what the weekend of the JFK assassination was to my generation—a violent tragedy that froze them in front of their TV sets and made them remember, forever after, where and how they heard the news. (For most, it was an in-classroom assigned event built around the first schoolteacher in space, making it even more traumatic.) Some students talked of being frightened into sleeplessness by the depiction of nuclear annihilation in ABC's fictional *The Day After*—not by the program, but merely by the on-air promos. Others remembered being riveted by such recent real-life TV offerings as the Jessica McClure rescue, the Iran–Contra hearings, the Congressional debate prior to giving the authorization for use of force in the Gulf, and the Gulf War coverage itself.

On the entertainment side, some students talked enthusiastically about what *The Muppet Show* meant to them, and one admitted crying after learning of Jim Henson's death. Her classmates, instead of laughing at her, nodded their heads in sympathetic unison. Fred Rogers was mentioned, and *The Electric Company,* and *The Twilight Zone,* and even (sigh) *Hart to Hart*—though not, thank goodness, as a contemporary urban myth.

The dominant topic of conversation, though, was Fox's *Beverly Hills,*

90210, the merits and faults of which were debated so vociferously by the students that I flew back from Chicago and wrote a column pegging *90210* as the hot new show among teens. A month later, with new summer episodes feeding that frenzy, *Beverly Hills, 90210* became a hit in the ratings, its cast members adorning every magazine cover this side of *U.S. News & World Report.* My head start—courtesy of insider-trading information gathered from those enthusiastic and watchful youngsters—was a clear case of a supposed expert learning something from his students.

If all the students' responses that night were collected into a book, that book might rightly be titled *Our Television Made Children*—and would help put TV in its proper perspective. Judging from those responses, it's clear the students of today already take TV quite seriously. The teachers have only to catch up—and, if given the chance, the children shall lead them.

CONCLUSION

Rather than reiterating the arguments from the preceding pages, I would prefer to end this book by stressing a conclusion I do *not* want anyone to reach—namely, that I'm soft on television. There is a difference between seeing a medium's potential and being its cheerleader, between admiring its finest achievements and embracing everything with equal enthusiasm. Yet I believe, unapologetically, the best way to play an active part in improving television is to seek out, acknowledge, and support its most important and impressive efforts.

Nothing is wrong with getting excited about the likes of *Northern Exposure* and *The American Experience*. Something is wrong, however, if nothing on television excites us at all. Blaming television for that no longer works, because the quality and quantity is there for the viewing. So the fault, dear Brutus, is not in our TV sets, but in ourselves.

Also, I'd like to conclude by presenting a last-minute update on some of the issues and ideas covered in the book, and by offering one final observation about TV's future.

The Gulf War. Television noted the first anniversary of the start of the conflict with a series of news specials, most notably CNN's *Desert Storm: One Year Later* and the Discovery Channel's multipart *The Gulf Crisis: The Road to War*. And though many critics charged that the war was forgotten by television after its official resolution, specials keyed to the war and its aftermath continued to appear.

In the first month of 1992, there were many such specials. CNN's *Iraq: One Year Later*, anchored live in Baghdad by John Holliman, revisited such controversial wartime sites as the baby-milk factory and the underground bomb shelter. ABC's *Nightline* teamed with *U.S. News & World Report* to present a special look at "The Unreported History of the Persian Gulf War." And PBS's *Nova* presented two specials dealing with the environmental aftermath of the Gulf War: *Hell Fighters of Kuwait* (a study of the crews hired to extinguish the raging oil fires) and *Saddam's War on Wildlife*, a profile of one man's official attempts to protect and preserve animals during the Gulf War.

Breaking news. As this book goes to press in May 1992, the year's biggest story was the rioting that followed the verdicts in the case of the LAPD officers who had beaten Rodney King. Graphic footage of truck drivers being dragged from their vehicles and beaten—footage photographed from local TV-news helicopters and broadcast live—was like watching the Rodney King "video" all over again, only from an aerial view and with the races reversed. Other recent major media events occurred in December 1991. One was the overplayed William Kennedy Smith trial, the media response to which was circuslike, recalling the worst days of the Bruno Hauptmann trial after the Lindbergh kidnapping. (The Smith case belonged on the specialized Courtroom Television Network, if anywhere, but not as a live "drama" on CNN.) The other was the tastefully handled Magic Johnson press conference, at which the Los Angeles Lakers basketball star, forthrightly and with dignity, revealed he had been infected by the HIV virus. The media response to Johnson's revelations was a series of stories aimed at informing young fans about the dangers of AIDS—features and news items that probably reached more viewers, and had more impact, than 100 public service announcements.

Television and children. The heightened respect with which TV has begun to treat children is reflected in recent actions by three of the contributors to this book.

Prior to ABC's Saturday-morning coverage of the Anita Hill–Clarence Thomas confrontation, Peter Jennings—once again displaying a sensitivity to younger viewers—offered a preface specifically for "those of you who are little." After gingerly describing the conflict at issue, Jennings vividly described the stakes at hand, and the dilemma facing the committee members:

> Think how awful it would be if they made the wrong decision, and the Supreme Court had a man on it who had been mean to a woman and lied about it, and was going to make a lot of decisions about the way other women are treated. Think how awful it would be if she were not telling the truth, and senators believed her and told the judge he couldn't sit on the court.

Later, at the start of 1992, Peggy Charren announced her intention to disband Action for Children's Television by the end of the year, thanks to advances made in federal regulations for children's TV. "For more than 20 years ACT has tried to get the public interest laws that govern broadcasting to apply to children," Charren said in a press conference announcing her organization's impending dissolution. "With the passage of the 1990 Children's Television Act, this goal has been achieved; people who want better TV for kids now have Congress on their side."

Finally, in March 1992, Linda Ellerbee mounted and cohosted *Nickelodeon Special Edition: A Conversation with Magic,* a brilliant and important special in which Magic Johnson and a group of youngsters discussed AIDS and HIV.

Teleliteracy. Examples of allusions, jokes, and other forms of direct and indirect appreciation of TV, or other media by TV, continue to proliferate. Michael Jackson's "Dangerous" video, while sparking a controversy for its inappropriate (and subsequently discarded) violent, crotch-grabbing dance climax, included homages to everything from *Singin' in the Rain* and *Die Hard 2* to previous music videos, including his own. Another, even more blatant example was Julie Brown's *Medusa: Dare to be Truthful*, a full-length, wickedly detailed Showtime satire of Madonna's *Truth or Dare*. It was the most intricate and accurate parody since *The Rutles*, in which Eric Idle and company lampooned the lives and legacy of the Beatles. Finally, for a graduate-level course in teleliteracy, there were the weekly doses of pop-culture references in the joke-filled running commentary on Comedy Central's *Mystery Science Theater 3000*.

The resonance of television past. During one week in December 1991, the two most popular movies in America were *Star Trek VI: The Undiscovered Country* and *The Addams Family*. (When *The Addams Family* opened in November, it shot to the top with an opening take of 24.1 million dollars, the biggest fall weekend in film history.) Demand for the original *Addams Family* TV series was stoked again, and an animated version was scheduled by ABC for fall 1992. In February, a movie based on the *Saturday Night Live* "Wayne's World" sketches was released, ranking as the most popular movie for more than a month, and the large-screen *Twin Peaks: Fire Walk with Me* was scheduled for fall 1992.

On network TV, CBS brought back *All in the Family* for yet another prime-time repeat run in 1992, and Miles Inc. tapped into video nostalgia by planning to repeat, in their entirety, old Alka-Seltzer ads, including ones with the animated Speedy Alka-Seltzer character and the durable catch phrases "I can't believe I ate the whole thing" and "Try it, you'll like it." The appeal is obvious: on home video, collections of old commercials, and vintage TV shows, are among the top sellers in the nontheatrical categories. One video retailer told the *New York Times*, "People want the shows they were raised on."

And as a return of sorts to the TV practices of yesteryear, the Fox network broadcast live prime-time editions of *In Living Color* and *Roc* in 1992.

Television being attacked. My favorite attack on TV during the period in which I was writing the book was "Turn Off the TV Day," a one-day protest organized by such groups as Morality in Media, the American Family Association, and Concerned Viewers for Quality Television (not to be confused with Viewers for Quality Television, which prefers to steer viewers in the direction of good shows rather than away from TV entirely). Not so incidentally, another advocacy group endorsing "Turn Off the TV Day" was the National Coalition on Television Violence, the organization with Dr. Thomas Radecki as its chairman and research director.

Not only did "Turn Off the TV Day" have no effect on the national ratings, but it was laughably easy to argue against. TV Critic Mark Dawidziak, in a column attacking that particular attack on television, pointed out the types of TV offerings you missed if you went along with Turn Off Your TV Day on October 29, 1991. "You missed a shattering *Frontline* documentary about the lingering impact of the Gulf War . . . a *Homefront* episode about racism, and a moving Home Box Office *America Undercover* report on Alzheimer's Disease. Yes, sir, you really sent a signal to programmers, didn't you?"

And as a serious postscript regarding Radecki himself, the NCTV chairman signed a consent order in April 1992 surrendering his medical license and practice for at least five years. According to the *State Journal-Register* of Springfield, Illinois, the state's Department of Professional Regulation had investigated Radecki after receiving allegations of "immoral conduct of an unprofessional nature with a patient."

Following the investigation, Radecki waived his right to a hearing on the charges, apologized for "a lapse in professional judgment," and severed his connection with the NCTV, which he founded in 1980. (According to the Illinois Department of Public Aid, he also repaid more than 250,000 dollars in state Medicaid money—improperly billed public aid for fiscal years 1988 and 1989.) After temporarily laying off members of its staff, however, the NCTV regrouped, appointed a new leader, and plans to continue its monitoring efforts . . . without Radecki.

Television being defended. My favorite defense of television during the same period came in Meg Greenfield's *Newsweek* column of December 23, 1991, raising "The Television Question" in the light of the media furor over the William Kennedy Smith televised trial. Greenfield wrote:

> Our lives have already been irreversibly transformed in ways that make the pre-television America of less than 50 years ago seem like the dark ages—literally. My opinion is that this has been almost without exception for the good and that our fitful complaining about it rests on turning legitimate worries about the role of TV coverage in a few specific circumstances into a mindless condemnation of the whole.

She even employed the history of TV wisely, comparing the electronically obscured face of the accuser in the Smith case (who, after the trial, went public, identifying herself as Patricia Bowman, on ABC's *PrimeTime Live)* to the fidgeting hands of mob figure Frank Costello during the 1951 Kefauver hearings on organized crime.

Television as literature. One quick quote to underscore the value of the miniseries form when it comes to literary adaptations. Fay Weldon, the author who was served so much better by the TV miniseries version of *The Life and Loves of a She-Devil* than by the movie *She-Devil*, was asked at a press conference in January 1992 to compare the two media.

"It always shows television up so well, doesn't it?" she replied. "You know, I think there's a great advantage—that novels do move quite well into television, and that, depending on who does them, don't necessarily go very well into film."

Even in the short form, TV handles itself well in this particular category. The first installment of Showtime's *Kurt Vonnegut's Monkey House* won an ACE Award (honoring excellence in cable programming) for Outstanding Dramatic Special, and the cable network committed to a minimum of four additional adaptations of Vonnegut stories.

Television taken seriously. This glacier hasn't moved much since I began the book, and the barriers between TV and film seem as artificial yet formidable as ever. David Rosenberg's 1991 book of collected essays, in which nearly two-dozen writers identify and describe *The Movie That Changed My Life*, was received as an interesting diversion and a tacit admission by a collection of intellectuals that movies meant something. How many decades will it be, though, before someone publishes a collection called *The TV Show That Changed My Life?*

On TV, film critics Gene Siskel and Roger Ebert raved about the documentary *Hearts of Darkness: A Filmmaker's Apocalypse* (a behind-the-scenes account of the making of Francis Ford Coppola's *Apocalypse Now),* which was released in American theaters only after being shown on the cable network Showtime and applauded by most TV critics. The duo insisted the only way to see *Hearts of Darkness* was on a large movie screen, but of course it wasn't. The documentary worked just fine on TV, and, if not for its acclaimed TV exposure, might never have made it to those large screens at all.

A much less provincial attitude was demonstrated, once again, by Dawidziak of the *Akron Beacon Journal.* He changed beats in 1992 to become, in all likelihood, the country's first multimedia movie critic—a person whose job is to review movies, whether they are produced for theatrical distribution, broadcast or cable television, or even home video. After two months on the job, Dawidziak laughed at the glut of TV-inspired material showing up at his movie-critic preview screenings.

"Last month I saw *Star Trek VI* and *The Addams Family,* Monday I saw *Wayne's World,* and we've got *Twin Peaks* coming up," he says, adding sarcastically, "I'm so glad I left the TV beat."

And Ann Magnuson, the performance artist whose credits include the movie *Making Mr. Right* and the ABC series *Anything but Love,* defended her eclectic resume with a properly open-minded and unbiased approach. "Neo-vaudevillian? Info-tainer?" Magnuson said to an interviewer. "Oh, I don't care what you call me, just call me."

Television taking itself seriously. Here, at least, there was lots of movement as *Teleliteracy* went to press. In addition to such predictable yet perspective-adding prime-time anniversaries as NBC's *Today at 40*, there were specific efforts in which television looked closely at its past contributions and missteps, as well as its recent tricks and treats.

HBO's two-part *Play by Play: A History of Sports Television* cut across network lines to give an overall picture of the development of sports TV, and the same network's *Buy Me That Too!: A Kid's Survival Guide to TV Advertising* warned children (and adults), once again, about the deceptive practices in certain TV ads. On the PBS series *The American Experience,* an episode called *The Quiz Show Scandal,* recounting the revelations about certain rigged quiz shows in the midfifties, looked back at a particularly embarrassing but formative period in TV's history, and an episode of *Nova* asked, *Can You Believe TV Ratings?*

On an *ABC World News Tonight* report, White House correspondent Brit Hume showed President Bush at an "informal lunch," chatting about how something had to be done to improve roadway conditions in New Hampshire. However, Hume simultaneously yanked the political teeth out of that particular "sound bite" by explaining the images were photographed exclusively by a New Hampshire local TV station, and that the station had been given access by the White House to eavesdrop on their supposedly casual chat.

By pointing out the political maneuvering intended to sway New Hampshire voters prior to the presidential primary, Hume managed to relay the day's "photo opportunity" while revealing its calculated intentions. Along with a fact-checking assessment of political ads, it is the kind of laying bare of the TV process in politics that will, and properly should, be a part of the 1992 presidential campaign. And Bill Moyers, too, set out to observe election-year events closely, in a weekly PBS series called *Listening to America.*

Also, there are the perspectives presented by the PBS popular culture series *Edge,* which provides more coherent, clever, and significant media criticism than any other TV forum, as well as the continued fine work by such outside observers and analysts as the Freedom Forum Media Studies Center at New York's Columbia University and the same city's Museum of Television & Radio. The former's analysis of the Gulf War was invaluable, and the latter's retrospective of the works of Dennis Potter (offering American premieres of more than a dozen compelling British teleplays) was a revelatory and thrilling experience.

Television taking risks. Sadly, I have to admit that 1991, while a great year for TV news, ended up a relatively poor year for TV entertainment. The most daring weekly series—especially NBC's *Shannon's Deal* and ABC's *Twin Peaks, China Beach,* and *Equal Justice*—all were canceled, with not much comparable in the drama genre to take their place. *I'll Fly Away* evolved into a gripping study of race relations, and George Lucas's *The Young Indi-*

ana Jones Chronicles proved a wonderful way to teach children while entertaining them. But television, like any other art form, is cyclical, and encouraging projects loom on the horizon.

Among the most tantalizing: *TNT Screenworks*, a trio of new cable TV dramas produced by Steven Spielberg's Amblin Entertainment. Even film snobs should be impressed by the contributors, if not the result, of these efforts. *The Water Engine*, written by David Mamet, will star Joe Mantegna. *The Habitation of Dragons*, written by Horton Foote, stars Jean Stapleton and Frederic Forrest. And *The Heart of Justice*, written by playwright Keith Reddin, stars Eric Stoltz and Jennifer Connelly.

The future of television. From a technological sense, it will continue to be dizzying. *Interactive CDs, CD-ROM, multimedia,* and other buzzwords will continue buzzing until they settle on a format, direction, and application that appeal to the American public. It's not necessary to get spooked by the new technology or terminology, because it will be the message, not the medium, that counts. As personal computers columnist Peter H. Lewis noted in the *New York Times,* "The real importance of multimedia is not in the hardware . . . but in the software, just as the significance of television is not in the picture tube but in the programming."

It is for precisely that reason that television must get bolder, not more timid, in the years ahead. Rather than cling desperately to old formulas in hopes of maintaining old audience levels, TV should—make that *must*—recognize what it does best, and do more of it. As Richard Austin Smith noted in a *Fortune* article about television:

> The mounting pressure of costs on sponsors and networks alike has weakened the will to experiment. . . . Yet as the medium loses its capacity to excite, to create and to lead, its audiences will inevitably shrink. And as audiences shrink, more pressure to stick to "successful" formats and eschew the unknown may well follow.

The amazing thing is, that observation was made in 1958—more than 30 years ago.

Another blast from the past with a message about TV's future comes from a very respected, and very unlikely, source: veteran theater critic Walter Kerr, who turned his attention to the small screen in a 1962 *Horizon* magazine essay called "What Good Is Television?"

Kerr praised the contributions of such TV figures as Ed Murrow, Mike Wallace, David Susskind, Jack Paar, and Leonard Bernstein, and was particularly enthusiastic about the unique way in which television brought him closer to the art and understanding of dance. Remarking on the first of Agnes de Mille's essays on choreography for the arts series *Omnibus,* Kerr wrote:

> Watching the de Mille show, I was thunderstruck—not so much by the quality of the program, which was superb, but by my own realization that there was nowhere else in the world I could go for this. . . .

What I was watching, I told myself, was an entirely new form: the visual essay. And because television had managed to arrange its resources in such an individual way that no rival medium could claim, or even aspire, to offer precisely the same experience, television had, for me, acquired an identity.

Thereafter I knew what sort of program I could not afford to miss. I could miss the Westerns, and catch them at Loew's. I could miss the dramas, and see better on Broadway. I could skip the news analysis, and read Walter Lippmann. But I could not miss the "visual essay" and expect to make up my loss.

In the subsequent thirty years, television has improved substantially in almost all respects. Instead of *Hopalong Cassidy* as an example of the TV Western, we have *Lonesome Dove*. The drama and news programs are mounted in a more sophisticated fashion, and the "visual essay," an evocative mixture of sights and sounds, has remained one of the medium's most evocative exercises. About the only area where TV has not improved is in the profit-and-loss column, but even there the possibility exists that economic adversity, in the long run, will help television more than harm it. It was something else Kerr foresaw back in 1962:

> The danger is not that television is limited in its own right, but that it may never discover what its own right is, that it will never subject itself to a proper show of strength. When the living is easy, no muscles are flexed, and the living is very easy just now. A television professional can go to sleep counting money so long as millions of feet of old film keep rolling down the Hollywood hillside.
>
> It will be interesting to see whether television becomes a mere convenience to be replaced by more convenient conveniences, or whether it makes a stubborn little place for itself in the memory of man.

No network, certainly not the ones in the red, would claim the living is easy right now. Therefore, it's time for TV to do some flexing and take some chances. With the mass audience fragmenting, it no longer makes sense to seek to please all of the people all of the time, or to generate and regenerate the same old formulas. Television has grown a lot in the last thirty years, and learned a lot, but one thing it still has not learned is its lesson.

Plainly put, television doesn't try hard enough most of the time. And when it does, and succeeds in presenting something truly special, neither its creators nor its viewers take it seriously enough. It's a two-way street that, all too often, leads to opposite dead ends: television does not give enough credit to itself or its audience, and does not get enough credit from those who watch it.

Will things change in the coming years? Will television be taken seriously—and take it upon itself to do even more ambitious, experimental, and meaningful endeavors? We'll see.

And, without question, we'll watch.

BIBLIOGRAPHY

Of the twenty chapters in this book, three are largely historical, and thus deserving of a slightly more focused form of annotation. Complete publishing information on the works listed in the notes below will be provided in the subsequent bibliography.

Chapter 3. Mass Media and Mass Contempt

For a detailed analysis of Plato and television, see Alexander Nehamas's essay "Plato and the Mass Media"—and, from the original source, Plato's *The Republic.*

For a well-researched, delightfully entertaining compilation of critical bad notices given to actors and plays from the legitimate stage, see Diana Rigg's *No Turn Unstoned.*

The last two volumes of Daniel Boorstin's *The Americans* trilogy were an invaluable resource, especially in their detail and insights regarding the impact of various print and electronic media on American society.

The telling details in Erik Barnouw's three-volume *History of Broadcasting* series were very helpful in both establishing and checking chronologies in Chapters 3 and 4.

For an invaluable argument-settling source of film-industry firsts, lasts, biggests, and bests, see Patrick Robertson's *The Guinness Book of Movie Facts & Feats.* It was of great help not only in chapter 3, but in chapters 4 and 17 as well.

For a precedent-seeking, precedent-setting book about legal cases regarding censorship of the cinema, see the very entertaining, never sensational *Banned Films: Movies, Censors, and the First Amendment,* by Edward De Grazia and Roger K. Newman.

For a generous and well-selected sampling of film criticism, pro and con, from the first decades of the cinema, see Stanley Kauffmann's *Early Film Criticism,* which I found especially interesting.

Finally, for an invaluable artifact of "movie phobia" in the thirties, see Henry James Forman's allegedly, but not convincingly, objective collection of social-studies essays on children and the cinema, *Our Movie Made Children.*

Chapter 4. Instant Replay: A Broad Look at Broadcast History

For details about the early days of radio and television, especially those details that were either unique or more reliable than those in other texts, I'm particularly indebted to the aforementioned works by Barnouw and Robertson, and to three others: David Halberstam's *The Powers That Be,* William Hawes's *American Television Drama: The Experimental Years,* and Irving Settel's *Pictorial History* books covering radio and television.

For delightful essays on TV and theater, respectively, see E. B. White's "Removal" piece in *One Man's Meat* and Robert Benchley's *Benchley at the Theatre.*

For TV news and reviews, the collected volumes of *Variety Television Reviews* were rich with contemporaneous opinion and detail. One unexpected bonus when dealing with this early material: the East and West coast editions of *Variety* were concerned with very different programs and issues, providing an ongoing comparison of the fall of New York TV and the rise of TV in Hollywood.

The fiftieth-anniversary *Broadcasting* magazine series, each week summarizing a different year in broadcast history, contributed large and small details to this and many other chapters.

Just as a way of saying thanks, I'd like to point out the joy I experienced, through the years, in reading the words and hearing the songs of Mason Williams, represented here by *The Mason Williams F.C.C. Rapport.*

This chapter also relied a good deal on the three books I feel are most indispensable to any working TV critic: *The Complete Directory to Prime Time Network TV Shows, 1946–Present* by Tim Brooks and Earle Marsh, *Leonard Maltin's TV Movies and Video Guide,* and Alex McNeil's *Total Television.*

Chapter 17. *The Civil War* and the Gulf War

The two most reliable and exhaustive sources for this chapter are part of larger works well worth enjoying in their entirety.

Edwin Emery's *The Press and America: An Interpretative History of the Mass Media* was the source of many key facts and parallels, particularly regarding the Civil War.

Also, I am deeply indebted to the chronologies outlined in David Stebenne's "The Military and the Media: The Gulf Conflict in Historical Perspective," one of many splendid scholarly efforts in Columbia University's Gannett Foundation Media Center (now known as the Freedom Forum) publication *The Media at War: The Press and the Persian Gulf Conflict.*

In these chapters and elsewhere, I relied heavily on the comments of those whom I interviewed, and would like to take this opportunity to thank them one final time for giving me their cooperation and trust.

Adler, Jerry. "Revisiting the Civil War," *Newsweek* (October 8, 1990), pp. 58–64.

Agee, James. *Agee on Film, Volume 1.* New York: Perigee, 1983.

"All About Television," *60 Minutes*, CBS-TV. March 5, 1989.

Alleman, Richard. *The Movie Lover's Guide to New York.* New York: Harper & Row, 1988.

Allen, Fred. *Treadmill to Oblivion.* New York: Little, Brown, 1954.

Alter, Jonathan. "Clippings From the Media War," *Newsweek* (March 11, 1991), p. 52.

———. "Does Bloody Footage Lose Wars?," *Newsweek* (February 11, 1991), p. 38.

———. "Showdown at 'Fact Gap,' " *Newsweek* (February 4, 1991), pp. 61–2.

Arlen, Michael. *The Camera Age.* New York: Farrar, Straus and Giroux, 1981.

———. *Living-Room War.* New York: Viking Press, 1969.

Attenborough, David. Interview with author. May 1991.

Barber, David W. *Bach, Beethoven, and the Boys.* Toronto: Sound and Vision, 1986.

Barber, Red. *The Broadcasters.* New York: Dial Press, 1970.

Barnouw, Erik. *Documentary.* Revised edition. New York: Oxford University Press, 1983.

———. *The Golden Web: A History of Broadcasting in the United States, Volume II—1933 to 1953.* New York: Oxford University Press, 1968.

———. *The Image Empire: A History of Broadcasting in the United States, Volume III—From 1953.* New York: Oxford University Press, 1970.

———. *A Tower in Babel: A History of Broadcasting in the United States, Volume I—to 1933.* New York: Oxford University Press, 1966.

———. *Tube of Plenty*, 2nd edition. New York: Oxford University Press, 1990.

Barton, Mary Ann. "Writer Calls C-SPAN 'Network of the '90s,' " *C-SPAN Update* (July 7, 1991), pp. 1, 4.

Bates, Stephen. *If No News, Send Rumors.* New York: Henry Holt and Company, 1989.

Bazin, André. *What is Cinema?, Volume I.* Berkeley: University of California Press, 1967.

Beck, Melinda. "Video Vigilantes," *Newsweek* (July 22, 1991), pp. 42–47.

Benchley, Robert. *Benchley at the Theatre.* Ipswich, Massachusetts: Ipswich Press, 1985.

Benjamin, Christopher, and Dennis E. Eckes. *The Sport Americana Price Guide to the Non-Sports Cards.* Cleveland, Ohio: Edgewater Book Company, 1988.

Bergan, Ronald, Graham Fuller, and David Malcolm. *Academy Award Winners.* New York: Crescent Books, 1986.

Bernstein, Richard. "Will the Gulf War Produce Endearing Art?" *New York Times* (June 9, 1991), p. 2:22.

Beschloss, Steven. "Local vs. Central: Civil War at PBS," *Channels* (December 3, 1990), pp. 52–53.

"Best Sellers," *New York Times Book Review* (July 14, 1991), p. 30.

Bianculli, David. "Beyond Betamax," *Fort Lauderdale News* (May 25, 1980), pp. G1, G11.

———. "A Gentlemen's Disagreement over 'Hill Street Blues,' " *Akron Beacon Journal* (June 12, 1983), p. B8.

———. "A Growing Trend: Plot Lines that Leak Before TV Shows Air," *Philadelphia Inquirer* (February 16, 1986), pp. H1, H15.

———. "Sound Tells the Story: War Breaks Out on Evening News," *New York Post* (January 17, 1991), p. 76.

———. "Teleliteracy," *Taxi*, November 1989.

Billington, Michael. "Made-For-TV Chekhov, From Mamet and Mosher," *New York Times* (February 17, 1991), p. 2:29.

Blackbeard, Bill, and Martin Williams. *The Smithsonian Collection of Newspaper Comics.*

Copublished by Washington, DC's Smithsonian Institution Press and New York's Harry S. Abrams, 1977.

Bloodworth-Thomason, Linda. Interview with author. August 1991.

Bloom, Allan. *The Closing of the American Mind.* New York: Simon and Schuster, 1987.

Boddy, William. *Fifties Television.* Urbana: University of Illinois Press, 1990.

Boorstin, Daniel J. *The Americans: The Colonial Experience.* New York: Random House, 1958.

———. *The Americans: The Democratic Experience.* New York: Random House, 1973.

———. *The Image.* New York: Atheneum, 1961.

Boot, William. "The Pool," *Columbia Journalism Review* (May/June 1991), pp. 24–27.

Bower, Robert T. *The Changing Television Audience in America.* New York: Columbia University Press, 1985.

Brand, Stewart. *The Media Lab: Inventing the Future at MIT.* New York: Viking, 1987.

Britman, Susan. Interview with author. June 1991.

Brittell, Timothy. Interview with author. July 1991.

Brooks, James L. Interview with author. August 1991.

Brooks, Tim. *The Complete Directory to Prime Time TV Stars.* New York: Ballantine Books, 1987.

Brooks, Tim, and Earle Marsh. *The Complete Directory to Prime Time Network TV Shows, 1946-Present.* 4th edition. New York: Ballantine Books, 1988.

Brown, Les. *The New York Times Encyclopedia of Television.* New York: Times Books, 1977.

Brown, Patricia Leigh. "TV After Fifty Years: In Search of a Shape," *New York Times* (October 4, 1990), pp. C1, C12.

Browne, David. "It Ain't Stealing, It's Video Homage," *Entertainment Weekly* (November 29, 1991), p. 42.

Burke, James. Interview with author. November 1990.

Burns, James MacGregor. "In Minor Dramas Lurk Major Sagas," *New York Times* (May 12, 1991), pp. 2:33, 44.

Burns, Ken. Interview with author. May 1991.

———. "The Painful, Essential Images of War," *New York Times* (January 27, 1991), pp. 2:1, 35.

Burrows, James. Interview with author. June 1991.

Campbell, Joseph. *The Power of Myth: Joseph Campbell, With Bill Moyers.* Betty Sue Flowers, editor. New York: Doubleday, 1988.

Cannon, Mark. "WNET Aims for Media Literacy," *Current* (March 4, 1991), p. 4.

Case, Frederick. "Is TV Spawning a Generation of Non-Thinkers?" *Fort Lauderdale Sun-Sentinel* (April 28, 1991), pp. 1E, 4E.

Cater, Douglass, and Michael J. Nyhan, editors. *The Future of Public Broadcasting.* New York: Praeger Publishers, 1976.

Channels 1991 Field Guide. December 3, 1990.

Charren, Peggy. Interview with author. May 1991.

Charren, Peggy, and Carol Hulsizer. *TV, Books, & Children.* Cambridge, Massachusetts: Action for Children's Television, 1990.

Coakley, Mary Lewis. *Rated X: The Moral Case Against TV.* New Rochelle, New York: Arlington, 1977.

Cohn, Lawrence, compiler. "All-time Film Rental Champs," *Variety* (May 6, 1991), pp. 82–100.

Colombo, John Robert, editor. *Wit and Wisdom of the Moviemakers.* London: Hamlyn, 1979.

Cooke, Patrick. "TV or Not TV," *In Health* (December/January 1992), pp. 33–43.

Corey, Melinda, and George Ochoa, compilers. *The Man in Lincoln's Nose.* New York: Simon & Schuster, 1990.

Corliss, Richard. "Czar of Bizarre," *Time* (October 1, 1990), pp. 84–88.

———. *Talking Pictures.* Woodstock, New York: Overlook Press, 1974.

Cosby, Bill. "Cosby on TV & Kids," *Parents* (May 1991), pp. 93–94.

———. Interview with author. April 1991.

Cowan, Geoffrey. *See No Evil.* New York: Simon and Schuster, 1979.

Cronin, Brenda J. "Nike to Aid CTW's New Literacy Show," *Current* (May 27, 1991), pp. 1, 6.

Cronkite, Walter. "What Is There to Hide?" *Newsweek* (February 25, 1991), p. 43.

Dawidziak, Mark. *The Columbo Phile.* New York: Mysterious Press, 1988.

————. Interview with author. July 1991.

————. "TV Can Be a Gold Mine, If You Look Hard Enough," *The Akron Beacon Journal* (November 7, 1991), pp. D1, D5.

De Grazia, Edward, and Roger K. Newman. *Banned Films: Movies, Censors, and the First Amendment.* New York: R. R. Bowker, 1982.

della Cava, Marco R. "The Publishing World Embraces Masculinity," *USA Today* (July 31, 1991), p. D1.

Denisoff, R. Serge. *Inside MTV.* New Brunswick: Transaction Books, 1988.

de Vries, Hilary. "For Actors, TV can Upstage Broadway," *New York Times* (January 19, 1992), p. 2:31.

Diamond, Edwin. "How CNN Does It," *New York* (February 11, 1991), pp. 30–35, 38–39.

Donlon, Brian. "Medium Is the Message at Broadcast Museum," *USA Today* (October 7, 1991), p. D3.

————. "Network Correspondents on the Front Line," *USA Today* (January 15, 1991), p. D3.

————. "Peace Catches Up to Gulf War Reporters," *USA Today* (August 2, 1991), p. D3.

Dunning, John. *Tune in Yesterday.* Englewood Cliffs, New Jersey: Prentice-Hall, 1976.

Duvall, Shelley. Interview with author. August 1991.

Dyer, Gwynne. *War.* New York: Crown Publishers, 1985.

Ellerbee, Linda. Interview with author. July 1991.

Ellison, Harlan. *The Glass Teat.* 2nd edition. New York: Pyramid Books, 1975.

————. *The Other Glass Teat.* New York: Pyramid Books, 1975.

Eisner, Joel. *The Official Batman Batbook.* Chicago: Contemporary Books, 1986.

Emery, Edwin. *The Press and America: An Interpretative History of the Mass Media.* 3rd edition. Englewood Cliffs, New Jersey: Prentice-Hall, 1972.

Enright, D. J. *Fields of Vision.* Oxford: Oxford University Press, 1990.

Erickson, Hal. *Syndicated Television: The First Forty Years, 1947–1987.* Jefferson, North Carolina: 1989.

Ewen, Stuart. *All Consuming Images.* New York: Basic Books, 1988.

"The Failure of Teacher Ed," *Newsweek* (October 1, 1990), pp. 58–60.

Farren, Julie. "Students Are Breaking Free from the Tyranny of TV," *USA Today* (September 30, 1991), p. D6.

Fecher, Charles A., editor. *The Diary of H. L. Mencken.* New York: Random House, 1989.

Feuer, Jane, Paul Kerr, and Tise Vahimagi. *MTM: Quality Television.* London: British Film Institute, 1984.

Fineman, Howard. "Schwarzkopf for President?" *Newsweek* (April 1, 1991), p. 24.

Fischer, Stuart. *Kids' TV: The First 25 Years.* New York: Facts on File Publications, 1983.

Fiske, John. *Television Culture.* London: Routledge, 1989.

Forman, Henry James. *Our Movie Made Children.* New York: Macmillan, 1933.

Frey, Tom. "And Now a Word From Our Sponsor," *Antique Toy World* (June 1991), pp. 102–105.

Friendly, Fred W. Interview with author. March 1991.

Frost, Mark. Interview with author. November 1990.

Gallen, Ira. Interview with author. October 1991.

Gehr, Richard. "The Mediocre Is the Message," *Village Voice* (March 21, 1989), pp. 45–46.

Geller, Robert. Interview with author. May 1991.

Gerani, Gary, and Paul H. Schulman. *Fantastic Television.* New York: Harmony Books, 1977.

Gerbner, George, Larry Gross, Nancy Signorielli, and Michael Morgan. *Television's Mean World: Violence Profile No. 14–15.* Philadelphia: University of Pennsylvania Annenberg School of Communications, 1986.

Goethals, Gregor T. *The TV Ritual: Worship at the Video Altar.* Boston: Beacon Press, 1981.

Goldberger, Paul. "A Post-modern Museum for Television, Sans Irony," *New York Times* (September 22, 1991), p. 2:36.

Goldman, William. *Adventures in the Screen Trade.* New York: Warner Books, 1983.

Goodman, Walter. "Literacy Does Not Mean Looking at the Pictures," *New York Times* (December 27, 1990), p. C17.

Gorman, James. "Miss the War? Here's How to Catch Up," *New York Times* (June 30, 1991), p. 2:19.

Granger, Rod. "Off-network Helps Cable, Study Says," *Electronic Media* (July 15, 1991), p. 8.

Greene, Graham. *The Pleasure Dome.* New York: Oxford University Press, 1980.

Greenfield, Jeff. "America Rallies 'Round the TV Set," *TV Guide* (February 16, 1991), pp. 4–7.

———. *Television.* New York: Harry N. Abrams, 1977.

Greenfield, Meg. "The Television Question," *Newsweek* (December 29, 1991), p. 74.

"A Grim Photo," *Newsweek* (February 25, 1991), p. 9.

Greppi, Michele. "Pentagon Directs the Show," *New York Post* (January 21, 1991), p. 76.

Grossman, Gary H. *Saturday Morning TV.* New York: Dell, 1981.

Gunter, Barrie, and Jill L. McAleer. *Children and Television: The One Eyed Monster?* London: Routledge, 1990.

Gussow, Mel. "Theater in Review," *New York Times* (October 2, 1991), p. C18.

Halberstam, David. *The Powers That Be.* New York: Dell, 1979.

Halliwell, Leslie. *Halliwell's Film Guide.* 6th edition. New York: Charles Scribner's Sons, 1987.

Harris, Jay S., editor and compiler. *TV Guide: The First 25 Years.* New York: Simon and Schuster, 1978.

Hartsfield, Larry. "TV, Seriously," *Sky* (September 1990), pp. 84–90.

Haskell, Molly. "Why Cinema Literacy," *Entertainment Weekly* (May 19, 1991), pp. 18–19.

Hawes, William. *American Television Drama: The Experimental Years.* University, Alabama: University of Alabama Press, 1986.

Hedges, Chris. "The Unilaterals," *Columbia Journalism Review* (May/June 1991), pp. 27–29.

Hewitt, Don. Interview with author. April 1991.

———. *Minute by Minute . . .* New York: Random House, 1985.

Hill, Doug, and Jeff Weingrad. *Saturday Night.* New York: Beech Tree Books, 1986.

Hirsch, E. D., Jr. *Cultural Literacy.* New York: Houghton Mifflin, 1987.

———, Joseph F. Kett, and James Trefil. *The Dictionary of Cultural Literacy.* Boston: Houghton Mifflin, 1988.

Holston, Noel. "Fresh from the Loony Bin, 'Tiny Toon' Animates TV," *Minneapolis Star Tribune* (May 12, 1991), pp. F1, F12.

Horowitz, Joy. "Life, Loss, Death and 'Thirtysomething,'" *New York Times* (February 10, 1991), pp. 2:29, 2:35.

Howlett, Debbie. "Routing Iraq: Strategy, Sleight of Hand," *USA Today* (February 28, 1991), pp. A6–7.

Hylsky, Jay. "Gulf War Via Satellite," *Satellite Orbit* (April 1991), pp. 4–5.

Jeannechild, Penny. "Once Again, It's Howdy Doody Time," *Philadelphia Inquirer,* "Weekend" (September 27, 1991), p. 32.

"Jeffrey Zaun," *People Extra* (Spring/Summer 1991), p. 30.

Jennings, Peter. Interview with author. March 1991.

Jowett, Garth S. "The Selling of the Pentagon: Television Confronts the First Amendment," *America History/American Television.* New York: Frederick Ungar, 1983, pp. 256–78.

Kael, Pauline. *Kiss Kiss Bang Bang.* Boston: Little, Brown, 1968.

Kass, Judith M. *Robert Altman: American Innovator.* New York: Popular Library, 1978.

Kauffmann, Stanley, with Bruce Henstell. *American Film Criticism: From the Beginnings to Citizen Kane.* New York: Liveright, 1972.

Kehr, David. "The Star," *Gannett Center Journal* (Summer 1989), pp. 45–57.

Kerr, Walter. *The Theater in Spite of Itself.* New York: Simon & Schuster, 1963.

Key, Wilson Bryan. *Subliminal Seduction.* New York: Prentice-Hall, 1973.

Lackmann, Ron. *Remember Television.* New York: G. P. Putnam's Sons, 1971.

LaGuardia, Robert. *Soap World.* New York: Arbor House, 1983.

Law, Lindsay. Interview with author. March 1991.

Lax, Eric. *Woody Allen.* New York: Alfred A. Knopf, 1991.

Leab, Daniel J. "See It Now: A Legend Reassessed," *American History/American Television.* New York: Frederick Ungar, 1983, pp. 1–32.

Lear, Norman. Interview with author. March 1991.

Lee, Jessica. "Bush: TV Hurting Kids," *USA Today* (September 4, 1991), p. A1.

Leroy, David, and Judith Leroy. "A Tiger by the Tail: How 'The Civil War' Surprised Public TV," *Current* (November 5, 1990), pp. 8–9.

Levinson, Richard and William Link. *Off Camera*. New York: Plume, 1986.

———. *Stay Tuned*. New York: St. Martin's Press, 1981.

Lewis, Gregg. *Telegarbage*. Nashville: Thomas Nelson, 1977.

Lewis, Peter. "Importance of Being Multimedia," *New York Times* (November 5, 1991), p. C5.

"Lights! Action! Disk Drives!" *Newsweek* (July 22, 1991), p. 54.

Link, William. Interview with author. May 1991.

Lucas, Tim. "Blood 'n Doughnuts: Notes on Twin Peaks," *Video Watchdog* (No. 2, 1990), pp. 32–49.

Lynn, Kenneth S. *Huckleberry Finn: Text, Sources and Criticism*. New York: Harcourt, Brace & World, 1961.

Maltin, Leonard. *Leonard Maltin's TV Movies and Video Guide*. 1991 Edition. New York: Signet, 1990.

Marc, David. *Comic Visions*. Boston: Unwin Hyman, 1989.

———. "The World of Alda and Hawkeye," *Television Quarterly* (Vol. XXIII, No. IV, 1988), pp. 15–24.

———, and Robert Thompson. *Architects of the Air: The Makers of American Television*. New York: Little, Brown, 1992.

Marill, Alvin H. *Movies Made for Television: The Telefeature and the Mini-Series, 1964–1986*. New York: Zoetrope Press, 1987.

Mathews, Tom. "A Soldier of Conscience," *Newsweek* (March 11, 1991), pp. 32–34.

Matza, Michael. "Checking Out PBS Classics," *Philadelphia Inquirer* (June 9, 1988), pp. D1, D4.

McCarty, John, and Brian Kelleher. *Alfred Hitchcock Presents*. New York: St. Martin's Press, 1985.

McLuhan, Marshall. *The Gutenberg Galaxy: The Making of Typographic Man*. Toronto: University of Toronto Press, 1962.

———. *Understanding Media: The Extensions of Man*. New York: McGraw-Hill, 1964.

McMurtry, Larry. *Film Flam*. New York: Touchstone Books, 1987.

McNeil, Alex. *Total Television*. 3rd edition. New York: Penguin Books, 1991.

Merrow, John. "Title Goes Here," *Gannett Center Journal* (Winter 1991), pp. 39–49.

Meyrowitz, Joshua. *No Sense of Place: The Impact of Electronic Media on Social Behavior*. New York: Oxford University Press, 1984.

Michaels, Lorne. Interview with author. July 1991.

Michener, James A. "A Hit—In Any Language," *TV Guide: The First 25 Years*. New York: Simon and Schuster, 1978, pp. 169–171.

Miller, Arthur. *Death of a Salesman*. New York: Viking Penguin, 1949.

Miller, Mark Crispin. *Boxed In*. 3rd edition. Evanston, Illinois: Northwestern University Press, 1989.

———. "Deride and Conquer," *Watching Television*, Todd Gitlin, ed. New York: Pantheon Books, 1986, pp. 183–228.

Minow, Newton. *How Vast the Wasteland Now?* New York: Gannett Foundation Media Center, 1991.

Mobilio, Albert. "Auteur! Auteur!," *VLS (Voice Literary Supplement) 91* (December 1990), p. 22.

Moore, Martha T. "Alka-Seltzer Brings Back Old Spice," *USA Today* (November 29, 1991), p. B1.

Morris, Edmund. *The Rise of Theodore Roosevelt*. New York: Coward, McCann & Geoghegam, 1979.

Moyers, Bill. Interview with author. April 1991.

———. "The Power of Television," *KCET Magazine* (September 1988), pp. 45–47.

———. *A World of Ideas II*. New York: Doubleday, 1990.

Mulkern, Lou. "Not Without Home Video," *Entertainment Weekly* (July 12, 1991), p. 62.

Murrow, Edward R., and Fred W. Friendly, editors. *See It Now*. New York: Simon and Schuster, 1955.

Nehamas, Alexander. Interview with author. August 1989.

———. "Serious Watching," *The South Atlantic Quarterly* 89:I (Winter 1990), pp. 157–180.

———. "Plato and the Mass Media," *Monist* 71 (Spring 1988), pp. 214–234.

Newcomb, Horace. *Television: The Critical View.* 2nd edition. New York: Oxford University Press, 1979.

Nichols, Peter M. "Video Settles Down to Its Second Decade," *New York Times* (December 30, 1990), p. 2:26.

———. "Home Video," *New York Times* (December 12, 1991), p. C22.

O'Brien, Tom. *The Screening of America.* New York: Continuum, 1990.

O'Connor, John E. *American History/American Television.* New York: Frederick Ungar, 1983.

Olivier, Carolyn. Interview with author. July 1991.

Ordovensky, Pat. "SAT Finds Teens at Loss For Words," *USA Today* (August 27, 1991), pp. D1-D2.

———. "TV Adds to Math Problems," *USA Today* (June 10, 1991), pp. D2.

Orlik, Peter B. *Critiquing Radio and Television Content.* Boston: Allyn and Bacon, 1988.

Paley, William S. *As It Happened.* New York: Doubleday, 1979.

Palmer, Edward L. *Television and America's Children: A Crisis of Neglect.* New York: Oxford University Press, 1988.

Pavlik, John, and Mark Thalhimer. "The Charge of the E-Mail Brigade," *The Media at War: The Press and the Persian Gulf Conflict.* New York: Gannett Foundation Media Center, Columbia University, 1991, pp. 34–37.

"PBS Series on 'The Civil War' Draws Critical Raves," *TCA News* (December 1990), pp. 4–5.

Persico, Joseph E. *Edward R. Murrow: An American Original.* New York: Laurel Books, 1988.

"Peter Arnett," *People Extra* (Spring/Summer 1991), pp. 34–36.

Plato. *The Republic of Plato.* A. D. Lindsay, translator. New York: E. P. Dutton, 1950.

Postman, Neil. *Amusing Ourselves to Death.* New York: Elisabeth Sifton Books, 1985.

Potter, Dennis. *Waiting For the Boat.* London: Faber and Faber, 1984.

Premiere: One Hundred Years of Moviemaking, Winter 1991.

"Prince of the Global Village," *Time* (January 6, 1992), pp. 22–3.

Prouty, Howard H., editor. *Variety Television Reviews, Volume 5: 1954–1956.* New York: Garland Publishing, 1989.

———, editor. *Variety Television Reviews, Volume 3: 1923–1950.* New York: Garland Publishing, 1989.

Rather, Dan, with Mickey Herskowitz. *The Camera Never Blinks.* New York: William Morrow, 1977.

Rawson, Hugh, and Margaret Miner, editors. *The New International Dictionary of Quotations.* New York: E. P. Dutton, 1986.

Reinholz, Mary. "Upper West Side Story," *Nostalgia* (March 1991), pp. 62–68.

Rense, Rip. "The Mainstreaming of Matt Groening," *Emmy* (July/August 1990), pp. 104–108.

Rigg, Diana, compiler. *No Turn Unstoned.* New York: Doubleday, 1982.

Robertson, Patrick. *The Guinness Book of Movie Facts & Feats.* Great Britain: Guinness Books, 1988.

Rodman, Howard A. "The Series that Will Change TV," *Connoisseur* (September 1989), pp. 139–144.

Rogers, Fred. Interview with author. July 1991.

Rogers, Dave. *The Complete Avengers.* New York: St. Martin's Press, 1989.

Rogers, Michael. "MTV, IBM, Tennyson and You," *Newsweek* special edition (September 1990), pp. 50–52.

Rolling Stone Rock Almanac. New York: Collier, 1983.

Rosenberg, Donald. Interview with author. July 1991.

Rothenberg, Randall. "Art or Schlock: Is TV Suitable for Framing?" *New York Times* (August 25, 1991), pp. 2:1, 21.

———. "For Students in an Electronic Age, Lessons on Watching Television," *New York Times* (December 10, 1990), pp. A1, B8.

———. "Yesterday's Boob Tube is Today's High Art," *New York Times* (October 7, 1990), pp. 2:1, 39.

Roush, Matt. "Live from Kuwait City, CBS Regains Some Glory," *USA Today* (February 27, 1991), p. D1.

Schumer, Arlen. *Visions From the Twilight Zone.* San Francisco: Chronicle Books, 1990.

Schwartz, Tony. *Media: The Second God.* Garden City, New York: Anchor Books, 1983.

Settel, Irving. *A Pictorial History of Radio.* New York: Grosset & Dunlap, 1967.

————. *A Pictorial History of Television.* 2nd, enlarged edition. New York: Frederick Ungar, 1983.

————, and William Laas. *A Pictorial History of Television.* New York: Grosset & Dunlap, 1969.

Shales, Tom. "The 10 Best TV-Movies Ever Made," *Panorama* (February 1981), pp. 50–52, 87–90.

————. "Troubling, Transcendent 'Twin Peaks,' " *Washington Post* (April 8, 1990), p. G1.

Sharbutt, Jay. " 'Cheers' has Link to Early Saloon Hit," *Philadelphia Inquirer* (September 6, 1991), p. D5.

Shirer, William L. *The Nightmare Years, 1930–1940.* New York: Little, Brown, 1984.

Shister, Gail. "Brokaw to Host a Show for the Classroom," *Philadelphia Inquirer* (November 22, 1991), p. D4.

Shulman, Arthur, and Roger Youman. *How Sweet It Was.* New York: Bonanza Books, 1966.

Siegel, Scott, and Barbara Siegel. *The Encyclopedia of Hollywood.* New York: Avon Books, 1990.

Silver, Alain, and Elizabeth Ward. *Film Noir.* Woodstock, New York: Overlook Press, 1979.

Singer, Dorothy G., and Jerome L. Singer. *The House of Make-Believe.* Cambridge: Harvard University Press, 1990.

Singer, Stephen. "The Midas Touch of 'The Civil War,' " *Current* (October 8, 1990), pp. 1, 13.

Slonimsky, Nicholas. *The Lexicon of Musical Invective: Critical Assaults on Composers Since Beethoven's Time.* Seattle: University of Washington Press, 1953.

Smolowe, Jill. "Iraq's Horror Picture Show," *Time* (February 4, 1991), pp. 34–35.

Smythe, Ted C., and George A Mastroianni, editors. *Issues in Broadcasting: Radio, Television, and Cable.* Palo Alto, California: Mayfield Publishing, 1975.

Sperber, A. M. *Murrow: His Life and Times.* New York: Freundlich Books, 1986.

Stapen, Candyce H., editor. "The First 50 Years of Broadcasting: 1932," *Broadcasting* (October 20, 1980), pp. 55–60.

————. "The First 50 Years of Broadcasting: 1933," *Broadcasting* (October 27, 1980), pp. 97–102.

————. "The First 50 Years of Broadcasting: 1938," *Broadcasting* (December 1, 1980), pp. 113–117.

————. "The First 50 Years of Broadcasting: 1939," *Broadcasting* (December 8, 1980), pp. 87–90.

————. "The First 50 Years of Broadcasting: 1944," *Broadcasting* (January 19, 1981), pp. 111–15.

————. "The First 50 Years of Broadcasting: 1948," *Broadcasting* (February 16, 1981), pp. 103–111.

————. "The First 50 Years of Broadcasting: 1951," *Broadcasting* (March 9, 1981), pp. 161–165.

————. "The First 50 Years of Broadcasting: 1952," *Broadcasting* (March 16, 1981), pp. 231–235.

————. "The First 50 Years of Broadcasting: 1955," *Broadcasting* (April 6, 1981), pp. 147–151.

Stebenne, David. "The Military and the Media: The Gulf Conflict in Historical Perspective," The Media at War: The Press and the Persian Gulf Conflict. New York: Gannett Foundation Media Center, Columbia University, 1991, pp. 8–25.

Stein, Ben. *The View from Sunset Boulevard.* New York: Basic Books, 1979.

Stempel, Tom. *FrameWork.* Expanded edition. New York: Continuum, 1991.

Streitfeld, David. "Michener the Mighty," *Entertainment Weekly* (May 31, 1991), pp. 30–32.

Stuart, Fredric. *The Effects of Television on the Motion Picture and Radio Industries.* New York: Arno Press, 1976.

Talty, Stephan. "Absolute Images," *Film Comment* (May-June 1991), pp. 52.

Taylor, Ella. *Prime-Time Families.* Berkeley: University of California Press, 1989.

Taylor, Robert. *Fred Allen: His Life and Wit.* New York: International Polygonics, 1989.

"Television's Blinding Power," *U.S. News & World Report* (July 27, 1987), pp. 18–21.

Terrace, Vincent. *Encyclopedia of Television: Series, Pilots and Specials, 1937–73*. New York: Zoetrope, 1986.

———. *Encyclopedia of Television: Series, Pilots and Specials, 1974–1984*. New York: Zoetrope, 1986.

———. *Radio's Golden Years*. San Diego: A. S. Barnes, 1981.

"TV and Jobs Cut into Reading Time," *USA Today* (March 26, 1991), p. D4.

Thompson, Frank. "Fade Out," *American Film* (August 1991), pp. 34–38, 46.

Thompson, Robert J. "The 'Garbage' on Television is Worth Including in the College Curriculum," *Chronicle of Higher Education* (October 26, 1988), pp. B2-B3.

———. Interview with author. March 1991.

Thoreau, Henry David. *Walden, and on the Duty of Civil Disobedience*. New York: Harper & Row, 1965.

Truffaut, Francois. *Hitchcock/Truffaut*. Revised edition. New York: Touchstone Books, 1985.

Valeriani, Richard. "Talking Back to the Tube," *Columbia Journalism Review* (March/April 1991), pp. 24–28.

"Videotape of Beating by Officers Puts Full Glare on Brutality Issue," *New York Times* (March 18, 1991), pp. A1, B7.

Vonnegut, Kurt. *Between Time and Timbuktu, or Prometheus-5*. New York: Delta, 1972.

———. Interview with author. March 1991.

———. *Slaughterhouse-Five*. New York: Dell, 1968.

Wallechinsky, David, and Irving Wallace. *The People's Almanac*. New York: Doubleday, 1975.

———. *The People's Almanac #3*. New York: Bantam, 1981.

Ward, Alex. "TV's Tormented Master," *New York Times Magazine* (November 13, 1988), pp. 38–41, 86–90.

Ward, Geoffrey C., with Ric Burns and Ken Burns. *The Civil War: An Illustrated History*. New York: Alfred A. Knopf, 1990.

Waters, Harry F. "Prime Time's New Star," *Newsweek* (October 8, 1990), pp. 60–61.

Weinraub, Bernard. " 'Am I Nervous? You Bet I Am,' " *New York Times* (October 15, 1991), pp. C13, C18.

Wertheim, Arthur Frank. "The Rise and Fall of Milton Berle," *American History/American Television*, John E. O'Connor, editor. New York: Frederick Ungar, 1985.

Wetterau, Bruce. *The New York Public Library Book of Chronologies*. New York: Prentice Hall, 1990.

"What You Watch," *Radio Times* (September 14–20, 1991), p. 10.

White, E. B. "Removal," One Man's Meat. New York: Harper, 1942.

Wicking, Christopher, and Tise Vahimagi. *The American Vein*. New York: E. P. Dutton, 1979.

Williams, Mason. *The Mason Williams F.C.C. Rapport*. New York: Liveright Publishing, 1969.

Willis, John. *Screen World 1990*. New York: Crown, 1990.

———. *Screen World 1989*. New York: Crown, 1989.

———. *Screen World 1988*. New York: Crown, 1988.

Winn, Marie. *The Plug-in Drug*. New York: Penguin Books, 1985.

Winokur, Jon, editor and compiler. *Writers on Writing*. Philadelphia: Running Press, 1990.

Winship, Michael. *Television*. New York: Random House, 1988.

Witchel, Alex. "On Stage and Off," *The New York Times* (September 6, 1991), p. C2.

Wloszczyna, Susan. "Video Does Right by Bullwinkle," *USA Today* (February 8, 1991), pp. D1-D2.

Zadan, Craig. *Sondheim & Co*. New York: Macmillan, 1974.

Zeman, Ned. "Seventies Something," *Newsweek* (June 10, 1991), pp. 62–63.

Zicree, Marc Scott. *The Twilight Zone Companion*. New York: Bantam Books, 1982.

Zoglin, Richard. "Is TV Ruining Our Children?" *Time* (October 15, 1990), pp. 75–76.

———. "Volleys on the Information Front," *Time* (February 4, 1991), pp. 44–45.

Zurawik, David. Interview with author. July 1991.

INDEX OF NAMES

INDEX OF TITLES